Limited Classical Reprint Library

THE

SECOND BOOK OF KINGS

BY

F. W. FARRAR, D.D., F.R.S.

LATE FELLOW OF TRINITY COLLEGE, CAMBRIDGE; ARCHDEACON OF
WESTMINSTER

Foreword by
Dr. Cyril J. Barber

Klock & Klock Christian Publishers, Inc.
2527 GIRARD AVE. N.
MINNEAPOLIS, MINNESOTA 55411

Originally published by
Hodder & Stroughton
London, 1903

ISBN: 0-86524-036-1

Printed by Klock & Klock in the U.S.A.
1981 Reprint

CONTENTS

CHAPTER XIII

CHAPTER XIV

CHAPTER XV

CHAPTER XVI

CHAPTER XX

CHAPTER XXI

CHAPTER XXII

CHAPTER XXIII

CHAPTER XXIV

CHAPTER XXV

CHAPTER XXVI

THE SECOND BOOK OF KINGS

I

"Theories of inspiration which impaginate the Everlasting Spirit, and make each verse a cluster of objectless and mechanical miracles, are not seriously believed by any one: the Bible itself abides in its endless power and unexhausted truth. All that is not of asbestos is being burned away by the restless fires of thought and criticism. That which remains is enough, and it is indestructible."—BISHOP OF DERRY.

CHAPTER I

AHAZIAH BEN-AHAB OF ISRAEL

B.C. 855—854

2 KINGS i. 1—18

"Ye know not of what spirit are ye."—LUKE ix. 55.
" He is the mediator of a better covenant, which hath been enacted upon better promises."—HEB. viii. 6.

AHAZIAH, the eldest son and successor of Ahab, has been called "the most shadowy of the Israelitish kings."[1] He seems to have been in all respects one of the most weak, faithless, and deplorably miserable. He did but reign two years—perhaps in reality little more than one ; but this brief space was crowded with intolerable disasters. Everything that he touched seemed to be marked out for ruin or failure, and in character he showed himself a true son of Jezebel and Ahab.

What results followed the defeat of Ahab and Jehoshaphat at Ramoth-Gilead we are not told. The

---

[1] Rawlinson, *Kings of Israel and Judah*, p. 86. "The name of Ahaziah ('the Lord taketh hold'), like that of all Ahab's sons, testifies to the fact that the husband of Jezebel still worshipped Jehovah. Among the names of the judges and kings before Ahab in Israel, and Asa in Judah, scarcely a single instance occurs of names compounded with Jehovah; thenceforward they became the rule" (Wellhausen, *Israel and Judah*, Es 1, p. 66).

3

war must have ended in terms of peace of some kind—
perhaps in the cession of Ramoth-Gilead ; for Ahaziah
does not seem to have been disturbed during his brief
reign by any Syrian invasion. Nor were there any
troubles on the side of Judah. Ahaziah's sister was
the wife of Jehoshaphat's heir, and the good understanding between the two kingdoms was so closely cemented,
that in both royal houses there was an identity of
names—two Ahaziahs and two Jehorams.

But even the Judæan alliance was marked with
misfortune. Jehoshaphat's prosperity and ambition, together with his firm dominance over Edom—in which
country he had appointed a vassal, who was sometimes
allowed the courtesy title of king [1]—led him to emulate
Solomon by an attempt to revive the old maritime
enterprise which had astonished Jerusalem with ivory,
and apes, and peacocks imported from India. He
therefore built " ships of Tarshish " at Ezion-Geber to
sail to Ophir. They were called " Tarshish-ships,"
because they were of the same build as those which
sailed to Tartessus, in Spain, from Joppa. Ahaziah
was to some extent associated with him in the enterprise. But it turned out even more disastrously than
it had done in former times. So unskilled was the
seamanship of those days among all nations except
the Phœnicians, that the whole fleet was wrecked and
shattered to pieces in the very harbour of Ezion-Geber
before it had set sail.

Ahaziah, whose affinity with the King of Tyre
and possession of some of the western ports had
given his subjects more knowledge of ships and
voyages, then proposed to Jehoshaphat that the vessels

---

[1] 1 Kings xxii. 47; 2 Kings iii. 9: comp. viii. 20.

should be manned with sailors from Israel as well as Judah. But Jehoshaphat was tired of a futile and expensive effort. He refused a partnership which might easily lead to complications, and on which the prophets of Jehovah frowned. It was the last attempt made by the Israelites to become merchants by sea as well as by land.

Ahaziah's brief reign was marked by one immense humiliation. David, who extended the dominion of the Hebrews in all directions, had smitten the Moabites, and inflicted on them one of the horrible atrocities against which the ill-instructed conscience of men in those days of ignorance did not revolt.[1] He had made the male warriors lie on the ground, and then, measuring them by lines, he put every two lines to death and kept one alive. After this the Moabites had continued to be tributaries. They had fallen to the share of the Northern Kingdom, and yearly acknowledged the suzerainty of Israel by paying a heavy tribute of the fleeces of a hundred thousand lambs and a hundred thousand rams. But now that the warrior Ahab was dead, and Israel had been crushed by the catastrophe at Ramoth-Gilead, Mesha, the energetic viceroy of Moab, seized his opportunity to revolt and to break from the neck of his people the odious yoke. The revolt was entirely successful. The sacred historian gives us no details, but one of the most priceless of modern archæological discoveries has confirmed the Scriptural reference by securing and translating a

---

[1] 2 Sam. viii. 2. On the ethics of these wars of extermination, such as are commanded in the Pentateuch, and were practised by Joshua, Samuel, Saul, David, and others, see Josh. vi. 17 ; 1 Sam. xv. 3, 33 ; 2 Sam. viii. 2, etc., and Mozley's *Lectures on the Old Testament*, pp. 83–103.

fragment of Mesha's own account of the annals of his reign. We have, in what is called "The Moabite Stone," the memorial written in glorification of himself and of his god Chemosh, "the abomination of the children of Ammon," by a contemporary of Ahab and Jehoshaphat.[1] It is the oldest specimen which we possess of Hebrew writing; perhaps the only specimen, except the Siloam inscription, which has come down to us from before the date of the Exile. It was discovered in 1878 by the German missionary Klein, amid the ruins of the royal city of Daibon (Dibon, Num. xxi. 30), and was purchased for the Berlin Museum in 1879. Owing to all kinds of errors and intrigues, it did not remain in the hands of its purchaser, but was broken into fragments by the nomad tribe of Beni Hamide, from whom it was in some way obtained by M. Clermont-Ganneau. There is no ground for questioning its perfect genuineness, though the discovery of its value led to the forgery of a number of spurious and often indecent inscriptions. There can be no reasonable doubt that when we look at it we see before us the identical memorial of triumph which the Moabite emîr erected in the days of Ahaziah on the *bamah* of Chemosh at Dibon, one of his chief towns.

This document is supremely interesting, not only for its historical allusions, but also as an illustration of customs and modes of thought which have left their traces in the records of the people of Jehovah, as well as in those of the people of Chemosh.[2] Mesha tells us that his father reigned in Dibon for thirty years, and

---

[1] See Stade, i. 86. He gives a photograph and translation of it at p. 534.

[2] See *Records of the Past*, xi. 166, 167.

that he succeeded. He reared this stone to Chemosh in the town of Karcha, as a memorial of gratitude for the assistance which had resulted in the overthrow of all his enemies. Omri, King of Israel, had oppressed Moab many days, because Chemosh was wroth with his people. Ahaziah wished to oppress Moab as his father had done. But Chemosh enabled Mesha to recover Medeba, and afterwards Baal-Meon, Kirjatan, Ataroth, Nebo, and Jahaz, which he reoccupied and rebuilt. Perhaps they had been practically abandoned by all effective Israelite garrisons. In some of these towns he put the inhabitants under a ban, and sacrificed them to Moloch in a great slaughter. In Nebo alone he slew seven thousand men. Having turned many towns into fortresses, he was enabled to defy Israel altogether, to refuse the old burdensome tribute, and to re-establish a strong Moabite kingdom east of the Dead Sea; for Israel was wholly unable to meet his forces in the open field. Month after month of the reign of the miserable son of Ahab must have been marked by tidings of shame, defeat, and massacre.

Added to these public calamities, there came to Ahaziah a terrible personal misfortune. As he was coming down from the roof of his palace, he seems to have stopped to lean against the lattice of some window or balcony in his upper chamber in Samaria.[1] It gave way under his weight, and he was hurled down into the courtyard or street below. He was so seriously hurt that he spent the rest of his reign on a sick-bed in pain and weakness, and ultimately died of the injuries he had received.

A succession of woes so grievous might well have

---

[1] 2 Kings i. 2; Heb., *be'ad hass'bakāh*; LXX., διὰ τοῦ δικτυωτοῦ: lg., *per cancellos* (comp. 1 Kings vii. 18; 2 Chron. iv. 12).

awakened the wretched king to serious thought. But
he had been trained under the idolatrous influences of
his mother. As though it were not enough for him to
walk in the steps of Ahab, of Jezebel, and of Jeroboam,
he had the fatuity to go out of his way to patronise
another and yet more odious superstition. Ekron was
the nearest town to him of the Philistine Pentapolis,
and at Ekron was established the local cult of a particular Baal known as Baal-Zebub ("the lord of flies ").[1]
Flies, which in temperate countries are sometimes an
intense annoyance, become in tropical climates an
intolerable plague. Even the Greeks had their Zeus
Apomuios ("Zeus the averter of flies"), and some Greek
tribes worshipped Zeus Ipuktonos ("Zeus the slayer of
vermin"), and Zeus Muiagros and Apomuios, and Apollo
Smintheus ("the destroyer of mice ").[2] The Romans, too,
among the numberless quaint heroes of their Pantheon,
had a certain Myiagrus and Myiodes, whose function
it was to keep flies at a distance.[3] This fly-god, Baal-
Zebub of Ekron, had an oracle, to whose lying responses

---

[1] LXX., Βάαλ μυῖαν θεὸν ᾿Ακκαρών. So, too, Jos., *Antt.*, IX. ii. 1. It is
possible that the god was represented holding a fly as the type of pestilence, just as the statue of Pthah held in its hands a mouse (Herod.,
ii. 141). Flies convey all kinds of contagion (Plin., *H. N.*, x. 28).

[2] Pausan., v. 14, § 2.

[3] The name, or a derisive modification of it, was given by the Jews
in the days of Christ to the prince of the devils. In Matt. xii. 24 the
true reading is Βεελζεβούλ, which perhaps means (in contempt) "the
lord of dung "; but might mean "the lord of the [celestial] habita-
tion " (οἰκοδεσπότην). Comp. Matt. x. 25; Eph. ii. 2; "Baal Shamaim,"
the Belsamen of Augustine (Gesen., *Monum. Phœnic.*, 387; Movers,
Phönizier, i. 176). For "opprobrious puns" applied to idols, see
Lightfoot, *Exercitationes ad Matt.*, xii. 24. The common word for idols,
gilloolim, is perhaps connected with *galal*, "dung." Hitzig thinks
that the god was represented under the symbol of the *Scarabæus
pillularius*, or dung-beetle.

the young and superstitious prince attached implicit
credence.   That a king of Israel professing any sort
of allegiance to Jehovah, and having hundreds of
prophets in his own kingdom, should send an embassy
to the shrine of an abominable local divinity in a town
of the Philistines—whose chief object of worship was

> "That twice-battered god of Palestine,
>   Who mourned in earnest when the captive ark
>   Maimed his brute image on the grunsel edge
>   Where he fell flat, and shamed his worshippers"—

was, it must be admitted, an act of apostasy more outrage-
ously insulting than had ever yet been perpetrated by
any Hebrew king.   Nothing can more clearly illustrate
the callous indifference shown by the race of Jezebel to
the lessons which God had so decisively taught them
by Elijah and by Micaiah.

But

> *Quem vult Deus perire, dementat prius;*

and in this "dementation preceding doom" Ahaziah
sent to ask the fly-god's oracle whether he should
recover of his injury.   His infatuated perversity became
known to Elijah, who was bidden by "the angel," or
messenger, "of the Lord"—which may only be the
recognised phrase in the prophetic schools, putting in a
concrete and vivid form the voice of inward inspiration
—to go up, apparently on the road towards Samaria,
and meet the messengers of Ahaziah on their way to
Ekron.   Where Elijah was at the time we do not know.
Ten years had elapsed since the calling of Elisha and
four since Elijah had confronted Ahab at the door of
Naboth's vineyard.   In the interval he has not once
been mentioned, nor can we conjecture with the least
certainty whether he had been living in congenial

solitude or had been helping to train the Sons of the Prophets in the high duties of their calling. Why he had not appeared to support Micaiah we cannot tell. Now, at any rate, the son of Ahab was drawing upon himself an ancient curse by going a-whoring after wizards and familiar spirits, and it was high time for Elijah to interfere.[1]

The messengers had not proceeded far on their way when the prophet met them, and sternly bade them go back to their king, with the denunciation, "Is it because there is no God in Israel that ye go to inquire of Baal-Zebub, the god of Ekron? Now, therefore, thus saith Jehovah, 'Thou shalt not descend from that bed on which thou art gone up, but dying thou shalt die.'"

He spoke, and after his manner vanished with no less suddenness.

The messengers, overawed by that startling apparition, did not dream of daring to disobey. They at once went back to the king, who, astonished at their reappearance before they could possibly have reached the oracle, asked them why they had returned.

They told him of the apparition by which they had been confronted. That it was a prophet who had spoken to them they knew; but the appearances of Elijah had been so few, and at such long intervals, that they knew not who he was.

"What sort of man was he that spoke to you?" asked the king.

"He was," they answered, "a lord of hair,[2] and girded about his loins with a girdle of skin."[3]

---

[1] Lev. xx. 6.

[2] בַּעַל שֵׂעָר (LXX., δασύς), whether in reference to his long shaggy locks, or his sheepskin *addereth*, μηλωτή (Zech. xiii. 4; Heb. xii. 37).

[3] ζώνη δερματίνη (Matt. iii. 4).

Too well did Ahaziah recognise from this description the enemy of his guilty race! If he had not been present on Carmel, or at Jezreel, on the occasions when that swart and shaggy figure of the awful Wanderer had confronted his father, he must have often heard descriptions of this strange Bedawy ascetic who " feared man so little because he feared God so much."

"It is Elijah the Tishbite!" he exclaimed, with a bitterness which was succeeded by fierce wrath; and with something of his mother's indomitable rage he sent a captain with fifty soldiers to arrest him.

The captain found Elijah sitting at the top of "the hill," perhaps of Carmel; and what followed is thus described :—

"Thou man of God," he cried, "the king hath said, Come down."

There was something strangely incongruous in this rude address. The title "man of God" seems first to have been currently given to Elijah, and it recognises his inspired mission as well as the supernatural power which he was believed to wield. How preposterous, then, was it to bid a man of God to obey a king's order and to give himself up to imprisonment or death!

"If I be a man of God," said Elijah, "then let fire come down from heaven, to consume thee and thy fifty."[1]

The fire fell and reduced them all to ashes.[2]

Undeterred by so tremendous a consummation, the king sent another captain with his fifty, who repeated the order in terms yet more imperative.[3]

---

[1] There is perhaps an intentional play of words between "man אִישׁ) of God " and "fire (אֵשׁ) of God " (Klostermann).

[2] Hebrew.   [3] "Come down *quickly*" (2 Kings i. 9).

Again Elijah called down the fire from heaven, and the second captain with his fifty soldiers was reduced to ashes.

For the third time the obstinate king, whose infatuation must indeed have been transcendent, despatched a captain with his fifty. But he, warned by the fate of his predecessors, went up to Elijah and fell on his knees, and implored him to spare the life of himself and his fifty innocent soldiers.

Then "the angel of the Lord" bade Elijah go down to the king with him and not be afraid.

What are we to think of this narrative?

Of course, if we are to judge it on such moral grounds as we learn from the spirit of the Gospel, Christ Himself has taught us to condemn it. There have been men who so hideously misunderstood the true lessons of revelation as to applaud such deeds, and hold them up for modern imitation. The dark persecutors of the Spanish Inquisition, nay, even men like Calvin and Beza, argued from this scene that "fire is the proper instrument for the punishment of heretics." To all who have been thus misled by a false and superstitious theory of inspiration, Christ Himself says, with unmistakable plainness, as He said to the Sons of Thunder at Engannim, "Ye know not what spirit ye are of. I am not come to destroy men's lives, but to save."[1] In the abstract, and judged by Christian standards, the

---

[1] Luke ix. 51–56. This is a more than sufficient answer to the censure of Theodoret, that "they who condemn the prophet are wagging their tongues against God." The remark is based on utter misapprehension; and if we are to form no judgment on the morality of Scripture examples, they would be of no help for us. Compare the striking remark of the minister to Balfour of Burleigh in Scott's *Old Mortality*.

calling down of lightning to consume more than a hundred soldiers, who were but obeying the orders of a king—the protection of personal safety by the miraculous destruction of a king's messengers—could only be regarded as a deed of horror. "There are few tracks of Elijah that are ordinary and fit for common feet," says Bishop Hall; and he adds, "Not in his own defence would the prophet have been the death of so many, if God had not, by a peculiar instinct, made him an instrument of His just vengeance."[1]

For myself, I more than doubt whether we have any right to appeal to these "peculiar instincts" and unrecorded inspirations; and it is so important that we should not form utterly false views of what Scripture does and does not teach, that we must once more deal with this narrative quite plainly, and not beat about the bush with the untenable devices and effeminate euphemisms of commentators, who give us the "to-and-fro-conflicting" apologies of *a priori* theory instead of the clear judgments of inflexible morality.

"It is impossible not to feel," says Professor Milligan,[2] "that the events thus presented to us are of a very startling kind, and that it is not easy to reconcile them either with the conception that we form of an honoured servant of God, or with our ideas of eternal justice. Elijah rather appears to us at first sight as a proud, arrogant, and merciless wielder of the power committed to him: we wonder that an answer should have been given to his prayer; we are shocked at the destruction of so many men, who listened only to the command of their captain and their king; and we cannot help contrasting Elijah's conduct, as a whole, with the

---

[1] Quoted by Rev. Professor Lumby, *ad loc.*
[2] *Elijah*, p. 146.

beneficent and loving tenderness of the New Testament dispensation."

Professor Milligan proceeds rightly to set aside the attempts which have been made to represent the first two captains and their fifties as especially guilty—which is a most flimsy hypothesis, and would not in any case touch the heart of the matter. He says that the event stands on exactly the same footing as the slaughter of the 450 prophets of Baal at Kishon, and of the 3000 idolaters by order of Moses at Sinai; the swallowing up of Korah, Dathan, and Abiram; the ban of total extirpation on Jericho and on Canaan; the sweeping massacre of the Amalekites by Saul; and many similar instances of recorded savagery. But the reference to analogous acts furnishes no justification for those acts. What, then, is their justification, if any can be found?

Some would defend them on the grounds that the potter may do what he likes with the clay. That analogy, though perfectly admissible when used for the purpose to which it is applied by St. Paul, is grossly inapplicable to such cases as this. St. Paul uses it simply to prove that we cannot judge or understand the purposes of God, in which, as he shows, mercy often lies behind apparent severity. But, when urged to maintain the rectitude of sweeping judgments in which a man arms his own feebleness with the omnipotence of Heaven, they amount to no more than the tyrant's plea that "might makes right." "Man is a reed," said Pascal, "but he is a *thinking* reed." He may not therefore be indiscriminately crushed. He was made by God in His image, after His likeness, and therefore his rights have a Divine and indefeasible sanction.

All that can be said is that these deeds of wholesale severity were not in disaccord with the conscience even of many of the best Old Testament saints. They did not feel the least compunction in inflicting judgments on whole populations in a way which would argue in us an infamous callousness. Nay, their consciences approved of those deeds; they were but acting up to the standard of their times, and they regarded themselves as righteous instruments of divinely directed vengeance.[1] Take, for instance, the frightful Eastern law which among the Jews no less than among Babylonians and Persians thought nothing of overwhelming the innocent with the guilty in the same catastrophe; which required the stoning, not only of Achan, but of all Achan's innocent family, as an expiation for his theft; and the stoning, not only of Naboth, but also of Naboth's sons, in requital for his asserted blasphemy. Two reasons may be assigned for the chasm between their moral sense and ours on such subjects—one was their amazing indifference to the sacredness of human life, and the other their invariable habit of regarding men in their corporate relations rather than in their individual capacity. Our conscience teaches us that to slay the innocent with the guilty is an action of monstrous injustice;[2] but they, regarding each person as indissolubly mixed up with all his family and tribe, magnified the conception

---

[1] This is practically the sum-total of the answer given again and again by Canon Mozley in his *Lectures on the Old Testament*, 2nd edition, 1878. For instance, he says that "the Jewish idea of justice gives us the reason why the Divine commands (of exterminating wars, etc.) were then adapted to man as the agent for executing them, and are not adapted now" (p. 102).

[2] Comp. Ezek. xviii, 2–30.

of *corporate responsibility,* and merged the individual
in the mass.

It is clear that, if we take the narrative literally,
Elijah would not have felt the least remorse in calling
fire from heaven to consume these scores of soldiers,
because the prophetic narrator who recorded the story,
perhaps two centuries later, must have understood
the spirit of those days, and certainly felt no shame
for the prophet's act of vengeance. On the contrary,
he relates it with entire approval for the glorification
of his hero. We cannot blame him for not rising
above the moral standard of his age. He held that
the natural manifestation of an angry Jehovah was,
literally or metaphorically, in consuming fire. Considering the slow education of mankind in the most
elementary principles of mercy and righteousness, we
must not judge the views of prophets who lived so
many ages before Christ by those of religious teachers
who enjoy the inherited experience of two millenniums
of Christianity. Thus much is plainly taught us by
Christ Himself, and there perhaps we might be content to leave the question. But we are compelled
to ask, Do we not too much form all our judgments
of the Scripture narratives on *a priori* traditions and
unreasoned prejudices? Can we with adequate knowledge and honest conviction declare our certainty
that this scene of destruction ever occurred as a
literal fact? If we turn to any of the great students
and critics of Germany, to whom we are indebted for
the floods of light which their researches have thrown
on the sacred page, they with almost consentient voice
regard these details of this story as legendary. There
is indeed every reason to believe the account of Ahaziah's
accident, of his sending to consult the oracle of Baal-

Zebub, of the turning back of his messengers by
Elijah, and of the menace which he heard from the
prophet's lips. But the calling down of lightning to
consume his captains and soldiers to ashes belongs to
the cycle of Elijah-traditions preserved in the schools
of the prophets ; and in the case of miracles so startling
and to our moral sense so repellent—miracles which
assume the most insensate folly on the part of the
king, and the most callous ruthlessness on the part of
the prophet—the question may be fairly asked, Is
there any proof, is there anything beyond dogmatic
assertion to convince us, that we were intended to
accept them *au pied de la lettre*? May they not be
the formal vehicle chosen for the illustration of the undoubted powers and righteous mission of Elijah as the
upholder of the worship of Jehovah ? In a literature
which abounds, as all Eastern literature abounds, in
vivid and concrete methods of indicating abstract truths,
have we any cogent proof that the supernatural details,
of which some may have been introduced into these
narratives by the scribes in the schools of the prophets,
were not, in some instances, *meant* to be regarded as
imaginative apologues ? The most orthodox divines,
both Jewish and Christian, have not hesitated to treat
the Book of Jonah as an instance of the use of fiction
for purposes of moral and spiritual edification. Were
any critic to maintain that the story of the destruction
of Ahaziah's emissaries belongs to the same class of
narratives, I do not know how he could be refuted,
however much he might be denounced by stereotyped
prejudice and ignorance. I do not, however, myself
regard the story as a mere parable composed to show
how awful was the power of the prophets, and how
fearfully it might be exercised. I look upon it rather

as possibly the narrative of some event which has been imaginatively embellished, and intermingled with details which we call supernatural.[1] Circumstances which we consider natural would be regarded as directly miraculous by an Eastern enthusiast, who saw in every event the immediate act of Jehovah to the exclusion of all secondary causes, and who attributed every ocurrence of life to the intervention of those "millions of spiritual creatures," who

> " walk the earth
> Unseen both when we wake and when we sleep."

If such a supposition be correct and admissible—and assuredly it is based on all that we increasingly learn of the methods of Eastern literature, and of the forms in which religious ideas were inculcated in early ages —then all difficulties are removed.   We are not dealing with the mercilessness of a prophet, or the wielding of Divine powers in a manner which higher revelation condemns, but only with the well-known fact that the Elijah-spirit was not the Christ-spirit, and that the scribes of Ramah or Gilgal, and "the men of the tradition" and the "men of letters" who lived at Jabez, when they used the methods of Targum and Haggadah in handling down the stories of the prophets, had not received that full measure of enlightenment which came only when the Light of the World had shone.[2]

---

[1] For the *idea* involved see Num. xi. 1 ; Deut. iv. 24 ; Psalm xxi. 9 ; Isa. xxvi. 11 ; Heb. x. 27, etc.

[2] 1 Chron. ii. 55, where "Shimeathites" means "men of the tradition," and "scribes," "men of letters."

CHAPTER II

THE ASCENSION OF ELIJAH

2 KINGS ii. 1—18

'Ηλίας ἐξ ἀνθρώπων ἠφανίσθη, καὶ οὐδεὶς ἔγνω μεχρὶς τῆς σήμερον αὐτοῦ τὴν τελεύτην.—Jos., *Antt.*, IX. ii. 2.

Γεγόνασιν ἀφανεῖς, θάνατον δὲ αὐτῶν οὐδεὶς οἶδεν.—St. Ephræm Syrus.

THE date of the assumption of Elijah is wholly uncertain, and it becomes still more so because of the confusion of chronological order which results from the composite character of the records here collected. It appears from various scattered notices that Elijah lived on till the reign of Jehoram of Judah, whereas the narrative in this chapter is placed before the death of Jehoshaphat.

When the time came that " Jehovah would take up Elijah by a whirlwind into heaven," the prophet had a prevision of his approaching end, and determined for the last time to visit the hills of his native Gilead. The story of his end, though not written in rhythm, is told in a style of the loftiest poetry, resembling other ancient poems in its simple and solemn repetitions. On his way to Gilead, Elijah desires to visit ancient sanctuaries where schools of the prophets were now established, and accompanied by Elisha, whose faithful ministrations he had enjoyed for ten almost silent years, he went to Gilgal. This was not the Gilgal in the Jordan valley so famous in the days of Joshua,[1] but *Jiljilia* in the hills of Ephraim,[2] where many young prophets were in course of training.[3]

Knowing that he was on his way to death, Elijah felt the imperious instinct which leads the soul to seek solitude at the supreme crises of life. He would have preferred that even Elisha should leave him, and he bade him stop at Gilgal, because the Lord had sent him as far as Bethel. But Elisha was determined to see the end, and exclaimed with strong asseveration, "As Jehovah liveth, and as thy soul liveth, I will not leave thee."

So they went on to Bethel, where there was another school of prophets, under the immediate shadow of Jeroboam's golden calf, though we are not told whether they continued the protest of the old nameless seer from Judah, or not.[4] Here the youths of the college came respectfully to Elisha—for they were prevented by a sense of awe from addressing Elijah—and asked him "whether he knew that that day God would take away his master." "Yes, I know it," he answers; but—for this is no subject for idle talk—"hold ye your peace."

Once more Elijah tries to shake off the attendance of his friend and disciple. He bids him stay at Bethel, since Jehovah has sent him on to Jericho. Once more Elisha repeats his oath that he will not leave him,

---

[1] Josh. iv. 19; v. 9, 10.

[2] Deut. xi. 30. It is on a hill south-west of Shiloh (*Seilun*), near the road to Jericho (Hos. iv. 15; Amos iv. 4). The name means "a circle," and there may have been an ancient circle of sacred stones there.

[3] 2 Kings iv. 38.

[4] 1 Kings xiii.

and once more the sons of the prophets at Jericho, who warn him of what is coming, are told to say no more.

But little of the journey now remains.   In vain Elijah urges Elisha to stay at Jericho; they proceed to Jordan.   Conscious that some great event is impending, and that Elijah is leaving these scenes for ever, fifty of the sons of the prophets watch the two as they descend the valley to the river.   Here they saw Elijah take off his mantle of hair, roll it up, and smite the waters with it.   The waters part asunder, and the prophets pass over dry-shod.[1]   As they crossed over Elijah asks Elisha what he should do for him, and Elisha entreats that a double portion of Elijah's spirit may rest upon him.   By this he does not mean to ask for twice Elijah's power and inspiration, but only for an elder son's portion, which was twice what was inherited by the younger sons.[2]   "Thou hast asked a hard thing," said Elijah; "but if thou seest me when I am taken hence, it shall be so."

The sequel can be only told in the words of the text: "And it came to pass, as they still went on, and talked, that, behold, there appeared a chariot of fire,

---

[1] As there are fords at Jericho, the object of this miracle, as of the one subsequently ascribed to Elisha, is not self-evident.   Nothing is more certain than that there is a Divine economy in the exercise of supernatural powers.   The pomp and prodigality of superfluous portents belong, not to Scripture, but to the *Acta sanctorum*, and the saint-stories of Arabia and India.

[2] Deut. xxi. 17.   The Hebrew is פִּי־שְׁנַיִם, "a mouthful, or ration of two."   Comp. Gen. xliii. 34.   Even Ewald's " *Nur Zweidrittel und auch diese kaum* " is too strong (*Gesch.*, iii. 517).   In no sense was Elisha greater than Elijah: he wrought more wonders, but he left little of his teaching, and produced on the mind of his nation a far less strong impression.

and horses of fire,[1] and parted them both asunder ; and Elijah went up by a whirlwind into heaven. And Elisha saw it, and he cried, ' My father, my father, the chariots of Israel, and the horsemen thereof!'[2] And he saw him no more."

Respecting the manner in which Elijah ended his earthly career, we know nothing beyond what is conveyed by this splendid narrative. His death, like that of Moses, was surrounded by mystery and miracles, and we can say nothing further about it. The question must still remain unanswered for many minds whether it was intended by the prophetic annalists for literal history, for spiritual allegory, or for actual events bathed in the colourings of an imagination to which the providential assumed the aspect of the supernatural.[3] We are twice told that " Elijah went up by a whirlwind into heaven,"[4] and in that storm—which would have seemed a fit scene for the close of a career of storm—God, in the high poetry of the Psalmist, may have made the winds His angels, and the flames of fire His ministers. For us it must suffice to say of Elijah,

---

[1] In 2 Kings vi. 17 the stormblast (*sā'ārāh*) and chariots and horses of fire are part of a vision of the Divine protection. Comp. Isa. lxvi. 15 ; Job xxxviii. 1 ; Nah. i. 3 ; Psalms xviii. 6-15, civ. 3.

[2] That is, the protection and defence of Israel by thy prayers.

[3] Even the Church-father St. Ephræm Syrus evidently felt some misgivings. He says : " Suddenly there came from the height a storm of fire, and in the midst of the flame the form of a chariot and horses, and parted them both asunder ; the one of them it left on the earth, the other it carried to the height ; but whether the wind carried him, or in what place it left him, the Scripture has not informed us, but it says that after some years, a terrifying letter from him full of menaces, was delivered to King Jehoram of Judah " (quoted by Keil *ad loc.*) See 2 Chron. xxi. 12. The letter is called " a writing " (*miktâb*).

[4] 2 Kings ii. 11 ; Ecclus. xlviii. 12. The LXX. curiously says ἐν συσσεισμῷ ὡς εἰς τὸν οὐρανόν. So too the Rabbis, *Sucah*, f. 5.

as the Book of Genesis says of Enoch, that " he was not, for God took him."

Elisha signalised the removal of his master by a burst of natural grief. He seized his garments and rent them in twain. Elijah had dropped his mantle of skin, and his grieving disciple took it with him as a priceless relic.[1] The legendary St. Antony bequeathed to St. Athanasius the only thing which he had, his sheep-skin mantle ; and in the mantle of Elijah his successor inherited his most characteristic and almost his sole possession. He returned to Jordan, and with this mantle he smote the waters as Elijah had done. At first they did not divide ;[2] but when he exclaimed, " Where is the Lord, the God of Elijah, even He ? " they parted hither and thither. Seeing the portent, the sons of the prophets came with humble prostrations, and acknowledged him as their new leader.

They were not, however, satisfied with what they had seen, or had heard from Elisha, of the departure of the great prophet, and begged leave to send fifty strong men to search whether the wind of the Lord had not swept him away to some mountain or valley. Elisha at first refused, but afterwards yielded to their persistent importunity. They searched for three days among the hills of Gilead, but found him not, either living or dead, as Elisha had warned them would be the case.

From that time forward Elijah has taken his place in all Jewish and Mohammedan legends as the mysterious and deathless wanderer. Malachi spoke of him as

---

[1] The circumstance has left its trace in the proverbs of nations, and in the German word *Mantelkind* for a spiritual successor.

[2] 2 Kings ii. 14. LXX., καὶ οὐ διῃρέθη; Vulg., *Percussit aquas, et non sunt divisæ.*

destined to appear again to herald the coming of the Messiah,[1] and Christ taught His disciples that John the Baptist had come in the spirit and power of Elijah. In Jewish legend he often appears and disappears. A chair is set for him at the circumcision of every Jewish child. At the Paschal feast the door is set open for him to enter. All doubtful questions are left for decision until he comes again. To the Mohammedans he is known as the wonder-working and awful El Khudr.[2]

Elisha is mentioned but once in all the later books of Scripture ; but Elijah is mentioned many times, and the son of Sirach sums up his greatness when he says : "Then stood up Elias as fire, and his word burned like a torch. O Elias, how wast thou honoured in thy wondrous deeds ! and who may glory like unto thee— who anointed kings to take revenge, and prophets to succeed after him—who wast ordained for reproof in their times, to pacify the wrath of the Lord's judgment before it broke forth into fury, and to turn the heart of the father unto the son, and to restore the tribes of Jacob ! Blessed are they that saw thee and slept in love ; for we shall surely live ! "

---

[1] Mal. iv. 4-6.

[2] *Bava-Metzia*, f. 37, 2, etc. His name is used for incantations in the Kabbala. *Kitsur Sh'lh*, f. 71, 1 (Hershon, *Talmudic Miscellany*, p. 340). The chair set for him is called "the throne of Elijah." For many Rabbinic legends see Hershon, *Treasures of the Talmud*, pp. 172–178. The Persians regard him as the teacher of Zoroaster.

CHAPTER III

ELISHA

2 KINGS ii. 1—25

"He did wonders in his life, and at death even his works were marvellous. For all this the people repented not."—ECCLUS. xlviii. 14, 15.

AT this point we enter into the cycle of supernatural stories, which gathered round the name of Elisha in the prophetic communities. Some of them are full of charm and tenderness; but in some cases it is difficult to point out their intrinsic superiority over the ecclesiastical miracles with which monkish historians have embellished the lives of the saints. We can but narrate them as they stand, for we possess none of the means for critical or historical analysis which might enable us to discriminate between essential facts and accidental elements.

We see at once that the figure of Elisha [1] is far less impressive than that of Elijah. He inspires less of awe and terror. He lives far more in cities and amid the ordinary surroundings of civilised life. The honour with which he was treated was the honour of respect and admiration for his kindliness. He plays his part in no stupendous scenes like those at Carmel and at Horeb, and nearly all his miracles were miracles of

---

[1] The name Elisha means "My God is salva 'on."

mercy. Other remarkable differences are observable in the records of Elijah and Elisha. In the case of the former his main work was the opposition to Baal-worship; but although Baal-worship still prevailed (2 Kings x. 18–27) we read of no protests raised by Elisha against it. " With him "—perhaps it should be more accurately said, in the narrative which tells us of him—" the miracles are everything, the prophetic work nothing." The conception of a prophet's mission in these stories of him differs widely from that which dominates the splendid *midrash* of Elijah.

His separate career began with an act of beneficence. He had stopped for a time at Jericho. The curse of the rebuilding of the town upon a site which Joshua had devoted to the ban had expended itself on Hiel, its builder. It was now a flourishing city, and the home of a large school of prophets. But though the situation was pleasant as "a garden of the Lord,"[1] the water was bad, and the land "miscarried." In other words, the deleterious spring caused diseases among the inhabitants, and caused the trees to cast their fruit. So the men of the city came to Elisha, and humbly addressing him as "my lord," implored his help. He told them to bring him a new cruse full of salt, and going with it to the fountain cast it into the springs, proclaiming in Jehovah's name that they were healed, and that there should be no more death or miscarrying land. The gushing waters of the Ain-es-Sultân, fed by the spring of Quarantania, are to this day pointed out as the Fountains of Elisha, as they have been since the days of Josephus.[2]

The anecdote of this beautiful interposition to help

---

[1] Gen. xiii. 10. " The city of palms " (Deut. xxxiv. 3).

[2] Jos., *B. J.*, IV. viii. 3 ; Robinson, *Bibl. Researches*, i. 554.

a troubled city is followed by one of the stories which
naturally repel us more than any other in the Old
Testament. Elisha, on leaving Jericho, returned to
Bethel, and as he climbed through the forest up the
ascent leading to the town through what is now called
the Wady Suweinît, a number of young lads—with the
rudeness which in boys is often a venial characteristic
of their gay spirits or want of proper training, and which
to this day is common among boys in the East—laughed
at him, and mocked him with the cry "Go up, round-
head! go up, round-head!"[1] What struck these ill-
bred and irreverent youngsters was the contrast between
the rough hair-skin garb and unkempt shaggy locks
of Elijah, "the lord of hair," and the smooth civilised
aspect and shorter hair of his disciple. If the word
quereach means "bald"[2] we see an additional reason
for their ill-mannered jeers, since baldness was a cause
of reproach and suspicion in the East, where it is
comparatively rare. No doubt, too, the conduct of
these young scoffers was the more offensive, and even
the more wicked, because of the deeper reverence for
age which prevails in Eastern countries, and above all
because Elisha was known as a prophet. Perhaps,
too, if some other reading lies behind the ἐλίθαζον
of one MS. of the Septuagint, they pelted him with

---

[1] Abarbanel's notion that they meant "Ascend to heaven as Elijah
did " is absurd.

[2] קֵרֵחַ. This means bald at the back of the head, as גִּבֵּחַ (*gibbeach*),
means "forehead-bald" (Ewald, iii. 512). Elisha could not have
been bald from old age, since he lived on for nearly sixty years, and
must have been a young man. Baldness involved a suspicion of
leprosy, and was disliked by Easterns (Lev. xxi. 5, xiii. 43;
Isa. iii. 17, 24, xv. 2), as much as by the Romans (Suet., *Jul. Cæs.*, 45;
Domit., 18). Elisha's prophetic activity lasted through the reigns of
Joram, Jehu, Jehoahaz, and Joash (*i.e.*, 12 + 28 + 17 + 2 years).

stones.[1] That Elisha should have rebuked them, and
that seriously—that he should even have inflicted some
punishment upon them to reform their manners—would
have been natural; but we cannot repress the shudder
with which we read the verse, "And he turned back
and looked on them, and cursed them in the name
of the Lord. And there came forth two she-bears out
of the wood, and tare forty-and-two children of them."
Surely the punishment was disproportionate to the
offence! Who could doom so much as a single rude
boy, not to speak of forty-two, to a horrible and
agonising death for shouting after any one? It is the
chief exception to the general course of Elisha's compassionate interpositions. Here, too, we must leave
the narrative where it is; but we hold it quite admissible
to conjecture that the incident, in some form or other,
really occurred—that the boys were insolent, and that
some of them may have been killed by the wild beasts
which at that time abounded in Palestine—and yet that
the *nuances* of the story which cause deepest offence
to us may have suffered from some corruption of the
tradition in the original records, and may admit of being
represented in a slightly different form.

After this Elisha went for a time to the ancient
haunts of his master on Mount Carmel, and thence
returned to Samaria, the capital of his country, which
he seems to have chosen for his most permanent
dwelling-place.

---

[1] The κατέπαιζον of the Vat. LXX. implies persistent and vehement
insult. The Post-Mishnic Rabbis, however, say that Elisha was
punished with sickness for this deed (*Bava-Metzia*, f. 87, 1).

CHAPTER IV

THE INVASION OF MOAB

2 KINGS iii. 4—27

"What reinforcement we may gain from hope,
If not, what resolution from despair."
MILTON, *Paradise Lost*, i. 190.

AHAZIAH, as Elijah had warned him, never recovered from the injuries received in his fall
through the lattice, and after his brief and luckless
reign died without a child. He was succeeded by his
brother Jehoram ("Jehovah is exalted"), who reigned
for twelve years.[1]

---

[1] There are great difficulties in the statement (2 Kings iii. 1) that
he began to reign in the eighteenth year of Jehoshaphat. I have not
entered, nor shall I enter, into the minute and precarious conjectures
necessitated by the uncertainties and contradictions of this synchronism introduced into the narrative by some editor. Suffice it
that with the aid of the Assyrian records we have certain *points de
repère*, from which we can, with the assistance of the historian,
conjecturally restore the main data. In the dates given at the head
of the chapters I follow Kittel, as a careful inquirer. Some of the
approximately fixed dates are (see Appendix I.):—

854. Battle of Karkar (Ahab and Benhadad against Shalmaneser II.)
738. Tribute of Menahem to Tiglath-Pileser II.
732. Fall of Damascus.
722. Capture of Samaria by Sargon.
720. Defeat of Sabaco by Sargon in battle of Raphia.
705. Accession of Sennacherib.
701. Campaign against Hezekiah.
608. Death of Josiah.

Jehoram began well. Though it is said that he did "that which was evil in the sight of the Lord," we are told that he was not so guilty as his father or his mother. He did not, of course, abolish the worship of Jehovah under the cherubic symbol of the calves; no king of Israel thought of doing that, and so far as we know neither Elijah, nor Elisha, nor Jonah, nor Micaiah, nor any genuine prophet of Israel before Hosea, ever protested against that worship, which was chiefly disparaged by prophets of Judah like Amos and the nameless seer.[1] But Jehoram at least removed the *Matstsebah* or stone obelisk which had been reared in Baal's honour in front of his temple by Ahab, or by Jezebel in his name.[2] In this direction, however, his reformation must have been exceedingly partial, for until the sweeping measures taken by Jehu the temple and images of Baal still continued to exist in Samaria under his very eyes, and must have been connived at if not approved.

The first great measure which occupied the thoughts of Jehoram was to subdue the kingdom of Moab, which had been restored to independence by the bravery of the great pastoral-king Mesha;[3] or at any rate to avenge the series of humiliating defeats which Mesha had inflicted on his brother Ahaziah. A war of forty years' duration[4] had ended in the complete success of Moab. The loss of a tribute of the fleeces of one

---

[1] But neither the man of God from Judah nor Amos directly denounce the calf-worship, so much as its concomitant sins and irregularities.

[2] Perhaps the true reading is "pillars" (LXX., Vulg., Arab.).

[3] He is called "a sheep-master," *noked*; LXX., νωκήδ. Elsewhere the word occurs only in Amos i. 1. The Alex. LXX. has ἦν φέρων φόρον.

[4] According to the Moabite Stone.

hundred thousand lambs and one hundred thousand rams was too serious to be lightly faced.[1] Jehoram laid his plans well. First he ordered a muster of all the men of war throughout his kingdom, and then appealed for the co-operation of Jehoshaphat and his vassal-king of Edom. Both kings consented to join him. Jehoshaphat had already been the victim of a powerful and wanton aggression on the part of King Mesha,[2] from which he had been delivered by the panic of his foes in the Valley of Salt. Though the king of Edom had, on that occasion, been an ally of Mesha, the forces of Edom had fallen the first victims of that internecine panic. Both Judah and Edom, therefore, had grave wrongs to avenge, and eagerly seized the opportunity to humble the growing pride of the people of Chemosh. The attack was wisely arranged. It was determined to advance against Moab from the south, through the territory of Edom, by a rough and mountainous track, and, as far as possible, to take the nation by surprise. The combined host took a seven days' circuit round the south of the Dead Sea, hoping to find an abundant supply of water in the stream which flows through the Wady-el-Ahsa, which separates Edom from Moab.[3] But owing to recent droughts the Wady was waterless, and the armies, with their horses, suffered all the agonies of thirst. Jehoram gave way

---

[1] It is not clear whether the lambs and rams were sent with the fleeces. The A.V. says "lambs and rams with their wool," in accordance with Josephus — μυριάδας εἴκοσι προβάτων σὺν τοῖς πόκοις. The LXX. has the vague ἐπὶ πόκων, and implies that this was a special fine after a defeat in the revolt (ἐν τῇ ἐπαναστάσει): but comp. Isa. xvi. 1.

[2] 2 Chron. xx. 1-30.

[3] Robinson (*Bibl. Res.*, ii. 157) identifies it with the brook *Zered*. Deut. ii. 13; Num. xxi. 12. The name means "valley of water-pits," W. R. Smith quotes Doughty, *Travels*, i. 26.

to despair, bewailing that Jehovah should have brought together these three kings to deliver them a helpless prey into the hands of Moab. But the pious Jehoshaphat at once thinks of "inquiring of the Lord" by some true prophet, and one of Jehoram's courtiers informs him that no less a person than Elisha, the son of Shaphat, who had been the attendant of Elijah, is with the host.[1] We are surprised to find that his presence in the camp had excited so little attention as to be unknown to the king;[2] but Jehoshaphat, on hearing his name, instantly acknowledged his prophetic inspiration. So urgent was the need, and so deep the sense of Elisha's greatness, that the three kings in person went on an embassy "to the servant of him who ran before the chariot of Ahab." Their humble appeal to him produced so little elation in his mind that, addressing Jehoram, who was the most powerful, he exclaimed, with rough indignation : "What have I to do with thee? Get thee to the prophets of thy father,"—nominal prophets of Jehovah, who will say to thee smooth things and prophesy deceits, as four hundred of them did to Ahab—"and to the Baal-prophets of thy mother." Instead of resenting this

---

[1] Comp. I Kings xxii. 7. The phrase "who poured water on the hands of Elijah" is a touch of Oriental custom which the traveller in remote parts of Palestine may still often see. Once, when driven by a storm into the house of the Sheykh of a tribe which had a rather bad reputation for brigandage, I was most hospitably entertained ; and the old white-haired Sheykh, his son, and ourselves were waited on by the grandson, a magnificent youth, who immediately after the meal brought out an old richly chased ewer and basin, and poured water over our hands, soiled by eating out of the common dish, of course without spoons or forks.

[2] This seems to have struck Josephus (*Antt.*, IX. iii. 1), who says that "he *chanced* to be in a tent (ἔτυχε κατεσκηνωκώς) outside the host.

scant respect Jehoram, in utmost distress, deprecated
the prophet's anger, and appealed to his pity for the
peril of the three armies.   But Elisha is not mollified.
He tells Jehoram that but for the presence of Jehoshaphat
he would not so much as look at him : so completely
was the destiny of the people mixed up with the
character of their kings!   Out of respect for Jehoshaphat
Elisha will do what he can.   But all his soul is in a
tumult of emotion.   For the moment he can do nothing.
He needs to be calmed from his agitation by the spell
of music, and bids them send a minstrel to him.   The
harper came, and as Elisha listened his soul was composed, and "the hand of the Lord came upon him" to
illuminate and inspire his thoughts.[1]   The result was
that he bade them dig trenches in the dry wady, and
promised that, though they should see neither wind nor
rain, the valley should be filled with water to quench
the thirst of the fainting armies, their horses and their
cattle.   After this God would also deliver the Moabites
into their hand ; and they were bidden to smite the
cities, fell the trees, stop the wells, and mar the smiling
pasture-lands, which constituted the wealth of Moab,
with stones.   That the hosts of Judah and Israel and
jealous Edom should be prone to afflict this awfully
devastating vengeance on a power by which they had
been so severely defeated on past occasions, and on
which they had so many wrongs and blood-feuds to
avenge, was natural; but it is surprising to find a
prophet of the Lord giving the commission to ruin the
gifts of God and spoil the innocent labours of man,
and thus to inflict misery on generations yet unborn.

---

[1] Comp. I Sam. x. 5 ; I Chron. xxv. 1; Ezek. i. 3, xxxiii. 22.
Menaggēn is one who plays on a stringed instrument, *n'gināh*. The
Pythagoreans used music in the same way (Cic., *Tusc. Disp.*, iv. 2).

The behest is directly contrary to rules of international war which have prevailed even between non-Christian nations, among whom the stopping or poisoning of wells and the cutting down of fruit trees has been expressly forbidden. It is also against the rules of war laid down in Deuteronomy.[1] Such, however, was the command attributed to Elisha; and, as we shall see, it was fulfilled, and seems to have led to disastrous consequences.

Cheered by the promise of Divine aid which the prophet had given them, the host retired to rest. The next morning at day-dawn, when the *minchah* of fine flour, oil, and frankincense was offered,[2] water, which, according to the tradition of Josephus, had fallen at three days' distance on the hills of Edom, came flowing from the south and filled the wady with its refreshing streams.

The incident itself is highly instructive. It throws light both upon the general accuracy of the ancient narrative, and on the fact that events to which a directly supernatural colouring is given are, in many instances, not so much supernatural as providential. The deliverance of Israel was due, not to a portent wrought by Elisha, but to the pure wisdom which he derived from the inspiration of God. When the counsels of princes were of none effect, and for lack of the spirit of counsel the people were perishing, his mind alone, illuminated by a wisdom from on high, saw what was the right step to take. He bade the soldiers dig trenches in the dry torrent bed,—which was the very step most likely to ensure their deliverance from the torment of thirst, and which would be done under similar circumstances to

---

[1] Deut. xx. 19, 20.
[2] Lev. ii. 1.   Comp. 1 Kings xviii. 36.

this day. They saw neither wind nor rain ; but there had been a storm among the farther hills, and the swollen watercourses discharged their overflow into the trenches of the wady which were ready prepared for them, and offered the path of least resistance.

Moab, meanwhile, had heard of the advance of the three kings through the territories of Edom. The whole military population had mustered in arms, and stood on the frontier, on the other side of the dry wady, to oppose the invasion. For they knew this would be a struggle of life and death, and that if defeated they would have no mercy to expect. When the sun rose, and its first rays burned on the wady, which had been dry on the previous evening, the water which, unknown to the Moabites, had filled the trenches in the night, looked red as blood. Doubtless it may have been stained, as Ewald says, by the red soil which gave its name to the red land of the "red king, Edom"; but as it gleamed under the dawn the Moabites thought that those seemingly crimson pools had been filled with the blood of their enemies, who had fallen by each other's swords. Their own recent experience when Jehoshaphat met them in the Valley of Salt showed them how easy it was for temporary allies to be seized by panic, and to fight among themselves.[1]

The army of their invaders was composed of heterogeneous and mutually conflicting elements. Between Israel and Judah there had been nearly a century of war,[2] and only a brief reunion ; and Edom, recently the willing and natural ally of Moab, was not likely to fight very zealously for Judah, which had reduced her to vassalage. So the Moabites said to one another,

---

[1] This dreadful result crippled the revolt of Vindex against Nero.
[2] Jeroboam I., B.C. 937 ; Joram, 854.

as they pointed to the unexpected apparition of those red pools: "This is blood. The kings are surely destroyed, and they have smitten each man his fellow. Moab to the spoil !" They rushed down tumultuously on the camp of Israel, and found the soldiers of Jehoram ready to receive them. Taken by surprise, for they had expected no resistance, they were hurled back in utter confusion and with immense slaughter. The three kings pushed their advantage to the utmost. They went forward into the land, driving and smiting the Moabites before them, and ruthlessly carrying out the command attributed to Elisha. They beat down the cities—most of which in a land of flocks and herds were little more than pastoral villages; they rendered the green fields useless with stones; they filled up all the wells with earth ; they felled every fruit-bearing tree of any value. At last only one stronghold, Kir-haraseth, the chief fenced town of Moab, held out against them.[1] Even this fortress was sore bested. The slingers, for which Israel, and specially the tribe of Benjamin, was so famous, advanced to drive its defenders from the battlements. King Mesha fought with undaunted heroism. He decided to take the seven hundred warriors who were left to him, and cut his way through the besieging host to the king of Edom. He thought that even now he might persuade the Edomites to abandon this new and unnatural alliance, and turn the battle against their common

[1] Isa. xv. 1, Kir of Moab; Jer. xlviii. 31, Kir-heres. It is built on a steep calcareous rock, surrounded by a deep, narrow glen, which thence descends westward to the Dead Sea, under the name of the Wady Kerak. We know that the armies of Nineveh habitually practised these brutal modes of devastation in the districts which they conquered. See Layard, *passim* ; Rawlinson, *Ancient Monarchies,* ii. 84.

enemies. But the numbers against him were too strong, and he found the plan impossible. Then he formed a dreadful resolution, dictated to him by the extremity of his despair. His inscription at Karcha shows that he was a profound and even fanatical believer in Chemosh, his god. Chemosh could still deliver him. If Chemosh was, as Mesha says in his inscription, " angry with his land "—if, even for a time, he allowed his faithful people and his devoted king to be afflicted—it could not be for any lack of power on his part, but only because they had in some way offended him, so that he was wroth, or because he had gone on a journey, or was asleep, or deaf.[1] How could he be appeased? Only by the offering of the most precious of all the king's possessions ; only by the self-devotion of the crown-prince, on whom were centred all the nation's hopes. Mesha would force Chemosh to help him for very shame. He would offer to Chemosh a human sacrifice, the sacrifice of his eldest son that should have reigned in his stead. Doubtless the young prince gave himself up as a willing offering, for that was essential to the holocaust being valid and acceptable.[2]

So upon the wall of Kir-haraseth, in the sight of all the Moabites, and of the three invading armies, the brave and desperate hero of a hundred fights, who had inflicted so many reverses upon these enemies, and received so many at their hands, but who, having liberated his country, now saw all the efforts of his life ruined at one blow—took his eldest son, kindled the

---

[1] 1 Kings xviii. 27. Comp. Psalm xxxv. 23, xliv. 23, lxxxiii. 1, etc.

[2] Comp. Micah vi. 7. This is an entirely different incident from that alluded to in Amos ii. 1.

sacrificial fire, and then and there solemnly offered that horrible burnt-offering.[1]

And it proved effectual, though far otherwise than Mesha had expected. He was delivered; and, doubtless, if ever he reared, at Kirharaseth or elsewhere, another memorial stone, he would have attributed his deliverance to his national god. But here, in the annals of Elisha, the result is hurried over, and a veil is, so to speak, dropped upon the dreadful scene with the one ambiguous expression, "And there was great wrath against Israel : and they departed from him, and returned to their own land."

The phrase awakens but does not satisfy our curiosity. We are not certain of the translation, or of the meaning. It may be, as in the margin of the Revised Version, "there came great wrath upon Israel."[2] But wrath from whom? and on what account? The word "wrath" all but invariably denotes divine wrath; but we cannot imagine (as some critics do) that any Israelite of the schools of the prophets would sanction the notion that the chosen people were allowed to suffer from the kindled wrath of Chemosh. Can we then suppose that the desperate act of King Mesha was a proof that Israel, who was no doubt the most interested and the most remorseless of the invaders, had pressed the Moabites too hard, and carried his vengeance much too far? That is by no means impossible. The prophet Amos denounces upon Moab in after years

---

[1] Eusebius (*Præp. Evang.*, iv. 16) quotes from Philo's Phœnician history a reference to human sacrifices (τοῖς τιμωροῖς δαίμοσιν) at moments of desperation.

[2] The rendering is doubtful. LXX., καὶ ἐγένετο μετάμελος μέγας ἐπὶ Ἰσράηλ; Vulg., indignatio *in* Israel; Luther, *Da ward Israel sehr zornig*.

the doom that fire should devour the palaces of Kirioth,
and that Moab should perish with shoutings, and all
his royal line be cut off, for the far less offence of having
burned into lime the bones of the king of Edom.[1]   The
command of Elisha did not exempt the Israelites from
their share of moral responsibility.   Jehu was commissioned to be an executioner of vengeance upon the
house of Ahab.   Yet Jehu is expressly condemned by
the prophet Hosea for the tiger-like ferocity and
horrible thoroughness with which he had carried out
his destined work.[2]   Only one other explanation is
possible.   If "wrath" here has the unusual sense of
human indignation, the clause can only imply that the
armies of Judah and Edom were roused to anger by
the unpitying spirit which Israel had displayed.   The
horrible tragedy enacted upon the wall of Kirharaseth
awoke their consciences to the sense of human compassion.   These, after all, were fellow-men—fellow-men
of kindred blood to their own—whom they had driven
to straits so frightful as to cause a king to burn his
own heir alive as a mute appeal to his god in the hour
of overwhelming ruin.   They had done enough:

"Sunt lacrimæ rerum et mentem mortalia tangunt."

They hastily broke up the league, dissolved the alliance,
returned horror-stricken to their own land.   They left
Moab indeed in possession of his last fortress, but they
had reduced his territory to a wilderness before they
retired and called it peace.

---

[1] Amos ii. 1-3.
[2] Hos. i. 4: "I will avenge the blood of Jezreel upon the house
of Jehu."

CHAPTER V

ELISHA'S MIRACLES

2 Kings iv. 1—44

WE are now in the full tide of Elisha's miracles, and as regards many of them we can do little more than illustrate the text as it stands. The record of them clearly comes from some account prevalent in the schools of the prophets, which is however only fragmentary, and has been unchronologically pieced into the annals of the kings of Israel.

The story of Elisha abounds far more in the supernatural than that of Elijah, and is believed by most critics to be of earlier date. Yet the scenes and portents of his life are almost wholly lacking in the element of grandeur which belong to those of the elder seer. His personality, if on the whole softer and more beneficent, inspires less of awe, and the whole tone of the biography which recorded these isolated incidents is lacking in the poetic and impassioned elevation which marks the episodes of Elijah's history. We see in the records of Elisha, as in the biographies—so rich in prodigies—of fourth-century hermits and mediæval saints, how little impressive in itself is the exercise of abnormal powers; how it derives its sole grandeur from the accompaniment of great moral lessons and spiritual revelations. John the Baptist "did no miracle," yet our Lord placed him not only far above Elisha, but even above Moses and Samuel and Elijah, when He said of him, "Verily I say unto you, of them that have been born of women there hath not risen a greater than John the Baptist."

It is impossible not to be struck with the singular parallelism between the powers exercised by Elisha and those which are attributed to his predecessor. "How true an heir is Elisha of his master," says Bishop Hall, "not in his graces only, but in his actions! Both of them divided the waters of Jordan, the one as his last act, the other as his first. Elijah's curse was the death of the captains and their troops; Elisha's curse was the death of the children. Elijah rebuked Ahab to his face; Elisha, Jehoram. Elijah supplied the drought of Israel by rain from heaven; Elisha supplied the drought of the three kings by waters gushing out of the earth; Elijah increased the oil of the Sareptan, Elisha increased the oil of the prophet's widow; Elijah raised from death the Sareptan's son, Elisha the Shunammite's; both of them had one mantle, one spirit; both of them climbed up one Carmel, one heaven." The resemblance, however, is not at all in character, but only in external and miraculous circumstances. In all other respects Elisha furnishes a contrast to Elijah which startles us quite as much as any superficial resemblances. Elijah was a free, wild Bedawy prophet, hating and shunning as his ordinary residence the abodes of men, making his home in the rocky wady or in the mountain glades, appearing and disappearing suddenly as the wind. He asserted his power most often in ministries of retribution. Clad in the sheepskin of a Gadite shepherd or mountaineer, he was not one of those who wear soft clothing or are found in kings' houses. He usually met monarchs as their enemy and their reprover, but for the most part avoided them. He never intervened for years together even in national events of the utmost importance, whether military or religious, unless he received the direct call of God, or there appeared to him to be a "*dignus Vindice nodus.*" Elisha, on the other hand, makes his home in cities, and chiefly in Samaria. He is familiar with kings and moves about with armies, and has no long retirements into unknown solitudes ; and though he could speak roughly to Jehoram, he is often on the friendliest terms with him and with other sovereigns.

The stories of Elisha give us many interesting glimpses into the social life of Israel in his day. As to their literal historic accuracy, those must make positive affirmation who feel that they can do so in accordance alike with adequate authority and with the sacredness of truth. Many will be unable to escape the opinion that they bear some resemblance to other Jewish haggadoth, written for edification, with every innocent intention, in the schools of the Prophets, but no more intended for perfectly literal acceptance in all their details than the Life of St. Paul the Hermit, by St. Jerome ; or that of St. Antony, attributed erroneously to St. Athanasius ; or that of St. Francis in the Fioretti ; or the lives of humble saints of the people called *Kisar-el-anbiah*, which are so popular among poor Mohammedans. Into that question there is no need to enter further. *Abundet quisque in sensu suo.*

I. On one occasion a widow of one of the Sons of the Prophets—for these communities, though cœnobitic, were not celibate—came to him in deep distress. Her husband—the Jews, with their usual guesswork, most improbably identify him with Obadiah, the chamberlain of Ahab [1]—had died insolvent.　As she had nothing to pay, her creditor under the grim provision of the law was about to exercise his right of selling her two sons into slavery to recoup himself for the debt.[2]　Would Elisha help her?

Prophets were never men of wealth, so that he could not pay her debt.　He asked her what she possessed to satisfy the demand.　"Nothing," she said, "but a pot of the common oil, used for anointing the body after a bath."

Elisha bade her go and borrow from her neighbours all the empty vessels she could, then to return home, shut the door, and pour the oil into the vessels.

She did so.　They were all filled, and she asked her son to bring yet another.　But there was not another to be had, so she went out and told the Man of God. He bade her sell the miraculously multiplied oil to pay the debt, and live with her sons on the proceeds of. what was over.

II.　We next find Elisha at Shunem, famous as the abode of the fair maiden—probably Abishag, the nurse of David's decrepitude—who is the heroine of the Song of Songs.　It is a village, now called Solam, on the slopes of Little Hermon (Jebel-el-Duhy), three miles north of Jezreel.　At this place there lived a lady of wealth and influence, whose husband owned the surrounding land.　There were but few khans in Palestine, and even where they now exist the traveller has in most cases to supply his own food.　Elisha, in his journeys to and fro among the schools of the Prophets,

---

[1] Jos., *Antt.*, IX. iv. 2.　This perhaps is only suggested by the reminiscences of 1 Kings xviii. 2, 3, 12.

[2] Lev. xxv. 39–41 ; Matt. xviii. 25.

had often enjoyed the welcome hospitality eagerly pressed upon him by the lady of Shunem. Struck with his sacred character, she persuaded her husband to take a step unusual even to the boundless hospitality of the East. She begged him to do honour to this holy Man of God by building for him a little chamber (*alïyah*) on the flat roof of the house, to which he might have easy and private access by the outside staircase.[1] The chamber was built, and furnished, like any other simple Eastern room, with a bed, a divan to sit on, a table, and a lamp ; and there the weary prophet on his journeys often found a peaceful, simple, and delightful resting-place.

Grateful for the reverence with which she treated him, and the kind care with which she had supplied his needs, Elisha was anxious to recompense her in whatever way might be possible. The thought of money payment was of course out of the question : merely to hint at it would have been a breach of manners. But perhaps he might be of use to her in some other way. At this time, and for years afterwards during his long ministry of perhaps fifty-six years, he was attended by a servant named Gehazi, who stood to him in the same sort of relation which he had held to Elijah. He told Gehazi to summon the Shunammite lady. In the deep humility of Eastern womanhood she came and stood in his presence. Even then he did not address her. So downtrodden was the position of women in the East that any dignified person, much more a great prophet, could not converse with a woman without compromising his dignity. The more

---

[1] 2 Kings iv. 10. Not "a little chamber on the wall " (A.V.), but " an *alïyah* with walls " (margin, R.V.).

scrupulous Pharisees in the days of Christ always carefully gathered up their garments in the streets, lest they should so much as touch a woman with their skirts in passing by, as the modern Chakams in Jerusalem do to this day.[1] The disciples themselves, sophisticated by familiarity with such teachers, were astonished that Jesus at the well of Shechem should talk with a woman.[2] So, though the lady stood there, Elisha, instead of speaking to her directly, told Gehazi to thank her for all the devout respect and care, all 'the modesty of fearful duty,'[3] which she had displayed towards them, and to ask her if he should say a good word for her to the King or the Captain of the Host. This is just the sort of favour which an Eastern would be likely to value most.[4] The Shunammite, however, was well provided for ; she had nothing to complain of, and nothing to request. She thanked Elisha for his kindly proposal, but declined it, and went away.

"Is there, then, nothing which we can do for her ? " asked Elisha of Gehazi.[5]

There was. Gehazi had learnt that the sorrow of her life—a sorrow and a source of reproach to any Eastern household, but most of all to that of a wealthy householder—was her childlessness.

" Call her," he said.

---

[1] Frankl., *Jews in the East.*

[2] John iv. 27 : " Then came His disciples, and marvelled that He was *talking* (μετὰ γυναικὸς) *with a woman.*"

[3] 2 Kings iv. 13 : "Behold, thou hast been careful for us with all this care" (LXX., πᾶσαν τὴν ἔκστασιν ταύτην).

[4] The Sheykh with whom I stayed at Bint es Jebeil could think of no return which I could offer for his hospitality so acceptable as if I would say a good word for him to the authorities at Beyrout.

[5] Gehazi is usually called the *na'ar* or "lad" of Elisha—a term implying lower service than Elisha's "ministry" to Elijah.

She came back, and stood reverently in the doorway. "When the time comes round," he said to her, "you shall embrace a son."

The promise raised in her heart a thrill of joy. It was too precious to be believed. "Nay," she said, "my lord, thou Man of God, do not lie unto thine handmaid."

But the promise was fulfilled, and the lady of Shunem became the happy mother of a son.

III. The charming episode then passes over some years. The child had grown into a little boy, old enough now to go out alone to see his father in the harvest fields and to run about among the reapers. But as he played about in the heat he had a sunstroke, and cried to his father, "O my head, my head!" Not knowing how serious the matter was, his father simply ordered one of his lads to carry the child home to his mother. The fond mother nursed him tenderly upon her knees, but at noon he died.

Then the lady of Shunem showed all the faith and strength and wisdom of her character. "The good Shunammite," says Bishop Hall, "had lost her son; her faith she lost not." Overwhelming as was this calamity —the loss of an only child—she suppressed all her emotions, and, instead of bursting into the wild helpless wail of Eastern mourners, or rushing to her husband with the agonising news, she took the little boy's body in her arms, carried it up to the chamber which had been built for Elisha, and laid it upon his bed. Then, shutting the door, she called to her husband to send to her one of his reapers and one of the asses, for she was going quickly to the Man of God and would return in the cool of the evening. "Why should you go to-day particularly?" he asked. "It is neither new

moon, nor sabbath." "It is all right," she said;[1] and
with perfect confidence in the rectitude of all her
purposes, he sent her the she-ass, and a servant to
drive it and to run beside it for her protection on the
journey of sixteen miles.

"Drive on the ass," she said. "Slacken me not the
riding unless I tell you." So with all possible speed
she made her way—a journey of several hours—from
Shunem to Mount Carmel.

Elisha, from his retreat on the hill, marked her
coming from a distance, and it rendered him anxious.
"Here comes the Shunammite," he said to Gehazi.
"Run to meet her, and ask Is it well with thee? is it
well with thy husband? is it well with the child?"

"All well," she answered, for her message was not
to Gehazi, and she could not trust her voice to speak;
but pressing on up-hillwards, she flung herself before
Elisha and grasped his feet. Displeased at the
familiarity which dared thus to clasp the feet of his
master, Gehazi ran up to thrust her away by force,
but Elisha interfered. "Let her alone," he cried; "she
is in deep affliction, and Jehovah has not revealed to
me the cause." Then her long pent-up emotion burst
forth. "Did I desire a son of my lord?" she cried.
"Did I not say do not deceive me?"

It was enough—though she seemed unable to bring
out the dreadful words that her boy was dead. Catch-
ing her meaning, Elisha said to Gehazi, "Gird up thy
loins, take my staff, and without so much as stopping
to salute any one, or to return a salutation,[2] lay my
staff on the dead child's face." But the broken-hearted

---

[1] 2 Kings iv. 23. Hebrew "Peace"; A.V., "It shall be well."

[2] Salutations occupy some time in the formally courteous East.
Comp. Luke x. 4.

mother refused to leave Elisha.   She imagined that the servant, the staff, might be severed from Elisha ; but she knew that wherever the prophet was, there was power.   So Elisha arose and followed her, and on the way Gehazi met them with the news that the child lay still and dead, with the fruitless staff upon his face.

Then Elisha in deep anguish went up to the chamber and shut the door, and saw the boy's body lying pale upon his bed.   After earnest prayer he outstretched himself over the little corpse, as Elijah had done at Zarephath.   Soon it began to grow warm with returning life, and Elisha, after pacing up and down the room, once more stretched himself over him.   Then the child opened his eyes and sneezed seven times, and Elisha called to Gehazi to summon the mother.

" Take up thy son," he said.   She prostrated herself at his feet in speechless gratitude, and took up her recovered child, and went.

IV. We next find Elisha at Gilgal, in the time of the famine of which we read his prediction in a later chapter.[1]   The sons of the prophets were seated round him, listening to his instructions ; the hour came for their simple meal, and he ordered the great pot to be put on the fire for the vegetable soup, on which, with bread, they chiefly lived.   One of them went out for herbs, and carelessly brought his outer garment (the *abeyah*)[2] full of wild poisonous coloquinths,[3] which, by ignorance or inadvertence, were shred into the pottage. But when it was cooked and poured out they perceived

---

[1] 2 Kings viii. 1.

[2] Not "lap," as in A.V. (Heb., *beged*) ; LXX. συνέλιξε πλῆρες τὸ ἱμάτιον αὐτοῦ ; Vulg., *implevit vestem suam* (both correctly).

[3] Heb., *paquoth* ; LXX., τολύπην ἀγρίαν ; Vulg., *colocynthidas agri.* Hence the name *cucumis prophetarum.*

the poisonous taste, and cried out, "O Man of God, death in the pot!"

"Bring meal," he said, for he seems always to have been a man of the fewest words.

They cast in some meal, and were all able to eat of the now harmless pottage. It has been noticed that in this, as in other incidents of the story, there is no invocation of the name of Jehovah.

V. Not far from Gilgal was the little village of Baalshalisha,[1] at which lived a farmer who wished to bring an offering of firstfruits and *karmel* (bruised grain) in his wallet to Elisha as a Man of God.[2] It was a poor gift enough—only twenty of the coarse barley loaves which were eaten by the common people, and a sack[3] full of fresh ears of corn.[4] Elisha told his servitor[5]—perhaps Gehazi—to set them before the people present. "What?" he asked, "this trifle of food before a hundred men!" But Elisha told him in the Lord's name that it should more than suffice; and so it did.

---

[1] Lord of the Chain and "Three lands." Three wadies meet a this spot, a little west of Bethel.

[2] 2 Kings iv. 42. Karmel, Lev. ii. 14. Perhaps a sort of frumenty.

[3] The word for "wallet" (*tsiqlon*; Vulg., *pera*) occurs here only. Peshito, "garment." The Vatican LXX. omits it. The Greek version has ἐν κωρύκῳ αὐτοῦ.

[4] See Lev. ii. 14, xxiii. 14.

[5] 2 Kings iv. 43. The word for "his servitor" (*m'chartho*) is used also of Joshua. It does not mean a mere ordinary attendant. LXX., λειτουργός; Vulg., *minister*.

CHAPTER VI

THE STORY OF NAAMAN

2 Kings v. 1—27

Matt. viii. 3 : Θέλω, καθαρίσθητι

AFTER these shorter anecdotes we have the longer episode of Naaman.[1]

A part of the misery inflicted by the Syrians on Israel was caused by the forays in which their light-armed bands, very much like the borderers on the marches of Wales or Scotland, descended upon the country and carried off plunder and captives before they could be pursued.

In one of these raids they had seized a little Israelitish girl and sold her to be a slave. She had been purchased for the household of Naaman, the captain of the Syrian host, who had helped his king and nation to win important victories either against Israel or against Assyria. Ancient Jewish tradition identified him with the man who had "drawn his bow at a venture" and slain King Ahab. But all Naaman's valour and rank and fame, and the honour felt for him by his king, were valueless to him, for he was suffering from the horrible affliction of leprosy. Lepers do not seem to

---

[1] It is curiously omitted by Josephus, though he mentions him (Ἄμανος) as the slayer of Ahab (*Antt.*, VIII. xv. 5). The name is an old Hebrew name (Num. xxvi. 40).

have been segregated in other countries so strictly as
they were in Israel, or at any rate Naaman's leprosy
was not of so severe a form as to incapacitate him from
his public functions.

But it was evident that he was a man who had won
the affection of all who knew him ; and the little slave
girl who waited on his wife breathed to her a passionate
wish that Naaman could visit the Man of God in
Samaria, for he would recover him from his leprosy.
The saying was repeated, and one of Naaman's friends
mentioned it to the king of Syria. Benhadad was
so much struck by it that he instantly determined to
send a letter, with a truly royal gift to the king of
Israel, who could, he supposed, as a matter of course,
command the services of the prophet. The letter came
to Jehoram with a stupendous present of ingots of
silver to the value of ten talents, and six thousand
pieces of gold, and ten changes of raiment.[1] After the
ordinary salutations, and a mention of the gifts, the
letter continued "And now, when this letter is come
to thee, behold I have sent Naaman my servant, that
thou mayest recover him of his leprosy."

Jehoram lived in perpetual terror of his powerful
and encroaching neighbour. Nothing was said in the
letter about the Man of God ; and the king rent his
clothes, exclaiming that he was not God to kill and to
make alive, and that this must be a base pretext for
a quarrel. It never so much as occurred to him, as
it certainly would have done to Jehoshaphat, that the
prophet, who was so widely known and honoured,
and whose mission had been so clearly attested in the
invasion of Moab, might at least help him to face this

---

[1] The word *l'boosh* means a gala dress. Comp. v. 5; Gen. xlv. 22.
χιτῶνες ἐπημοιβοί (Hom., *Od.*, xiv. 514). Comp. viii. 249.

problem.   Otherwise the difficulty might indeed seem insuperable, for leprosy was universally regarded as an incurable disease.

But Elisha was not afraid : he boldly told Jehoram to send the Syrian captain to him.   Naaman, with his horses and his chariots, in all the splendour of a royal ambassador, drove up to the humble house of the prophet.   Being so great a man, he expected a deferential reception, and looked for the performance of his cure in some striking and dramatic manner.   "The prophet," so he said to himself, "will come out, and solemly invoke the name of his God Jehovah, and wave his hand over the leprous limbs, and so work the miracle."[1]

But the servant of the King of kings was not exultantly impressed, as false prophets so often are, by earthly greatness.   Elisha did not even pay him the compliment of coming out of the house to meet him. He wished to efface himself completely, and to fix the leper's thoughts on the one truth that if healing was granted to him, it was due to the gift of God, not to the thaumaturgy or arts of man.   He simply sent out his servant to the Syrian commander-in-chief with the brief message, "Go and wash in Jordan seven times, and be thou clean."

Naaman, accustomed to the extreme deference of many dependants, was not only offended, but enraged, by what he regarded as the scant courtesy and procrastinated boon of the prophet.   Why was he not received as a man of the highest distinction ?   What necessity could there be for sending him all the way to the Jordan ?   And why was he bidden to wash in that wretched, useless, tortuous stream, rather than in

---

[1] Elisha would not be likely to *touch* the place.

the pure and flowing waters of his own native Abanah and Pharpar?[1] How was he to tell that this "Man of God" did not design to mock him by sending him on a fool's errand, so that he would come back as a laughing-stock both to the Israelites and to his own people? Perhaps he had not felt any great faith in the prophet, to begin with; but whatever he once felt had now vanished. He turned and went away in a rage.

But in this crisis the affection of his friends and servants stood him in good stead. Addressing him, in their love and pity, by the unusual term of honour "my father," they urged upon him that, as he certainly would not have refused some *great* test, there was no reason why he should refuse this simple and humble one.

He was won over by their reasonings, and descending the hot steep valley of the Jordan, bathed himself in the river seven times. God healed him, and, as Elisha had promised, "his flesh," corroded by leprosy, "came again like the flesh of a little child, and he was clean."

This healing of Naaman is alluded to by our Lord to illustrate the truth that the love of God extended farther than the limits of the chosen race; that His Fatherhood is co-extensive with the whole family of man.

It is difficult to conceive the transport of a man cured of this most loathsome and humiliating of all earthly afflictions. Naaman, who seems to have possessed "a mind naturally Christian," was filled with gratitude. Unlike the thankless Jewish lepers whom Christ cured as He left Engannim, this alien returned

---

[1] Now the *Burâda* ("cold") and the Nahr-el-Awâj.

to give glory to God. Once more the whole imposing
cavalcade rode through the streets of Samaria, and
stopped at Elisha's door. This time Naaman was
admitted into his presence. He saw, and no doubt
Elisha had strongly impressed on him the truth, that
his healing was the work not of man but of God; and
as he had found no help in the deities of Syria, he
confessed that the God of Israel was the only true God
among those of the nations. In token of his thankful-
ness he presses Elisha, as God's instrument in the
unspeakable mercy which has been granted to him to
accept "a blessing" (*i.e.*, a present) from him—"from
thy servant," as he humbly styled himself.

Elisha was no greedy Balaam. It was essential that
Naaman and the Syrians should not look on him as on
some vulgar sorcerer who wrought wonders for "the
rewards of divination." His wants were so simple that
he stood above temptation. His desires and treasures
were not on earth. To put an end to all importunity,
he appealed to Jehovah with his usual solemn formula—
"As the Lord liveth before whom I stand, I will receive
no present."[1]

Still more deeply impressed by the prophet's incorruptible superiority to so much as a suspicion of low
motives, Naaman asked that he might receive two
mules' burden of earth wherewith to build an altar to
the God of Israel of His own sacred soil.[2] The very

---

[1] Compare the answer of Abraham to the King of Sodom (Gen.
xiv. 23.)

[2] The feeling which influenced Naaman is the same which led
the Jews to build Nahardea in Persia of stones from Jerusalem.
Altars were to be of earth (Exod. xx. 24), but no altar is mentioned
in 2 Kings v. 17, and the LXX. does not even specify *earth* (γόμος
ζεῦγος ἡμιόνων).

soil ruled by such a God must, he thought, be holier
than other soil; and he wished to take it back to
Syria, just as the people of Pisa rejoiced to fill their
Campo Santo with mould from the Holy Land, and
just as mothers like to baptize their children in water
brought home from the Jordan.   Henceforth, said
Naaman, I will offer burnt-offering and sacrifice to no
God but unto Jehovah.   Yet there was one difficulty
in the way.   When the King of Syria went to worship
in the temple of his god Rimmon it was the duty of
Naaman to accompany him.[1]   The king leaned on his
hand, and when he bowed before the idol it was
Naaman's duty to bow also.   He begged that for this
concession God would pardon him.

Elisha's answer was perhaps different from what
Elijah might have given.   He practically allowed
Naaman to give this sign of outward compliance with
idolatry, by saying to him, "Go in peace."   It is from
this circumstance that the phrase "to bow in the house
of Rimmon" has become proverbial to indicate a
dangerous and dishonest compromise.   But Elisha's
permission must not be misunderstood.   He did but
hand over this semi-heathen convert to the grace of
God.   It must be remembered that he lived in days
long preceding the conviction that proselytism is a part
of true religion; in days when the thought of missions
to heathen lands was utterly unknown.   The position
of Naaman was wholly different from that of any

---

[1] This is the only place in Scripture where Rimmon is mentioned,
though we have the name Tab-Rimmon ("Rimmon is good"), 1 Kings
xv. 18, and Hadad-Rimmon (Zech. xii. 11).   He was the god of the
thunder.   The word means "pomegranate," and some have fancied
that this was one of his symbols.   But the resemblance may be
accidental, and the name was properly *Ramman.*

Israelite.   He was only the convert, or the half-convert
of a day, and though he acknowledged the supremacy
of Jehovah as alone worthy of his worship, he probably
shared in the belief—common even in Israel—that there
were other gods, local gods, gods of the nations, to
whom Jehovah might have divided the limits of their
power.[1]   To demand of one who, like Naaman, had
been an idolater all his days, the sudden abandonment
of every custom and tradition of his life, would have
been to demand from him an unreasonable, and, in his
circumstances, useless and all but impossible self-
sacrifice.   The best way was to let him feel and see
for himself the futility of Rimmon-worship.   If he
were not frightened back from his sudden faith in
Jehovah, the scruple of conscience which he already
felt in making his request might naturally grow within
him and lead him to all that was best and highest.
The temporary condonation of an imperfection might
be a wise step towards the ultimate realisation of a truth.
We cannot at all blame Elisha, if, with such knowledge
as he then possessed, he took a mercifully tolerant view
of the exigencies of Naaman's position.   The bowing
in the house of Rimmon under such conditions probably
seemed to him no more than an act of outward respect
to the king and to the national religion in a case where
no evil results could follow from Naaman's example.[2]

---

[1] See Deut. xxxii. 8, where the LXX. has κατὰ ἀριθμὸν ἀγγέλων.

[2] The moral difficulty must have been early felt, for the Alexandrian
LXX. reads καὶ προσκυνήσω ἅμα αὐτῷ ἐγὼ Κυρίῳ τῷ Θεῷ μου.   But
he would still be bowing in the House of Rimmon, though he might
in his heart worship God.   "Elisha, like Elijah" (says Dean Stanley),
"made no effort to set right what had gone so wrong.   Their mission
was to make the best of what they found; not to bring back a rule
of religion which had passed away, but to dwell on the Moral Law
which could be fulfilled everywhere, not on the Ceremonial Law

But the general principle that *we* must *not* bow in
the house of Rimmon remains unchanged.   The light
and knowledge vouchsafed to us far transcend those
which existed in times when men had not seen the
days of the Son of Man.   The only rule which sincere
Christians can follow is to have no truce with Canaan,
no halting between two opinions, no tampering, no
compliance, no connivance, no complicity with evil,—
even no tolerance of evil as far as their own conduct
is concerned.   No good man, in the light of the Gospel
dispensation, could condone himself in seeming to
sanction—still less in doing—anything which in his
opinion ought not to be done, or in saying anything
which implied his own acquiescence in things which he
knows to be evil.   "Sir," said a parishioner to one
of the non-juring clergy : "there is many a man who has
made a great gash in his conscience ; cannot you make a
little nick in yours ?"   No ! a *little* nick is, in one sense,
as fatal as great gash.   It is an abandonment of *the
principle* ; it is a violation of the Law.   The wrong of
it consists in this—that all evil begins, not in the commission of great crimes, but in the slight divergence
from right rules.   The angle made by two lines may be
infinitesimally small, but produce the lines and it may
require infinitude to span the separation between the
lines which inclose so tiny an angle.   The wise man
gave the only true rule about wrong-doing, when he
said, "Enter not into the path of the wicked and go not
in the way of evil men.   Avoid it, pass not by it, turn

---

which circumstances seemed to have put out of their reach : 'not
sending the Shunammite to Jerusalem' (says Cardinal Newman), 'not
eager for a proselyte in Naaman, yet making the heathen fear the
Name of God, and proving to them that there was a prophet in
Israel'" (Stanley, *Lectures*, ii. 377 ; Newman, *Sermons*, viii. 415).

from it and pass away."[1]   And the reason for his rule
is that the beginning of sin—like the beginning of
strife—"is as when one letteth out water."[2]

The proper answer to all abuses of any supposed
concession to the lawfulness of bowing in the house
of Rimmon—if that be interpreted to mean the doing
of anything which our consciences cannot wholly approve—is *Obsta principiis*—avoid the beginnings of evil.

> "We are not worst at once; the course of evil
>   Begins so slowly, and from such slight source,
>   An infant's hand might stem the breach with clay;
>   But let the stream grow wider, and philosophy,
>   Age, and religion too, may strive in vain
>   To stem the headstrong current."

The mean cupidity of Gehazi, the servant of Elisha,
gives a deplorable sequel to the story of the prophet's
magnanimity.   This man's wretched greed did its
utmost to nullify the good influence of his master's
example.   There may be more wicked acts recorded
in Scripture than that of Gehazi, but there is scarcely
one which shows so paltry a disposition.

He had heard the conversation between his master
and the Syrian marshal, and his cunning heart despised
as a futile sentimentality the magnanimity which had
refused an eagerly proffered reward.   Naaman was
rich : he had received a priceless boon ; it would be
rather a pleasure to him than otherwise to return for
it some acknowledgment which he would not miss.
Had he not even seemed a little hurt by Elisha's refusal
to receive it ?   What possible harm could there be in
taking what he was anxious to give ?   And how useful
those magnificent presents would be, and to what
excellent uses could they be put !   He could not
approve of the fantastic and unpractical scrupulosity

---

[1] Prov. iv. 14, 15.   [2] Prov. xvii. 14.

which had led Elisha to refuse the "blessing" which
he had so richly earned. Such attitudes of unworldli-
ness seemed entirely foolish to Gehazi.

So pleaded the Judas-spirit within the man. By
such specious delusions he inflamed his own covetousness, and fostered the evil temptation which had taken
sudden and powerful hold upon his heart, until it took
shape in a wicked resolve.

The mischief of Elisha's quixotic refusal was done,
but it could be speedily undone, and no one would be
the worse. The evil spirit was whispering to Gehazi :—

> "Be mine and Sin's for one short hour ; and then
> Be all thy life the happiest man of men."

"Behold," he said, with some contempt both for
Elisha and for Naaman, "my master hath let off this
Naaman the Syrian ; but as the Lord liveth I will run
after him, and take somewhat of him."

"As the Lord liveth!" It had been a favourite
appeal of Elijah and Elisha, and the use of it by
Gehazi shows how utterly meaningless and how very
dangerous such solemn words become when they are
degraded into formulæ.[1] It is thus that the habit of
swearing begins. The light use of holy words very
soon leads to their utter degradation. How keen is
the satire in Cowper's little story :—

> "A Persian, humble servant of the sun,
> Who, though devout, yet bigotry had none,
> Hearing a lawyer, grave in his address,
> With adjurations every word impress,—
> Supposed the man a bishop, or, at least,
> God's Name so often on his lips—a priest.
> Bowed at the close with all his gracious airs,
> And begged an interest in his frequent prayers!"

---

[1] On Gehazi's lips it meant no more than the incessant *Wallah*, "by
God," of Mohammedans.

Had Gehazi felt their true meaning—had he realised that on Elisha's lips they meant something infinitely more real than on his own, he would not have forgotten that in Elisha's answer to Naaman they had all the validity of an oath, and that he was inflicting on his master a shameful wrong, when he led Naaman to believe that, after so sacred an adjuration, the prophet had frivolously changed his mind.

Gehazi had not very far to run,[1] for in a country full of hills, and of which the roads are rough, horses and chariots advance but slowly. Naaman, chancing to glance backwards, saw the prophet's attendant running after him. Anticipating that he must be the bearer of some message from Elisha, he not only halted the cavalcade, but sprang down from his chariot,[2] and went to meet him with the anxious question, "Is all well?"

"Well," answered Gehazi; and then had ready his cunning lie. "Two youths," he said, " of the prophetic schools had just unexpectedly come to his master from the hill country of Ephraim; and though he would accept nothing for himself, Elisha would be glad if Naaman would spare him two changes of garments, and one talent of silver for these poor members of a sacred calling."[3]

Naaman must have been a little more or a little less than human if he did not feel a touch of disappointment on hearing this message. The gift was nothing to him.

---

[1] 2 Kings v. 19. Heb., *kib'rath aretz*, "a little way"—literally, "a space of country." (The Vatican LXX. follows another reading, εἰς Δεββαθὰ τῆς γῆς ; Vulg., *electo terræ tempore* [?].)

[2] LXX., κατεπήδησεν.

[3] A talent of silver was worth about £400—an enormous sum for two half-naked youths.

It was a delight to him to give it, if only to lighten
a little the burden of gratitude which he felt towards
his benefactor.   But if he had felt elevated by the
magnanimous example of Elisha's disinterestedness, he
must have thought that this hasty request pointed to
a little regret on the prophet's part for his noble self-
denial.   After all, then, even prophets were but men,
and gold after all was gold!   The change of mind
about the gift brought Elisha a little nearer the ordinary
level of humanity, and, so far, it acted as a sort of
disenchantment from the high ideal exhibited by his
former refusal.   And so Naaman said, with alacrity,
" Be content : take two talents."

The fact that Gehazi's conduct thus inevitably com-
promised his master, and undid the effects of his
example, is part of the measure of the man's apostacy.
It showed how false and hypocritical was his position,
how unworthy he was to be the ministering servant of
a prophet.   Elisha was evidently deceived in the man
altogether.   The heinousness of his guilt lies in the
words *Corruptio optimi pessima.*   When religion is used
for a cloak of covetousness, of usurping ambition, of
secret immorality, it becomes deadlier than infidelity.
Men raze the sanctuary, and build their idol temples
on the hallowed ground.   They cover their base
encroachments and impure designs with the "cloke
of profession, doubly lined with the fox-fur of hypocrisy,"
and hide the leprosy which is breaking out upon their
foreheads with the golden *petalon* on which is inscribed
the title of "holiness to the Lord."

At first Gehazi did not like to take so large a sum
as two talents ; but the crime was already committed,
and there was not much more harm done in taking two
talents than in taking one.   Naaman urged him, and

it is very improbable that, unless the chances of detection weighed with him, he needed much urging. So the Syrian weighed out silver ingots to the amount of two talents, and putting them in two satchels laid them on two of his servants and told them to carry the money before Gehazi to Elisha's house. But Gehazi had to keep a look-out lest his nefarious dealings should be observed, and when they came to Ophel—the word means the foot of the hill of Samaria, or some part of the fortifications [1]—he took the bags from the two Syrians, dismissed them, and carried the money to some place where he could conceal it in the house. Then, as though nothing had happened, with his usual smooth face of sanctimonious integrity, the pious Jesuit went and stood before his master.

He had not been unnoticed! His heart must have sunk within him when there smote upon his ear Elisha's question,—

"Whence comest thou, Gehazi?"

But one lie is as easy as another, and Gehazi was doubtless an adept at lying.

"Thy servant went no whither," he replied, with an air of innocent surprise.

"*Went not* my beloved one?" [2] said Elisha—and he must have said it with a groan, as he thought how utterly unworthy the youth, whom he thus called "my loving heart" or "my dear friend,"—"when the man turned from his chariot to meet thee?" It may be

---

[1] 2 Kings v. 24. The LXX. (εἰς τὸ σκοτεινὸν) seems to have read אֹפֶל (*ophel*); "darkness," a treasury or secret place, for עֹפֶל, and so the Vulgate *jam vesperi*.

[2] 2 Kings v. 26. The verse is so interpreted by some critics, especially Ewald, followed by Stanley. Margin, R.V.: "Mine heart went not from me, when " etc.

that from the hill of Samaria Elisha had seen it all, or
that he had been told by one who had seen it. If not, he
had been rightly led to read the secret of his servant's
guilt. "Is it a time," he asked, "to act thus?" Did
not my example show thee that there was a high object
in refusing this Syrian's gifts, and in leading him to
feel that the servants of Jehovah do His bidding with
no afterthought of sordid considerations? Are there
not enough troubles about us actual and impending,
to show that this is no time for the accumulation of
earthly treasures? Is it a time to receive money—
and all that money will procure? to receive garments,
and olive-yards and vineyards, and oxen, and men-
servants and maid-servants? Has a prophet no higher
aim than the accumulation of earthly goods, and are his
needs such as earthly goods can supply? And hast
thou, the daily friend and attendant of a prophet, learnt
so little from his precepts and his example?

Then followed the tremendous penalty for so grievous
a transgression—a transgression made up of meanness,
irreverence, greed, cheating, treachery, and lies.

"The leprosy therefore of Naaman shall cleave unto
thee, and unto thy seed for ever!" "Oh heavy talents
of Gehazi!" exclaims Bishop Hall: "Oh the horror
of the one unchangeable suit! How much better had
been a light purse and a homely coat, with a sound
body and a clean soul!"

"And he went out from his presence a leper as white
as snow." [1]

It is the characteristic of the leprous taint in the
system to be thus suddenly developed, and apparently
in crises of sudden and overpowering emotion it might
affect the whole blood. And one of the many morals

---

[1] Exod. iv. 6; Num. xii. 10.

which lie in Gehazi's story is again that moral to which the world's whole experience sets its seal—that though the guilty soul may sell itself for a desired price, the sum-total of that price is nought. It is Achan's ingots buried under the sod on which stood his tent. It is Naboth's vineyard made abhorrent to Ahab on the day he entered it. It is the thirty pieces of silver which Judas dashed with a shriek upon the Temple floor. It is Gehazi's leprosy for which no silver talents or changes of raiment could atone.

The story of Gehazi—of the son of the prophets who would naturally have succeeded Elisha as Elisha had succeeded Elijah—must have had a tremendous significance to warn the members of the prophetic schools from the peril of covetousness. That peril, as all history proves to us, is one from which popes and priests, monks, and even nominally ascetic and nominally pauper communities, have never been exempt;—to which, it may even be said, that they have been peculiarly liable. Mercenariness and falsity, displayed under the pretence of religion, were never more overwhelmingly rebuked. Yet, as the Rabbis said, it would have been better if Elisha, in repelling with the left hand, had also drawn with the right.[1]

The fine story of Elisha and Naaman, and the fall and punishment of Gehazi, is followed by one of the anecdotes of the prophet's life which appears to our unsophisticated, perhaps to our imperfectly enlightened judgment, to rise but little above the ecclesiastical portents related in mediæval hagiologies.

[1] The later Rabbis thought that Elisha was too severe with Gehazi, and was punished with sickness because " he repelled him with both his hands" (*Bava-Metsia*, f. 87, 1, and *Yalkut Jeremiah*).

At some unnamed place—perhaps Jericho—the house of the Sons of the Prophets had become too small for their numbers and requirements, and they asked Elisha's leave to go down to the Jordan and cut beams to make a new residence. Elisha gave them leave, and at their request consented to go with them. While they were hewing, the axe-head of one of them fell into the water, and he cried out, "Alas! master, it was borrowed!" Elisha ascertained where it had fallen. He then cut down a stick,[1] and cast it on the spot, and the iron swam and the man recovered it.

The story is perhaps an imaginative reproduction of some unwonted incident. At any rate, we have no sufficient evidence to prove that it may not be so. It is wholly unlike the economy invariably shown in the Scripture narratives which tell us of the exercise of supernatural power. All the eternal laws of nature are here superseded at a word, as though it were an every-day matter, without even any recorded invocation of Jehovah, to restore an axe-head, which could obviously have been recovered or resupplied in some much less stupendous way than by making iron swim on the surface of a swift-flowing river. It is easy to invent conventional and à priori apologies to show that religion demands the unquestioning acceptance of this prodigy, and that a man must be shockingly wicked who does not feel certain that it happened exactly in the literal sense ; but whether the doubt or the defence be morally worthier, is a thing which God alone can judge.[2]

---

[1] The Hebrew word for "cut off" (*qatsab*) is very rare. LXX., ἀπέκνισε ξύλον ; Vulg., *præcidit lignum.*

[2] It must be further borne in mind that "the iron did swim" (A.V.) is less accurate than "made the iron to swim" (R.V.). The LXX. has ἐπεπόλασε, "brought to the surface." Von Gerlach says, "He thrust the stick into the water, and raised the iron to the surface."

CHAPTER VII

ELISHA AND THE SYRIANS

2 KINGS vi. 1—23

"Now there was found in the city a poor wise man, and he by his wisdom delivered the city."—ECCLES. ix. 15.

ELISHA, unlike his master Elijah, was, during a great part of his long career, intimately mixed up with the political and military fortunes of his country. The king of Israel who occurs in the following narratives is left nameless—always the sign of later and more vague tradition ; but he has usually been identified with Jehoram ben-Ahab, and, though not without some misgivings, we shall assume that the identification is correct. His dealings with Elisha never seem to have been very cordial, though on one occasion he calls him " my father." The relations between them at times became strained and even stormy.

His reign was rendered miserable by the incessant infestation of Syrian marauders. In these difficulties he was greatly helped by Elisha. The prophet repeatedly frustrated the designs of the Syrian king by revealing to Jehoram the places of Benhadad's ambuscades, so that Jehoram could change the destination of his hunting parties or other movements, and escape the plots laid to seize his person. Benhadad, finding himself thus frustrated, and suspecting that

it was due to treachery, called his servants together
in grief and indignation, and asked who was the
traitor among them. His officers assured him that
they were all faithful, but that the secrets whispered
in his bed-chamber were revealed to Jehoram by Elisha
the prophet in Israel, whose fame had spread into
Syria, perhaps because of the cure of Naaman. The
king, unable to take any step while his counsels were
thus published to his enemies, thought—not very consistently—that he could surprise and seize Elisha
himself, and sent to find out where he was. At that
time he was living in Dothan, about twelve miles north-
east of Samaria,[1] and Benhadad sent a contingent with
horses and chariots by night to surround the city, and
prevent any escape from its gates. That he could thus
besiege a town so near the capital shows the helpless-
ness to which Israel had been now reduced.

When Elisha's servitor rose in the morning he was
terrified to see the Syrians encamped round the city,
and cried to Elisha, " Alas ! my master, what shall we
do ? "

" Fear not," said the prophet : " they that be with
us are more than they that be with them." He
prayed God to grant the youth the same open eyes,
the same spiritual vision which he himself enjoyed ; and
the youth saw the mountain full of horses and chariots
of fire round about Elisha.

This incident has been full of comfort to millions,
as a beautiful illustration of the truth that—

> "The hosts of God encamp around
> The dwellings of the just ;
> Deliverance He affords to all
> Who on His promise trust.

---

[1] Gen. xxxvii. 17, *Dothain*, "two wells" (?).

> "Oh, make but trial of His love,
>   Experience will decide,
>   How blest are they, and only they,
>   Who in His truth confide."

The youth's affectionate alarm had not been shared by his master. He knew that to every true servant of God the promise will be fulfilled, "He shall defend thee under His wings; thou shalt be safe under His feathers; His righteousness and truth shall be thy shield and buckler." [1]

Were our eyes similarly opened, we too should see the reality of the Divine protection and providence, whether under the visible form of angelic ministrants or not. Scripture in general, and the Psalms in particular, are full of the serenity inspired by this conviction. The story of Elisha is a picture-commentary on the Psalmist's words: "The angel of the Lord encampeth round them that fear Him, and delivereth them." [2] "He shall give His angels charge over thee, to keep thee in all thy ways." [3] "And I will encamp about Mine house because of the army, because of him that passeth by, and because of him that returneth: and no oppressor shall pass through them any more: for now have I seen with Mine eyes." [4] "The angel of His presence saved them: in His love and in His pity He redeemed them; and He bare them, and carried them all the days of old." [5]

But what is the exact meaning of all these lovely promises? They do not mean that God's children and saints will always be shielded from anguish or defeat, from the triumph of their enemies, or even from apparently hopeless and final failure, or miserable death.

---

[1] Psalm xci. 4.
[2] Psalm xxxiv. 7.
[3] Psalm xci. 11.
[4] Zech. ix. 8.
[5] Isa. lxiii. 9.

The lesson is not that their persons shall be inviolable, or that the enemies who advance against them to eat up their flesh shall always stumble and fall. The experiences of tens of thousands of troubled lives and martyred ends instantly prove the futility of any such reading of these assurances. The saints of God, the prophets of God, have died in exile and in prison, have been tortured on the rack and broken on the wheel, and burnt to ashes at innumerable stakes ; they have been destitute, afflicted, tormented, in their lives—stoned, beheaded, sawn asunder, in every form of hideous death ; they have rotted in miry dungeons, have starved on desolate shores, have sighed out their souls into the agonising flame. The Cross of Christ stands as the emblem and the explanation of their lives, which fools count to be madness, and their end without honour. On earth they have, far more often than not, been crushed by the hatred and been delivered over to the will of their enemies. Where, then, have been those horses and chariots of fire ?

They have been there no less than around Elisha at Dothan. The eyes spiritually opened have seen them, even when the sword flashed, or the flames wrapped them in indescribable torment. The sense of God's protection has least deserted His saints when to the world's eyes they seemed to have been most utterly abandoned. There has been a joy in prisons and at stakes, it has been said, far exceeding the joy of harvest. "Pray for me," said a poor boy of fifteen, who was being burned at Smithfield in the fierce days of Mary Tudor. "I would as soon pray for a dog as for a heretic like thee," answered one of the spectators. "Then, Son of God, shine Thou upon me !" cried the boy-martyr ; and instantly, upon a dull and cloudy day, the sun shone out, and bathed his young face in glory; whereat, says the martyrologist, men greatly marvelled. But is there one death-bed of a saint on which that glory has not shone?

The presence of those horses and chariots of fire, unseen by the carnal eye—the promises which, if they be taken literally, all experience seems to frustrate—mean two things, which they who are the heirs of such promises, and who would without them be of all men most miserable, have clearly understood.

They mean, first, that as long as a child of God is on the path of duty, and until that duty has been fulfilled, he is inviolable and invulnerable. He shall tread upon the lion and the adder; the young lion and the dragon shall he trample under his feet. He shall take up the serpent in his hands; and if he drink any deadly thing, it shall not hurt him. He shall not be afraid of the terror by night, nor of the arrow that flieth by day; of the pestilence that walketh in darkness, nor of the demon that destroyeth in the noonday. A thousand shall fall at his right hand, and ten thousand beside him; but it shall not come nigh him. The histories and the legends of numberless marvellous deliverances all confirm the truth that, when a man fears the Lord, He will keep him in all his ways, and give His angels charge over him, lest at any time he dash his foot against a stone. God will not permit any mortal force, or any combination of forces, to hinder the accomplishment of the task entrusted to His servant. It is the sense of this truth which, under circumstances however menacing, should enable us to

> "bate no jot
> Of heart or hope, but still bear up, and steer
> Uphillward"

It is this conviction which has nerved men to face
insuperable difficulties, and achieve impossible and
unhoped-for ends. It works in the spirit of the cry,
" Who art thou, O great mountain ? Before Zerubbabel
be thou changed into a plain ! " It inspires the faith
as a grain of mustard seed which is able to say to this
mountain, " Be thou removed, and be thou cast into
the sea,"—and it shall obey. It stands unmoved upon
the pinnacle of the Temple whereon it has been
placed, while the enemy and the tempter, smitten by
amazement, falls. In the hour of difficulty it can cry,—

> "Rescue me, O Lord, in this mine evil hour,
> As of old so many by Thy mighty power,—
> Enoch and Elias from the common doom ;
> Noe from the waters in a saving home ;
> Abraham from the abounding guilt of heathenesse;
> Job from all his multiform and fell distress ;
> Isaac when his faither's knife was raised to slay;
> Lot from burning Sodom on the judgment day;
> Moses from the land of bondage and despair;
> Daniel from the hungry lions in their lair ;
> And the children three amid the furnace flame;
> Chaste Susanna from the slander and the shame;
> David from Golia, and the wrath of Saul ;
> And the two Apostles from their prison-thrall."

The strangeness, the unexpectedness, the apparently
inadequate source of the deliverance, have deepened the
trust that it has not been due to accident. Once, when
Felix of Nola was flying from his enemies, he took
refuge in a cave, and he had scarcely entered it before
a spider began to spin its web over the fissure. The
pursuer, passing by, saw the spider's web, and did not
look into the cave ; and the saint, as he came out into
safety, remarked : " *Ubi Deus est, ibi aranea murus, ubi
non est ibi murus aranea* " ("Where God is, a spider's

web is as a wall; where He is not, a wall is but as a spider's web ").

This is one lesson conveyed in the words of Christ when the Pharisees told Him that Herod desired to kill Him. He knew that Herod could not kill Him till He had done His Father's will and finished His work. "Go ye," He said, "and tell this fox, Behold, I cast out devils, and I do cures to-day and to-morrow, and the third day I shall be perfected. Nevertheless, I must walk to-day, and to-morrow, and the day following."

But had all this been otherwise—had Felix been seized by his pursuers and perished, as has been the common lot of God's prophets and heroes—he would not therefore have felt himself mocked by these exceeding great and precious promises. The chariots and horses of fire are still there, and are there to work a deliverance yet greater and more eternal. Their office is not to deliver the perishing body, but to carry into God's glory the immortal soul. This is indicated in the death-scene of Elijah. This was the vision of the dying Stephen. This was what Christian legend meant when it embellished with beautiful incidents such scenes as the death of Polycarp. This was what led Bunyan to write, when he describes the death of Christian, that "all the trumpets sounded for him on the other side." When poor Captain Allan Gardiner lay starving to death in that Antarctic isle with his wretched companions, he yet painted on the entrance of the cave which had sheltered them, and near to which his remains were found, a hand pointing downward at the words, "Though He slay me, yet will I put my trust in Him."

There was a touch of almost joyful humour in the

way in which Elisha proceeded to use, in the present
emergency, the power of Divine deliverance. He seems
to have gone out of the town and down the hill to the
Syrian captains,[1] and prayed God to send them illusion
($\dot{a}\beta\lambda\epsilon\psi\acute{\iota}a$), so that they might be misled.[2]   Then he
boldly said to them, " You are being deceived : you
have come the wrong way, and to the wrong city.   I
will take you to the man whom ye seek."   The incident
reminds us of the story of Athanasius, who, when he
was being pursued on the Nile, took the opportunity
of a bend of the river boldly to turn back his boat
towards Alexandria.   "Do you know where Athanasius
is ? " shouted the pursuers.   "He is not far off !"
answered the disguised Archbishop ; and the emissaries
of Constantius went on in the opposite direction from
that in which he made his escape.

Elisha led the Syrians in their delusion straight into
the city of Samaria, where they suddenly found themselves at the mercy of the king and his troops.   Delighted at so great a chance of vengeance, Jehoram eagerly
exclaimed, " My father, shall I smite, shall I smite ? "

Certainly the request cannot be regarded as unnatural, when we remember that in the Book of
Deuteronomy, which did not come to light till after this
period, we read the rule that, when the Israelites had
taken a besieged city, " thou shalt smite every male
thereof with the edge of the sword ";[3] and that when
Israel defeated the Midianites [4] they slew all the males,

---

[1] Adopting the reading of the Syriac version : "And when they
[Elisha and his servant] came down to them [the Syrians]."   The
ordinary reading is " to *him*," which makes the narrative less clear.

[2] 2 Kings vi. 19.   סַנְוֵרִים, *ἀορασία*, only found in Gen. xix. 11.

[3] Deut. xx. 13.

[4] Num. xxxi. 7.

and Moses was wroth with the officers of the host because they had not also slain all the women. He then (as we are told) ordered them to slay all except the virgins, and also—horrible to relate—"*every male among the little ones.*" The spirit of Elisha on this occasion was larger and more merciful. It almost rose to the spirit of Him who said, "It was said to them of old time, Thou shalt love thy neighbour and hate thine enemy; but I say unto you, Love your enemies; forgive them that hate you; do good unto them that despitefully use you and persecute you." He asked Jehoram reproachfully whether he would even have smitten those whom he had taken captive with sword and bow.[1] He not only bade the king to spare them, but to set food before them, and send them home. Jehoram did so at great expense, and the narrative ends by telling us that the example of such merciful generosity produced so favourable an impression that "the bands of Syria came no more into the land of Israel."

It is difficult, however, to see where this statement can be chronologically fitted in. The very next chapter —so loosely is the compilation put together, so completely is the sequence of events here neglected—begins with telling us that Benhadad with all his host went up and besieged Samaria. Any peace or respite gained by Elisha's compassionate magnanimity must, in any case, have been exceedingly short-lived. Josephus tries to get over the difficulty by drawing a sufficiently futile distinction between marauding bands and a direct invasion,[2] and he says that King Benhadad gave up his frays through *fear* of Elisha. But, in the first

---

[1] Vulg., *Non percuties; neque enim cepisti eos . . . ut percutias.*

[2] Jos., *Antt.,* IX. iv. 4, Κρύφα μὲν οὐκέτι . . . φανερῶς δέ.

place, the encompassing of Dothan had been carried out by "*a great host* with horses and chariots," which is hardly consistent with the notion of a foray, though it creates new difficulties as to the numbers whom Elisha led to Samaria; secondly, the substitution of a direct invasion for predatory incursions would have been no gain to Israel, but a more deadly peril; and, thirdly, if it was fear of Elisha which stopped the king's raids, it is strange that it had no effect in preventing his invasions. We have, however, no data for any final solution of these problems, and it is useless to meet them with a network of idle conjectures. Such difficulties naturally occur in narratives so vague and unchronological as those presented to us in the documents from the story of Elisha which the compiler wove into his history of Israel and Judah.[1]

---

[1] Kittel, following Kuenen, surmises that this story has got misplaced; that it does not belong to the days of Jehoram ben-Ahab and Benhadad II., but to the days of Jehoahaz ben-Jehu and Benhadad III., the son of Hazael (*Gesch. der Hebr.*, 249). In a very uncertain question I have followed the conclusion arrived at by the majority of scholars, ancient and modern.

CHAPTER VIII

THE FAMINE AND THE SIEGE

2 Kings vi. 24—vii. 20

"'Tis truly no good plan when princes play
The vulture among carrion; but when
They play the carrion among vultures—that
Is ten times worse."

LESSING, *Nathan the Wise*, Act I., Sc. 3.

IF the Benhadad, King of Syria, who reduced Samaria to the horrible straits recorded in this chapter, (2 Kings vi.) was the same Benhadad whom Ahab had treated with such impolitic confidence, his hatred against Israel must indeed have burned hotly. Besides the affair at Dothan, he had already been twice routed with enormous slaughter, and against those disasters he could only set the death of Ahab at Ramoth-Gilead. It is obvious from the preceding narrative that he could advance at any time at his will and pleasure into the heart of his enemy's country, and shut him up in his capital almost without resistance. The siege-trains of ancient days were very inefficient, and any strong fortress could hold out for years, if only it was well provisioned. Such was not the case with Samaria, and it was reduced to a condition of sore famine. Food so loathsome as an ass's head, which at other times the poorest would have spurned, was now sold for eighty shekels' weight of silver (about £8); and the fourth part of a *xestes* or *kab*—which was itself the smallest dry-measure, the sixth part of a *seah*—of the coarse, common pulse, or roasted chick-peas, vulgarly known as "dove's dung," fetched five shekels (about 12s. 6d.).[1]

While things were at this awful pass, "the King of Israel," as he is vaguely called throughout this story, went his rounds upon the wall to visit the sentries and encourage the soldiers in their defence. As he passed, a woman cried, "Help, my lord, O king!" In Eastern monarchies the king is a judge of the humblest; a suppliant, however mean, may cry to him. Jehoram thought that this was but one of the appeals which sprang from the clamorous mendicity of famine with which he had grown so painfully familiar. "The Lord curse you!" he exclaimed impatiently.[2] "How can I help you? Every barn-floor is bare, every wine-press drained." And he passed on.

But the woman continued her wild clamour, and turning round at her importunity, he asked, "What aileth thee?"

He heard in reply a narrative as appalling as ever smote the ear of a king in a besieged city. Among the curses denounced upon apostate Israel in the Pentateuch, we read, "Ye shall eat the flesh of your sons, and the flesh of your daughters shall ye eat";[3] or, as it is expressed more fully in the Book

---

[1] So *asafœtida* is called "devil's dung" in Germany; and the *Herba alcali*, "sparrow's dung" by Arabs. The *Q'ri*, however, supports the *literal* meaning; and compare 2 Kings xviii. 27; Jos., *B. J.*, V. xiii. 7. Analogies for these prices are quoted from classic authors. Plutarch (*Artax.*, xxiv.) mentions a siege in which an ass's head could hardly be got for sixty drachmas (£2 10s.), though usually the whole animal only cost £1. Pliny (*H. N.*, viii. 57) says that during Hannibal's siege of Casilinum a mouse sold for £6 5s.

[2] So Clericus. Comp. Jos. ἐπηράσατο αὐτῇ.   [3] Lev. xxvi. 29.

of Deuteronomy, " He shall besiege thee in all thy
gates throughout all thy land. . . . And thou shalt eat the
fruit of thine own body, the flesh of thy sons and thy
daughters, which the Lord thy God hath given thee,
in the siege, and in the straitness wherewith thine
enemies shall distress thee : so that the man that is
tender among you, and very delicate, his eye shall be
evil towards his brother, and towards the wife of his
bosom, and towards the remnant of his children which
he shall leave ; so that he shall not give to any of them
of the flesh of his children whom he shall eat, because
he hath nothing left him in the siege. . . . The tender and
delicate woman, which would not adventure to set the
sole of her foot upon the ground for delicateness and
tenderness, her eye shall be evil towards the husband
of her bosom, and towards her son, and towards her
daughter, and towards her children : for she shall eat
them for want of all things secretly in the siege and
the straitness, if thou wilt not observe to do all the
words of the law, . . . that thou mayest fear the glorious
and fearful name, *The Lord thy God.*"[1] We find almost
the same words in the prophet Jeremiah ;[2] and in
Lamentations we read : " The hands of the pitiful
women have sodden their own children : they were their
meat in the destruction of the daughter of My people."[3]

Isaiah asks, " Can a woman forget her sucking child,
that she should not have compassion on the son of her
womb ? " Alas ! it has always been so in those awful
scenes of famine, whether after shipwreck or in beleaguered cities, when man becomes degraded to an
animal, with all an animal's primitive instincts, and

---

[1] Deut. xxviii. 52-58.

[2] Jer. xix. 9.

[3] Lam. iv. 10: comp. ii. 20; Ezek. v. 10; Jos., *B. J.*, VI. iii. 4.

when the wild beast appears under the thin veneer of civilisation.   So it was at the siege of Jerusalem, and at the siege of Magdeburg, and at the wreck of the *Medusa*, and on many another occasion when the pangs of hunger have corroded away every vestige of the tender affections and of the moral sense.

And this had occurred at Samaria : her women had become cannibals and devoured their own little ones.

" This woman," screamed the suppliant, pointing her lean finger at a wretch like herself—" this woman said unto me, ' Give thy son, that we may eat him to-day, and we will afterwards eat my son.' I yielded to her suggestion.   We killed my little son, and ate his flesh when we had sodden it.   Next day I said to her, ' Now give thy son, that we may eat him ' ; and she hath hid her son ! "

How could the king answer such a horrible appeal ? Injustice had been done ; but was he to order and to sanction by way of redress fresh cannibalism, and the murder by its mother of another babe ?   In that foul obliteration of every natural instinct, what could he do, what could any man do ?   Can there be equity among raging wild beasts, when they roar for their prey and are unfed ?

All that the miserable king could do was to rend his clothes in horror and to pass on, and as his starving subjects passed by him on the wall they saw that he wore sackcloth beneath his purple, in sign, if not of repentance, yet of anguish, if not of prayer, yet of uttermost humiliation.[1]

But if indeed he had, in his misery, donned that sackcloth in order that at least the semblance of self-mortification might move Jehovah to pity, as it had

---

[1] 1 Kings xxi. 27 ; Isa. xx. 2, 3.

done in the case of his father Ahab, the external sign
of his humility had done nothing to change his heart.
The gruesome appeal to which he had just been forced
to listen only kindled him to a burst of fury.[1]　The
man who had warned, who had prophesied, who so far
during this siege had not raised his finger to help—
the man who was believed to be able to wield the
powers of heaven, and had wrought no deliverance for
his people, but suffered them to sink unaided into these
depths ef abjectness—should he be permitted to live?
If Jehovah would not help, of what use was Elisha?
"God do so to me, and more also," exclaimed Jehoram
—using his mother's oath to Elijah[2]—"if the head of
Elisha, the son of Shaphat, shall stand on him this
day."

Was this the king who had come to Elisha with
such humble entreaty, when three armies were perishing
of thirst before the eyes of Moab?　Was this the king
who had called Elisha "my father," when the prophet
had led the deluded host of Syrians into Samaria, and
bidden Jehoram to set large provision before them?
It was the same king, but now transported with fury
and reduced to despair.　His threat against God's
prophet was in reality a defiance of God, as when our
unhappy Plantagenet, Henry II., maddened by the loss
of Le Mans, exclaimed that, since God had robbed him
of the town he loved, he would pay God out by robbing
Him of that which He most loved in him—his soul.

Jehoram's threat was meant in grim earnest, and he
sent an executioner to carry it out.　Elisha was sitting
in his house with the elders of the city, who had come

---

[1] Compare the wrath of Pashur the priest in consequence of the
denunciation of Jeremiah (Jer. xx. 2).

[2] I Kings xix. 2.

to him for counsel at this hour of supreme need. He knew what was intended for him, and it had also been revealed to him that the king would follow his messenger to cancel his sanguinary threat. "See ye," he said to the elders, "how this son of a murderer "— for again he indicates his contempt and indignation for the son of Ahab and Jezebel—"hath sent to behead me ! When he comes, shut the door, and hold it fast against him. His master is following hard at his heels."

The messenger came, and was refused admittance. The king followed him,[1] and entering the room where the prophet and elders sat, he gave up his wicked design of slaying Elisha with the sword, but he overwhelmed him with reproaches, and in despair renounced all further trust in Jehovah. Elisha, as the king's words imply, must have refused all permission to capitulate : he must have held out from the first a promise that God would send deliverance. But no deliverance had come. The people were starving. Women were devouring their babes. Nothing worse could happen if they flung open their gates to the Syrian host. "Behold," the king said, "this evil is Jehovah's doing. You have deceived us. Jehovah does not intend to deliver us. Why should I wait for Him any longer ? " Perhaps the king meant to imply that his mother's Baal was better worth serving, and would never have left his votaries to sink into these straits.

And now man's extremity had come, and it was God's opportunity. Elisha at last was permitted to announce that the worst was over, that the next day

---

[1] In 2 Kings vi. 33 we should read *melek* (king) for *malkab* (messenger). Jehoram repented of his hasty order.

plenty should smile on the besieged city. "Thus saith
the Lord," he exclaimed to the exhausted and despondent
king, "To-morrow about this time, instead of an ass's
head being sold for eighty shekels, and a thimbleful
of pulse for five shekels, a peck of fine flour shall be
sold for a shekel, and two pecks of barley for a shekel,
in the gate of Samaria."

The king was leaning on the hand of his chief
officer, and to this soldier the promise seemed not
only incredible, but silly: for at the best he could
only suppose that the Syrian host would raise the
siege; and though to hope for that looked an absurdity,
yet even that would not in the least fulfil the immense
prediction. He answered, therefore, in utter scorn:
"Yes! Jehovah is making windows in heaven! But
even thus could this be?" It is much as if he should
have answered some solemn pledge with a derisive
proverb such as, "Yes! if the sky should fall, we
should catch larks!"

Such contemptuous repudiation of a Divine promise
was a blasphemy; and answering scorn with scorn, and
riddle with riddling, Elisha answers the mocker, "Yes!
and *you* shall see this, but shall not enjoy it."

The word of the Lord was the word of a true
prophet, and the miracle was wrought. Not only was
the siege raised, but the wholly unforeseen spoil of the
entire Syrian camp, with all its accumulated rapine,
brought about the predicted plenty.

There were four lepers [1] outside the gate of Samaria,
like the leprous mendicants who gather there to this
day. They were cut off from all human society, except
their own. Leprosy was treated as contagious, and
if "houses of the unfortunate" (*Biut-el-Masâkin*) were

---

[1] The Jews say Gehazi, and his three sons (**Jarchi**).

provided for them, as seems to have been the case at
Jerusalem, they were built outside the city walls.[1] They
could only live by beggary, and this was an aggrava-
tion of their miserable condition. And how could any
one fling food to these beggars over the walls, when
food of any kind was barely to be had within them?

So taking counsel of their despair, they decided that
they would desert to the Syrians : among them they
would at least find food, if their lives were spared;
and if not, death would be a happy release from their
present misery.

So in the evening twilight, when they could not be
seen or shot at from the city wall as deserters, they
stole down to the Syrian camp.

When they reached its outermost circle, to their
amazement all was silence. They crept into one of
the tents in fear and astonishment. There was food
and drink there, and they satisfied the cravings of
their hunger. It was also stored with booty from the
plundered cities and villages of Israel. To this they
helped themselves, and took it away and hid it. Having
spoiled this tent, they entered a second. It was likewise deserted, and they carried a fresh store of treasures to their hiding-place. And then they began to
feel uneasy at not divulging to their starving fellow-
citizens the strange and golden tidings of a deserted
camp. The night was wearing on ; day would reveal
the secret. If they carried the good news, they would
doubtless earn a rich guerdon. If they waited till
morning, they might be put to death for their selfish
reticence and theft. It was safest to return to the city,
and rouse the warder, and send a message to the
palace. So the lepers hurried back through the night,

---

[1] Lev. xiii. 46; Num. v. 2, 3.

and shouted to the sentinel at the gate, "We went to the Syrian camp, and it was deserted! Not a man was there, not a sound was to be heard. The horses were tethered there, and the asses, and the tents were left just as they were."

The sentinel called the other watchmen to hear the wonderful news, and instantly ran with it to the palace. The slumbering house was roused; and though it was still night, the king himself arose. But he could not shake off his despondency, and made no reference to Elisha's prediction. News sometimes sounds too good to be true. "It is only a decoy," he said. "They can only have left their camp to lure us into an ambuscade, that they may return, and slaughter us, and capture our city."

"Send to see," answered one of his courtiers. "Send five horsemen to test the truth, and to look out. If they perish, their fate is but the fate of us all."

So two chariots with horses were despatched, with instructions not only to visit the camp, but track the movements of the host.

They went, and found that it was as the lepers had said. The camp was deserted, and lay there as an immense booty; and for some reason the Syrians had fled towards the Jordan to make good their escape to Damascus by the eastern bank. The whole road was strewn with the traces of their headlong flight; it was full of scattered garments and vessels.

Probably, too, the messengers came across some disabled fugitive, and learnt the secret of this amazing stampede. It was the result of one of those sudden unaccountable panics to which the huge, unwieldy, heterogeneous Eastern armies, which have no organised system of sentries, and no trained discipline, are con-

stantly liable. We have already met with several
instances in the history of Israel. Such was the panic
which seized the Midianites when Gideon's three
hundred blew their trumpets; and the panic of the
Syrians before Ahab's pages of the provinces; and of
the combined armies in the Valley of Salt; and of the
Moabites at Wady-el-Ahsy; and afterwards of the
Assyrians before the walls of Jerusalem. Fear is
physically contagious, and, when once it has set in,
it swells with such unaccountable violence, that the
Greeks called these terrors "panic," because they
believed them to be directly inspired by the god Pan.
Well-disciplined as was the army of the Ten Thousand
Greeks in their famous retreat, they nearly fell victims
to a sudden panic, had not Clearchus, with prompt
resource, published by the herald the proclamation
of a reward for the arrest of the man who had let
the ass loose. Such an unaccountable terror—caused
by a noise as of chariots and of horses which rever-
berated among the hills—had seized the Syrian host.
They thought that Jehoram had secretly hired an army
of the princes of the Khetas[1] and of the Egyptians
to march suddenly upon them. In wild confusion, not
stopping to reason or to inquire, they took to flight,
increasing their panic by the noise and rush of their
own precipitance.

No sooner had the messengers delivered their glad
tidings, than the people of Samaria began to pour
tumultuously out of the gates, to fling themselves on the
food and on the spoil. It was like the rush of the dirty,
starving, emaciated wretches which horrified the keepers

---

[1] The capitals of the ancient Hittites—a nation whose fame had
been almost entirely obliterated till a few years ago—were Karchemish,
Kadesh, Hamath, and Helbon (Aleppo).

of the reserved stores at Smolensk in Napoleon's retreat from Moscow, and forced them to shut the gates, and fling food and grain to the struggling soldiers out of the windows of the granaries   To secure order and prevent disaster, the king appointed his attendant lord to keep the gate.   But the torrent of people flung him down, and they trampled on his body in their eagerness for relief.   He died after having seen that the promise of Elisha was fulfilled, and that the cheapness and abundance had been granted, the prophecy of which he thought only fit for his sceptical derision.

"The sudden panic which delivered the city," says Dean Stanley, "is the one marked intervention on behalf of the northern capital.   No other incident could be found in the sacred annals so appropriately to express, in the Church of Gouda, the pious gratitude of the citizens of Leyden, for their deliverance from the Spanish army, as the miraculous raising of the siege of Samaria."[1]

---

[1] *Lectures,* ii. 345.

CHAPTER IX

THE SHUNAMMITE AND HAZAEL

2 KINGS viii. 1—6, 7—15. (Circ. B.C. 886.)

"Our acts still follow with us from afar,
And what we have been makes us what we are."
GEORGE ELIOT.

THE next anecdote of Elisha brings us once more into contact with the Lady of Shunem. Famines, or dearths, were unhappily of very frequent occurrence in a country which is so wholly dependent, as Palestine is, upon the early and latter rain. On some former occasion Elisha had foreseen that " Jehovah had called for a famine"; for the sword, the famine, and the pestilence are represented as ministers who wait His bidding.[1] He had also foreseen that it would be of long duration, and in kindness to the Shunammite had warned her that she had better remove for a time into a land in which there was greater plenty. It was under similar circumstances that Elimelech and Naomi, ancestors of David's line, had taken their sons Mahlon and Chilion, and gone to live in the land of Moab; and, indeed, the famine which decided the migration of Jacob and his children into Egypt had been a turning-point in the history of the Chosen People.

---

[1] Jer. xxv. 29; Ezek. xxxviii. 21.

The Lady of Shunem had learnt by experience the weight of Elisha's words. Her husband is not mentioned, and was probably dead; so she arose with her household, and went for seven years to live in the plain of Philistia. At the end of that time the dearth had ceased, and she returned to Shunem, but only to find that during her absence her house and land were in possession of other owners, and had probably escheated to the Crown. The king was the ultimate, and to a great extent the only, source of justice in his little kingdom, and she went to lay her claim before him and demand the restitution of her property. By a providential circumstance she came exactly at the most favourable moment. The king—it must have been Jehoram—was at the very time talking to Gehazi about the great works of Elisha. As it is unlikely that he would converse long with a leper, and as Gehazi is still called "the servant of the man of God," the incident may here be narrated out of order. It is pleasant to find Jehoram taking so deep an interest in the prophet's story. Already on many occasions during his wars with Moab and Syria, as well as on the occasion of Naaman's visit, if that had already occurred, he had received the completest proof of the reality of Elisha's mission, but he might be naturally unaware of the many private incidents in which he had exhibited a supernatural power. Among other stories Gehazi was telling him that of the Shunammite, and how Elisha had given life to her dead son. At that juncture she came before the king, and Gehazi said, "My lord, O king, this is the very woman, and this is her son whom Elisha recalled to life." In answer to Jehoram's questions she confirmed the story, and he was so much impressed by the narrative that he not only ordered the immediate restitution of her land, but also of the value of its products during the seven years of her exile.

We now come to the fulfilment of the second of the commands which Elijah had received so long before at Horeb. To complete the retribution which was yet to fall on Israel, he had been bidden to anoint Hazael to be king of Syria in the room of Benhadad. Hitherto the mandate had remained unfulfilled, because no opportunity had occurred; but the appointed time had now arrived. Elisha, for some purpose, and during an interval of peace, visited Damascus, where the visit of Naaman and the events of the Syrian wars had made his name very famous. Benhadad II., grandson or great-grandson of Rezin, after a stormy reign of some thirty years, marked by some successes, but also by the terrible reverses already recorded, lay dangerously ill. Hearing the news that the wonder-working prophet of Israel was in his capital, he sent to ask of him the question, "Shall I recover?" It had been the custom from the earliest days to propitiate the favour of prophets by presents, without which even the humblest suppliant hardly ventured to approach them.[1] The gift sent by Benhadad was truly royal, for he thought perhaps that he could purchase the intercession or the miraculous intervention of this mighty thaumaturge. He sent Hazael with a selection "of every good thing of Damascus," and, like an Eastern, he endeavoured to make his offering seem more magnificent [2] by distributing it on the backs of forty camels.

At the head of this imposing procession of camels

---

[1] See the cases of Samuel (1 Sam. ix. 7), of Ahijah (1 Kings xiv. 3), and of Elisha himself (2 Kings iv. 42).

[2] As Jacob did in sending forward his present to Esau. Comp. Chardin, *Voyages*, iii. 217.

walked Hazael, the commander of the forces, and stood
in Elisha's presence with the humble appeal, "Thy son
Benhadad, King of Syria, hath sent me to thee, saying,
Shall I recover of this disease?"

About the king's munificence we are told no more,
but we cannot doubt that it was refused. If Naaman's
still costlier blessing had been rejected, though he was
about to receive through Elisha's ministration an inestimable boon, it is unlikely that Elisha would accept
a gift for which he could offer no return, and which,
in fact, directly or indirectly, involved the death of
the sender. But the historian does not think it necessary to pause and tell us that Elisha sent back the
forty camels unladen of their treasures. It was not
worth while to narrate what was a matter of course.
If it had been no time, a few years earlier, to receive
money and garments, and olive-yards and vineyards, and
men-servants and maid-servants, still less was it a time
to do so now. The days were darker now than they
had been, and Elisha himself stood near the Great White
Throne. The protection of these fearless prophets lay
in their utter simplicity of soul. They rose above
human fears because they stood above human desires.
What Elisha possessed was more than sufficient for the
needs of the plain and humble life of one whose com-
muning was with God. It was not wonderful that
prophets should rise to an elevation whence they could
look down with indifference upon the superfluities of
the lust of the eyes and the pride of life, when even
sages of the heathen have attained to a similar independence of earthly luxuries. One who can climb such
mountain-heights can look with silent contempt on
gold.

But there is a serious difficulty about Elisha's answer

to the embassage.   "Go, say unto him"—so it is
rendered in our Authorised Version—"Thou mayest
certainly recover: howbeit the Lord hath showed me
that he shall surely die."

It is evident that the translators of 1611 meant the
emphasis to be laid on the "*mayest*," and understood
the answer of Elisha to mean, "Thy recovery is quite
possible; and yet"—he adds to Hazael, and not as
part of his answer to the king—"Jehovah has shown
me that dying he shall die,"—not indeed of this disease,
but by other means before he has recovered from it.

Unfortunately, however, the Hebrew will not bear
this meaning.   Elisha bids Hazael to go back with the
distinct message, "Thou shalt surely recover," as it is
rightly rendered in the Revised Version.

This, however, is the rendering, not of the *written*
text as it stands, but of the margin.   Every one knows
that in the Masoretic original the text itself is called
the K'thîb, or "what is written," whereas the margin
is called *Q'rî*, "read."   Now, our translators, both those
of 1611 and those of the Revision Committee, all but
invariably follow the Kethîb as the most authentic
reading.   In this instance, however, they abandon the
rule and translate the marginal reading.

What, then, is the written text?

It is the reverse of the marginal reading, for it has:
"Go, say, Thou shalt *not* recover."

The reader may naturally ask the cause of this
startling discrepancy.

It seems to be twofold.

(I.) Both the Hebrew word *lo*, "not" (לֹא), and the
word *lo*, "to him" (לוֹ), have precisely the same pro-
nunciation.   Hence this text might mean either "Go,
say *to him*, Thou shalt certainly recover," or "Go,

say, Thou shalt *not* recover." The same identity of the
negative and the dative of the preposition has made
nonsense of another passage of the Authorised Version,
where "Thou hast multiplied the nation, and *not* increased the joy : they joy before Thee according to
the joy of harvest," should be "Thou hast multiplied
the nation, and increased *its* joy." So, too, the verse
"It is He that hath made us, and *not* we ourselves,"
may mean "It is He that hath made us, and *to Him*
we belong." In the present case the adoption of the
negative (which would have conveyed to Benhadad the
exact truth) is not possible ; for it makes the next
clause and its introduction by the word "Howbeit"
entirely meaningless.

But (II.) this confusion in the text might not have
arisen in the present instance but for the difficulty of
Elisha's appearing to send a deliberately false message
to Benhadad, and a message which he tells Hazael at
the time is false.

Can this be deemed impossible ?

With the views prevalent in "those times of ignorance," I think not. Abraham and Isaac, saints and
patriarchs as they were, both told practical falsehoods
about their wives. They, indeed, were reproved for
this, though not severely ; but, on the other hand, Jael
is not reproved for her treachery to Sisera ; and Samuel,
under the semblance of a Divine permission, used a
diplomatic ruse when he visited the household of Jesse ;
and in the apologue of Micaiah a lying spirit is represented as sent forth to do service to Jehovah ; and
Elisha himself tells a deliberate falsehood to the Syrians
at Dothan. The sensitiveness to the duty of always
speaking the exact truth is not felt in the East with
anything like the intensity that it is in Christian lands ;

and reluctant as we should be to find in the message
of Elisha another instance of that *falsitas dispensativa*
which has been so fatally patronised by some of
the Fathers and by many Romish theologians, the
love of truth itself would compel us to accept this
view of the case, if there were no other possible interpretation.

I think, however, that another view is possible. I
think that Elisha may have said to Hazael, "Go, say
unto him, Thou shalt surely recover," with the same
accent of irony in which Micaiah said at first to the
two kings, "Go up to Ramoth-Gilead, and prosper; for
the Lord shall deliver it into the hand of the king." I
think that his whole manner and the tone of his voice
may have shown to Hazael, and may have been meant
to show him, that this was not Elisha's real message
to Benhadad.   Or, to adopt the same line of explanation with an unimportant difference, Elisha may have
meant to imply, "Go, follow the bent which I know you
will follow; go, carry back to your master the lying
message that I said he would recover.   But that is
not *my* message.   My message, whether it suits your
courtier instincts or not, is that Jehovah has warned
me that he shall surely die."

That some such meaning as this attaches to the
verse seems to be shown by the context.   For not only
was some reproof involved in Elisha's words, but he
showed his grief still more by his manner.   It was as
though he had said, "Take back what message you
choose, but Benhadad will certainly die"; and then
he fastened his steady gaze on the soldier's countenance, till Hazael blushed and became uneasy.   Only
when he noted that Hazael's conscience was troubled
by the glittering eyes which seemed to read the inmost

secrets of his heart did Elisha drop his glance, and burst into tears. " Why weepeth, my lord ? " asked Hazael, in still deeper uneasiness. Whereupon Elisha revealed to him the future. " I weep," he said, " because I see in thee the curse and the avenger of the sins of my native land. Thou wilt become to them a sword of God ; thou wilt set their fortresses on fire ; thou wilt slaughter their youths ; thou wilt dash their little ones to pieces against the stones ; thou wilt rip up their women with child." That he actually inflicted these savageries of warfare on the miserable Israelites we are not told, but we are told that he smote them in all their coasts ; that Jehovah delivered them into his hands ; that he oppressed Israel all the days of Jehoahaz.[1] That being so, there can be no question that he carried out the same laws of atrocious warfare which belonged to those times and continued long afterwards. Such atrocities were not only inflicted on the Israelites again and again by the Assyrians and others,[2] but they themselves had often inflicted them, and inflicted them with what they believed to be Divine approval, on their own enemies.[3] Centuries after, one of their own poets accounted it a beatitude to him who should dash the children of the Babylonians against the stones.[4]

As the answer of Hazael is usually read and interpreted, we are taught to regard it as an indignant declaration that he could never be guilty of such vile deeds. It is regarded as though it were " an abhorrent repudiation of his future self." The lesson often drawn

---

[1] 2 Kings x. 32, xiii. 3, 22.
[2] Isa. xiii. 15, 16 ; Hos. x. 14, xiii. 16 ; Nah. iii. 10.
[3] See Josh. vi. 17, 21 ; 1 Sam. xv. 3 ; Lev. xxvii. 28, 29.
[4] Psalm cxxxvii. 9.

from it in sermons is that a man may live to do, and
to delight in, crimes which he once hated and deemed
it impossible that he should ever commit.

The lesson is a most true one, and is capable of
a thousand illustrations. It conveys the deeply needed
warning that those who, even in thought, dabble with
wrong courses, which they only regard as venial pecca-
dilloes, may live to commit, without any sense of horror,
the most enormous offences. It is the explanation of
the terrible fact that youths who once seemed innocent
and holy-minded may grow up, step by step, into
colossal criminals. "Men," says Scherer, "advance
unconsciously from errors to faults, and from faults
to crimes, till sensibility is destroyed by the habitual
spectacle of guilt, and the most savage atrocities come
to be dignified by the name of State policy."

> "Lui-même à son portrait forcé de rendre hommage,
> Il frémira d'horreur devant sa propre image."

But true and needful as these lessons are, they are
entirely beside the mark as deduced from the story
of Hazael. What he said was not, as in our Authorised
Version, "But what, is thy servant a dog, that he
should do this great thing?" nor by "great thing" does
he mean "so deadly a crime." His words, more
accurately rendered in our Revision, are, "But what
is thy servant, which is but a dog, that he should do
this great thing?" or, "But what is the dog, thy
servant?" It was a hypocritic deprecation of the
future importance and eminence which Elisha had prophesied for him. There is not the least sense of horror
either in his words or in his thoughts. He merely
means 'A mere dog, such as I am, can never accom-
plish such great designs." A dog in the East is utterly

despised ;[1] and Hazael, with Oriental irony, calls himself
a dog, though he was the Syrian commander-in-chief—
just as a Chinaman, in speaking of himself, adopts the
periphrasis " this little thief."

Elisha did not notice his sham humility, but told him,
" The Lord hath showed me that thou shalt be King
over Syria." The date of the event was B.C. 886.

The scene has sometimes been misrepresented to
Elisha's discredit, as though he suggested to the general
the crimes of murder and rebellion. The accusation
is entirely untenable. Elisha was, indeed, in one sense,
commissioned to anoint Hazael King of Syria, because
the cruel soldier had been predestined by God to that
position ; but, in another sense, he had no power
whatever to give to Hazael the mighty kingdom of
Aram, nor to wrest it from the dynasty which had now
held it for many generations. All this was brought
about by the Divine purpose, in a course of events
entirely out of the sphere of the humble man of God.
In the transferring of this crown he was in no sense
the agent or the suggester. The thought of usurpation must, without doubt, have been already in Hazael's
mind. Benhadad, as far as we know, was childless.
At any rate he had no natural heirs, and seems to
have been a drunken king, whose reckless undertakings
and immense failures had so completely alienated the
affections of his subjects from himself and his dynasty,
that he died undesired and unlamented, and no hand
was uplifted to strike a blow in his defence. It hardly
needed a prophet to foresee that the sceptre would
be snatched by so strong a hand as that of Hazael from
a grasp so feeble as that of Benhadad II. The utmost
that Elisha had done was, under Divine guidance, to

----

[1] I Sam. xxiv. 14 ; 2 Sam. ix. 8.

read his character and his designs, and to tell him that the accomplishment of these designs was near at hand.

So Hazael went back to Benhadad, and in answer to the eager inquiry, "What said Elisha to thee?" he gave the answer which Elisha had foreseen that he meant to give, and which was in any case a falsehood, for it suppressed half of what Elisha had really said. "He told me," said Hazael, "that thou shouldest surely recover."

Was the sequel of the interview the murder of Benhadad by Hazael?

The story has usually been so read, but Elisha had neither prophesied this nor suggested it. The sequel is thus described. "And it came to pass on the morrow, that *he* took the coverlet,[1] and dipped it in water, and spread it on his face, so that he died: and Hazael reigned in his stead." The repetition of the name Hazael in the last clause is superfluous if he was the subject of the previous clause, and it has been consequently conjectured that "he took" is merely the impersonal idiom "one took." Some suppose that, as Benhadad was in the bath, his servant took the bath-cloth, wetted it, and laid its thick folds over the mouth of the helpless king; others, that he soaked the thick quilt, which the king was too weak to lift away.[2] In either case it is hardly likely that a great officer like Hazael would

---

[1] מַכְבֵּר. Jos., *Antt.*, IX. iv. 6, δίκτυον διάβροχον. Aquila, Symmachus, τὸ στρῶμα. Michaelis supposed it to be the mosquito-net (κωνωπεῖον). Comp. 1 Sam. xix. 13. Ewald suggested "bath-mattress" (iii. 523). Sir G. Grove (*s.v.* "Elisha," *Bibl. Dict.*, ii. 923) mentions that Abbas Pasha is said to have been murdered in the same manner. Some, however, think that the measure was taken by way of cure (Bruce, *Travels*, iii. 33. Klostermann, *ad loc.*, alters the text at his pleasure).

[2] 2 Kings viii. 15; LXX., τὸ μαχβάρ; Vulg., *stragulum*; lit., "woven cloth."

7

have been in the bath-room or the bed-room of the dying king. Yet we must remember that the Prætorian Præfect Macro is said to have suffocated Tiberius with his bed-clothes. Josephus says that Hazael strangled his master with a net; and, indeed, he has generally been held guilty of the perpetration of the murder. But it is fair to give him the benefit of the doubt. Be that as it may, he seems to have reigned for some forty-six years (B.C. 886–840), and to have bequeathed the sceptre to a son on whom he had bestowed the old dynastic name of Benhadad.

CHAPTER X

(1) *JEHORAM BEN-JEHOSHAPHAT OF JUDAH*
B.C. 851—843

(2) *AHAZIAH BEN-JEHORAM OF JUDAH*
B.C. 843—842

2 KINGS viii. 16—24, 25—29

"Bear like the Turk, no brother near the throne."—POPE.

THE narrative now reverts to the kingdom of
Judah, of which the historian, mainly occupied
with the great deeds of the prophet in Israel, takes
at this period but little notice.

He tells us that in the fifth year of Jehoram of Israel,
son of Ahab, his namesake and brother-in-law, Jehoram
of Judah, began to reign in Judah, though his father,
Jehoshaphat, was then king.[1]

The statement is full of difficulties, especially as
we have been already told (i. 17) that Jehoram ben-
Ahab of Israel began to reign in the *second* year of

---

[1] The following genealogy may help to elucidate the troublesome
identity of names:—

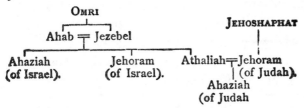

99

Jehoram ben-Jehoshaphat of Judah, and (iii. 1) in the eighteenth year of Jehoshaphat. It is hardly worth while to pause here to disentangle these complexities in a writer who, like most Eastern historians, is content with loose chronological references. By the current mode of reckoning, the twenty-five years of Jehoshaphat's reign may merely mean twenty-three and a month or two of two other years; and some suppose that, when Jehoram of Judah was about sixteen, his father went on the expedition against Moab, and associated his son with him in the throne. This is only conjecture. Jehoshaphat, of all kings, least needed a coadjutor, particularly so weak and worthless a one as his son; and though the association of colleagues with themselves has been common in some realms, there is not a single instance of it in the history o Israel and Judah—the case of Uzziah, who was a leper, not being to the point.[1]

The kings both of Israel and of Judah at this period, with the single exception of the brave and good Jehoshaphat, were unworthy and miserable. The blight of the Jezebel-marriage and the curse of Baal-worship lay upon both kingdoms. It is scarcely possible to find such wretched monarchs as the two sons of Jezebel—Ahaziah and Jehoram in Israel, and the son-in-law and grandson of Jezebel, Jehoram and Ahaziah, in Judah. Their respective reigns are annals of shameful apostasy, and almost unbroken disaster.

Jehoram ben-Jehoshaphat of Judah was thirty-two years old when he began his independent reign, and reigned for eight deplorable years. The fact that his mother's name is (exceptionally) omitted seems to

---

[1] Jotham ben-Uzziah was not the colleague of his father, but his public representative.

imply that his father Jehoshaphat set the good example of monogamy.[1] Jehoram was wholly under the influence of Athaliah, his wife, and of Jezebel, his mother-in-law, and he introduced into Judah their alien abominations. He "walked in their way, and did evil in the sight of the Lord." The Chronicler fills up the general remark by saying that he did his utmost to foster idolatry by erecting *bamoth* in the mountains of Judah, and compelled his people to worship there, in order to decentralise the religious services of the kingdom, and so to diminish the glory of the Temple. He introduced Baal-worship into Judah, and either he or his son was the guilty builder of a temple to Baalim, not only on the "opprobrious mount" on which stood the idolatrous chapels of Solomon, but on the Hill of the House itself. This temple had its own high priest, and was actually adorned with treasures torn from the Temple of Jehovah.[2] So bad was Jehoram's conduct that the historian can only attribute his non-destruction to the "covenant of salt" which God had made with David, "to give him a lamp for his children always."

But if actual destruction did not come upon him and his race, he came very near such a fate, and he certainly experienced that "the path of transgressors is hard." There is nothing to record about him but crime and catastrophe. First Edom revolted. Jehoshaphat had subdued the Edomites, and only allowed them to be governed by a vassal; now they threw off the yoke. The Jewish King advanced against them to

---

[1] The only other king of Judah whose mother's name is not mentioned (perhaps because his father Jotham had but one wife) is Ahaz.

[2] 2 Kings xi. 18; 2 Chron. xxi. 11, xxiv. 7.

"Zair"—by which must be meant apparently either Zoar (through which the road to Edom lay), or their capital, Mount Seir.[1] There he was surrounded by the Edomite hosts; and though by a desperate act of valour he cut his way through them at night in spite of their reserve of chariots, yet his army left him in the lurch. Edom succeeded in establishing its final independence, to which we see an allusion in the one hope held out to Esau by Isaac in that "blessing" which was practically a curse.

The loss of so powerful a subject-territory, which now constituted a source of danger on the eastern frontier of Judah, was succeeded by another disaster on the south-west, in the Shephelah or lowland plain. Here Libnah revolted,[3] and by gaining its autonomy contracted yet farther the narrow limits of the southern kingdom.

The Book of Kings tells us no more about the Jewish Jehoram, only adding that he died and was buried with his fathers, and was succeeded by his son Ahaziah. But the Book of Chronicles, which adds far darker touches to his character, also heightens to an extraordinary degree the intensity of his punishment. It tells us that he began his reign by the atrocious murder of his six younger brothers, for whom, following the old precedent of Rehoboam, Jehoshaphat had provided

---

[1] Vulg., *Seira*; Arab., *Sa'ir* (but the historian never uses the name Mount Seir); LXX., Σιώρ. There is perhaps some corruption in the text, and the reading of the Chronicler "with his princes" shows that it may have once been עִם־שָׂרָיו.

[2] 2 Kings viii. 21. "The people" (*i.e.*, the army of Judah) "fled to their tents." Apparently this means that they slunk away home. The word "tents" is a reminiscence of their nomad days, like the treasonable cry, "To your tents, O Israel."

[3] Josh. x. 29–39.

by establishing them as governors of various cities. As
his throne was secure, we cannot imagine any motive
for this brutal massacre except the greed of gain, and
we can only suppose that, as Jehoram ben-Jehoshaphat
became little more than a friendly vassal of his kinsmen
in Israel, so he fell under the deadly influence of his
wife Athaliah, as completely as his father-in-law had
done under the spell of her mother Jezebel. With his
brothers he also swept away a number of the chief
nobles, who perhaps embraced the cause of his murdered
kinsmen. Such conduct breathes the known spirit of
Jezebel and of Athaliah. To rebuke him for this
wickedness, he received the menace of a tremendous
judgment upon his home and people in a writing from
Elijah, whom we should certainly have assumed to
be dead long before that time. The judgment itself
followed. The Philistines and Arabians invaded Judah,
captured Jerusalem, and murdered all Jehoram's own
children, except Ahaziah, who was the youngest. Then
Jehoram, at the age of thirty-eight, was smitten with an
incurable disease of the bowels, of which he died two
years later, and not only died unlamented, but was
refused burial in the sepulchres of the kings. In any
case his reign and that of his son and successor were
the most miserable in the annals of Judah, as the
reigns of their namesakes and kinsmen, Ahaziah ben-
Ahab and Jehoram ben-Ahab, were also the most
miserable in the annals of Israel.

Jehoram was succeeded on the throne of Judah by
his son Ahaziah. If the chronology and the facts be
correct, Ahaziah ben-Jehoram of Judah must have been
born when his father was only eighteen, though he
was the youngest of the king's sons, and so escaped
from being massacred in the Philistine invasion. He

succeeded at the age of twenty-two, and only reigned a single year. During this year his mother, the Gebîrah Athaliah, the daughter of Ahab and Jezebel, and grand-daughter of the Tyrian Ethbaal, was all-supreme. She bent the weak nature of her son to still further apostasies. She was "his counsellor to do wickedly," and her Baal-priest Mattan was more important than the Aaronic high priest of the despised and desecrated Temple. Never did Judah sink to so low a level, and it was well that the days of Ahaziah of Judah were cut short.

The only event in his reign was the share he took with his uncle Jehoram of Israel in his campaign to protect Ramoth-Gilead from Hazael. The expedition seems to have been successful in its main purpose. Ramoth-Gilead, the key to the districts of Argob and Bashan, was of immense importance for commanding the country beyond Jordan. It seems to be the same as Ramath-Mizpeh (Josh. xiii. 26); and if so, it was the spot where Jacob made his covenant with Laban. Ahab, or his successors, in spite of the disastrous end of the expedition to Ahab personally, had evidently recovered the frontier fortress from the Syrian king.[1] Its position upon a hill made its possession vital to the interests of Gilead; for the master of Ramah was the master of that Trans-Jordanic district. But Hazael had succeeded his murdered master, and was already beginning to fulfil the ruthless mission which Elisha had foreseen with tears. Jehoram ben-Ahab seems to have held his own against Hazael for a time; but in the course of the campaign at Ramoth he was so severely wounded that he was compelled to leave his army under the command of Jehu, and to return to Jezreel, to be

---

[1] Jos., *Antt.*, IX. vi. 1.

healed of his wounds. Thither his nephew Ahaziah
of Judah went to visit him ; and there, as we shall hear,
he too met his doom. That fate, the Chronicler tells
us, was the penalty of his iniquities. " The destruction
of Ahaziah was of God by coming to Joram."

We have no ground for accusing either king of any
want of courage ; yet it was obviously impolitic of
Jehoram to linger unnecessarily in his luxurious capital,
while the army of Israel was engaged in service on a
dangerous frontier. The wounds inflicted by the
Syrian archers may have been originally severe. Their
arrows at this time played as momentous a part in
history as the cloth-yard shafts of our English bowmen
which "sewed the French ranks together" at Poictiers,
Creçy, and Azincour. But Jehoram had at any rate
so far recovered that he could ride in his chariot ; and
if he had been wise and bravely vigorous, he would
not have left his army under a subordinate at so perilous an epoch, and menaced by so resolute a foe. Or
if he were indeed compelled to consult the better
physicians at Jezreel, he should have persuaded his
nephew Ahaziah of Judah—who seems to have been
more or less of a vassal as well as a kinsman—to keep
an eye on the beleaguered fort. Both kings, however,
deserted their post,—Jehoram to recover perfect health ;
and Ahaziah, who had been his comrade—as their
father and grandfather had gone together to the same
war—to pay a state visit of condolence to the royal
invalid. The army was left under a popular, resolute,
and wholly unscrupulous commander, and the results
powerfully affected the immediate and the ultimate
destiny of both kingdoms.

CHAPTER XI

THE REVOLT OF JEHU

B.C. 842

2 KINGS ix. 1—37

"Te semper anteit sæva Necessitas
Clavos trabales et cuneos manu,
Gestans ahenâ." HORAT., *Od.*, I. xxxv. 17.

A LONG period had elapsed since Elijah had received the triple commission which was to mark the close of his career. Two of those Divine behests had now been accomplished. He had anointed Elisha, son of Shaphat, of Abel-Meholah, to be prophet in his room;[1] and Elisha had anointed Hazael to be king over Syria;[2] the third and more dangerous commission, involving nothing less than the overthrow of the mighty dynasty of Omri, remained still unaccomplished.

If the name of Jehu ("Jehovah is He")[3] had been actually mentioned to Elijah, the dreadful secret must have remained buried in the breast of the prophet and in that of his successor for many years. Further, Jehu was yet a very young man, and to have marked him out as the founder of a dynasty would have been to doom him to certain destruction. An Eastern king,

---

[1] 1 Kings xix. 15, 16.
[2] 2 Kings viii. 12, 13.
[3] The name was not uncommon, 1 Chron. ii. 38, iv. 35, xii. 3.

whose family has once securely seated itself on the throne, is hedged round with an awful divinity, and demands an unquestioning obedience. Elijah had been removed from earth before this task had been fulfilled, and Elisha had to wait for his opportunity. But the doom was passed, though the judgment was belated. The sons of Ahab were left a space to repent, or to fill to the brim the cup of their father's iniquities.

> "The sword of Heaven is not in haste to smite,
>   Nor yet doth linger."

Ahaziah, Ahab's eldest son, after a reign of one year, marked only by crimes and misfortunes, had ended in overwhelming disaster his deplorable career. His brother Jehoram had succeeded him, and had now been on the throne for at least twelve years, which had been chiefly signalised by that unsuccessful attempt to recover the territory of revolted Moab, to which we owe the celebrated Stone of Mesha. We have already narrated the result of the campaign which had so many vicissitudes. The combined armies of Israel, Judah, and Edom had been delivered by the interposition of Elisha from perishing of thirst beside the scorched-up bed of the Wady-el-Ahsy ; and availing themselves of the rash assault of the Moabites, had swept everything before them. But Moab stood at bay at Kir-Haraseth (Kerak), his strongest fortress, six miles from Ar or Rabbah, and ten miles east of the southern end of the Dead Sea. It stood three thousand feet above the level of the sea, and is defended by a network of steep valleys. Nevertheless, Israel would have subdued it, but for the act of horrible despair to which the King of Moab resorted in his extremity, by offering up his eldest son as a burnt-offering to Chemosh upon the wall of the city. Horror-stricken by the catastrophe, and terrified with the dread that the vengeance of Chemosh could not but be aroused by so tremendous a sacrifice, the besieging host had retired. From that moment Moab had not only been free, but assumed the *rôle* of an aggressor, and sent her marauding bands to harry and carry the farms and homesteads of her former conqueror.[1]

Then followed the aggressions of Benhadad which had been frustrated by the insight of Elisha, and which owed their temporary cessation to his generosity.[2] The reappearance of the Syrians in the field had reduced Samaria to the lowest depths of ghastly famine. But the day of the guilty city had not yet come, and a sudden panic, caused among the invaders by a rumoured assault of Hittites and Egyptians, had saved her from destruction.[3] Taking advantage of the respite caused by the change of the Syrian dynasty, and pressing on his advantage, Jehoram, with the aid of his Judæan nephew, had once more got possession of Ramoth-Gilead before Hazael was secure on the throne which he had usurped.

This then was the situation :—The allied and kindred kings of Israel and Judah were idling in the pomp of hospitality at Jezreel ; their armies were encamped about Ramoth-Gilead ; and at the head of the host of Israel was the crafty and vehement grandson of Nimshi.

Elisha saw and seized his opportunity. The day of vengeance from the Lord had dawned. Things had not materially altered since the days of Ahab. If Jehovah

---

[1] 2 Kings xiii. 20, xxiv. 2 ; Jer. xlviii.
[2] 2 Kings vi. 8-23.
[3] 2 Kings vii. 6.

was nominally worshipped, if the very names of the
kings of Israel bore witness to His supremacy,[1] Baal
was worshipped too. The curse which Elijah had
pronounced against Ahab and his house remained
unfulfilled. The credit of prophecy was at stake.
The blood of Naboth and his slaughtered sons cried
to the Lord from the ground ; and hitherto it seemed
to have cried in vain. If the *Nebîim* (the prophetic
class) were to have their due weight in Israel, the hour
had come, and the man was ready.

The light which falls on Elisha is dim and inter-
mittent. His name is surrounded by a halo of nebulous
wonders, of which many are of a private and personal
character. But he was a known enemy of Ahab and
his house. He had, indeed, more than once interposed
to snatch them from ruin, as in the expedition against
Moab, and in the awful straits of the siege of Samaria
by the Syrians. But his person had none the less
been hateful to the sons of Jezebel, and his life had
been endangered by their bursts of sudden fury. He
could hardly again have a chance so favourable as that
which now offered itself, when the armed host was at
one place and the king at another. Perhaps, too, he
may have been made aware that the soldiers were not
well pleased to find at their head a king who was so
far a *fainéant* as to leave them exposed to a powerful
enemy, and show no eagerness to return. His "urgent
private affairs" were not so urgent as to entitle him to
take his ease at luxurious Jezreel.

Where Elisha was at the time we do not know—
perhaps at Dothan, perhaps at Samaria. Suddenly he
called to him a youth—one of the Sons of the Prophets,
on whose speed and courage he could rely—placed in

---

[1] Jehoram == Jehovah is exalted. Ahaziah == Jehovah holds.

his hands a vial of the consecrated anointing oil,[1] told
him to gird up his loins,[2] and to speed across the Jordan
to Ramoth-Gilead. When he arrived, he was to bid
Jehu rise up from the company of his fellow-captains
to hurry him into "a chamber within a chamber,"[3] to
shut the door for secrecy, to pour the consecrating oil
upon his head, to anoint him King of Israel in the
name of Jehovah, and then to fly without a moment's
delay.[4]

The messenger—the Rabbis guess that he was
Jonah, the son of Amittai[5]—knew well that his was a
service of immense peril, in which his life might easily
pay the forfeit of his temerity. How was he to guess
that at once, without striking a blow, the host of
Israel would fling to the winds its sworn allegiance to
the son of the warrior Ahab, the fourth monarch of
the powerful dynasty of Omri? Might not any one
of a thousand possible accidents thwart a conspiracy of
which the success depended on the unflinching courage
and promptitude of his single hand?

He was but a youth, but he was the trained pupil of
a master who had, again and again, stood before kings,
and not been afraid. He sprang from a community
which inherited the splendid traditions of the Prophet
of Flame.

He did not hesitate a moment. He tightened the
camel's hide round his naked limbs, flung back the

---

[1] Vial (*pak*) only here and in 1 Sam. x. 1. "*The* oil" (LXX., τὸν
φακὸν τοῦ ἐλαίου).

[2] "His habit fit for speed *succinct*" (Milton).

[3] Inner chamber, 1 Kings xx. 30.

[4] Perhaps, if Elisha had gone in person, suspicion might have been
aroused. He was not more than fifty at this time, and lived forty-
three years more.

[5] *Seder Olam*, c. 18.

long dark locks of the Nazarite, and sped upon his way. A true son of the schools of Jehovah's prophets has, and can have, no fear of man. The armies of Israel and Judah saw the wild, flying figure of a young man, with his hairy garment and streaming locks, rush through the camp. Whatever might be their sur- misings, he brooked no questions. Availing himself of the awe with which the shadow of Elijah had covered the sacrosanct person of a prophetic messenger, he made his way straight to the war-council of the captains; and brushing aside every attempt to impede his progress with the plea that he was the bearer of Jehovah's message, he burst into the council of the astonished warriors, who were assembled in the private courtyard of a house in the fortress-town.[1]

He knew the fame of Jehu, but did not know his person, and dared not waste time. "I have an errand to thee, O captain," he said to the assembly generally. The message had been addressed to no one in parti- cular, and Jehu naturally asked, "Unto which of all of us?" With the same swift intuition which has often enabled men in similar circumstances to recognise a leader—as Josephus recognised Vespasian, and St. Severinus recognised Odoacer, and Joan of Arc re- cognised Charles VI. of France—he at once replied, "To thee, O captain." Jehu did not hesitate a moment. Prophets had shown, many a time, that their messages might not be neglected or despised. He rose, and followed the youth, who led him into the most secret recess of the house, and there, emptying on his head the fragrant oil of consecration, said, "Thus saith Jehovah, God of Israel, I have anointed thee

---

[1] It seems as though they were *inside* the town to defend it, not a beleaguring host outside.

king over the people of Jehovah, even over Israel."[1] He was to smite the house of his master Ahab in vengeance for the blood of Jehovah's prophets and servants whom Jezebel had murdered. Ahab's house, every male of it, young and old, bond and free,[2] is doomed to perish, as the houses of Jeroboam and of Baasha had perished before them, by a bloody end. Further, the dogs should eat Jezebel by the rampart of Jezreel,[3] and there should be none to bury her.

One moment sufficed for his daring deed, for his burning message; the next he had flung open the door and fled. The soldiers of the camp must have whispered still more anxiously together as they saw the same agitated youth rushing through their lines with the same impetuosity which had marked his entrance. In those dark days the sudden appearance of a prophet was usually the herald of some terrific storm.[4]

Jehu was utterly taken by surprise; but according to the reading preserved by Ephraem Syrus in 2 Kings ix. 26, he had on the previous night seen in a dream the blood of Naboth and his sons. If the thought of revolt had ever passed for a moment through his mind, it had never assumed a definite shape. True, he had

---

[1] The expression is remarkable, as showing how completely the prerogative of the Chosen People was supposed to rest with the Ten Tribes, as the most important representatives of the seed of Abraham.

[2] "Him that is shut up, and him that is left at large in Israel" (2 Kings ix. 8; 1 Kings xiv. 10, xvi. 3, 4).

[3] The A.V. has, less accurately, "in the *portion* of Jezreel." See 1 Kings xxi. 23. Heb., חֵלֶק. The חֵיל of an Eastern town is the ditch and empty space—a sort of external *pomœrium* around it. It is the place of offal, and the haunt of vultures and pariah dogs.

[4] 1 Sam. xvi. 4: "Comest thou peaceably?"

been a warrior from his youth. True, he had been
one of Ahab's bodyguard, and had ridden before him
in a chariot at least twenty years earlier, and had now
risen by valour and capacity to the high station of
captain of the host. True, also, that he had heard
the great curse which Elijah had pronounced on Ahab
at the door of Naboth's vineyard ; but he heard it
while he was yet an obscure youth, and he had little
dreamed that his was the hand which should carry
it into execution. Who was he ? And had not the house
of Omri been, in some sense, sanctioned by Heaven ?
And were not the words of the prophet "wild and
wandering cries," of which the issues might be averted
by such a repentance as that of Ahab ?

And he felt another misgiving. Might not this
scene be the plot of some secret enemy ? Might it
not at any rate be a reckless jest palmed upon him by
his comrades ? If any jealous member of the confederacy of captains betrayed the fact that Jehu had
tampered with their allegiance, would his head be safe
for a single hour ? He would act warily. He came
back to his fellow-captains and said nothing.

But they were burning with curiosity. Something
must be impending. Prophets did not rush in thus
tumultuously for no purpose. Must not the youth's
mantle of hair be some standard of war ?

"Is all right?" they shouted. "Why did this
frantic fellow come to thee ?"[1]

"You know all about it," answered Jehu, with wary
coolness. "You know more about it than I do. You
know the man, and what his talk was."

---

[1] 2 Kings ix. 11, הַמְשֻׁגָּע. LXX., ὁ ἐπίληπτος. Comp. ver. 20, "he
driveth *furiously*" (בְּשִׁגָּעוֹן)

8

"Lies!" bluntly answered the rough soldiers.[1] "Tell us now."

Then Jehu's eye took measure of them and their feelings. A judge of men and of men's countenances, he saw conspiracy flashing in their faces. He saw that they suspected the true state of things, and were on fire to carry it out. Perhaps they had caught sight of the vial of oil under the youth's scant dress. Could any quickened observation at least fail to notice that the soldier's dark locks were shining and fragrant, as they had not been a moment ago, with consecrated oil?

Then Jehu frankly told them the perilous secret. Thus and thus had the young prophet spoken, and had said, "Thus saith Jehovah, I have anointed thee king over Israel."

The message was met with a shout of answering approbation. That shout was the death-knell of the house of Omri. It showed that the reigning dynasty had utterly forfeited its popularity. No luck had followed the sons of Naboth's murderer. Israel was weary of their mother Jezebel. Why was this king Jehoram, this king of evil auspices, who had been repudiated by Moab and harried by Syria—why, in the first gleam of possible prosperity, was he being detained at Jezreel by wounds which rumour said were already sufficiently healed to allow him to return to his post? Down with the seed of the murderer and the sorceress! Let brave Jehu be king, as Jehovah has said!

So the captains sprang to their feet, and then and there seized Jehu, and carried him in triumph to the top of the stairs which ran round the inside of the courtyard, and stripped off their mantles to extemporise

---

[1] Ver. 12, a lie! (שֶׁקֶר).

for him the semblance of a cushioned throne.[1] Then
in the presence of such soldiers as they could trust
they blew a sudden blast of the ram's horn, and
shouted, " Jehu is king !"

Jehu was not the man to let the grass grow under
his feet. Nothing tries a man's vigour and nerve so
surely as a sudden crisis. It is this swift resolution
which has raised many a man to the throne, as it raised
Otho, and Napoleon I. and Napoleon III. The history
of Israel is specially full of *coups d'état*, but no one of
them is half so decisive or overwhelming as this. Jehu
instantly accepted the office of Jehovah's avenger on
the house of Ahab.[2] Everything, as Jehu saw,
depended on the suddenness and fury with which the
blow was delivered. "If you want me to be your
king,"[3] he said, "keep the lines secure, and guard the
fortress walls. I will be my own messenger to Jehoram.
Let no deserter go forth to give him warning."[4]

It was agreed ; and Jehu, only taking with him
Bidkar, his fellow-officer, and a small band of followers,
set forth at full speed from Ramoth-Gilead.

The fortress of Ramoth, now the important town of
Es-Salt, a place which must always have been the key

---

[1] What is meant by the *gerem* of the staircase is uncertain. The
word means "a bone" (Aquila, ὀστῶδες), and is, in this connection, an
ἅπαξ λεγόμενον. The Targum explains it as the top vane of a stair-
dial. The margin of the R.V. renders it "on the bare steps." The
Vulgate renders it *in similitudinem tribunalis*, as though *gerem*
meant *tselem*. The LXX. conceal their perplexity by simply translating the word ἐπὶ τὸ γαρέμ. Grotius and Clericus, *in fastigio
graduum*. Symmachus, ἐπὶ μίαν τῶν ἀναβαθμίδων.

[2] 2 Kings ix. 14: "So Jehu *conspired* against Joram." The same
word is used in 2 Chron. xxiv. 25, 26.

[3] 2 Kings ix. 15, R.V: "If this be your mind."

[4] So far as we know, he never returned to Ramoth-Gilead, of which
indeed we hear no more.

of Gilead, was built on the summit of a rocky headland, fortified by nature as well as by art. It is south of the river Jabbok, and lies at the head of the only easy road which runs down westward to the Jordan and eastward to the rich plateau of the interior.[1] Crossing the fords of the Jordan, Jehu would soon be able to join the main road, which, passing Tirzah, Zaretan, and Beth-shean, and sweeping eastward of Mount Gilboa, gives ready access to Jezreel.

The watchman on the lofty watchtower of the summer palace caught sight of a storm of dust careering along from the eastward up the valley towards the city.[2] The times were wild and troublous. What could it be? He shouted his alarm, "I see a troop!" The tidings were startling, and the king was instantly informed that chariots and horsemen were approaching the royal city. "Send a horseman to meet them," he said, "with the message, 'Is all well?'"

Forth flew the rider, and cried to the rushing escort, "The king asks, 'Is all well? Is it peace?" For probably the anxious city hoped that there might have been some victory of the army against Hazael, which would fill them with joy.

"What hast thou to do with peace? Turn thee behind me," answered Jehu; and perforce the horseman, whatever may have been his conjectures, had to follow in the rear.

"He reached them," cried the sentry on the watch-tower, "but he does not return."

The news was enigmatical and alarming; and the

---

[1] Tristram, *Land of Moab.*

[2] Heb., *Shiph'hath,* "a dust-storm" (LXX., κονιορτόν, *al.* ὄχλον; Vulg., *globum*), not as in A.V. and R.V., "a company." Comp. Isa. lx. 6; Ezek. xxvi. 10.

troubled king sent another horseman.   Again the same
colloquy occurred, and again the watchman gave the
ominous message, adding to it the yet more perplexing
news that, in the mad and headlong driving[1] of the
charioteer, he recognises the driving of Jehu, the son
of Nimshi.[2]

What had happened to his army ?   Why should the
captain of the host be driving thus furiously to Jezreel ?

Matters were evidently very critical, whatever the
swift approach of chariots and horsemen might por-
tend.   "Yoke my chariot," said Jehoram ; and his
nephew Ahaziah, who had shared his campaign, and
was no less consumed with anxiety to learn tidings
which could not but be pressing, rode by him in another
chariot to meet Jehu.   They took with them no escort
worth mentioning.   The rebellion was not only sudden,
but wholly unexpected.

The two kings met Jehu in a spot of the darkest
omen.   It was the plot of ground which had once been
the vineyard of Naboth, at the door of which Ahab
had heard from Elijah the awful message of his doom.
As the New Forest was ominous to our early Norman
kings as the witness of their cruelties and encroachments, so was this spot to the house of Omri, though
it was adjacent to their ivory palace, and had been
transformed from a vineyard into a garden or pleasance.

"Is it peace, Jehu ?" shouted the agitated king ; by

---

[1] Clearly the rendering "he driveth furiously " is right.   The word
"furiously" is *beshigga'ōn* (Vulg., *præceps*), and is connected with
"mad," ver. 11.   LXX., ἐν παραλλαγῇ.   Arab. Chald., "quietly."
Josephus, "leisurely, and in good order."   Such an approach would
not, however, have been at all in accordance with the perilous
urgency of his intent.

[2] Jehu, the son of Jehoshaphat, is named from his grandfather Nimshi,
who seems to have been the founder of the greatness of his house.

which probably he only meant to ask, "Is all going well in the army at Ramoth?"

The fierce answer which burst from the lips of his general fatally undeceived him. "What peace," brutally answered the rebel, "so long as the whoredoms of thy mother Jezebel and her witchcrafts are so many?" She, after all, was the *fons et origo mali* to the house of Jehoram. Hers was the dark spirit of murder and idolatry which had walked in that house. She was the instigator and the executer of the crime against Naboth. She had been the foundress of Baal- and Asherah-worship; she was the murderess of the prophets; she had been specially marked out for vengeance in the doom pronounced both by Elijah and Elisha.

The answer was unmistakable. This was a revolt, a revolution. "Treachery, Ahaziah!" shouted the terrified king, and instantly wheeled round his chariot to flee.[1] But not so swiftly as to escape the Nemesis which had been stealing upon him with leaden feet, but now smote him irretrievably with iron hand. Without an instant's hesitation, Jehu snatched his bow from his attendant charioteer, "filled his hands with it," and from its full stretch and resonant string sped the arrow, which smote Jehoram in the back with fatal force, and passed through his heart.[2] Without a word the unhappy king sank down upon his knees[3] in his chariot, and fell face forward, dead.

"Take him up," cried Jehu to Bidkar,[4] "and fling him down where he is,—here in this portion of the field of Naboth the Jezreelite. Here, years ago, you

---

[1] 2 Kings ix. 23 : "Turned his hands." Comp. 1 Kings xxii. 34.
[2] Ver. 24. Vulg., *inter scapulas.*   [3] LXX., reading עַל בִּרְכָּיו.
[4] Bidkar, perhaps Bar-dekar, "Son of stabbing." Comp. 1 Kings iv. 9.

and I, as we rode behind Ahab,[1] heard Elijah utter his
oracle on this man's father, that vengeance should meet
him here. Where the dogs licked the blood of Naboth
and his sons, let dogs lick the blood of the son of Ahab."[2]

But Jehu was not the man to let the king's murder
stay his chariot-wheels when more work had yet to be
done. Ahaziah of Judah, too, belonged to Ahab's house,
for he was Ahab's grandson, and Jehoram's nephew
and ally. Without stopping to mourn or avenge the
tragedy of his uncle's murder, Ahaziah fled towards
Bethgan or Engannim,[3] the fountain of gardens, south
of Jezreel, on the road to Samaria and Jerusalem. Jehu
gave the laconic order, "Smite him also";[4] but fright
added wings to the speed of the hapless King of Judah.
His chariot-steeds were royal steeds, and were fresh;
those of Jehu were spent with the long, fierce drive
from Ramoth. He got as far as the ascent of Gur
before he was overtaken.[5] There, not far from
Ibleam, the rocky hill impeded his flight, and he was
wounded by the pursuers. But he managed to struggle
onwards to Megiddo, on the south of the plain of Jezreel,
and there he hid himself.[6] He was discovered, dragged

---

[1] Heb., *ts'madim*, "in pairs"; LXX., ἐπιβεβηκότες ἐπὶ ζεύγη. It is
uncertain whether Jehu and Bidkar were in the same chariot as
Ahab, as Josephus says (καθεζομένους ὄπισθεν τοῦ ἅρματος), or in a
separate chariot.

[2] 2 Kings ix. 26: "Saith the Lord." Ephraem Syrus omits these
words. He says that the night before Jehu had seen the blood
of Naboth and his sons in a dream. Comp. Hom., *Od.*, iii. 258:
Τῷ κε οἱ οὐδὲ θανόντι χυτὴν ἐπὶ γαῖαν ἔχευαν 'Αλλ' ἄρα τόνγε κύνες τε
καὶ οἰωνοὶ κατέδαψαν Κείμενον ἐν πεδίῳ.

[3] A.V., "By the way of the garden-house." LXX., Βαιθγάν.

[4] The text is a little uncertain.

[5] Thenius supposes "Gur" to mean "a caravanserai." Comp.
2 Chron. xxvi. 7, *Gur-Baal*; Vulg., *Hospitium Baalis*.

[6] The account of the Chronicler (2 Chron. xxii. 9) differs from that
of the earlier historian. It may, however, be (uncertainly) reconciled

out, and slain.   Even Jehu's fierce emissaries did not
make war on dead bodies, any more than Hannibal did,
or Charles V.   They left such meanness to Jehu himself, and to our Charles II.   They did not interfere with
the dead king's remains.   His servants carried them
to Jerusalem, and there he was buried with his fathers
in the sepulchre of the kings, in the city of David.   As
there was nothing more to tell about him, the historian
omits the usual formula about the rest of the acts of
Ahaziah, and all that he did.   His death illustrates the
proverb *Mitgegangen mitgefangen* : he was the comrade
of evil men, and he perished with them.

Jehu speedily reached Jezreel, but the interposition
of Jehoram and the orders for the pursuit of Ahaziah
had caused a brief delay, and Jezebel had already been
made aware that her doom was imminent.

Not even the sudden and dreadful death of her son,
and the nearness of her own fate, daunted the steely
heart of the Tyrian sorceress.   If she was to die, she
would meet death like a queen.   As though for some
Court banquet, she painted her eyelashes and eyebrows
with antimony, to make her eyes look large and lus-
trous,[1] and put on her jewelled head-dress.[2]   Then she

---

with it as in the text, if we suppose the words "he was hid in
Samaria" to mean in Megiddo, in the territory of Samaria.   Obviously,
however, the traditions varied.   There are difficulties about the story,
for Ibleam is on the west towards Megiddo, and not between Jezreel
and Samaria.

[1] פּוּךְ, "Lead-glance."   A mixture of pulverised antimony (*stibium*)
and zinc is still used by women in the East for this purpose.   *In calli-
blepharis dilatat oculos* (Plin., *H. N.*, xxxiii.).   Keren-Happuk, the name
given by Job to one of his daughters, means "horn of stibium."   The
object could hardly have been to *attract* Jehu (as Ephraem Syrus
thinks), for Jezebel had already a *grandson* twenty-three years old
(viii. 26).

[2] A.V., "*Tired* her head."   Comp. *tiara*.   Lit., "made good";
LXX., ἠγάθυνε.

mounted the palace tower, and, looking down through the lattice above the city gate, watched the thundering advance of Jehu's chariot, and hailed the triumphant usurper with the bitterest insult she could devise. She knew that Omri, her husband's father, had taken swift vengeance on the guilt of the usurper Zimri, who had been forced to burn himself in the harem at Tirzah after one month's troubled reign. Her shrill voice was heard above the roar of the chariot-wheels in the ominous taunt,—

"Is it peace, thou Zimri, thou murderer of thy master?"[1]

No!—She meant, "There is no peace for thee nor thine, any more than for me or mine! Thou mayest murder us; but thee too, thy doom awaiteth!"

Stung by the ill-omened words, Jehu looked up at her and shouted,—

"Who is on my side? Who?"

The palace was apparently rife with traitors. Ahab had been the first polygamist among the kings of Israel, and therefore the first also to introduce the odious atrocity of eunuchs. Those hapless wretches, the portents of Eastern scraglios, the disgrace of humanity, are almost always the retributive enemies of the societies of which they are the helpless victims. Fidelity or gratitude are rarely to be looked for from natures warped into malignity by the ruthless misdoing of men. Nor was the nature of Jezebel one to inspire affection. One or two eunuchs[2] immediately thrust out of the

---

[1] Josephus gives the sense very well: Καλὸς δοῦλος ὁ ἀποκτείνας τὸν δεσπότην (*Antt.*, IX. vi. 4). The same question might have been addressed to Baasha, Shallum, Menahem, Pekah, and Hoshea; but at least Jehu might plead a prophet's call.

[2] "Two or three." Lit., "two three," like the old English "two three" for "several."

windows their bloated and beardless faces. " Fling her down ! " Jehu shouted. Down they flung the wretched queen (has any queen ever died a death so shamelessly ignominious ?), and her blood spirted upon the wall, and on the horses. Jehu, who had only stopped for an instant in his headlong rush, drove his horses over her corpse,[1] and entered the gate of her capital with his wheels crimson with her blood. History records scarcely another instance of such a scene, except when Tullia, a century later, drove her chariot over the dead body of her father Servius Tullius in the *Vicus Sceleratus* of ancient Rome.[2]

But what cared Jehu ? Many a conqueror ere now has sat down to the dinner prepared for his enemy ; and the obsequious household of the dead tyrants, ready to do the bidding of their new lord, ushered the hungry man to the banquet provided for the kings whom he had slain. No man dreamt of uttering a wail ; no man thought of raising a finger for dead Jehoram or for dead Jezebel, though they had all been under *her* sway for at least five-and-thirty years. " The wicked perish, and no man regardeth." "When the wicked perish, there is shouting."[3]

We may be startled at a revolution so sudden and so complete ; yet it is true to history. A tyrant or a cabal may oppress a nation for long years. Their word may be thought absolute, their power irresistible. Tyranny seems to paralyse the courage of resistance, like the fabled head of Medusa. Remove its fascination

---

[1] Ver. 33. Heb., "He trod her underfoot." LXX., Συνεπάτησαν αὐτήν; Vulg., *Conculcaverunt eam.*

[2] Liv., i. 46–48.

[3] Prov. xi. 10. Compare the remark of Voltaire, who saw "le peuple ivré de vin et de joie de la mort de Louis XIV."

of corruption, and men become men, and not machines, once more.   Jehu's daring woke Israel from the lethargy which had made her tolerate the murders and enchantments of this Baal-worshipping alien.   In the same way in one week Robespierre seemed to be an invincible autocrat ; the next week his power had crumbled into dust and ashes at a touch.

It was not until Jehu had sated his thirst and hunger after that wild drive, which had ended in the murder of two kings and a queen and in his sudden elevation to a throne, that it even occurred to this new tiger-king to ask what had become of Jezebel.   But when he had eaten and drunk, he said, "Go, see now to this cursed woman, and bury her : for she is a king's daughter." That she had been first Princess, then Queen, then Gebîrah in Israel for nearly a full lifetime was nothing : it was nothing to Jehu that she was a wife, and mother, and grandmother of kings and queens both of Israel and Judah ;—but she was also the daughter of Ethbaal, the priest-king of Tyre and Sidon, and therefore any shameful treatment of her remains might kindle trouble from the region of Phœnicia.[1]

But no one had taken the trouble so much as to look after the corpse of Jezebel.   The populace of Jezreel were occupied with their new king.   Where Jezebel fell, there she had been suffered to lie ; and no one, apparently, cared even to despoil her of the royal robes, now saturated with bloodshed.   Flung from the palace-tower, her body had fallen in the open space just outside the walls—what is called "the mounds" of an Eastern city.   In the strange carelessness of sanitation which

---

[1] I Kings xvi. 31.   At this time Ethbaal was dead.   He reigned probably from B.C. 940–908, and died at the age of sixty-eight (Jos., *Antt.*, VIII. xiii. 1, IX. vi. 6 ; *c. Ap.*, i. 18).

describes as "fate" even the visitation of an avoidable pestilence, all sorts of offal are shot into this vacant space to fester in the tropic heat. I myself have seen the pariah dogs and the vultures feeding on a ghastly dead horse in a ruined space within the street of Beit-Dejun ; and the dogs and the vultures—"those national undertakers"—had done their work unbidden on the corpse of the Tyrian queen. When men went to bury her, they only found a few dog-mumbled bones—the skull, and the feet, and the palms of the hands.[1] They brought the news to Jehu as he rested after his feast. It did not by any means discompose him. He at once recognised that another levin-bolt had fallen from the thunder-crash of Elijah's prophecy, and he troubled himself about the matter no further. Her carcase, as the man of God had prophesied, had become as dung upon the face of the field, so that none could say, "This is Jezebel."[2]

---

[1] 1 Kings xxi. 23.

[2] Comp. Psalm lxxxiii. 10. Her name remained a by-word till the latest days (Rev. ii. 20), and the Spanish Jews called their persecutress Isabella the Catholic "Jezebel."

CHAPTER XII

JEHU ESTABLISHED ON THE THRONE

B.C. 842—814

2 KINGS x. 1—17

"The devil can quote Scripture for his purpose."
SHAKESPEARE.

BUT the work of Jehu was not yet over. He was established at Jezreel; he was lord of the palace and seraglio of his master; the army of Israel was with him. But who could be sure that no civil war would arise, as between the partisans of Zimri and Omri, as between Omri and Tibni? Ahab, first of the kings of Israel, had left many sons. There were no less than seventy of these princes at Samaria. Might there not be among them some youth of greater courage and capacity than the murdered Jehoram? And could it be anticipated that the late dynasty was so utterly unfortunate and execrated as to have none left to do them reverence, or to strike one blow on their behalf, after more than half a century of undisputed sway? [1] Jehu's *coup de main* had been brilliantly successful. In one day he had leapt into the throne. But Samaria was strong upon its watch-tower hill. It was full of Ahab's sons, and had not yet declared on Jehu's side. It might

---

[1] Omri, 12 years; Ahab, 22; Ahaziah, 18; Jehoram, 12.

125

be expected to feel some gratitude to the dynasty
which Jehu had supplanted, seeing that it owed to the
grandfather of the king whom he had just slain its very
existence as the capital of Israel.

He would put a bold face on his usurpation, and
strike while the iron was hot. He would not rouse
opposition by seeming to assume that Samaria would
accept his rebellion. He therefore wrote a letter to the
rulers of Samaria [1]—which was but a journey of nine
hours' distance from Jezreel—and to the guardians of
the young princes, reminding them that they were
masters in a strong city, protected with its own contingent of chariots and horses, and well supplied with
armour. He suggested that they should select the most
promising of Ahab's sons, make him king, and begin a
civil war on his behalf.

The event showed how prudent was this line of conduct. As yet Jehu had not transferred the army from
Ramoth-Gilead. He had doubtless taken good care to
prevent intelligence of his plans from reaching the
adherents of Jehoram in Samaria. To them the
unknown was the terrible. All they knew was that
"Behold, two kings stood not before him!" The army
must have sanctioned his revolt : what chance had
they ? As for loyalty and affection, if ever they had
existed towards this hapless dynasty, they had vanished
like a dream. The people of Samaria and Jezreel had
once been obedient as sheep to the iron dominance of
Jezebel. They had tolerated her idol-abominations,
and the insolence of her army of dark-browed priests.

---

[1] The reading of 2 Kings x. 1, "Unto the rulers of *Jezreel*," is clearly
wrong. The LXX. reads, "Unto the rulers of Samaria." Unless
"Jezreel" be a clerical error for Israel, we must read, "He sent letters
from Jezreel unto the rulers of Samaria."

They had not risen to defend the prophets of Jehovah, and had suffered even Elijah, twice over, to be forced to flee for his life. They had borne, hitherto without a murmur, the tragedies, the sieges, the famines, the humiliations, with which during these reigns they had been familiar. And was not Jehovah against the waning fortunes of the Beni-Omri? Elijah had undoubtedly cursed them, and now the curse was falling. Jehu must doubtless have let it be known that he was only carrying out the behest of their own citizen the great Elisha, who had sent to him the anointing oil. They could find abundant excuses to justify their defection from the old house, and they sent to the terrible man a message of almost abject submission:— Let him do as he would; they would make no king: they were his servants, and would do his bidding.

Jehu was not likely to be content with verbal or even written promises. He determined, with cynical subtlety, to make them put a very bloody sign-manual to their treaty, by implicating them irrevocably in his rebellion. He wrote them a second mandate.

"If," he said, "ye accept my rule, prove it by your obedience. Cut off the heads of your master's sons, and see that they are brought to me here to-morrow by yourselves before the evening."

The ruthless order was fulfilled to the letter by the terrified traitors. The king's sons were with their tutors, the lords of the city. On the very morning that Jehu's second missive arrived, every one of these poor guiltless youths was unceremoniously beheaded. The hideous, bleeding trophies were packed in fig-baskets and sent to Jezreel.[1]

---

[1] Fig-baskets, Jer. xxiv. 2. The word *dudim* is rendered "pots"

When Jehu was informed of this revolting present it was evening, and he was sitting at a meal with his friends.[1] He did not trouble himself to rise from his feast or to look at "death made proud by pure and princely beauty." He knew that those seventy heads could only be the heads of the royal youths. He issued a cool and brutal order that they should be piled in two heaps[2] until the morning on either side the entrance of the city gates. Were they watched? or were the dogs and vultures and hyænas again left to do their work upon them? We do not know. In any case it was a scene of brutal barbarism such as might have been witnessed in living memory in Khiva or Bokhara;[3] nor must we forget that even in the last century the heads of the brave and the noble rotted on Westminster Hall and Temple Bar, and over the Gate of York, and over the Tolbooth at Edinburgh, and on Wexford Bridge.

The day dawned, and all the people were gathered at the gate, which was the scene of justice. With the calmest air imaginable the warrior came out to them, and stood between the mangled heads of those who but yesterday had been the pampered minions of fortune and luxury. His speech was short and politic in its brutality. "Be yourselves the judges," he said. "Ye are righteous. Jezebel called me a Zimri. Yes! I conspired against my master and slew him: but"— and here he casually pointed to the horrible, bleeding heaps—"who smote all these?" The people of Jezreel

---

in 1 Sam. ii. 14. LXX., ἐν καρτάλλοις; Vulg., *in cophinis.* In Psalm lxxxi. 6 the LXX. has ἐν τῷ κοφίνῳ.

[1] Jos., *Antt.*, IX. vi. 5.

[2] Heb., *Tsibourim*; LXX., βουνούς.

[3] Comp. 1 Sam. xvii. 54; 2 Macc. xv. 30.

and the lords of Samaria were not only passive witnesses of his rebellion ; they were active sharers in it. They had dabbled their hands in the same blood. Now they could not choose but accept his dynasty : for who was there besides himself ? And then, changing his tone, he does not offer " the tyrant's devilish plea, necessity," to cloak his atrocities, but—like a Romish inquisitor of Seville or Granada—claims Divine sanction for his sanguinary violence. This was not *his* doing. He was but an instrument in the hands of fate. Jehovah is alone responsible. He is doing what He spake by His servant Elijah. Yes ! and there was yet more to do ; for no word of Jehovah's shall fall to the ground.

With the same cynical ruthlessness, and cold indifference to smearing his robes in the blood of the slain, he carried out to the bitter end his task of policy which he gilded with the name of Divine justice. Not content with slaying Ahab's sons, he set himself to extirpate his race, and slew all who remained to him in Jezreel, not only his kith and kin, but every lord and every Baal-priest who favoured his house, until he left him none remaining.

But what a frightful picture do these scenes furnish us of the state of religion and even of civilisation in Jezreel ! There was this man-eating tiger of a king wallowing in the blood of princes, and enacting scenes which remind us of Dahomey and Ashantee, or of some Tartary khanate where human hands are told out in the market-place after some avenging raid. And amid all this savagery, squalor, and Turkish atrocity, the man pleads the sanction of Jehovah, and claims, unrebuked, that he is only carrying out the behests of Jehovah's prophets ! It is not until long afterwards that the voice of a prophet is heard repudiating his plea and denouncing his bloodthirstiness.

> "An evil soul producing holy witness
> Is like a villain with a smiling cheek—
> A goodly apple rotten at the core."

---

[1] Hos. i. 4.

CHAPTER XIII

FRESH MURDERS—THE EXTIRPATION OF BAAL-WORSHIP (B.C. 842)

2 KINGS x. 12—28

> "Jéhu, sur les hauts lieux, enfin osant offrir
> Un téméraire encens que Dieu ne peut souffrir,
> N'a pour servir sa cause et venger ses injures
> Ni le cœur assez droit, ni les mains assez pures."
>
> RACINE.

AFTER such abject subservience had been shown him by the lords of Samaria and Jezreel, Jehu evidently had no further shadow of apprehension. He seems to have loved blood for its own sake—to have been seized by a vertigo of blood-poisoning. Having waded through slaughter to a throne, he loved to wash his footsteps in the blood of the slain, and to stretch to the very uttermost—to stretch until it cracked all its ravelled threads—the Divine sanction claimed by his fanaticism or his hypocrisy.

When he had finished his massacres at Jezreel, he went to Samaria. It was only a journey of a few hours. On the high road he met a company of travelers, whose escort and rich apparel showed that they vere persons of importance. They were about to halt, erhaps for refreshment, at the shearing-house of the shepherds—the place in which the sheep were gathered before they were shorn.[1]

"Who are ye?" he asked.

They answered that they were princes of the house of Judah, the brethren of Ahaziah,[2] on their way to see the two kings at Jezreel, and to salute their cousins, the children of Jehoram, and their kinsfolk the children of Jezebel the Gebîrah.[3]　The answer sealed their fate. Jehu ordered his followers to take them alive. At first he had not decided what he would do with them. But half measures had now become impossible. This cavalcade of princes little knew that they were on their way to greet the dead children of a dead king and a dead queen.　Jehu felt that the possibilities of an endless *vendetta* must be quenched in blood. He gave orders to slay them, and there in one hour forty-two more scions of the royal houses of Judah and Israel were done to death.[4]　With the usual reckless insouciance of the East, where any tank or well is made the natural receptacle for corpses regardless of ultimate consequences, their bodies were flung into the cistern of the shearing-house, in which the sheep were washed before shearing, just as the bodies of Gedaliah's followers were flung by Ishmael into the well at Mizpah, and the bodies of our own murdered countrymen were

---

[1] 2 Kings x. 12.　The shepherds' House of Meeting (*Beth-equed-haroim*).　LXX., ἐν Βαιθακάθ ; Vulg., *ad cameram pastorum* ; Aquila, οἶκος κάμψεως.　It has been conjectured by Klostermann that it belonged to the Rechabites, that they had been persecuted by Jezebel, and that they were glad to help in taking vengeance on her descendants.

[2] The Chronicler (2 Chron. xxii. 8) says "*sons* of the brethren of Ahaziah."

[3] LXX., ἡ δυναστεύουσα.

[4] 2 Kings x. 14, A.V., "at the pit."　Lit., "in" or "into the cistern."

flung into the well of Cawnpore. He did not leave one of them alive.

Thus Jehu "murdered two kings, and one hundred and twelve princes, and gave Queen Jezebel to dogs to eat; and if priests had but noticed how even Hosea condemns and denounces his savagery, they would have abstained from some of their glorifications of assassins and butchers, nor would they have appealed to this man's hideous example, as they have done, to excuse some of their own revolting atrocities."[1] But

> "Crime was ne'er so black
> As ghostly cheer and pious thanks to lack.
> Satan is modest. At heaven's door he lays
> His evil offspring, and in Scriptural phrase
> And saintly posture gives to God the praise
> And honour of his monstrous progeny."[2]

One cruel deed more or less was nothing to Jehu. Leaving this tank choked with death and incarnadined with royal blood, he went on his way as if nothing particular had happened. He had not proceeded far when he saw a man well known to him, and of a spirit kindred to his own. It was the Arab ascetic and Nazarite Jehonadab, the son of Rechab (or "The Rider"), the chief of the tribe of Kenites who had flung in their lot with the children of Israel since the days of Moses.[3] It was the tribe which had produced a Jael; and Jehonadab had something of the fierce, fanatical

---

[1] See Martin, *Hist. de France*, ix. 114.

[2] Whittier.

[3] Jer. xxxv. 1–19. Josephus (*Antt.*, IX. vi. 6) calls him "a good man and a just, who had long been a friend of Jehu." "He was," says Ewald (*Gesch.*, iii. 543), "of a society of those who despaired of being able to observe true religion undisturbedly in the midst of the nation with the stringency with which they understood it, and therefore withdrew into the desert."

spirit of the ancient chieftainess, who, in her own tent, had dashed out with the tent-peg the brains of Sisera. His very name, "The Lord is noble," indicated that he was a worshipper of Jehovah, and his fierce zeal showed him to be a genuine Kenite. Disgusted with the wickedness of cities, disgusted above all with the loathly vice of drunkenness, which, as we see from the contemporary prophets, had begun in this age to acquire fresh prominence in luxurious and wealthy communities, he exacted of his sons a solemn oath that neither they nor their successors would drink wine nor strong drink, and that, shunning the squalor and corruption of cities, they would live in tents, as their nomad ancestors had done in the days when Jethro and Hobab were princes of pastoral Midian. We learn from Jeremiah, nearly two and a half centuries later, how faithfully that oath had been observed; and how, in spite of all temptation, the vow of abstinence was maintained, even when the strain of foreign invasion had driven the Rechabites into Jerusalem from their desolated pastures.[1]

Jehu knew that the stern fanaticism of the Kenite Emîr would rejoice in his extirminating zeal, and he recognised that the friendship and countenance of this "good man and just," as Josephus calls him, would add strength to his cause, and enable him to carry out his dark design. He therefore blessed him.[2]

"Is thine heart right with my heart, as my heart is with thy heart?" he asked, after he had returned the greeting of Jehonadab.

---

[1] Jer. xxxv. (written about B.C. 604). Communities of Nazarites seem to have sprung up at this epoch, perhaps as a protest against the prevailing luxury (Amos ii. 11).

[2] In Josephus it is Jehonadab who blesses the king.

"It is, it is !" answered the vehement Rechabite.[1]

"Then give me thy hand," he said ; and grasping the Arab by the hand,[2] he pulled him up into his chariot—the highest distinction he could bestow upon him—and bade him come and witness his zeal for Jehovah.

His first task on arriving at Samaria was to tear up the last fibres of Ahab's kith and destroy all his partisans. This was indeed to push to a self-interested extreme the denunciation which had been pronounced upon Ahab ; but the crime helped to secure his fiercely founded throne.

One deep-seated plot was yet unaccomplished. It was the total extermination of Baal-worship. To drive out for ever this orgiastic, corrupt, and alien idolatry was right ; but there is nothing to show that Jehu would have been unable to effect this purpose by one stern decree, together with the destruction of Baal's images and temple. A method so simply righteous did not suit this Nero-Torquemada, who seemed to be never happy unless he united Jesuitical cunning with the pouring out of rivers of massacre.

He summoned the people together ; and as though he now threw off all pretence of zeal for orthodoxy, he proclaimed that Ahab had served Baal a little, but Jehu would serve him much. The Samaritans must have been endowed with infinite gullibility if they could suppose that the king who had ridden into the city side by side with such a man as Jehonadab—"the warrior in his coat of mail, the ascetic in his shirt of hair "—who had already exhibited an unfathomable

---

[1] Heb., יֵשׁ וָיֵשׁ.

[2] Striking hands was a sign of good faith (Job xvii. 3 ; Prov. xxii. 26).

cunning, and had swept away the Baal-priests of Jezreel, was indeed sincere in this new conversion.[1] Perhaps they felt it dangerous to question the sincerity of kings. The Baal-worshippers of former days were known, and Jehu proclaimed that if any one of them was missing at the great sacrifice which he intended to offer to Baal he should be put to death. A solemn assembly to Baal was proclaimed, and every apostate from God to nature-worship from all Israel was present, till the idol's temple was thronged from end to end.[2] To add splendour to the solemnity, Jehu bade the wardrobe-keeper to bring out all the rich vestments of Tyrian dye and Sidonian broidery, and clothe the worshippers.[3] Solemnly advancing to the altar with the Rechabite by his side, he warned the assembly to see that their gathering was not polluted by the presence of a single known worshipper of Jehovah. Then, apparently, he still further disarmed suspicion by taking a personal part in offering the burnt-offering. Meanwhile, he had surrounded the temple and blocked every exit with eighty armed warriors, and had threatened that any

---

[1] He did it "in subtilty" (בְּעָקְבָה). This substantive occurs nowhere else, but is connected with the name Jacob. LXX., ἐν πτερνισμῷ, "in taking by the heel," with reference to the name Jacob, "supplanter."

[2] Lit., "mouth to mouth." LXX., στόμα ἐς στόμα.

[3] Ver. 22, מֶלְתָּחָה, Vestiarum, occurs here only. The LXX. omits it or puts it in Greek letters. Targum, κάμπτραι, "chests" Sil. Italicus (iii. 23) describes the robes of the priests of the Gaditanian Hercules,—

> " Nec discolor ulli,
> Ante aras cultus ; velantur corpora lino
> Et Pelusiaco praefulget stamine vertex."
>
> KEIL, ad loc.

It was a mixture of "the rich dye of Tyre and the rich web of Nile."

one of them should be put to death if he let a single Baal-worshipper escape. When he had finished the offering,[1] he went forth, and bade his soldiers enter, and slay, and slay, and slay till none were left. Then flinging the corpses in a heap, they made their way to the fortress of the Temple, where some of the priests may have taken refuge. They dragged out and burnt the *matstseboth* of Baal,[2] broke down the great central idol, and utterly dismantled the whole building. To complete the pollution of the dishallowed shrine, he made it a common midden for Samaria, which it continued to be for centuries afterwards.[3] It was his last voluntary massacre. The House of Ahab was no more. Baal-worship in Israel never survived that exterminating blow.

Happily for the human race, such atrocities committed in the name of religion have not been common. In Pagan history we have but few instances, except the slaughter of the Magians at the beginning of the reign of Darius, son of Hystaspes. Alas that other parallels should be furnished by the abominable tyranny of a false Christianity, blessed and incited by popes and priests ! The persecutions and massacres of the Albigenses, preached by Arnold of Citeaux, and instigated by Pope Innocent III. ; the expulsion of the Jews from Spain ; the deadly work of Torquemada ; the murderous furies of Alva among the hapless Netherlanders, urged and approved by Pope Pius V. ; the massacre of St.

---

[1] The phrase may be impersonal, "when one [*i.e.*, they] had finished the sacrifice"; but the narrative seems to imply that Jehu offered it himself (LXX., ὡς συνετέλεσαν ποιοῦντες τὴν ὁλοκαύτωσιν Vulg., *cum completum esset holocaustum*).

[2] A.V., images; R.V., pillars.

[3] Comp. Ezra vi. 11 ; Dan. ii. 5.

Bartholomew, for which Pope Gregory and his cardinals sang their horrible Te Deum in their desecrated shrines, —these are the parallels to the deeds of Jehu. He has found his chief imitators among the votaries of a blood-stained and usurping sacerdotalism, which has committed so many crimes and inflicted so many horrors on mankind.

And did God approve all this detestable mixture of zealous enthusiasm with lying deceit and the insatiate thirst of blood?

If right be right, and wrong be wrong, the answer must not be an elaborate subterfuge, but an uncompromising "No!" We need be under no doubt on that subject. Christ Himself reproved His Apostles for savage zealotry, and taught them that the Elijah-spirit was not the Christ-spirit. Nor is the Elisha-spirit the Christian spirit any the more if these deeds of hypocrisy and blood were in any sense approved by him who is sometimes regarded as the mild and gentle Elisha. Where was he? Why was he silent? Could he possibly approve of this murderer's fury? We do not, indeed, know how far Elisha lent his sanction to anything more than the general end. Ahab's house had been doomed to vengeance by the voice which gave utterance to the verdict of the national conscience. The doom was just; Jehu was ordained to be the executioner. In no other way could the judgment be carried out. The times were not sentimental. The murder of Jehoram was not regarded as an act of tyrannicide, but of divinely commissioned justice. Elisha *may* have shrunk from the unreined furies of the man whom he had sent his emissary to anoint. On the other hand, we have not the least proof that he did so. He partook, probably, of the wild spirit of

the times, when such deeds were regarded with feelings
very different from the abhorrence with which we,
better taught by the spirit of love, and more enlightened
by the widening dawn of history, now justly regard
them. No remonstrance of *contemporary* prophecy,
however faint, is recorded as having been uttered
against the doings of Jehu. The fact that, several
centuries later, they could be recorded by the historian
without a syllable of reprobation shows that the education of nations in the lessons of righteousness is slow,
and that we are still amid the annals of the deep night
of moral imperfection. But the nation was on the eve
of purer teaching, and in the prophets Amos and Hosea
we read the clear condemnation of deeds of cruelty in
general, and specially of the king who felt no pity.
Amos condemns even the idolatrous King of Edom,
"because he did pursue his brother with the sword,
and did cast off all pity, and his anger did tear perpetually, and he kept his wrath for ever."[1] He condemns no less severely the Chemosh-worshipping King
of Moab even for an insult done to the dead : " Because
he burned the bones of the King of Edom into lime."[2]
Jehu had warred pitilessly upon the living, and had
shamelessly insulted the dead. He had flung the heads
of seventy princes in two bleeding heaps on the common
road for all eyes to stare upon, and he had polluted
the cistern of Beth-equed-haroim with the dead bodies
of forty-two youths of the royal house of Judah. He
might plead that he was but carrying out to the full
the commission of Jehovah, imposed upon him by
Elisha ; but Hosea, a century later, gives God's message
against his house : " Yet a little while, and I will avenge

---

[1] Amos i. 11.   [2] Amos ii. 1.

the blood of Jezreel upon the house of Jehu, **and will** cause to cease the kingdom of the house of Israel."[1]

Nay, more! If, as is possible, the ghastly story of the siege of Samaria, narrated in the memoirs of Elisha, is displaced, and if it really belongs to the reign of Jehoahaz ben-Jehu, then Elisha himself brands the cruelty of the rushing thunderbolt of vengeance which his own hand had launched. For he calls the unnamed " King of Israel" " the son of a murderer."

Men who are swords of God, and human executioners of Divine justice, may easily deceive themselves. God works the ends of His own providence, and He uses their ministry. " The fierceness of man shall turn to Thy praise, and the fierceness of them shalt Thou refrain."[2] But they can never make their plea of prophetic sanction a cloak of maliciousness. Cromwell had stern work to do. Rightly or wrongly, he deemed it inevitable, and did not shrink from it. But he hated it. Over and over again, he tells us, he had prayed to God that He would not put him to this work. To the best of his power he avoided, he minimised, every act of vengeance, even when the sternness of his Puritan sense of righteousness made him look on it as duty. Far different was the case of Jehu. He loved murder and cunning for their own sakes, and, like Joab, he dyed the garments of peace with the blood of war.

How little was his gain! It had been happier for him if he had never mounted higher than the captaincy of the host, or even so high. He reigned for twenty-eight years (842–814)—longer than any king except his great-grandson Jeroboam II. ; and in recognition of any element of righteousness which had actuated his revolt,

---

[1] Hos. i. 4.   [2] Psalm lxxvi. 10.

his children, even to the fourth generation, were suffered
to sit upon the throne. His dynasty lasted for one
hundred and thirteen years.[1] But his own reign was
only memorable for defeat, trouble, and irreparable
disaster.

For Hazael, who had seized the throne ot his murdered lord Benhadad, was a fierce and able warrior.
He held his own against the overweening might of his
northern neighbour Assyria; and whenever he obtained
a respite from this desperate warfare, he indemnified
himself for all losses by enlarging his dominion out ot
the territories of the Ten Tribes. "In those days the
Lord began to cut Israel short, and Hazael smote them
in all the borders of Israel." Jehu had the mortification
of seeing the fairest and most fruitful regions of his
dominion, those which had belonged to Israel from the
most ancient times, wrenched out of his grasp. From
this time forwards Israel lost half the fair Promised
Land which God had given to their fathers. It was
the beginning of the end. Henceforth the tribal inheritance of Reuben, Gad, and the half tribe of Manasseh
was an oppressed dependency of Aram. Hazael overran and annexed the land of Bashan from the spurs
of Mount Hermon to the Lake of Gennezareth; Gaulan,
and volcanic Argob, and Hauran the entire ancient
kingdom of Og, King of Bashan, with all the herds and
pasture-lands. Southward of this he seized the whole
forest-clad plateau of Gilead, with its lovely ravines,
north of the Jabbok, the territory of Gad; and pushing

---

[1] Jehu . . . . . . 842—814.
Jehoahaz . . . . . 814—797.
Joash . . . . . . 797—781.
Jeroboam II. . . . . 781—740.
Zechariah . . . . . 740.

still southward, established his sway over the district, of the Ammonites and the tribe of Reuben, as far as the city of Aroer, on the other side of the great chasm of Arnon (Wady Mojib). All the fatness of Bashan and Rabbah with her watery plain of the Beni-Ammon, and the grass-covered uplands which fed the enormous flocks of Mesha, the great Emîr and sheep-master of Moab, passed from Israel to Syria, never to be recovered. What made the humiliation more terrible was that the invasion and conquest were accompanied with acts of unwonted cruelty. Elisha had wept to think what evil Hazael would do the children of Israel[1]—how he would set their strongholds on fire, and slay their young men with the sword, and dash in pieces their little ones, and rip up their women with child. These atrocities were in those horrible days the ordinary incidents of warfare;[2] but Hazael seems to have been pre-eminent in brutal fierceness. It was this which called down on him and his people the "burdens" of Amos. "Thus saith the Lord; For three transgressions of Damascus, and for four, I will not turn away the punishment thereof; because they have threshed Gilead with threshing instruments of iron : but I will send a fire into the house of Hazael, which shall devour the palaces of Benhadad."[3]

We can imagine rather than describe the anguish of Jehu when he was compelled to look impotently on, while his powerful Syrian neighbour laid waste his dominion with fire and sword, and the cry of his despoiled and slaughtered subjects was uplifted to him in vain. Nor was this all. Emboldened by these re-

---

[1] 2 Kings viii. 12.

[2] Isa. xiii. 11—16; Hos. x. 14, xiii. 16; Nah. iii. 10.

[3] Amos i. 3, 4.

verses, a host of other enemies, once subjugated and despised, began to wreak their revenge and insolence on humbled Israel. The Philistines eagerly undertook the sale of the wretched captives who were brought to them in gangs from the burnt Trans-Jordanic towns.[1] The old "brotherly covenant" with the Tyrian, which had once been formed by Solomon, and had been cemented by the marriage of Jezebel with Ahab, was cancelled by Jehu's insults, and the Tyrians emulously outbad the Philistines in the purchase of Israelitish slaves. The Edomites and the Ammonites also helped Hazael in his marauding raids, and enlarged their own domains at the expense of Samaria. Such insults and humiliations might well go far to break the heart of an impetuous and warrior-king.

Of Jehu the Books of Kings and Chronicles have no more to tell us, but we gain fresh insight into his degradation from the Black Obelisk of Shalmaneser II. (860–824), now in the British Museum. From the inscription we find that, in 842, Jehu—"the son of Omri," as he is erroneously called—was one of the vassal kings who subjected themselves to the Assyrian conqueror,[2] and sent him tribute, which may have euphemistically passed under the name of presents.

---

[1] Amos i. 6–15.

[2] See Appendix I., Schrader, *Keilinschriften u. das Alte Test.*, 208 ff. ; Sayce, *Records of the Past*, v. 41 ; Layard, *Nineveh*, p. 613; Rawlinson, *Herodotus*, i. 469. He is twice mentioned in inscriptions of Shalmaneser II. (861–825). He is called Ja-hu-a, son of Omri. The name of Omri was familiar in Nineveh; for Ahab had fought as a vassal of Assyria at the battle of Karkar, and Samaria was called Beth-Khumri. Shalmaneser would not trouble himself with the fact that Jehu had extirpated the old dynasty. His black stèlè was found by Layard, and is figured in *Monuments of Nineveh*, i., pl. 53. The name of Jehu was first deciphered by Dr. Hincks in 1851.

The despot of Nineveh twice speaks of it as a tribute. On this obelisk we see a picture of Jehu's ambassadors —perhaps of Jehu himself. On the left stands the Assyrian King with the winged circle over his head. He holds a beaker of wine in his hand, and two eunuchs stand behind him, one of whom covers him with a sunshade. Before him kneels and grovels in adoration the Jewish King, with his beard sweeping the ground. In long array behind him come his servants—first two eunuchs, then a number of bearded figures, who carry the tribute. They are dressed in long richly fringed robes, exactly resembling those of the Assyrians themselves, and they wear shoes which turn up at the toes. They are carrying figures of gold and silver, goblets, golden vessels, ingots of precious metals, spear-shafts, a kingly sceptre, baskets, bags, and trays of treasure, the contribution of which must have fallen with crushing weight on the impoverished kingdom.[1]

This tribute must have been sent in 842, the eighteenth year of Shalmaneser II.'s reign. Doubtless Jehu thought he might be delivered from his furious neighbour Hazael by propitiating the Northern tyrant, who at the same time received the submission of the Tyrians and Sidonians. But if so, Jehu's hopes were dashed to the ground. Shalmaneser was the enemy of Hazael (Ha-sa-ilu), who had gone out to meet him at Antilibanus, and there had fought a desperate battle. The Syrian King was routed, and driven back, and Shalmaneser had besieged Damascus. But he had failed to take it, and indeed had not troubled Syria again till 832, when he made an excursion of minor importance. His troubles on the north and east of

---

[1] Schrader (E. T.), ii. 199.

Assyria had diverted his attention from Damascus;
and this, together with the inferiority of his son
Samsiniras (*d.* 811), had given Hazael a free hand to
avenge himself on Israel as the ally of Assyria. Of
Jehu we hear no more. After his long reign of twenty-
eight years he slept with his fathers, and was buried
in Samaria, and Jehoahaz his son reigned in his stead.
Savage as had been his measures, his victory over
alien idolatries was by no means complete. What
Micah calls "the statutes of Omri, and the works of
the House of Ahab,"[1] were still kept; and men, both in
Israel and Judah, walked in their old sins. Even in
the reign of Jehu's own son Jehoahaz there still
remained in Samaria the Asherah, or tree consecrated
to the nature-goddess, which Jehu seems to have put
away, but not to have destroyed.[2] As he grovelled in
the dust before Shalmaneser, did no memory of his
own ferocities darken his humiliated soul? Must not
he, like our Henry II., have been inclined to utter the
wailing cry, "Shame, shame on a conquered king!"

---

[1] Mic. vi. 16.   [2] 2 Kings xiii. 6.

CHAPTER XIV

ATHALIAH (B.C. 842—836)—JOASH BEN-AHAZIAH OF JUDAH (B.C. 836—796)

2 KINGS xi. 1—xii. 21

"Par cette fin terrible, et due à ses forfaits,
Apprenez, Roi des Juifs, et n'oubliez jamais,
Que les rois dans le ciel ont un juge sevère,
L'innocence un vengeur, et les orphelins un père!"

RACINE, *Athalie.*

"Regardless of the sweeping whirlwind's sway,
That, hushed in grim repose, expects its evening prey."

GRAY.

BEFORE we follow the destinies of the House of Jehu we must revert to Judah, and watch the final consequences of ruin which came in the train of Ahab's Tyrian marriage, and brought murder and idolatry into Judah, as well as into Israel.

Athaliah, who, as queen-mother, was more powerful than the queen-consort (*malekkah*), was the true daughter of Jezebel. She exhibits the same undaunted fierceness, the same idolatrous fanaticism, the same swift resolution, the same cruel and unscrupulous wickedness.

It might have been supposed that the miserable disease of her husband Jehoram, followed so speedily by the murder, after one year's reign, of her son Ahaziah, might have exercised over her character the

146

softening influence of misfortune. On the contrary, she
only saw in these events a short path to the consum
mation of her ambition.

Under Jehoram she had been queen : under Ahaziah
she had exercised still more powerful influence as
Gebîrah, and had asserted her sway alike over her
husband and over her son, whose counsellor she was
to do wickedly. It was far from her intention tamely
to sink from her commanding position into the abject
nullity of an aged and despised dowager in a dull
provincial seraglio. She even thought that

> "To reign is worth ambition, though in hell;
> Better to reign in hell than serve in heaven."

The royal family of the House of David, numerous
and flourishing as it once was, had recently been
decimated by cruel catastrophes. Jehoram, instigated
probably by his heathen wife, had killed his six younger
brothers.[1] Later on, the Arabs and Philistines, in their
insulting invasion, had not only plundered his palace,
but had carried away his sons ; so that, according to
the Chronicler, "there was never a son left him, save
Jehoahaz [*i.e.*, Ahaziah], the youngest of his sons."[2]
He may have had other sons after that invasion ; and
Ahaziah had left children, who must all, however, have
been very young, since he was only twenty-two or
twenty-three when Jehu's servants murdered him.
Athaliah might naturally have hoped for the regency ;
but this did not content her. When she saw that her
son Ahaziah was dead, "she arose and destroyed all the
seed royal." In those days the life of a child was but
little thought of ; and it weighed less than nothing with
Athaliah that these innocents were her grandchildren.

---

[1] 2 Chron. xxi. 2–4.   [2] 2 Chron. xxi. 17.

She killed all of whose existence she was aware, and
boldly seized the crown. No queen had ever reigned
alone either in Israel or in Judah. Judah must have
sunk very low, and the talents of Athaliah must have
been commanding, or she could never have established
a precedent hitherto undreamed of, by imposing on the
people of David for six years the yoke of a woman, and
that woman a half-Phœnician idolatress. Yet so it was!
Athaliah, like her cousin Dido, felt herself strong enough
to rule.

But a woman's ruthlessness was outwitted by a
woman's cunning. Ahaziah had a half-sister on the
father's side,[1] the princess Jehosheba, or Jehoshabeath,
who was then or afterwards (we are told) married to
Jehoiada, the high priest.[2] The secrets of harems are
hidden deep, and Athaliah may have been purposely
kept in ignorance of the birth to Ahaziah of a little
babe whose mother was Zibiah of Beersheba, and who
had received the name of Joash. If she knew of his
existence, some ruse must have been palmed off upon
her, and she must have been led to believe that he too
had been killed. But he had not been killed. Jehosheba
"stole him from among the king's sons that were slain,"
and, with the connivance of his nurse, hid him from the
murderers sent by Athaliah in the palace store-room
in which beds and couches were kept.[3] Thence, at the
first favourable moment, she transferred the child and
nurse to one of the chambers in the three storeys of

[1] ὁμοπάτριος ἀδελφή (Jos.).
[2] 2 Chron. xxii. 11. There are undoubted difficulties about the
statement (see *infra*). There is no other instance of the marriage
of a princess with a priest.
[3] Jos., *Antt.*, IX. vii. 1 : τὸ ταμεῖον τῶν κλινῶν. The chamber of beds
was a sort of unoccupied wardrobe-room.

chambers which ran round the Temple, and were variously used as wardrobes or as dwelling-rooms.

The hiding-place was safe; for under Athaliah the Temple of Jehovah fell into neglect and disrepute, and its resident ministers would not be numerous. It would not have been difficult, in the seclusion of Eastern life, for Jehosheba to pass off the babe as her own child to all but the handful who knew the secret.

Six years passed away, and the iron hand of Athaliah still kept the people in subjection. She had boldly set up in Judah her mother's Baal-worship. Baal had his temple not far from that of Jehovah; and though Athaliah did not imitate Jezebel in persecuting the worshippers of Jehovah, she made her own high priest, Mattan, a much more important person than Jehoiada for all who desired to propitiate the favours of the Court.

Joash had now reached his seventh year, and a Jewish prince in his seventh year is regarded as something more than a mere child. Jehoiada thought that it was time to strike a blow in his favour, and to deliver him from the dreadful confinement which made it impossible for him to leave the Temple precincts.

He began secretly to tamper with the guards both of the Temple and of the palace. Upon the Levitic guards, indignant at the intrusion of Baal-worship, he might securely count, and the Carites and queen's runners were not likely to be very much devoted to the rule of the manlike and idolatrous alien-queen. Taking an oath of them in secrecy, he bound them to allegiance to the little boy whom he produced from the Temple chamber as their lawful lord, and the son of their late king.

The plot was well laid. There were five captains of the five hundred royal body-guards, and the priest

secretly enlisted them all in the service.[1]   The Chronicler
says that he also sent round to all the chief Levites,
and collected them in Jerusalem for the emergency.
The arrangements of the Sabbath gave special facility
to his plans; for on that day only one of the five
divisions of guards mounted watch at the palace, and
the others were set free for the service of the Temple.[2]
It had evidently been announced that some great
ceremony would be held in the shrine of Jehovah; for
all the people, we are told, were assembled in the courts
of the house of the Lord.   Jehoiada ordered one of the
companies to guard the palace; another to be at the
" gate Sur," or the gate " of the Foundation ";[3] another
at the gate behind the barracks (?) of the palace-runners,
to be a barrier[4] against any incursion from the palace.
Two more were to ensure the safety of the little king
by watching the precincts of the Temple.   The Levitic
officers were to protect the king's person with serried
ranks.   Jehoiada armed them with spears and shields,
which David had placed as trophies in the porch; and
if any one tried to force his way within their lines he
was to be slain.   The only danger to be apprehended
was from any Carite mercenaries, or palace-servants
of the queen: among all others Jehoiada found a widespread defection.   The people, the Levites, even the
soldiers, all hated the Baal-worshipping usurper.[5]

At the fateful moment the guards were arranged in

---

[1] 2 Kings xi. 4 : " The centurions of the Carians and of the runners."

[2] This is the second time that the word " Sabbath " occurs, or that
the institution is alluded to, in the history of either monarchy.

[3] Nothing is known of סוּר, Sur, or יְסוֹד y'sôd, the Foundation
(2 Chron. xxiii. 5).   They are not mentioned elsewhere.   LXX., ἐν τῇ
πύλῃ τῶν ὁδῶν, and (in Chronicles) ἐν τῇ πύλῃ τῇ μέσῃ.

[4] Not as in A.V., " that it be not broken down."

[5] In reading side by side the narratives in the Books of Kings and

two dense lines, beginning from either side of the porch, till their ranks met beyond the altar, so as to form a hedge round the royal boy. Into this triangular space the young prince was led by the high priest, and placed beside the *Matstsebah*—some prominent pillar in the Temple court, either one of Solomon's pillars Jachin and Boaz, or some special erection of later days.[1] Round him stood the princes of Judah, and there, in the midst of them, Jehoiada placed the crown upon his head, and in significant symbol also laid lightly upon it for a moment "The Testimony"—perhaps the Ten Commandments and the Book of the Covenant—the most ancient fragment of the Pentateuch[2]—which was treasured up with the pot of manna inside or in front of the Ark. Then he poured on the child's head the consecrated oil, and said, "Let the king live!"

The completion of the ceremony was marked by the blare of the rams' horns, the softer blast of the silver trumpets, and the answering shouts of the soldiers and the people. The tumult, or the news of it, reached

---

Chronicles (2 Chron. xxiii.), it is difficult to avoid the conclusion that the main anxiety of the Chronicler is to leave the impression that the work in the Temple was chiefly done by the Levites, and that the sacred precincts were not polluted by the presence of alien troops. He evidently stumbled at the notion, conveyed by the older narrative, that Carians and suchlike semi-heathen mercenaries should have stood by the altar at a high priest's command; so he substitutes Levites for guardsmen, and the profane laymen are relegated outside. In details the two accounts are only reconcilable by a special pleading which would reconcile *any* discrepancy.

[1] 1 Kings vii. 21. Comp., however, 2 Kings xxiii. 3.

[2] See Exod. xxv. 16, 21, xvi. 34. הָעֵדוּת (see 2 Chron. xxiii. 11). Kimchi takes it to mean "a royal robe," and other Rabbis a phylactery on the coronet (Deut. vi. 8). In the Targum to Chronicles it is explained to mean the costly jewel (2 Sam. xii. 30), of which none but a descendant of David could bear the weight. For *ha'edôth* Klostermann therefore suggests *hats'adôth*, "the royal bracelets."

the ears of Athaliah in the neighbouring palace, and, with all the undaunted courage of her mother, she instantly summoned her escort, and went into the Temple to see for herself what was taking place.[1]   She probably mounted the ascent which Solomon had made from the palace to the Temple court, though it had long been robbed of its precious metals and scented woods. She led the way, and thought to overawe by her personal ascendency any irregularity which might be going on ; for in the deathful hush to which she had reduced her subjects she does not seem to have dreamt of rebellion.   No sooner had she entered than the guards closed behind her, excluding and menacing her escort.[2]

A glance was sufficient to reveal to her the significance of the whole scene.   There, in royal robes, and crowned with the royal crown, stood her little unknown grandson beside the *Mats!sebah*,[3] while round him were the leaders of the people and the trumpeters, and the multitudes were still rolling their tumult of acclamation from the court below.   In that sight she read her doom. Rending her clothes, she turned to fly, shrieking, " Treason ! treason ! "   Then the commands of the priest rang out : " Keep her between the ranks,[4] till you have got her outside the area of the Temple ; and if any of her guards follow or try to rescue her, kill him with the sword.   But let not the sacred courts be polluted with her blood."   So they made way for

---

[1] So says Josephus (μετὰ τῆς ἰδίας στρατίας), and it is certain that she would hardly go unattended.

[2] Jos., *Antt.*, IX. vii. 3 : Τοὺς δὲ ἐπομένους ὁπλίτας εἷρξαν εἰσελθεῖν.

[3] The meaning of *al-ha'amôd* is uncertain (A.V., " by a pillar "; Vulg., " on the tribunal "). Comp. 2 Kings xxiii. 3 ; 2 Chron. xxiii. 13 ; 1 Kings viii. 22 ; 2 Chron. vi. 13.

[4] 2 Kings xi. 15.   Not as in A.V., " without the ranges." Heb., *kash'dêrôth* ; LXX., ἔσωθεν τῶν σαδηρώθ.

her,[1] and as she could not escape she passed between the rows of Levites and soldiers till she had reached the private chariot-road by which the kings drove to the precincts.[2] There the sword of vengeance fell. Athaliah disappears from history, and with her the dark race of Jezebel. But her story lives in the music of Handel and the verse of Racine.

This is the only recorded revolution in the history of Judah. In two later cases a king of Judah was murdered, but in both instances " the people of the land " restored the Davidic heir. Life in Judah was less dramatic and exciting than in Israel, but far more stable ;[3] and this, together with comparative immunity from foreign invasions, constituted an immense advantage.

Jehoiada, of course, became regent for the young king, and continued to be his guide for many years, so that even the king's two wives were selected by his advice. As the nation had been distracted with idolatries, he made the covenant between the king and the people that they should be loyal to each other,

---

[1] A.V., " And they laid hands on her "; LXX., ἐπέβαλον αὐτῇ χεῖρας; Vulg., *imposuerunt ei manus.* But R.V. as in the text, following the Targum, and the Jewish commentators, "They made for her two sides."

[2] This is usually understood to be the " horse gate " of the city (Neh. iii. 28), and so Josephus seems to have taken it, for he says that Athaliah was killed in " the Kedron Valley." Canon Rawlinson says that it was more probably in the Tyropœon Valley. But there could have been no object in dragging the wretched queen all this way. Jehoiada was only anxious that she should not stain the Temple with her blood, and " the way by which the horses came into the king's house" seems to be some private palace-gate. We are expressly told (ver. 16) that Athaliah was slain " at the king's house," probably in "the king's garden " (2 Kings xxv. 4).

[3] Wellhausen, *Isr. and Jud.*, p. 96.

and between Jehoiada and the king and the people that
they should be Jehovah's people.   Such covenants were
not infrequent in Jewish history.   Such a covenant
had been made by Asa [1] after Abijam's apostasy, as it
was afterwards made by Hezekiah [2] and by Josiah. [3]   The
new covenant, and the sense of awakenment from the
dream of guilty apostasy, evoked an outburst of spontaneous enthusiasm in the hearts of the populace.   Of
their own impulse they rushed to the temple of Baal
which Athaliah had reared, dismantled it, and smashed
to pieces his altars and images.   The riot was only
stained by a single murder.   They slew Mattan,
Athaliah's Baal-priest, before the altars of his god. [4]

With Jehoiada begins the title of "high priest."
Hitherto no higher name than "the priest" had been
given even to Aaron, or Eli, or Zadok ; but thenceforth
the title of "chief priest" is given to his successors,
among whom he inaugurated a new epoch. [5]

It was now Jehoiada's object to restore such splendour
and solemnity as he could to the neglected worship of
the Temple, which had suffered in every way from
Baal's encroachments.   He did this before the king's
second solemn inauguration.   Even the porters had
been done away with, so that the Temple could at any
time be polluted by the presence of the unclean, and

---

[1] 2 Chron. **xv.** 9-15.

[2] 2 Chron. **xxix.** 10.

[3] 2 Chron. **xxxiv.** 31.

[4] The name is perhaps an abbreviation from Mattan-Baal, "gift of
Baal."   Comp. "Methumballes" (Plaut.).   The names of Tyrian kings,
Mitinna, Mattun, occur in inscriptions of Tiglath-Pileser II.   See
Herod., vii. 98 (Bahr, *ad loc.*).   "Methumbaal of Arvad" is mentioned
on a monument of Tiglath-Pileser II. (Schrader, ii. 249).

[5] 2 Kings **xii.** 10; Jer. **xxix.** 26; 2 Chron. **xxiv.** 6. **Stanley**
Lectures, ii. **399.**

the whole service of priests and Levites had fallen into desuetude.

Then he took the captains, and the Carians, and the princes, and conducted the boy-king, amid throngs of his shouting and rejoicing people, from the Temple to his own palace. There he seated him on the lion-throne of Solomon his father, in the great hall ot justice, and the city was quiet and the land had rest. According to the historian, "Joash did right *all his days*, because Jehoiada the priest instructed him."[1] The stock addition that "howbeit the *bamoth* were not removed, and the people still sacrificed and offered incense there," is no derogation from the merits of Joash, and perhaps not even of Jehoiada, since if the law against the *bamoth* then existed, it had become absolutely unknown, and these local sanctuaries were held to be conducive to true religion.[2]

It was natural that the child of the Temple should have at heart the interests of the Temple in which he had spent his early days, and to the shelter of which he owed his life and throne. The sacred house had been insulted and plundered by persons whom the Chronicler calls "the sons of Athaliah, that wicked

---

[1] 2 Kings xii. 2. After "all his days," the R.V. and A.V. add "*wherein* Jehoiada instructed him." This, however, is not accurate. There is a stop at days, and "wherein" should be "*because*." There seems, however, from the LXX., to be some variation in the text, and according to the Chronicler Joash became an apostate. LXX., Πάσας τὰς ἡμέρας ἃς ἐφώτιζεν αὐτὸν ὁ ἱερεύς; Vulg., *Cunctis diebus quibus docuit eum Jojadas sacerdos.*

[2] The Chronicler (2 Chron. xxiv. 1, 2) *more suo* copies 2 Kings xii. 1, 2, but omits 3, because he dislikes the fact that not even his hero Jehoiada had anything to say against the *bamoth*. But it appears from 2 Kings xxiii. 9 that the *bamoth* had regular priests of their own, who "eat the priestly portions" (according to an old MS.) among their brethren.

woman,"[1] meaning, probably, her adherents. Not only
had its treasures been robbed to enrich the house of
Baal, but it had been suffered to fall into complete
disrepair. Breaches gaped in the outer walls, and the
very foundations were insecure. The necessity for
restoring it occurred, not, as we should have expected,
to the priests who lived at its altar, but to the boy-
king. He issued an order to the priests that they
should take charge of all the money presented to the
Temple for the hallowed things, all the money paid in
current coin, and all the assessments for various fines
and vows,[2] together with every freewill contribution.
They were to have this revenue entirely at their
disposal, and to make themselves responsible for the
necessary repairs. According to the Chronicler, they
were further to raise a subscription throughout the
country from all their personal friends.

The king's command had been urgent. Money had
at first come in, but nothing was done. Joash had
reached the twenty-third year of his reign, and was
thirty years old ; but the Temple remained in its old
sordid condition. The matter is passed over by the
king as lightly, courteously, and considerately as he
could ; but if he does not charge the priests with downright embezzlement, he does reproach them for most
reprehensible neglect. They were the appointed
guardians of the house : why did they suffer its
dilapidations to remain untouched year after year, while
they continued to receive the golden stream which
poured—but now, owing to the disgust of the people,

---

[1] 2 Chron. xxiv. 7.
[2] 2 Kings xii. 4: "The money that every man is set at." Lit.,
"Each the money of the souls of his valuation." Comp. Numb. xviii.
16; Lev. xxvii. 2.

in diminished volume—into their coffers? "Take no
more money, therefore," he said, "from your acquaint-
ances, but deliver it for the breaches of the house."
For what they had already received he does not call
them to account, but henceforth takes the whole matter
into his own hands. The neglectful priests were to
receive no more contributions, and not to be responsible
for the repairs. Joash, however, ordered Jehoiada to
take a chest and put it beside the altar on the right.[1]
All contributions were to be dropped into this chest.
When it was full, it was carried by the Levites unopened
into the palace,[2] and there the king's chancellor and
the high priest had the ingots weighed and the money
counted; its value was added up, and it was handed
over immediately to the architects, who paid it to the
carpenters and masons. The priests were left in
possession of the money for the guilt-offerings[3] and for
the sin-offerings, but with the rest of the funds they
had nothing to do. In this way was restored the
confidence which the management of the hierarchy had
evidently forfeited, and with renewed confidence in the
administration fresh gifts poured in. Even in the
cautious narrative of the Chronicler it is clear that
the priests hardly came out of these transactions with
flying colours. If their honesty is not formally im-
pugned, at least their torpor is obvious, as is the fact
that they had wholly failed to inspire the zeal of the
people till the young king took the affair into his own
hands.[4]

---

[1] The Chronicler says "at the gate."

[2] 2 Chron. xxiv. 11.

[3] Lev. v. 1-6, xiv. 13. "Trespass-money" is here first mentioned.

[4] 2 Chron. xxiv. 8-10. There is a difference between the historian
and the Chronicler respecting the vessels of the house.

The long reign of Joash ended in eclipse and murder.
If the later tradition be correct, it was also darkened
with atrocious ingratitude and crime.

For, according to the Chronicler, Jehoiada died at
the advanced age of one hundred and thirty, and was
buried, as an unwonted honour, in the sepulchres of the
kings.[1]   When he was dead, the princes of Judah
came to Joash, who had now been king for many years,
and with a strange suddenness tempted the zealous
repairer of the Temple of Jehovah into idolatrous
apostasy.   With soft speech they seduced him into the
worship of Asherim.   It was marvellous indeed if the
child of the Temple became its foe, and he who had
made a covenant with Jehovah fell away to Baalim.
But worse followed.   Prophets reproved him, and he
paid them no heed, in spite of "the greatness of the
burdens"—*i.e.*, the multitude of the menaces—laid upon
him.[2]   The stern, denunciative harangues were despised.
At last Zechariah, the son of his benefactor Jehoiada,
rebuked king and people.   He cried aloud from some
eminence in the court of the Temple, that "since they had
transgressed the commandments of Jehovah they could
not prosper : they had forsaken Him, and He would
forsake them."   Infuriated by this prophecy of woe,
the guilty people, at the command of their guiltier king,

---

[1] 2 Chron. xxiv. 15, 16.   The statement of the Chronicler is
(as so often) surrounded by difficulties and improbabilities.   If
Jehoiada was one hundred and thirty years old when he died, he
must have been ninety when Ahaziah was murdered, at the age of
twenty-three.   But as Ahaziah was (apparently) born when his
father Jehoram was eighteen, Jehosheba must have been under
eighteen, and must have been married to a man seventy years
older than herself !   See Lord Arthur Hervey, *On the Genealogies,*
p. 113.

[2] 2 Chron. xxiv. 27.

stoned him to death.[1]   As he lay dying, he exclaimed,
" The Lord look upon it, and require it ! "[2]

The entire silence of the elder and better authority
might lead us to hope that there may be room for
doubt as to the accuracy of the much later tradition.
Yet there certainly was a persistent belief that Zechariah
had been thus martyred.   A wild legend, related in the
Talmud,[3] tells us that when Nebuzaradan conquered
Jerusalem and entered the Temple he saw blood
bubbling up from the floor of the court, and slaughtered
ninety-four myriads, so that the blood flowed till it
touched the blood of Zechariah, that it might be
fulfilled which is said (Hos. iv. 2), " Blood toucheth
blood."   When he saw the blood of Zechariah, and
noticed that it was boiling and agitated, he asked,
" What is this ? " and was told that it was the spilled
blood of the sacrifices.   Finding this to be false, he
threatened to comb the flesh of the priests with iron
curry-combs if they did not tell the truth.   Then they
confessed that it was the blood of the murdered
Zechariah.   "Well," he said, "I will pacify him."
First he slaughtered the greater and lesser Sanhedrin :
but the blood did not rest.   Then he sacrificed young

---

[1] Stanley charitably thinks that Joash may have only burst into
hasty words like those of Henry II. against Becket.

[2] The Chronicler says that "the *sons* of Jehoiada" had helped
to crown him, and that he put "the *sons* of Jehoiada" to death
(2 Chron. xxiii. 11, xxiv. 25).

[3] Gittin, f. 57, 2 ; Sanhedrin, f. 96, 2 ; Hershon, *Treasures of the
Talmud*, p. 276 ; Lightfoot on Matt. xxiii. 35.   There can be little
doubt that the reading "Berechiah" is a later correction of some
one who remembered the murder narrated in Jos., *B. J.*, IV. v. 4,
and that the true reading is "son of Jehoiada."   This is the last
murder of a prophet mentioned in the Old Testament, and we learn
from the Gospel the fact that he was slain "between the Temple
and the altar."

men and maidens : but the blood still bubbled. At last he cried, " Zechariah, Zechariah, must I then slay them all ? " Then the blood was still, and Nebuzaradan, thinking how much blood he had shed, fled, repented, and became a Jewish proselyte !

Perhaps the worst feature of the story against Joash might have been susceptible of a less shocking colouring. He had naturally all his life been under the influence of priestly domination. The ascendency which Jehoiada had acquired as priest-regent had been maintained till long after the young king had arrived at full manhood. At last, however, he had come into collision with the priestly body. He was in the right ; they were transparently in the wrong. The Chronicler, and even the older historian, soften the story against the priests as much as they can ; but in both their narratives it is plain that Jehoiada and the whole hierarchy had been more careful of their own interests than of those of the Temple, of which they were the appointed guardians. Even if they can be acquitted of potential malfeasance, they had been guilty of reprehensible carelessness. It is clear that in this matter they did not command the confidence of the people ; for so long as they had the management of affairs the sources of munificence were either dried up or only flowed in scanty streams, whereas they were poured forth with glad abundance when the administration of the funds was placed mainly in the hands of laymen under the king's chancellor. It is probable that when Jehoiada was dead Joash thought it right to assert his royal authority in greater independence of the priestly party ; and that party was headed by Zechariah, the son of Jehoiada. The Chronicler says that he prophesied : that, however, would not necessarily constitute him a

prophet, any more than it constituted Caiaphas. If he
was a prophet, and was yet at the head of the priests,
he furnishes an all-but solitary instance of such a
position. The position of a prophet, occupied in the
great work of moral reformation, was so essentially
antithetic to that of priests, absorbed in ritual ceremonies, that there is no body of men in Scripture of
whom, as a whole, we have a more pitiful record than
of the Jewish priests. From Aaron, who made the
golden calf, to Urijah, who sanctioned the idolatrous
altar of Ahaz, and so down to Annas and Caiaphas,
who crucified the Lord of glory, they rendered few
signal services to true religion. They opposed Uzziah
when he invaded their functions, but they acquiesced
in all the idolatries and abominations of Rehoboam,
Abijah, Ahaziah, Ahaz, and many other kings, without
a syllable of recorded protest. When a prophet did
spring from their ranks, they set their faces with one
consent, and were confederate against him. They
mocked and ridiculed Isaiah. When Jeremiah rose
among them, the priest Pashur smote him on the cheek,
and the whole body persecuted him to death, leaving
him to be protected only by the pity of eunuchs and
courtiers. Ezekiel was the priestliest of the prophets,
and yet he was forced to denounce the apostasies
which they permitted in the very Temple. The pages
of the prophets ring with denunciations of their priestly
contemporaries.[1]

We do not know enough of Zechariah to say much
about his character; but priests in every age have
shown themselves the most unscrupulous and the most
implacable of enemies. Joash probably stood to him

---

[1] Isa. xxiv. 2; Jer. v. 31, xxiii. 11; Ezek. vii. 26, xxii. 26; Hos.
iv. 9; Mic. iii. 11, etc.

in the same relation that Henry II. stood to Thomas
à Becket. The priest's murder may have been due to
an outburst of passion on the part of the king's friends,
or of the king himself—gentle as his character seems
to have been—without being the act of black ingratitude which late traditions represented it to be. The
legend about Zechariah's blood represents the priest's
spirit as so ruthlessly unforgiving as to awaken the
astonishment and even the rebukes of the Babylonian
idolater. Such a legend could hardly have arisen in the
case of a man who was other than a most formidable
opponent. The murder of Joash may have been, in its
turn, a final outcome of the revenge of the priestly party.
The details of the story must be left to inference and
conjecture, especially as they are not even mentioned in
the earlier and more impartial annalists.

It is at least singular that while Joash, the king, is
blamed for continuing the worship at the *bamoth*,
Jehoiada, the high priest, is *not* blamed, though they
continued throughout his long and powerful regency.
Further, we have an instance of the priest-regent's
autocracy which can hardly be regarded as redounding
to his credit. It is preserved in an accidental allusion
on the page of Jeremiah. In Jer. xxix. 26 we read his
reproof and doom of the lying prophecy of the priest
Shemaiah the Nehelamite, because as a priest he had
sent a letter to the chief priest Zephaniah and all the
priests, urging them as the successors of Jehoiada to
follow the ruling of Jehoiada, which was to put Jeremiah
in a collar. For Jehoiada, he said, "had ordered the
priests, as officers [*pakidim*] in the house of Jehovah, to
put in the stocks every one that is mad and maketh
himself a prophet."[1] If, then, the Jehoiada referred to is

---

[1] Jer. xxix. 24–32.

the priest-regent, as seems undoubtedly to be the case,
we see that he hated all interference of Jehovah's
prophets with his rule. That the prophets were
usually regarded by the world and by priests as
"mad," we see from the fact that the title is given
by Jehu's captains to Elisha's emissary ;[1] and that this
continued to be the case we see from the fact that the
priests and Pharisees of Jerusalem said of John the
Baptist that he had a devil, and of Christ that He was
a Samaritan, and that He, too, had a devil. If Joash
was in opposition to the priestly party, he was in the
same position as all God's greatest saints and reformers
have ever been from the days of Moses to the days
of John Wesley. The dominance of priestcraft is the
invariable and inevitable death of true, as apart from
functional, religion. Priests are always apt to con-
centrate their attention upon their temples, altars,
religious practices and rites—in a word, upon the
externals of religion. If they gain a complete ascendency over their fellow-believers, the faithful become
their absolute slaves, religion degenerates into formalism, "and the life of the soul is choked by the
observance of the ceremonial law." It was a misfortune
for the Chosen People that, except among the prophets
and the wise men, the external worship was thought
much more of than the moral law. "To the ordinary
man," says Wellhausen, "it was not moral but litur-
gical acts which seemed to be religious." This accounts
for the monotonous iteration of judgments on the
character of kings, based primarily, not upon their
essential character, but on their relation to the *bamoth*
and the calves.

Although the historian of the Kings gives no hint of

---

[1] 2 Kings ix. 11.

this dark story of Zechariah's murder, or of the apostasy of Joash, and indeed narrates no other event of the long reign of forty years, he tells us of the deplorable close. Hazael's ambition had been fatal to Israel; and now, in the cessation of Assyrian inroads upon Aram, he extended his arms towards Judah. He went up against Gath and took it, and cherished designs against Jerusalem. Apparently he did not head the expedition in person, and the historian implies that Joash bought off the attack of his "general." But the Chronicler makes things far worse. He says that the Syrian host marched to Jerusalem, destroyed all the princes of the people, plundered the city, and sent the spoil to Hazael, who was at Damascus. Judah, he says, had assembled a vast army to resist the small force of the Syrian raid; but Joash was ignominiously defeated, and was driven to pay blackmail to the invader. As to this defeat in battle the historian is silent; but he mentions what the Chronicler omits—namely, that the only way in which Joash could raise the requisite bribe was by once more stripping the Temple and the palace, and sending to Damascus all the treasures which his three predecessors had consecrated,—though we are surprised to learn that after so many strippings and plunderings any of them could still be left.

The anguish and mortification of mind caused by these disasters, and perhaps the wounds he had received in the defeat of his army, threw Joash into "great diseases." But he was not suffered to die of these.[1] His servants—perhaps, if that story be authentic, to avenge the slain son of Jehoiada, but doubtless also in

---

[1] But from the Book of Kings we should not infer that there had been any fighting at all. The Syrian commander had been bribed to retire.

disgust at the national humiliation—rose in conspiracy against him, and smote him at Beth-Millo,[1] where he was lying sick. The Septuagint, in 2 Chron. xxiv. 27, adds the dark fact that *all his sons* joined in the conspiracy.[2] This cannot be true of Amaziah, who put the murderer to death. Such, however, was the deplorable end of the king who had stood by the Temple pillar in his fair childhood, amid the shouts and trumpet-blasts of a rejoicing people. At that time all things seemed full of promise and of hope. Who could have anticipated that the boy whose head had been touched with the sacred oil and over-shadowed with the Testimony—the young king who had made a covenant with Jehovah, and had initiated the task of restoring the ruined Temple to its pristine beauty—would end his reign in earthquake and eclipse ? If indeed he had been guilty of the black ingratitude and murderous apostasy which tradition laid to his charge, we see in his end the Nemesis of his ill-doing ; yet we cannot but pity one who, after so long a reign, perished amid the spoliation of his people, and was not even allowed to end his days by the sore sickness into which he had fallen, but was hurried into the next world by the assassin's knife.

It is impossible not to hope that his deeds were less black than the Chronicler painted. He had made the priests feel his power and resentment, and their Levitic recorder was not likely to take a lenient view of his offences. He says that though Joash was buried in the City of David, he was not buried in the sepulchres of his fathers. The historian of the Kings, however, expressly says that " they buried him with his fathers

---

[1] We cannot understand the addition "on the way that goeth down to Silla." Silla is nowhere else referred to.

[2] LXX., 2 Chron. xxiv. 27, καὶ οἱ υἱοὶ αὐτοῦ πάντες,

in the City of David," and he was peaceably succeeded by Amaziah his son.

There is a curious, though it may be an accidental, circumstance about the name of the two conspirators who slew him. They are called "Jozacar, the son of Shimeath, and Jehozabad, the son of Shomer, his servants." The names mean "Jehovah remembers," the son of "Hearer," and "Jehovah awards," the son of "Watcher"; and this strangely recalls the last words attributed in the Book of Chronicles to the martyred Zechariah. "Jehovah look upon it, and require it!" The Chronicler turns the names into "Zabad, the son of Shimeath, an Ammonitess, and Jehozabad, the son of Shimrith, a Moabitess." Does he record this to account for their murderous deed by the blood of hated nations which ran in their veins?

CHAPTER XV

AMAZIAH OF JUDAH

B.C. 796—783 (?)

2 KINGS xiv. 1—22

"All they that take the sword shall perish with the sword."—
MATT. xxvi. 52.

THE fate of Amaziah (" Jehovah is strong "), son of
Joash of Judah, resembles in some respects that
of his father. Both began to reign prosperously: the
happiness of both ended in disaster. Amaziah at his
accession was twenty-five years old. He was the son
of a lady of Jerusalem named Jehoaddin. He reigned
twenty-nine years, of which the later ones were passed
in misery, peril, and degradation, and, like the unhappy
Joash, and at about the same age, he fell the victim of
domestic conspiracy.

The hereditary principle was too strongly established
to enable the murderers of Joash to set it aside, but
Amaziah was not at first strong enough to make any
head against them. In time he became established in
his kingdom, and then his earliest act was to bring the
head conspirators, Jozacar and Jehozabad, to justice.
It was noted as a most remarkable circumstance that
he did not put to death their children, and extirpate
their houses. In acting thus, if he were influenced by

167

a spirit of mercy, he showed himself before his time, but such mercy was completely contrary to the universal custom, and was also regarded as most impolitic. Even the comparatively merciful Greeks had the proverb, "Fool, who has murdered the sire, and left his sons to avenge him!"[1]

In epochs of the wild justice of revenge, when blood-feuds are an established and approved institution, the policy of letting vengeance only fall on the actual offender was regarded as fatal. Perhaps Amaziah felt it beyond his power to do more than bring the actual murderers to justice, and it is possible that their children may have been among the conspirators who, in his hour of shame, ultimately destroyed him.

The historian, it is true, attributes his conduct to magnanimity, or rather to his obedience to the law, "The fathers shall not be put to death for the children, nor the children for the fathers; but every man shall die for his own sin." This is a reference to Deut. xxiv. 16, and is probably the independent comment of the writer who recorded the event two centuries later. In the gradual growth of a milder civilisation, and the more common dominance of legal justice, such a law may have come into force, as expressive of that voice of conscience which is to sincere nations the voice of God. That the Book of Deuteronomy, as a book, was not in existence in its present form till four reigns later we shall hereafter see strong reasons to believe. But even if any part of that book was in existence, it is not easy to understand how Amaziah would have been able to decide that the law which forbade the punishment of

---

[1] Νήπιος ὃς πατέρα κτείνας υἱοὺς καταλείπει. Comp. Q. Curtius, vi. 11: "Lege cautum erat ut propinqui eorum qui regi insidiati cum ipsis necarentur." Cic., *Ad Brut.*, 15.

the children with the offending parents was the law
which he was bound to follow, when Moses and Joshua
and other heroes of his race had acted on the olden
principle. The innocent families of Korah, Dathan,
and Abiram were represented as having been swallowed up with the ambitious heads of their houses.
Joshua and all Israel had not only stoned Achan, but
with him all his unoffending house. What, too, was
the meaning of the law which established the five Cities
of Refuge as the best way to protect the accidental
homicide from the recognised and unrebuked actions
of the Goel—the avenger of blood? The vengeance
of a Goel was regarded, as it is in the East and South
to this day, not as an implacable fierceness, but as a
sacred duty, the neglect of which would cover him with
infamy. Judging of our documents by the impartial light
of honest criticism, it seems impossible to deny that
the law of Deuteronomy was the law of an advancing
civilisation, which became more mild as justice became
firmer and more available. If Deuteronomy represents
the legislation of Moses, we can only say that in this
respect Amaziah was the first person who paid the
slightest attention to it. Such exceptional obedience
may well excite the notice of the historian, in whose
pages we see that prophets like Ahijah, Elijah, and
Elisha had, again and again, in accordance with the
spirit of their times, contemplated the total excision,
not only of erring kings, but even of their little children
and their most distant kinsfolk.

Further :—We are told that Amaziah "did that
which was right in the sight of Jehovah : he did
according to all things *as Joash his father did.*" The
Chronicler also bestows his eulogy on Amaziah ; but
having told such dark stories of the apostasy of Joash

to Asherah-worship and his murder of the prophets,
he could hardly add " as Joash his father did "; so he
omits those words.   The reservation that Amaziah did
right, "yet not like David his father" (2 Kings xiv. 3),
"but not with a perfect heart" (2 Chron. xxv. 2), is
followed by the stock abatement about the *bamoth*,
and the sacrifices and incense burnt in them.   This
was a crime in the eyes of writers in B.C. 540, but
certainly not in the eyes of any king before the
discovery of the "Book of the Law" in the reign of
Josiah, B.C. 621.   We are compelled, therefore, by
simple truth, to ask, How came it that Amaziah should
be so scrupulous as to observe the Deuteronomic law
by not slaying the sons of his father's murderers, while
he does not seem to be aware, any more than the
best of his predecessors, that while he obeyed one
precept he was violating the essence and spirit of the
entire code in which the precept occurs?   The one
main object, the constantly repeated law of Deuteronomy,
is the centralisation of all worship, and the rigid prohibition of every local place of sacrifice.   Strange that
Amaziah should have selected for attention a single
precept, while he is profoundly unconscious of, or indifferent to, the fact that he is setting aside the regulation
with which the law, as Deuteronomy represents it,
begins and ends, and on which it incessantly insists!

Joash had been something of a weakling, as though
the gloom of his early concealment in the Temple and
the shadow of priestly dominance had paralysed his
independence.   Amaziah, on the other hand, born in
the purple, was vigorous and restless.   When he was
secure upon the throne, and had done his duty to his
father's memory, he bent his efforts to recover Edom.
The Edomites had revolted in the days of his great-

grandfather Jehoram,[1] and since then " did tear perpetually," [2] harassing with incessant raids the miserable
fellahîn of Southern Judah.   They reaped the crops of
the settled inhabitants, cut down their fruit-trees, burnt
their farmsteads, and carried their children into cruel
and hopeless slavery.   One verse tells us all that the
historian knew, or cared to relate, of Amaziah's campaign.   He only says that it was eminently successful.
Amaziah confronted the Edomites in the Valley of
Salt,[3] on the border of Edom, to the south of the Dead
Sea, and inflicted upon them a signal defeat.   He not
only slaughtered ten thousand of them, but, advancing
southwards, he stormed and captured Selah or Petra,
their rocky capital, two days' journey north of Ezion-
Geber, on the gulf of Akabah.[4]   Considering the natural
strength of Petra, amid its mountain-fastnesses, this
was a victory of which he might well be proud, and
he marked his prowess by changing the name of the
city to Joktheel, "subdued by God."   The historian,
copying the ancient record before him, says that Selah
continued to be so called "to this day." [5]   This is a
curious instance of close transcription, for it is certain
that Selah can only have retained the name of Joktheel
for a very short period, and had lost it long before the
days of the Exile.   Even in the reign of Ahaz (B.C.
735-715) the Edomites had so completely recovered

---

[1] 2 Kings viii. 20–22.

[2] Amos i. 11.

[3] The Valley (*Gê*) of Salt is "the plain of the Sabkah," about two
miles broad, between the southern end of the Dead Sea and the
hills which separate the Ghôr from the Arabah (Seetzen, *Reisen*, ii.
356; Robinson, *Researches*, ii. 450, 488).   David had won a great
victory there (2 Sam. viii. 13; Psalm lx., *title*).

[4] Selah, "a rock" (Πέτρα).   Eusebius calls it Rekem.

[5] It is the name also of a city of Judah (Josh. xv. 38).

lost ground that they were able to make predatory
excursions into Judah, and to threaten Hebron, which
would have been obviously impossible if they were
not masters of their own chief capital.[1]   The district
which Amaziah seems to have conquered was mainly
west of the Arabah.   He wished to restore Elath, and
perhaps to carry out the old commerce with the Red
Sea which Solomon began, and which had fired the
ambition of Jehoshaphat.   The conquest of Selah
secured the road for his commercial caravans.

So far the older and better authorities.   The
Chronicler expands the story in his usual fashion, in
which historical and critical verity is so often compelled,
if not to suspect the disease of exaggeration and the
bias of Levitism, at least to feel uncertainty as to the
details.   He says that Amaziah collected an army of
three hundred thousand men of Judah, trained them
to a high state of discipline, and armed them with spear
and shield.   He hired in addition one hundred thousand
Israelitish mercenaries, mighty men of valour, at the
heavy cost of one hundred talents of silver.   He was
rebuked by a prophet for employing Israelites, "because
the Lord was not with them," so that if he used their
aid he would certainly be defeated.   Amaziah asked
what he was to do for the hundred talents, and the
prophet told him that Jehovah could give him much
more than this.[2]   So he dismissed his Ephraimites,
who, returning home in great fury, "fell upon the cities
of Judah," from Samaria even unto Beth-horon, killed
three thousand of their inhabitants, and took much
spoil.   Amaziah, however, defeated the Edomites without their aid, and not only slew ten thousand, but took

[1] 2 Chron. xxviii. 17 ; Jos., *Antt.*, XII. viii. 6.
[2] 2 Chron. xxv. 5–10, 13.

captive ten thousand more, all of whom he dashed to pieces by hurling them from the top of the rock of Petra.[1]

Then, by an apostasy much more astounding than even that of his father Joash, he took home with him the idols of Mount Seir, worshipped them, and burnt incense before them. Jehovah sends a prophet to rebuke him for his senseless infatuation in worshipping the gods of the Edomites whom he had just so utterly defeated; but Amaziah returns him the insolent answer, "Who made thee of the king's council? Be silent, or I will put thee to death." The prophet met his ironical sneer with words of deeper meaning: "If I am not on *your* council, I am on God's. Because thou hast not hearkened to my counsel, I know that God has counselled to destroy thee."

The later writer thus accounts for the folly and overthrow of this valorous and hitherto eminently pious king. Certain it is, as we shall narrate in the next chapter, that, in spite of warning, he had the temerity to challenge to battle the warlike Joash ben-Jehoahaz of Israel, grandson of Jehu. The kings met at Beth-Shemesh, and Amaziah was utterly routed, with consequences so shameful to himself and to Jerusalem that he was never able to hold up his head again. He could but eat away his own heart in despair, a ruined man. After this he "lived" rather than reigned fifteen years longer.[2] The wall of Jerusalem, broken down near the Damascus Gate, on the side towards

---

[1] Κατακρημνισμός. This mode of execution prevailed till quite recent times in the little republic of Andorra.

[2] 2 Kings xiv. 17. The phrase that "he *lived* fifteen years" is unusual, and seems to imply that the historian saw,—

"In more of life, true life no more."

Israel, for a space of four hundred cubits, was a standing witness of the king's infatuated folly. His people were ashamed of him, and weary of him ; and at last, seeing that nothing more could be expected of one whose spirit had evidently been broken from impetuosity into abjectness, they formed a conspiracy against him. To save his life he fled to the strong fort of Lachish, a royal Canaanite city, in the hills to the south-west of Judah.[1] But they pursued him thither, and even Lachish would not protect him. He was murdered. They threw the corpse upon a chariot, conveyed it to Jerusalem, and buried it in the sepulchres of his fathers. The people quietly elevated to the throne his son Azariah, then sixteen years old, who had been born the year before his father's crowning disgrace. What became of the conspirators we do not know. They were probably too strong to be brought to justice, and we are not told that Azariah even attempted to visit their crime upon their heads.

---

[1] **Josh. x. 6, 31, xv. 39;** 2 Kings xviii. 17 ; 2 Chron. xi. 9.

CHAPTER XVI

THE DYNASTY OF JEHU

"Them that honour Me I will honour, and they that despise Me shall be lightly esteemed."—I SAM. ii. 30.

ISRAEL had scarcely ever sunk to so low a nadir of degradation as she did in the reign of the son of Jehu. We have already mentioned that some assign to his reign the ghastly story which we have narrated in our sketch of the work of Elisha. It is told in the sixth chapter of the Second Book of Kings, and seems to belong to the reign of Jehoram ben-Ahab; but it may have got displaced from this epoch of yet deeper wretchedness. The accounts of Jehoahaz in 2 Kings xiii. are evidently fragmentary and abrupt.

Jehoahaz reigned seventeen years.[1] Naturally, he did not disturb the calf-worship, which, like all his

---

[1] I have not thought it worth while to unravel by a series of uncertain conjectures the careless, and often self-contradictory, synchronism of the reigns of the kings in the two kingdoms. The compiler of these books evidently attached little or no importance to accurate chronology. For instance, the data of 2 Kings xiii. 1, 10, do not coincide; and instead of entering into tedious, doubtful, and

predecessors and successors, he regarded as a perfectly innocent symbolic adoration of Jehovah, whose name he bore and whose service he professed. Why should he do so ? It had been established now for more than two centuries. His father, in spite of his passionate and ruthless zeal for Jehovah, had never attempted to disturb it. No prophet—not even Elijah nor Elisha, the practical establishers of his dynasty—had said one word to condemn it. It in no way rested on his conscience as an offence ; and the formal condemnation of it by the historian only reflects the more enlightened judgment of the Southern Kingdom and of a later age. But according to the parenthesis which breaks the thread of this king's story (2 Kings xiii. 5, 6), he was guilty of a far more culpable defection from orthodox worship ; for in his reign, the Asherah—the tree or pillar of the Tyrian nature-goddess—still remained in Samaria, and therefore must have had its worshippers. How it came there we cannot tell. Jezebel had set it up (1 Kings xvi. 33), with the connivance of Ahab. Jehu apparently had " put it away " with the great stêlê of Baal (2 Kings iii. 2), but, for some reason or other, he had not destroyed it. It now apparently occupied some public place, a symbol of decadence, and provocative of the wrath of Heaven.

Jehoahaz sank very low. Hazael's savage sword, not content with the devastation of Bashan and Gilead, wasted the west of Israel also in all its borders. The king became a mere vassal of his brutal neighbour at Damascus. So little of the barest semblance of

---

confusing guesses, I have contented myself throughout with giving for the reigns of the kings such dates, or approximate dates, as seem to result from the several notices compared with the contemporary annals of Assyria.

power was left him, that whereas, in the reign of David, Israel could muster an army of eight hundred thousand, and in the reign of Joash, the son and successor of Jehoahaz, Amaziah could hire from Israel one hundred thousand mighty men of valour as mercenaries, Jehoahaz was only allowed to maintain an army of ten chariots, fifty horsemen, and ten thousand infantry ! In the picturesque phrase of the historian, " the King of Syria had threshed down Israel to the dust," in spite of all that Jehoahaz did, or tried to do, and " all his might." How completely helpless the Israelites were is shown by the fact that their armies could offer no opposition to the free passage of the Syrian troops through their land. Hazael did not regard them as threatening his rear ; for, in the reign of Jehoahaz, he marched southwards, took the Philistine city of Gath, and threatened Jerusalem. Joash of Judah could only buy them off with the bribe of all his treasures, and according to the Chronicler they " destroyed all the princes of the people," and took great spoil to Damascus.[1]

Where was Elisha ? After the anointing of Jehu he vanishes from the scene. Unless the narrative of the siege of Samaria has been displaced, we do not so much as once hear of him for nearly half a century.

The fearful depth of humiliation to which the king was reduced drove him to repentance. Wearied to death of the Syrian oppression of which he was the daily witness, and of the utter misery caused by prowling bands of Ammonites and Moabites—jackals who waited on the Syrian lion—Jehoahaz " besought the Lord,[2] and the Lord hearkened unto him, and gave

---

[1] 2 Chron. xxiv. 23.

[2] 2 Kings xiii. 4; "besought," literally "*stroked the face of*" (1 Sam. xiii. 12 ; 1 Kings xiii. 6).

Israel a saviour, so that they went out from under the hand of the Syrians : and the children of Israel dwelt in their tents, as beforetime." If this indeed refers to events which come out of place in the memoirs of Elisha ; and if Jehoahaz ben-Jehu, not Jehoram ben-Ahab, was the king in whose reign the siege of Samaria was so marvellously raised, then Elisha may possibly be the temporary deliverer who is here alluded to.[1] On this supposition we may see a sign of the repentance of Jehoahaz in the shirt of sackcloth which he wore under his robes, as it became visible to his starving people when he rent his clothes on hearing the cannibal instincts which had driven mothers to devour their own children. But the respite must have been brief, since Hazael (ver. 22) oppressed Israel all the days of Jehoahaz. If this rearrangement of events be untenable, we must suppose that the repentance of Jehoahaz was only so far accepted, and his prayer so far heard, that the deliverance, which did not come in his own days, came in those of his son and of his grandson.

Of him and of his wretched reign we hear no more ; but a very different epoch dawned with the accession of his son Joash, named after the contemporary King of Judah, Joash ben-Ahaziah.

In the Books of Kings and Chronicles Joash of Israel is condemned with the usual refrains about the sins of Jeroboam. No other sin is laid to his charge ; and breaking the monotony of reprobation which tells us of every king of Israel without exception that " he did that which was evil in the sight of the Lord," Josephus boldly ventures to call him " a good man, and the antithesis to his father."

---

[1] The reference is usually explained of Jeroboam II.

He reigned sixteen years. At the beginning of his reign he found his country the despised prey, not only of Syria, but of the paltry neighbouring bandit-sheykhs who infested the east of the Jordan; he left it comparatively strong, prosperous, and independent.

In his reign we hear again of Elisha, now a very old man of past eighty years. Nearly half a century had elapsed since the grandfather of Joash had destroyed the house of Ahab at the prophet's command. News came to the king that Elisha was sick of a mortal sickness, and he naturally went to visit the death-bed of one who had called his dynasty to the throne, and had in earlier years played so memorable a part in the history of his country. He found the old man dying, and he wept over him, crying, " My father, my father! the chariot of Israel, and the horsemen thereof." [1] The address strikes us with some surprise. Elisha had indeed delivered Samaria more than once when the city had been reduced to direst extremity ; but in spite of his prayers and of his presence, the sins of Israel and her kings had rendered this chariot of Israel of very small avail. The names of Ahab, Jehu, Jehoahaz, call up memories of a series of miseries and humiliations which had reduced Israel to the very verge of extinction. For sixty-three years Elisha had been the prophet of Israel ; and though his public interpositions had been signal on several occasions, they had not been availing to prevent Ahab from becoming the vassal of Assyria, nor Israel from becoming the appanage of the dominion of that Hazael whom Elisha himself had anointed King of Syria, and who had become of all the enemies of his country the most persistent and the most implacable.

---

[1] Comp. 2 Kings ii. 12.

The narrative which follows is very singular. We
must give it as it occurs, with but little apprehension
of its exact significance.

Elisha, though Joash "did that which was evil in
the sight of the Lord," seems to have regarded him
with affection.   He bade the youth take his bow,[1] and
laid his feeble, trembling hands on the strong hands
of the king.   Then he ordered an attendant to fling
open the lattice, and told the king to shoot eastward
towards Gilead, the region whence the bands of Syria
made their way over the Jordan.   The king shot, and
the fire came back into the old prophet's eye as he
heard the arrow whistle eastward.   He cried, "The
arrow of Jehovah's deliverance, even the arrow of
victory over Syria : for thou shalt smite the Syrians
in Aphek, till thou have consumed them."[2]   Then he
bade the young king to take the sheaf of arrows, and
smite towards the ground, as if he was striking down
an enemy.   Not understanding the significance of the
act, the king made the sign of thrice striking the arrows
downwards, and then naturally stopped.[3]   But Elisha
was angry—or at any rate grieved.[4]   "You should
have smitten five or six times," he said, "and then you
would have smitten Syria to destruction.   Now you
shall only smite Syria thrice."   The king's fault seems
to have been lack of energy and faith.

There are in this story some peculiar elements which
it is impossible to explain, but it has one beautiful

---

[1] Lit., "Make thine hand to ride upon thy bow."   There is not the
slightest taint of belomancy in the story (comp. Ezek. xxi. 21), nor
does it allude to shooting an arrow into an enemy's country as a
declaration of war (Virg., Æn., ix. 57).

[2] Aphek, a name of good omen (1 Kings xx. 26–30).

[3] Thrice.   Comp. Num. xxii. 28 ; Exod. xxiii. 17, etc.

[4] LXX., ἐλυπήθη.

and striking feature. It tells us of the death-bed of
a prophet. Most of God's greatest prophets have
perished amid the hatred of priests and worldlings.
The progress of the truth they taught has been "from
scaffold to scaffold, and from stake to stake."

"Careless seems the Great Avenger. History's pages but record
　One death-grapple in the darkness 'twixt old systems and the
　　Word—
　Truth for ever on the scaffold, wrong for ever on the throne;
　Yet that scaffold sways the Future, and behind the dim unknown
　Standeth God within the shadow, keeping watch above His own!"

Now and then, however, as an exception, a great
prophetic teacher or reformer escapes the hatred of
the priests and of the world, and dies in peace.
Savonarola is burnt, Huss is burnt, but Wiclif dies
in his bed at Lutterworth, and Luther died in peace
at Eisleben. Elijah passed away in storm, and was
seen no more. A king comes to weep by the death-bed
of the aged Elisha. "For us," it has been said, "the
scene at his bedside contains a lesson of comfort and
even encouragement. Let us try to realise it. A man
with no material power is dying in the capital of Israel.
He is not rich : he holds no office which gives him any
immediate control over the actions of men ; he has but
one weapon—the power of his word. Yet Israel's king
stands weeping at his bedside—weeping because this
inspired messenger of Jehovah is to be taken from
him. In him both king and people will lose a mighty
support, for this man is a greater strength to Israel
than chariots and horsemen are. Joash does well to
mourn for him, for he has had courage to wake the
nation's conscience ; the might of his personality has
sufficed to turn them in the true direction, and rouse
their moral and religious life. Such men as Elisha

everywhere and always give a strength to their people above the strength of armies, for the true blessings of a nation are reared on the foundations of its moral force."

The annals are here interrupted to introduce a posthumous miracle—unlike any other in the whole Bible—wrought by the bones of Elisha. He died, and they buried him, "giving him," as Josephus says, "a magnificent burial." As usual, the spring brought with it the marauding bands of Moabites. Some Israelites who were burying a man caught sight of them, and, anxious to escape, thrust the man into the sepulchre of Elisha, which happened to be nearest at hand. But when he was placed in the rocky tomb, and touched the bones of Elisha, he revived, and stood up on his feet. Doubtless the story rests on some real circumstance. There is, however, something singular in the turn of the original, which says (literally) that the man *went and touched* the bones of Elisha;[1] and there is proof that the story was told in varying forms, for Josephus says that it was the Moabite plunderers who had killed the man, and that he was thrown by them into Elisha's tomb.[2] It is easy to invent moral and spiritual lessons out of this incident, but not so easy to see what lesson is intended by it. Certainly there is not throughout Scripture any other passage which even *seems* to sanction any suspicions of magic potency in the relics of the dead.[3]

But Elisha's symbolic prophecy of deliverance from Syria was amply fulfilled. About this time Hazael had died, and had left his power in the feebler hands of his

---

[1] See R.V., margin.

[2] *Antt.*, IX. viii. 6.

[3] See Ecclus. xlviii. 13: "When he was dead, he prophesied in the tomb." (But the clause may be spurious.)

son Benhadad III. Jehoahaz had not been able to make any way against him (2 Kings xiii. 3), but Joash his son thrice met and thrice defeated him at Aphek. As a consequence of these victories, he won back all the cities which Hazael had taken from his father on the west of Jordan. The east of Jordan was never recovered. It fell under the shadow of Assyria, and was practically lost for ever to the tribes of Israel.

Whether Assyria lent her help to Joash under certain conditions we do not know. Certain it is that from this time the terror of Syria vanishes. The Assyrian king Rammânirâri III. about this time subjugated all Syria and its king, whom the tablets call Mari, perhaps the same as Benhadad III. In the next reign Damascus itself fell into the power of Jeroboam II., the son of Joash.

One more event, to which we have already alluded, is narrated in the reign of this prosperous and valiant king.

Amity had reigned for a century between Judah and Israel, the result of the politic-impolitic alliance which Jehoshaphat had sanctioned between his son Jehoram and the daughter of Jezebel. It was obviously most desirable that the two small kingdoms should be united as closely as possible by an offensive and defensive alliance. But the bond between them was broken by the overweening vanity of Amaziah ben-Joash of Judah. His victory over the Edomites, and his conquest of Petra, had puffed him up with the mistaken notion that he was a very great man and an invincible warrior. He had the wicked infatuation to kindle an unprovoked war against the Northern Tribes. It was the most wanton of the many instances in which, if Ephraim did not envy Judah, at least Judah vexed Ephraim,

Amaziah challenged Joash to come out to battle, that they might look one another in the face. He had not recognised the difference between fighting with and without the sanction of the God of battles.

Joash had on his hands enough of necessary and internecine war to make him more than indifferent to that bloody game. Moreover, as the superior of Amaziah in every way, he saw through his inflated emptiness. He knew that it was the worst possible policy for Judah and Israel to weaken each other in fratricidal war, while Syria threatened their northern and eastern frontiers, and while the tread of the mighty march of Assyria was echoing ominously in the ears of the nations from afar. Better and kinder feelings may have mingled with these wise convictions. He had no wish to destroy the poor fool who so vaingloriously provoked his superior might. His answer was one of the most crushingly contemptuous pieces of irony which history records, and yet it was eminently kindly and good-humoured. It was meant to save the King of Judah from advancing any further on the path of certain ruin.

"The thistle that was in Lebanon" (such was the apologue which he addressed to his would-be rival) "sent to the cedar that was in Lebanon, saying: Give thy daughter to my son to wife.[1] The cedar took no sort of notice of the thistle's ludicrous presumption, but a wild beast that was in Lebanon passed by, and trod down the thistle."

It was the answer of a giant to a dwarf;[2] and to

---

[1] Possibly some matrimonial proposal may have lain behind the interchange of messages.

[2] Stade. For similar parables see Judg. ix. 8; Herod., i. 141 Rawlinson, *Anc. Mon.*, iii. 226.

make it quite clear to the humblest comprehension,
Joash good-naturedly added : "You are puffed up with
your victory over Edom : glory in this, and stay at
home.   Why by your vain meddling should you ruin
yourself and Judah with you ?   Keep quiet : I have
something else to do than to attend to you."

Happy had it been for Amaziah if he had taken
warning !   But vanity is a bad counsellor, and folly
and self-deception—ill-matched pair—were whirling him
to his doom.   Seeing that he was bent on his own
perdition, Joash took the initiative and marched to
Beth-Shemesh, in the territory of Judah.[1]   There the
kings met, and there Amaziah was hopelessly defeated.
His troops fled to their scattered homes, and he fell
into the hands of his conqueror.   Joash did not care
to take any sanguinary revenge ; but much as he
despised his enemy, he thought it necessary to teach
him and Judah the permanent lesson of not again
meddling to their own hurt.   He took the captive king
with him to Jerusalem, which opened its gates without
a blow.[2]   We do not know whether, like a Roman
conqueror, he entered it through the breach of four
hundred cubits which he ordered them to make in the
walls,[3] but otherwise he contented himself with spoil
which would swell his treasure, and amply compensate
for the expenses of the expedition which had been

---

[1] Beth-Shemesh, "the house of the sun."   It is mentioned in
I Sam. vi. 9, 12, and was a priestly city, and one of Solomon's store-
cities (I Kings iv. 9).   It ultimately fell into the hands of the
Philistines (2 Chron. xxviii. 18).   It is not the Beth-Shemesh of
Josh. xix. 22.

[2] Josephus says that this was the fault of Amaziah, whom Joash of
Israel threatened with death if Jerusalem resisted.

[3] This implies that at least half the northern wall was dismantled—
the wall towards Ephraim.

forced upon him.   He ransacked Jerusalem for silver and gold ; he made Obed-Edom, the treasurer, give up to him all the sacred vessels of the Temple, and all that was worth taking from the palace.   He also took hostages—probably from among the number of the king's sons—to secure immunity from further intrusions. It is the first time in Scripture that hostages are mentioned.   It is to his credit that he shed no blood, and was even content to leave his defeated challenger with the disgraced phantom of his kingly power, till, fifteen years later, he followed his father to the grave through the red path of murder at the hand of his own subjects.[1]

After this we hear no further records of this vigorous and able king, in whom the characteristics of his grandfather Jehu are reflected in softer outline.   He left his son Jeroboam II. to continue his career of prosperity, and to advance Israel to a pitch of greatness which she had never yet attained, in which she rivalled the grandeur of the united kingdom in the earlier days of Solomon's dominion.

---

[1] Some have conjectured that Amaziah of Judah became more or less the vassal of Joash of Israel, and that the vassalage continued till after the death of Jeroboam II. (1) For Jeroboam II. held Elath till his death, when Uzziah recovered it (2 Kings xiv. 22), and he certainly could not have held this southern Judæan port if Judah was entirely independent ; and (2) we read that Uzziah did not become king at all till the *twenty-seventh* year of Jeroboam II.   But if Amaziah only survived Joash of Israel fifteen years (2 Kings xiv. 17), Uzziah must have succeeded in the *fifteenth* year of Jeroboam.   Is the explanation to be found in the fact that up to that time—for twelve years—Jeroboam did not allow the Judæans to elect a king? or are these among the hopeless confusion of synchronism which cannot be reconciled at all with our present data ?

CHAPTER XVII

THE DYNASTY OF JEHU (*continued*)—JEROBOAM II

B.C. 781—740

2 KINGS xiv. 23—29

IF we had only the history of the kings to depend upon, we should scarcely form an adequate conception either of the greatness of Jeroboam II. or of the condition of society which prevailed in Israel during his long and most prosperous reign of forty-one years (B.C. 781–740). In the Books of Chronicles he is merely mentioned accidentally in a genealogy. The Second Book of Kings only devotes one verse to him (xiv. 25) beyond the stock formulæ of connection so often repeated. That verse, however, gives us at least a glimpse of his great importance, for it tells us that "he restored the coast of Israel from the entering of Hamath unto the sea of the plain." Those two lines sufficiently prove to us that he was by far the greatest and most powerful of all the kings of Israel, as he was also the longest-lived and had the longest reign. His victories flung a broad gleam of sunset over the afflicted kingdom, and, for a time, they might have beguiled the Israelites into lofty hopes for the future ; but with the death of Jeroboam the light instantly faded away, and there was no after-glow.

And this sudden brightness, if it deceived others, did not deceive the prophets of the Lord. It happened in accordance with the promise of Jehovah given by Jonah, the son of Amittai, of Gath-Hepher ;[1] but Amos and Hosea saw that the glory of the reign was hollow and delusive, and that the outward prosperity did but " skin and film the ulcerous place " below.

In truth, the possibility of this sudden outburst of success was due to the very enemy who, within a few years, was to grind Israel to powder. God pitied the deplorable overthrow of His chosen people : He saw that there was neither slave nor freeman—"neither any shut up, nor any left at large, nor any helper for Israel"; and in Jeroboam He gave them the saviour who had been granted to the penitence of Jehoahaz.[2] It was, so to speak, a last pledge to them of the love and mercy of Jehovah, which gave them a respite, and would fain have saved them altogether, if they had turned with their whole heart to Him. And, personally, Jeroboam II. seems to have been one of the better kings. Not a single crime is laid to his charge ; for under the circumstances of its deep-rooted continuance through the reigns of all his predecessors, it cannot be deemed a heinous crime that he did not put down the symbolic cult of Jehovah by the cherubic emblems at Dan and Bethel. The fact that he had been named after the founder of the kingdom of Israel

---

[1] 2 Kings xiv. 25–27. There are other allusions to the historic events in 2 Kings x. 32, 33, xiii. 3–7, 22–25. Hitzig conjectures that Isa. xv., xvi., are "a burden of Moab" quoted from Jonah.

[2] 2 Kings xiii. 5, "The Lord gave Israel a saviour"; xiv. 27, "And He saved them by the hand of Jeroboam, the son of Joash." Some suppose the saviour to be the Assyrian King.

shows that the kingdom was proud of the valiant and
Heaven-commissioned rebel who had thrown off the
yoke of the house of Solomon. The house of Jehu
admired his policy and his institutions. The son of
Nebat did not by any means appear in the eyes of
his people as only worthy of the monotonous epitaph,
"who made Israel to sin." It is true that now the
voice of prophecy in Israel itself began to denounce the
concomitants of the "calf-worship"; but the voices of
the Jewish herdsman of Tekoa and of the Israelite
Hosea probably raised but faint murmurs in the ears
of the warrior-king, with whom they do not seem to
have come into personal contact. In no case would
he rank them as equal in importance with the fiery
Elijah or the king-making Elisha, who had been for
four generations the counsellor of his race. Neither
of those great prophets had insisted on the Deuteronomic law of a centralised worship, nor had they
denounced the revered local sanctuaries with which
Israel had been so long familiar. Jonah, indeed—who,
if legend be correct, had been the boy of Zarephath,
and the personal attendant of Elijah—had predicted
the king's unbroken success, and had neither made it
conditional on a religious revolution, nor, so far as we
know, had in any way censured the existing institutions.

What rendered Jeroboam's glory possible was the
immediate paralysis and imminent ruin of the power
of Syria. The Israelitish king was probably on good
terms with Assyria, and, during this epoch, three
Assyrian monarchs had struck blow after blow against
the house of Hazael. Damascus and its dependencies
had received shattering defeats at the hands of
Rammânirâri III., Shalmaneser III. (782–772), and
Assurdan III. (772–754). Rammânirâri had made

expeditions against Damascus (773) and Hazael (772);
and Assurdan had invaded the Syrian domains in 767,
755, and 754. Syria had more than enough to do to
hold her own in a struggle for life and death against
her atrocious neighbour. With Uzziah in Judah,
Jeroboam II. seems to have been on the friendliest
terms; and probably Uzziah acted as a half-independent
vassal, united with him by common interests. The
day for Assyria to threaten Israel had not yet come.
Syria lay in the path; and Assurdan III. had been
succeeded by Assurnirari, who gave the world the
unusual spectacle of a peaceful Assyrian king.

Jeroboam II., therefore, was free to enlarge his
domains; and unless there be a little patriotic exaggeration in the extent and reality of his prowess, he
exercised at least a nominal suzerainty over a realm
nearly as extensive as that of David. He first advanced
against Damascus, and so far "recovered" it as to
make it acknowledge his rule.[1] His father Joash had
won back all the Israelite cities which Benhadad III.
had taken from Jehoahaz; and Jeroboam, if he did not
absolutely reconquer the district east of Jordan, yet
kept it in check and repressed the predatory incursions of the Emîrs of Moab and Ammon.[2] He thus

---

[1] It had owned the feudal supremacy of David (2 Sam. viii. 6), and
Ahab had extorted the privilege of having bazaars there (1 Kings
xx. 34). Considering how immense had been the resources of
Damascus (2 Kings vi. 14), which had once been able to send to
battle twelve thousand war-chariots (*Eponym Canon*, p. 108) under
Benhadad, we see how fearfully the Syrian capital must have been
weakened.

[2] If Isa. xv. 1, 2, refers to this invasion of Jeroboam II., as Hitzig
first conjectured, we infer that he had taken both Ar of Moab
(Rabbath) and Kir of Moab, a strong fortress on a hill, by night
assaults; and that he had also captured Dibon, Nebo, and Medeba,
and inflicted on them summary chastisement. It appears that the

extended the border of Israel to the sea of the Arabah
and "the brook of willows" which divides Edom from
Moab.[1] But this was not all. He pushed his conquests
two hundred miles northwards of Samaria, and became
lord of Hamath the Great. Ascending the gorge of
the Litâny between the chains of Libanus and Antilibanus, which formed the northern limit of Israel,
and following the river to its source near Baalbek,
he then descended the Valley of the Orontes, which
constitutes the "pass" or "entering in" of Hamath
Hamath was a town of the Hittites, the most powerful
race of ancient Canaan. They were not of Semitic
origin, but spoke a separate language. They were the
last great branch of the once famous and dominant
Khetas, whose former importance has only recently been
revealed by their deciphered inscriptions. A century
and a half earlier the Hamathites had thrown off the
yoke of Solomon, and they governed nearly a hundred
dependent cities. In alliance with the Phœnicians and
Syrians, they had been valuable members of a league,
which, though defeated, had long formed a barrier
against the southward movement of the Assyrians.
How striking was the conquest of this city by Jeroboam
is shown by the title of "Hamath the Great," bestowed
upon it by the contemporary prophets,[2] with whom
literary prophecy begins.

Moabites had advanced northwards from the Arnon, while Hazael
occupied Ramoth-Gilead, and had seized part of the tribe of Reuben.
Jeroboam II. first expelled them, and then invaded their own proper
country. Hitzig conjectures that Isa. xv., xvi., are really an old
prophecy—perhaps by Jonah, son of Amittai—which Isaiah quotes, and
to which he adds two verses (Isa. xvi. 12, 13). In such overthrow
Moab must have learnt to be ashamed of Chemosh (Jer. xlviii. 13).

[1] Isa. xv. 7 ; Amos vi. 14.
[2] Amos vi. 2.

The result of these conquests was unwonted peace. Agriculture once more became possible, when the farmers of Israel were secure that their crops would not be reaped by plundering Bedouîn. Intercourse with neighbouring nations was revived, as in the golden days of Solomon, though it was regarded with suspicion.[1] Civilisation softened something of the old brutality. Prophecy assumed a different type, and literature began to dawn.

But to this state of things there was, as we learn from the contemporary prophets Amos and Hosea, a darker side. Of Jonah we know nothing more; for it is impossible to see in the Book of Jonah much more than a beautiful and edifying story, which may or may not rest on some surviving legends. It differs from every other prophetic book by beginning with the word "And," and its late origin and legendary character cannot any longer be reasonably disputed.[2] We may hope, therefore, that the Northern prophet, whose home was not far from Nazareth, was not quite the morose and ruthless grumbler so strikingly portrayed in the book which bears his name. Of any historical intervention of his in the affairs of Jeroboam we know nothing further than the recorded promise of the king's prosperity.

---

[1] Merchandise had hitherto been considered discreditable for a pure Jew, so that a trader is called a Canaanite (Hos. xii. 7, 8).

[2] See the writer's *Minor Prophets* ("Men of the Bible" Series), pp. 231–243.

CHAPTER XVIII

AMOS, HOSEA, AND THE KINGDOM OF ISRAEL

2 KINGS xiv. 23—29; xv. 8—12

"In them is plainest taught and easiest learnt
What makes a nation happy and keeps it so,
What ruins kingdoms and lays cities flat."
MILTON, *Paradise Regained.*

"We see dimly in the Present what is small and what is great,
Slow of faith how weak an arm may turn the iron helm of Fate:
But the soul is still oracular: amid the market's din
List the ominous stern whisper from the Delphic cave within,
'They enslave their children's children who make compromise
with sin.'"
LOWELL.

AMOS and Hosea are the two earliest prophets whose "burdens" have come down to us. From them we gain a near insight into the internal condition of Israel in this day of her prosperity.

We see, first, that the prosperity was not unbroken. Though peace reigned, the people were not left to lapse unwarned into sloth and godlessness. The land had suffered from the horrible scourge of locusts, until every *carmel*—every garden of God on hill and plain—withered before them.[1] There had been widespread conflagrations;[2] there had been a visitation of pestilence; and, finally, there had been an earthquake so

---

[1] Amos vii. 1. Famine (iv. 6); drought (iv. 7, 8); yellow blight and locusts (iv. 9); pestilence (iv. 10); earthquake and burning (iv. 11).
[2] Amos vii. 4.

violent that it constituted an epoch from which dates were reckoned.[1] There were also two eclipses of the sun, which darkened with fear the minds of the superstitious.[2]

Nor was this the worst. Civilisation and commerce had brought luxury in their train, and all the bonds of morality had been relaxed. The country began to be comparatively depleted, and the innocent regularity of agricultural pursuits palled upon the young, who were seduced by the glittering excitement of the growing towns. All zeal for religion was looked on as archaic, and the splendour of formal services was regarded as a sufficient recognition of such gods as there were. As a natural consequence, the nobles and the wealthy classes were more and more infected with a gross materialism, which displayed itself in ostentatious furniture, and sumptuous palaces of precious marbles inlaid with ivory. The desire for such vanities increased the thirst for gold, and avarice replenished its exhausted coffers by grinding the faces of the poor, by defrauding the hireling of his wages, by selling the righteous for silver, the needy for handfuls of barley, and the poor for a pair of shoes. The degrading vice of intoxication acquired fresh vogue, and the gorgeous gluttonies of the rich were further disgraced by the shameful spectacle

---

[1] Amos i. 1, iii. 14, iv. 11, viii. 8; Zech. xiv. 5: "Ye shall flee like as ye fled before the earthquake in the days of Uzziah." Josephus says that in an earthquake a little before the birth of Christ ten thousand were buried under the ruined houses (*Antt.*, XV. v. 2), and he has many Rabbinic haggadoth to tell us about the earthquake, which, he says, happened at the moment when Uzziah burnt incense in the Temple (*Antt.*, IX. x. 4).

[2] According to Hind, they took place on June 15th, B.C. 763, and February 9th, B.C. 784. Amos alludes to the capture of Gath by Uzziah, of Calneh (*Ktesiphon*), and of Hamath (vi. 2; 2 Chron. xxvi. 6). Gath henceforth disappears from the Philistian Pentapolis (Amos i. 7, 8; Zeph. ii. 4; Zech. ix. 5).

of drunkards, who lolled for hours over the revelries which were inflamed by voluptuous music. Worst of all, the purity of family life was invaded and broken down. Throwing aside the old veiled seclusion of women in Oriental life, the ladies of Israel showed themselves in the streets in all "the bravery of their tinkling ornaments of gold," and sank into the adulterous courses stimulated by their pampered effrontery.

Such is the picture which we draw from the burning denunciations of the peasant-prophet of Tekoa. He was no prophet nor prophet's son, but a humble gatherer of sycomore-fruit, a toil which only fell to the humblest of the people.[1] Who is not afraid, he asks, when a lion roars? and how can a prophet be silent when the Lord God has spoken? Indignation had transformed and dilated him from a labourer into a seer, and had summoned him from the pastoral shades of his native village—whether in Judah or in Israel is uncertain—to denounce the more flagrant iniquities of the Northern capital.[2] First he proclaims

---

[1] Or "dresser of sycomore-trees" (R.V.). LXX., κνίζων συκάμινα; Vulg., *vellicans sycomoros.* The sycomore-fruit (fruit of the *Ficus sycomorus*, or wild fig) is ripened by puncturing it (Theoph., *H. Plant.*, iv. 2 ; Pliny, *H. N.*, xiii. 14).

[2] The well-known town of Tekoa had been Solomon's horse-fair, and had been fortified by Rehoboam (2 Chron. xi. 6). It lay in a wild country six miles south of Bethlehem (2 Chron. xx. 20; 1 Macc. ix. 33; Robinson, *Bibl. Res.*, i. 486). For a fuller account of these prophets, I must refer to my book on *The Minor Prophets* in the "Men of the Bible" Series. It has always been assumed that Amos belonged to the well-known Tekoa, and was therefore a subject of the Southern Kingdom. In recent days this has become uncertain. No sycomores grow or can grow on the bleak uplands of Tekoa (Tristram, *Nat. Hist. of the Bible*, p. 397) ; so that Jerome, in his preface to Amos, thinks that "brambles" are intended. Even Kimchi conjectured that Tekoa was an unknown town in the tribe of Asher. Amos's allusions to scenery are all applicable to the Northern landscape.

the vengeance of Jehovah upon the transgressions of
the Philistines, of Tyre, of Edom, of Ammon, of Moab,
and even of Judah ; and then he turns with a crash
upon apostatising Israel.[1]   He speaks with unsparing
plainness of their pitiless greed, their shameless
debauchery, their exacting usury, their attempts to
pervert even the abstinent Nazarites into intemperance,
and to silence the prophets by opposition and obloquy.
Jehovah was crushed under their violence.[2]   And did
they think to go unscathed after such black ingratitude?
Nay ! their mightiest should flee away naked in the
day of defeat.   Robbery was in their houses of ivory,
and the few of them who should escape the spoiler
should only be as when a shepherd tears out of the
mouth of a lion two legs and a piece of an ear ?[3]
As for Bethel, their shrine—which he calls Bethaven,
"House of Vanity," not Bethel, "House of God"—the
horns of its altars should be cut off.   Should oppression and licentiousness flourish ?   Jehovah would take
them with hooks, and their children with fish-hooks,
and their sacrifices at Bethel and Gilgal should be
utterly unavailing.   Drought, and blasting, and mildew,
and wasting plague, and earth-convulsions like those
which had swallowed Sodom and Gomorrha, from
which they should only be plucked as a "firebrand out
of the burning," should warn them that they must
prepare to meet their God.[4]   It was lamentable ; but
lamentation was vain, unless they would return to
Jehovah, Lord of hosts,[5] and abandon the false worship

---

[1] Amos i. 1–ii. 5.   [3] Amos iii. 9–15.
[2] Amos ii. 6–13.   [4] Amos iv. 1–13.
[5] This title, "Jehovah-Tsebaoth," now begins to occur. It is not
found in the Hexateuch.   It probably means "Lord of the *starry
hosts."*   Contact with Assyria first made the Israelites acquainted

of Bethel, Beersheba, and Gilgal, and listen to the
voice of the righteous, whom they now abhorred for
his rebukes. They talked hypocritically about "the
day of the Lord," but to them it should be blackness.
They relied on feast days, and services, and sacrifices;
but since they would not give the sacrifice of judgment
and righteousness, for which alone God cared, they
should be carried into captivity beyond Damascus:
yes! even to that terrible Assyria with whose king
they now were on friendly terms. They lay at ease
on their carved couches at their delicate feasts, drain-
ing the wine-bowls, and glistering with fragrant oils,
heedless of the impending doom which would smite
the great house with breaches and the little house with
clefts, and which should bring upon them an avenger
who should afflict them from their conquered Hamath
southwards even to the wady of the wilderness.[1]
The threatened judgments of locusts and fire had been
mitigated at the prophet's prayer, but nothing could
avert the plumb-line of destruction which Jehovah held
over them, and He would rise against the House of
Jeroboam with His sword.[2] We infer from all that
Amos and Hosea say that the calf-worship at Bethel
(for Dan is not mentioned in this connexion[3]) had

---

with star-worship. Amos alludes to the Pleiades and Orion (**v. 8**:
comp. Job ix. 9, xxxviii. 31). Star-worship is forbidden in Deuteronomy. In Amos v. 26 the true meaning is that the Israelites *would
take with them, on their road to exile,* Sakkuth (Moloch?) and Kewan
(the god-star Saturn).

[1] Amos vi. 1–14.

[2] Amos vii. 1–9.

[3] Strange as it may seem, the early authority for the existence of
any calf at Dan is very slight, and the extreme uncertainty of the
reading and interpretation in one main passage (1 Kings xii. 32)
makes it at least possible that there were *two calves at Bethel,* and that

degenerated into an idolatry far more abject than it originally was. The familiarity of such multitudes of the people with Baal-worship and Asherah-worship had tended to obliterate the sense that the "calves" were cherubic emblems of Jehovah; and were it not for some confusions of this kind, it is inconceivable that Jehoram ben-Jehu should have restored the Asherah which his father had removed. Be that as it may, Bethel and Gilgal seem to have become centres of corruption. Dan is scarcely once alluded to as a scene of the calf-worship.

Others, then, might be deceived by the surface-glitter of extended empire in the days of Jeroboam II. Not so the true prophets. It has often happened—as to Persia, when, in B.C. 388, she dictated the Peace of Antalcidas, and to Papal Rome in the days of the Jubilee of 1300, and to Philip II. of Spain in the year of the Armada, and to Louis XIV. in 1667—that a nation has seemed to be at its zenith of pomp and power on the very eve of some tremendous catastrophe. Amos and Hosea saw that such a catastrophe was at hand for Israel, because they knew that Divine punishment inevitably dogs the heels of insolence and crime. The loftiness of Israel's privilege involved the utterness of her ruin. "You only have I known of all the families of the earth: therefore I will visit upon you all your iniquities."[1]

Such prophecies, so eloquent, so uncompromising, so varied, and so constantly disseminated among the people, first by public harangues, then in writing, could

---

at Dan there was no calf, but only the old idolatrous ephod of Micah, still served by the servant of Moses. See additional note at the end of the volume.

[1] Amos iii. 2.

no longer be neglected. Amos, with his natural culture, his rhythmic utterances, and his inextinguishable fire, was far different from the wild fanatics, with their hairy garments, and sudden movements, and long locks, and cries, and self-inflicted wounds, with whom Israel had been familiar since the days of Elijah whom they all imitated. So long as this inspired peasant confined himself to moral denunciations the aristocracy and priesthood of Samaria could afford comfortably to despise him. What were moral denunciations to them? What harm was there in ivory palaces and refined feasts? This man was a mere red socialist who tried to undermine the customs of society. The hold of the upper classes on the people, whom their exactions had burdened with hopeless debt, and whom they could with impunity crush into slavery, was too strong to be shaken by the "hysteric gush" of a philanthropic faddist and temperance fanatic like this. But when he had the enormous presumption to mention publicly the name of their victorious king, and to say that Jehovah would rise against him with the sword, it was time for the clergy to interfere, and to send the intruder back to his native obscurity.

So Amaziah, the priest of Bethel,[1] invoked the king's authority. "Amos," he said to the king, "hath conspired against thee in the midst of the house of Israel." The charge was grossly false, but it did well enough to serve the priest's purpose. "The land is not able to bear all his words."

That was true; for when nations have chosen to abide by their own vicious courses, and refuse to listen

---

[1] That the chief priest of Bethel bore the name "Jehovah is strong" shows once more that "calf-worship" was in no sense a *substitute* for the worship of Jehovah.

to the voice of warning, they are impatient of rebuke. They refuse to hear when God calls to them.

> "For when we in our viciousness grow hard,
>   Oh misery on it! the wise gods seal our eyes;
>   In our own filth drop our clear judgments; make us
>   Adore our errors; laugh at us while we strut
>   To our confusion."

The priest tried further to inflame the king's anger by telling him two more of Amos's supposed predictions. He had prophesied (which was a false inference) that Israel should be led away captive out of their own land,[1] and had also prophesied (which was a perversion of the fact) "that Jeroboam *should die* by the sword."

At the first prophecy Jeroboam probably smiled. It might indeed come true in the long-run. If he was a man of prescience as well as of prowess, he probably foresaw that the elements of ruin lurked in his transient success, and that though, for the present, Assyria was occupied in other directions, it was unlikely that the weaker Israel would escape the fate of the far more powerful Syria. As for the personal prophecy, he was strong, and was honoured, and had his army and his guards. He would take his chance. Nor does it seem to have troubled any one that Amos looked for the ultimate union of Israel with Judah. Since the time of Joash the inheritance of David had been but as "a ruined booth" (ix. 11); but Amos prophesied its restoration. This touch may have been added later, when he wrote and published his "burdens"; but he

---

[1] This was not quite accurate; he had rather prophesied the devastation of the high places (vii. 9). In fact, his words had often been very vague. "*Thus* will I do unto thee" (iv. 12).

did not hesitate to speak as if the two kingdoms were really and properly one.[1]

We are not told that Jeroboam II. interfered with the prophet in any way.[2] Had he done so, he would have been rebuked and denounced for it. He probably went no further than to allow the priest and the prophet to settle the matter between themselves. Perhaps he gave a contemptuous permission that, if Amaziah thought it worth while to send the prophet back into Judah, he might do so.

Armed with this nonchalant mandate, Amaziah, with more mildness and good-humour than might have been expected from one of his class, said to Amos, "O Seer,[3] go home, and eat thy bread, and prophesy to thy heart's content at home ; but do not prophesy any more at Bethel, for it is the king's sanctuary and the king's court."

Amos obeyed perforce, but stopped to say that he had not prophesied out of his own mouth, but by Jehovah's bidding. He then hurled at the priest a message of doom as frightful as that which Jeremiah

---

[1] Amos ix. 11-15. Comp. Hos. iii. 5.

[2] The exaggerated haggadoth of later days say that Amaziah had Amos beaten with leaded thongs, and that he was carried home in a dying state (Epiphan., *Opp.*, ii. 145), to which there is a supposed allusion in Heb. xi. 35 : ἄλλοι δὲ ἐτυμπανίσθησαν.

[3] We cannot be sure that the term "Seer" was meant to be contemptuous, although from 1 Sam. ix. 9 we should infer that the title had become somewhat obsolete. Further, we must bear in mind that it may not have been always easy for worldlings to distinguish between true prophets and the unprincipled pretenders who, about this time, succeeded in making the name and aspect of a prophet so complete a disgrace that men had carefully to disclaim it (Zech. xiii. 2-6). It is true that the heading of Amos (i. 1), which may not, however, be by the prophet himself, tells us of "the words which he *saw*" (*i.e.*, spoke as a seer), and he also disclaims the name of prophet (vii. 14).

pronounced upon Pashur, when that priest smote him
on the face. His wife should be a harlot in the
city; his sons and daughters should be slain; his
inheritance should be divided; he should die in a
polluted land; and Israel should go into captivity.
And as for his mission, he justified it by the fact
that he was not one of an hereditary or a profes-
sional community; he was no prophet or prophet's
son. Such men might—like Zedekiah, the son of
Chenaanah, and his four hundred abettors—be led into
mere function and professionalism, into manufactured
enthusiasm and simulated inspiration. From such
communities freshness, unconventionality, courage, were
hardly to be expected. They would philippise at
times; they would get to love their order and their
privileges better than their message, and themselves
best of all. It is the tendency of organised bodies
to be tempted into conventionality, and to sink into
banded unions chiefly concerned in the protection of
their own prestige. Not such was Amos. He was a
peasant herdsman in whose heart had burned the
inspiration of Jehovah and the wrath against moral
misdoing till they had burst into flame. It was
indignation against iniquity which had called Amos
from the flocks and the sycomores to launch against
an apostatising people the menace of doom. In that
grief and indignation he heard the voice and received
the mandate of the Lord of hosts. He heads the long
line of literary prophets whose priceless utterances are
preserved in the Old Testament. The inestimable
value of their teaching lies most of all in the fact that
they were—like Moses—preachers of the moral law;
and that, like the Book of the Covenant, which is the
most ancient and the most valuable part of the Laws

of the Pentateuch, they count external service as no better than the small dust of the balance in comparison with righteousness and true holiness.

The rest of the predictions of Amos were added at a later date. They dwelt on the certainty and the awful details of the coming overthrow; the doom of the idolaters of Gilgal and Beersheba; the inevitable swiftness of the catastrophe in which Samaria should be sifted like corn in a sieve in spite of her incorrigible security.[1] Yet the ruin should not be absolute. "Thus saith Jehovah: As the shepherd teareth out of the mouth of the lion two legs and the piece of an ear, so shall the children of Israel be rescued, that sit in Samaria on the corner of a couch, and on the damask of a bed."

The Hebrew Prophets almost invariably weave together the triple strands of warning, exhortation, and hope. Hitherto Amos has not had a word of hope to utter. At last, however, he lets a glimpse of the rainbow irradiate the gloom. The overthrow of Israel should be accompanied by the restoration of the fallen booth of David, and, under the rule of a scion of that house, Israel should return from captivity to enjoy days of peaceful happiness, and to be rooted up no more.[2]

Hosea, the son of Beeri, was of a somewhat later date than Amos. He, too, "became electric," to flash into meaner and corrupted minds the conviction that formalism is nothing, and that moral sincerity is all in all. That which God requires is not ritual service, but truth in the inward parts. He is one of the

---

[1] Amos viii. 1–ix. 9, 10.   [2] Amos ix. 11–15.

saddest of the prophets; but though he mingles prophecies of mercy with his menaces of wrath, the
general tenor of his oracles is the same. He pictures
the crimes of Ephraim by the image of domestic un-
faithfulness, and bids Judah to take warning from the
curse involved in her apostasy.[1] Many of his allusions
touch upon the days of that deluge of anarchy which
followed the death of Jeroboam II. (iv.–vi. 3). That
he was a Northerner appears from the fact that he
speaks of the King of Israel as "our king" (vii. 5).
Yet he seems to blame the revolt of Jeroboam I.
(i. 11, viii. 4), although a prophet had originated it,
and he openly aspires after the reunion of the Twelve
Tribes under a king of the House of David (iii. 5).
He points more distinctly to Assyria, which he frequently names as the scourge of the Divine vengeance,
and indicates how vain is the hope of the party which
relied on the alliance of Egypt.[2] He speaks with far
more distinct contempt of the cherub at Bethel and
the shrine at Gilgal, and says scornfully, "Thy calf, O
Samaria, has cast thee off."[3] Shalmaneser had taken
Beth-Arbel, and dashed to pieces mother and children.
Such would be the fate of the cities of Israel.[4] Yet
Hosea, like Amos, cannot conclude with words of

[1] Hos. iv. 15–19.

[2] Hos. v. 13, vii. 11, viii. 9, ix. 3–6, xi. 5, xii. 1, xiv. 3. It
must be borne in mind that the cuneiform inscriptions prove that
Assyria had burst into sight like a lurid comet on the horizon far
earlier than we had supposed. Jehu had paid tribute to Shalmaneser
as far back as B.C. 842, more than a century before Menahem's
tribute in 738. The destruction which Hosea prophesied took place
within thirty-one years of his prophecies—probably in B.C. 722,
when Sargon finished the siege of Samaria begun by Shalmaneser.
The king Hoshea was perhaps taken captive before the siege.

[3] Hos. viii. 5, ix. 15.

[4] Hos. x. 13, 14.

wrath and woe, and he ends with a lovely song of the days when Ephraim should be restored, after her true repentance, by the loving tenderness of God.

Jeroboam II. must have been aware of some at least of these prophecies. Those of Hosea must have impressed him all the more because Hosea was a prophet of his own kingdom, and all of his allusions were to such ancient and famous shrines of Ephraim as Mizpeh, Tabor, Bethel, Gilgal, Shechem,[1] Jezreel, and Lebanon. He was the Jeremiah of the North, and a passionate patriotism breathes through his melancholy strains. Yet in the powerful rule of Jeroboam II. he can only see a godless militarism founded upon massacre (i. 4), and he felt himself to be the prophet of decadence. Page after page rings with wailing, and with denunciations of drunkenness, robbery, and whoredom—"swearing, lying, killing, stealing, and adultery" (iv. 2).

If Jeroboam was as wise and great as he seemed to have been, he must have seen with his own eyes the ominous clouds on the far horizon, and the deep-seated corruption which was eating like a cancer into the heart of his people. Probably, like many another great sovereign—like Marcus Aurelius when he noted the worthlessness of his son Commodus, like Charlemagne when he burst into tears at the sight of the ships of the Vikings—his thoughts were like those of the ancient and modern proverbs—"When I am dead, let earth be mixed with fire." We have no trace that Jeroboam treated Hosea as did those guilty priests to whom he was a rebuke, and who called him "a fool" and "mad" (ix. 7, 8, iv. 6–8, v. 2). Yet the aged king—he must have reached the unusual age

---

[1] Hos. vi. 9 : for " by consent " read " towards Shechem."

of seventy-three at least, before he ended the longest
and most successful reign in the annals of Israel—
could hardly have anticipated that within half a year
of his death his secure throne would be shaken to its
foundation, his dynasty be hurled into oblivion, and
that Israel, to whom, as long as he lived, mighty
kingdoms had curtsied, should,

> "Like a forlorn and desperate castaway,
> Do shameful execution on herself."

Yet so it was. Jeroboam II. was succeeded by no
less than six other kings, but he was the last who
died a natural death. Every one of his successors fell
a victim to the assassin or the conqueror. His son
Zachariah ("Remembered by Jehovah") succeeded him
(B.C. 740), the fourth in descent from Jehu. Considering the long reign of his father, he must have ascended
the throne at a mature age. But he was the child
of evil times. That he should not interrupt the "calf"-
worship was a matter of course ; but if he be the king
of whom we catch a glimpse in Hos. vii. 2–7, we see
that he partook deeply of the depravity of his day.
We are there presented with a deplorable picture.
There was thievishness at home, and bands of marauding
bandits began to appear from abroad. The king was
surrounded by a desperate knot of wicked counsellors,
who fooled him to the top of his bent, and corrupted
him to the utmost of his capacity. They were all
scorners and adulterers, whose furious passions the
prophet compares to the glowing heat of an oven heated
by the baker. They made the king glad with their
wickedness, and the princes with lying flatteries. On
the royal birthday, apparently at some public feast,
this band of infamous revellers, who were the boon

companions of Zachariah, first made him sick with
bottles of wine, and then having set an ambush in
waiting, murdered the effeminate and self-indulgent
debauchee before all the people.[1] The scene reads
like the assassination of a Commodus or an Elagabalus.
No one was likely to raise a hand in his favour. Like
our Edward II., he was a weakling who followed a
great and warlike father. It was evident that troublous
times were near at hand, and nothing but the worst
disasters could ensue if there was no one better than
such a drunkard as Zachariah to stand at the helm
of state.

So did the dynasty of the mighty Jehu expire like
a torch blown out in stench and smoke.

Its close is memorable most of all because it evoked
the magnificent moral and spiritual teaching of Hebrew
prophecy. The ideal prophet and the ordinary priest
are as necessarily opposed to each other as the saint
and the formalist. The glory of prophecy lies in its
recognition that right is always right, and wrong always
wrong, apart from all expediency and all casuistry,
apart from "all prejudices, private interests, and partial
affections." "What Jehovah demands," they taught,
"is righteousness—neither more nor less ; what He
hates is injustice. Sin or offence to the Deity is a
thing of purely moral character. Morality is that for

---

[1] Hos. vii. 3-7. The allusions are vague, but we see a drunken
king among his drunken princes, surrounded by wicked plotters who
have flattered his vices. He is ignorant of his peril. The subjects
aid the rulers in these abominations. All are blazing, like an oven,
with passion and infamy, and only rest (as the baker does) to acquire
new strength for inflaming their burning desires. At the dawn their
treachery blazes into the crime of murder, and in the wine-sick fever-
heat of the banquet the king is murdered by his corrupt intimates
(see my *Minor Prophets*, p. 78).

the sake of which all other things exist ; it is the most essential element of all sincere religion.   It is no postulate, no idea, but a necessity and a fact ; the most intensely living of human powers—Jehovah, the God of hosts.   In wrath, in ruin, this holy reality makes its existence known ; it annihilates all that is hollow and false." [1]

[1] Wellhausen, *Isr. and Jud.*, 85.

CHAPTER XIX

AZARIAH-UZZIAH (B.C. 783(?)—737)

JOTHAM (B.C. 737—735)

2 KINGS xv. 1—7, 32—38

"This is vanity, and it is a sore sickness."—ECCLES. vi. 2.

BEFORE we watch the last "glimmerings and decays" of the Northern Kingdom, we must once more revert to the fortunes of the House of David. Judah partook of the better fortunes of Israel. She, too, enjoyed the respite caused by the crippling of the power of Syria, and the cessation from aggression of the Assyrian kings, who, for a century, were either unambitious monarchs like Assurdan, or were engaged in fighting on their own northern and eastern frontiers. Judah, too, like Israel, was happy in the long and wise governance of a faithful king.

This king was Azariah ("My strength is Jehovah"), the son of Amaziah. He is called Uzziah by the Chronicler, and in some verses of the brief references to his long reign in the Book of Kings. It is not certain that he was the eldest son of Amaziah;[1] but he was so distinctly the ablest, that, at the age of sixteen, he was chosen king by "all the people." His official

---

[1] Hence, perhaps, the expression that the people "took him." If Amaziah died at fifty-nine, he probably had other sons.

title to the world must have been Azariah, for in that form his name occurs in the Assyrian records. Uzziah seems to have been the more familiar title which he bore among his people.[1] There seems to be an allusion to both names—Jehovah-his-helper, and Jehovah-his-strength—in the Chronicles: "God *helped him*, and made him to prosper; and his name spread far abroad, and he was marvellously helped, *till he was strong*."

The Book of Kings only devotes a few verses to him; but from the Chronicler we learn much more about his prosperous activity. His first achievement was to recover and fortify the port of Elath, on the Red Sea,[2] and to reduce the Edomites to the position they had held in the earlier days of his father's reign. This gave security to his commerce, and at once "his name spread far abroad, even to the entering in of Egypt."

He next subdued the Philistines; took Gath, Jabneh, and Ashdod; dismantled their fortifications, filled them with Hebrew colonists, and "smote all Palestine with a rod."[3]

He then chastised the roving Arabs of the Negeb or south country in Gur-Baal and Maon, and suppressed their plundering incursions.

His next achievement was to reduce the Ammonite

---

[1] Compare the interchange of the names Azariel and Uzziel (Exod. vi. 18) in 1 Chron. vi. 2, 18. Azariah means "Jehovah hath helped," and Uzziah "Strength of Jehovah." It is just possible that his name was changed at his accession, as the chief priest also was named Azariah, and confusion might otherwise have arisen.

[2] 2 Chron. xxvi. 2-15.

[3] Isa. xiv. 29. A mixed language arose in this district in consequence (Neh. xiii. 24; Zech. ix. 6). The word Palestine only applies strictly to the district of Philistia. Milton uses it, with his usual accuracy, in the description of Dagon as

That twice-battered god of Palestine."

Emîrs to the position of tributaries, and to enforce
from them rights of pasturage for his large flocks, not
only in the low country (*shephelah*), but in the southern
wilderness (*midbar*), and in the *carmels* or fertile
grounds among the Trans-Jordanic hills.

Having thus subdued his enemies on all sides, he
turned his attention to home affairs—built towers,
strengthened the walls of Jerusalem at its most assail-
able points, provided catapults and other instruments
of war, and rendered a permanent benefit to Jerusalem
by irrigation and the storing of rain-water in tanks.

All these improvements so greatly increased his
wealth and importance that he was able to renew
David's old force of heroes (Gibborim), and to increase
their number from six hundred to two thousand six
hundred, whom he carefully enrolled, equipped with
armour, and trained in the use of engines of war.
And he not only extended his boundaries southwards
and eastwards, but appears to have been strong enough,
after the death of Jeroboam II., to make an expedition
northwards, and to have headed a Syrian coalition
against Tiglath-Pileser III., in B.C. 738. He is mentioned in two notable fragments of the annals of the
eighth year of this Assyrian king. He is there called
Azrijahu, and both his forces and those of Hamath
seem to have suffered a defeat.[1]

It is distressing to find that a king so good and so
great ended his days in overwhelming and irretrievable

---

[1] Uzziah's opposition to Assyria—of which there seems to be no
doubt, for he must be the Azrijahu of the *Eponym Canon*—took place
about 738, and was a coalition movement. But it gives rise to great
chronological and other difficulties. As the solution of these is at
present only conjectural, I refer to Schrader (E. Tr.), ii. 211–219. He
is called Azrijahu Jahudai.

misfortune. The glorious reign had a ghastly conclusion. All that the historian tells us is that "the Lord smote the king, so that he was a leper, and dwelt in a several [*i.e.*, a separate] house." The word rendered "a several house" may perhaps mean (as in the margin of the A.V.) "a lazar house," like the *Beit el Massakin* or "house of the unfortunate," the hospital or abode of lepers, outside the walls of Jerusalem.[1] The rendering is uncertain, but it is by no means impossible that the prevalence of the affliction had, even in those early days, created a retreat for those thus smitten, especially as they formed a numerous class. Obviously the king could no more fulfil his royal duties. A leper becomes a horrible object, and no one would have been more anxious than the unhappy Azariah himself to conceal his aspect from the eyes of his people.[2] His son Jotham was set over the household ; and though he is not called a regent or joint-king—for this institution does not seem to have existed among the ancient Hebrews —he acted as judge over the people of the land.

We are told that Isaiah wrote the annals of this king's reign, but we do not know whether it was from Isaiah's biography that the Chronicler took the story of the manner in which Uzziah was smitten with leprosy. The Chronicler says that his heart was puffed up with his successes and his prosperity, and that he was consequently led to thrust himself into the priest's

---

[1] 2 Kings xv. 5 (2 Chron. xxvi. 21, "a house of sickness"). LXX., ἐν οἴκῳ ἀφφουσώθ ; Vulg., *in domo libera seorsim.* Comp. Lev. xiii. 46. Theodoret understands it that he was shut up privately in his own palace : ἔνδον ἐν θαλάμῳ ὑπ' οὐδένος ὁρώμενος. Symmachus, ἐγκεκλεισμένος.

[2] His misfortune must have made a deep impression, and is possibly alluded to in Hos. iv. 4 : "For thy people are as they that strive with the priest."

office by burning incense in the Temple.[1] Solomon
appears to have done the same without the least question
of opposition; but now the times were changed, and
Azariah, the high priest,[2] and eighty of his colleagues
went in a body to prevent Uzziah, to rebuke him, and
to order him out of the Holy Place.[3] The opposition
kindled him into the fiercest anger, and at this moment
of hot altercation the red spot of leprosy suddenly rose
and burned upon his forehead. The priests looked
with horror on the fatal sign; and the stricken king,
himself horrified at this awful visitation of God, ceased
to resist the priests, and rushed forth to relieve the
Temple of his unclean presence, and to linger out the
sad remnant of his days in the living death of that
most dishonouring disease. Surely no man was ever
smitten down from the summits of splendour to a lower
abyss of unspeakable calamity! We can but trust that
the misery only laid waste the few last years of his
reign; for Jotham was twenty-five when he began to
reign, and he must have been more than a mere boy
when he was set to perform his father's duties.

So the glory of Uzziah faded into dust and darkness.
At the age of sixty-eight death came as the welcome
release from his miseries, and "they buried him with
his fathers in the City of David." The Levitically

---

[1] The Chronicler attributes the good part of his reign to the influence of an unknown Zechariah, "who had understanding in the
visions of God"; and says that when Zechariah died Uzziah altered
for the worse.

[2] This high priest, Azariah, is only mentioned elsewhere in
2 Chron. xxvi. 17, 20.

[3] Josephus says that he had put on a priestly robe, and that a great
feast was going on, and that the earthquake (Amos i. 1; Zech. xiv. 5)
happened at the moment, which broke the Temple roof, so that a
sunbeam smote his head and produced the leprosy. We here see
the growth of the Haggadah.

scrupulous Chronicler adds that he was not laid in the actual sepulchre of his fathers, but in a field of burial which belonged to them—" for they said, He is a leper." The general outline of his reign resembled that of his father's. It began well ; it fell by pride ; it closed in misery.

The annals of his son Jotham were not eventful, and he died at the age of forty-one or earlier. He is said to have reigned sixteen years, but there are insuperable difficulties about the chronology of his reign, which can only be solved by hazardous conjectures.[1] He was a good king, "howbeit the high places were not removed." The Chronicler speaks of him chiefly as a builder. He built or restored the northern gate of the Temple, and defended Judah with fortresses and towns. But the glory and strength of his father's reign faded away under his rule. He did indeed suppress a revolt of the Ammonites, and exacted from them a heavy indemnity ; but shortly afterwards the inaction of Assyria led to an alliance between Pekah, King of Israel, and Rezin, King of Damascus ; and these kings harassed Jotham—perhaps because he refused to become a member of their coalition. The good king must also have been pained by the signs of moral degeneracy all around him in the customs of his own people. It was "in the year that King Uzziah died " that Isaiah saw his first vision, and he gives us a deplorable picture of contemporary laxity. Whatever the king may have been, the princes were no better than " rulers of Sodom," and the people were "people of Gomorrha." There was abundance of lip-worship, but little sincerity ; plentiful religionism, but no godliness. Superstition went

---

[1] For instance, two verses earlier (2 Kings xv. 30) we read of the twentieth year of Jotham.

hand in hand with formalism, and the scrupulosity of outward service was made a substitute for righteousness and true holiness. This was the deadliest characteristic of this epoch, as we find it portrayed in the first chapter of Isaiah. The faithful city had become a harlot—but not in outward semblance. She " reflected heaven on her surface, and hid Gomorrha in her heart." Righteousness had dwelt in her—but now murderers ; but the murderers wore phylacteries, and for a pretence made long prayers. It was this deep-seated hypocrisy, this pretence of religion without the reality, which called forth the loudest crashes of Isaiah's thunder. There is more hope for a country avowedly guilty and irreligious than for one which makes its scrupulous ceremonialism a cloak of maliciousness. And thus there lay at the heart of Isaiah's message that protest for bare morality, as constituting the end and the essence of religion, which we find in all the earliest and greatest prophets :—

" Hear the word of the Lord, ye rulers of Sodom ;
    Give ear unto the Law of our God, ye people of Gomorrha!
    To what purpose is the multitude of your sacrifices unto me ? saith
        the Lord.
    I am full of the burnt-offerings of rams, and the fat of fed beasts ;
    And I delight not in the blood of bullocks, or of lambs, or of
        he-goats.
    When ye come to see My face, who hath required this at your
        hands, to trample My courts ?
    Bring no more vain oblations !
    Incense is an abomination unto Me :
    New moon and sabbath, the calling of assemblies—
    I cannot away with iniquity and the solemn meeting. . . .
    Wash you ! make you clean ! " [1]

Of Jotham we hear nothing more. He died a natural

---

[1] Isa. i. 10-17.

death at an early age. If the years of his reign are counted from the time when his father's affliction devolved on him the responsibilities of office, it is probable that he did not long survive the illustrious leper, but was buried soon after him in the City of David his father.

CHAPTER XX

THE AGONY OF THE NORTHERN KINGDOM

	B.C.			B.C.
Shallum ...	... 740	Pekahiah	...	737—735
Menahem ...	... 740—737	Pekah ...	...	735—734

2 KINGS xv. 8—31

"Blood toucheth blood."—Hos. iv. 2.

"The revolters are profuse in murders."—Hos. v. 2.

"They have set up kings, but not by Me: they have made princes, and I knew it not."—Hos. viii. 4.

"Non tam reges fuere quam fures, latrones, et tyranni."—WITSIUS, *Decaph.*, 326.

WITH the death of Zachariah begins the acute agony of Israel's dissolution. Four kings were murdered in forty years. Indeed, within two centuries, at least nine kings—Nadab, Elah, Zimri, Tibni, Jehoram, Zachariah, Shallum, Pekahiah, Pekah—had made the steps of the throne slippery with blood. Except in the house of Omri, all the kings of Israel either left no sons or left them to be slain. Amos, by his vision of the basket of summer fruit, had intimated that the sins of Israel were ripe for punishment, and the lesson had been emphasised by the paronomasia of *quits*, "summer," and *queets*, "end."[1] The prophet had singled four out of many crimes as the cause of her ruin. They were (1) greedy oppression of the poor;

---

[1] Amos vi. 2.

(2) land-grabbing; (3) licentious and idolatrous revelries; (4) cruelty to poor debtors, and rioting on the proceeds of unjust gains.   In their drunkenness they even tempted God's Nazarites to break their vows. "Behold," saith Jehovah, "I am pressed under you, as a cart is pressed that is full of sheaves."   Even women shared in the common intoxication, and showed themselves utterly shameless, so that Amos contemptuously calls them "fat cows of Bashan upon the mountain of Samaria," whom in punishment the brutal conqueror should drag by the hair out of their ivory palaces, as a fisherman drags his prey out of the water by hooks.[1]

Shallum, son of Jabesh, the unknown murderer of Zachariah and the usurper of his throne, suffered the fate of Zimri, and only reigned for one month.   If his conspiracy was marked by the odious circumstances of treachery and corruption, which we infer from the allusions of Hosea, Shallum richly deserved the swift retribution which fell upon him.   He seems to have destroyed Zachariah by means of his best affections— under the guise of friendship, in the midst of boon companionship.   But the slayer of his master had no peace, and from the moment of his fruitless crime the unhappy country seems to have been plunged in the horrors of civil war.   Some dim glimpses of the evils of the day are gained from the earlier Zechariah,[2] just as some dim glimpses of the horrors of Rome in the days of the later Cæsars may be seen in the Apocalypse. The prophet speaks of three shepherds cut off in one

[1] Amos iv. 1–3.

[2] It is probable that our present Book of Zechariah is composed of the works of three prophets of different dates, each of whom may have borne that name.   See my *Minor Prophets* (" Men of the Bible " Series).

month, who abhorred God, and His soul was impatient
at them.[1]

Just as Galba, Otho, and Vitellius flit across the
stage of the Empire amid war and assassinations, so
Zachariah and Shallum are swept away by "dagger-
thrusts through the purple." Was there a third?
Ewald and others think that they detect a shadowy
outline of him and of his name in 2 Kings xv. 10. If
so, his name was Kobolam, but we know no more of
him beyond the fact that "he was, and is not." For
the sacred annals are but little concerned with this
bloody phantasmagoria of feeble kings, who ruled amid
usurpation, anarchy, hostile attacks from without, and
civil war within. "Israel," said Hosea, "hath cast off
the thing that is good: the enemy shall pursue him.
They have set up kings, but not by Me: they have
made princes, and I knew it not." "They are all as
hot as an oven, and have devoured their judges; all
their kings have fallen; there is none among them that
calleth upon Me."[2]

It was perhaps during this distracted epoch that for
one moment there was an attempt to place the ruling
authority of the nation in the hands of the prophet
himself. So it would appear from Zech. xi. 7–14. Of
course these chapters may be allegorical throughout, as,
in any case, they are in great part. But if so, it becomes
more difficult to understand the meaning. What the
prophet says is as follows:—

---

[1] Zech. xi. 8. In 2 Kings xv. 10 the LXX. read καὶ ἐπάταξεν αὐτὸν
ἐν κεβλαάμ; and Ewald thinks that "before the people" (קָבָלְ־עָם)
is really a proper name of the third king in one month—"and
Kobolam slew him." There is insufficient ground for this, though a
similar name is found in Assyrian records.

[2] Hos. viii. 3, vii. 7.

First, as though he saw the terrible conflagration of the Assyrian tyranny rolling southwards, and felt it to be irresistible, he bids Lebanon open her doors, that the fire may devour her cedars. There is perhaps an allusion to the death of Jeroboam II. in the words, "Howl fir tree, for the cedar is fallen." He sees in vision the forces of devastation raging among the oaks of Bashan, the forest and the vintage, while the shepherds cry, and the ousted lions roar in vain. Then Jehovah bids him feed "the flock of the slaughter"—the flock sold remorselessly by its rich possessors, and slain, and left unpitied, as the people were despoiled by its nobles and its kings. The prophet undertakes the charge of the miserable flock, and takes two staves, one of which he calls "Prosperity," and the other "Union." While he was thus engaged three shepherds were cut off in one month,[1] whom he loathed, and who abhorred him. But he finds his task hopeless, and flings it up; and in sign that his covenant with the people is broken, he breaks his staff "Prosperity." The nation refused to pay him anything for his services, except a paltry sum of thirty pieces of silver, and these he disdainfully flung into the sacred treasury.[2] Then seeing that all hope of union between Israel and Judah was at an end, he broke his staff "Union." Lastly, Jehovah says He will raise up a foolish, neglectful, cruel shepherd who would care for nothing but to eat the flesh of the fat and break the hoofs of the flock. And as for this worthless shepherd, the sword should be upon his arm and in his right eye; his arm shall be dried up, and his right eye utterly darkened.

By this cruel and self-seeking shepherd is probably

---

[1] Zachariah, Shallum, Kobolam (?).

[2] Zech. xi. 1-17 (Heb. 13).

meant Menahem.   He had been, according to Josephus, the captain of the guard, and was living at Tirzah, the old beautiful capital of the land.   From Tirzah, where he occupied the position of the captain of the chariots, he marched on the ill-supported Shallum.   Samaria apparently offered no protection to the usurper. Menahem defeated him and put him to death.   Then he proceeded to enforce the allegiance of the rest of the country.   An otherwise unknown town of the name of Tiphsach[1] ventured to resist him.   Menahem conquered it, and perhaps thinking, as Machiavelli thought, that princes had better exhibit their utmost cruelty at first, to deter any further opposition, he let loose his ferocity on the town in a way which created a shuddering remembrance.   As though he had been one of the ferocious heathen, who had never been restrained by the knowledge of God, he exhibited the extreme of callous brutality by ripping up all the women that were with child.[2]   In this he followed the remorseless example of Hazael.   Hosea had prophesied that this should be the fate of Samaria ;[3] Amos had denounced the Ammonities for acting thus in the cities of Gilead ;[4]

---

[1] That this was Thapsacus on the Euphrates (1 Kings iv. 24), and that Menahem was in a position to march northward three hundred miles, and offer so deadly and wanton an insult to the might of Assyria, is out of the question.   The name means "a ford," and might apply to any town on a river.   Thenius thinks the name is a clerical error for *Tappuach*, between Ephraim and Manasseh (Josh. xvii. 7, 8).

[2] Josephus says, ὠμότητος ὑπερβολὴν οὐ καταλιπὼν οὐδὲ ἀγριότητος. It is said that the same crime was committed in 1861 by a Mexican bandit.   Machiavelli says, "He who violently and without just right usurps a crown must use cruelty, if cruelty becomes necessary, once for all" (*De princ.*, 8).

[3] 2 Kings viii. 12 ; Hos. xiii. 16.

Amos i. 13.

Shalmaneser III. had, in B.C. 732, thus avenged himself on the resistance of Beth-Arbel,[1] and Assyria was ultimately to meet an analogous retribution,[2] as also was Babylon.[3] But that a king of Ephraim, of God's chosen people, should act thus to his own brethren was a horrible portent, ominous of swift destruction.

And the vengeance came. Menahem reigned, at least in name, for ten years; for the sword which had slain mothers with their unborn infants reduced the stricken people to terrified silence. But at this epoch Assyria woke once more from her lethargy, and became the scourge of God to the guilty people and their guiltier kings. For a whole century the Assyrians had either been governed by kings who had abjured the lust of blood and conquest, or had been too seriously occupied on their own eastern and northern frontiers to intermeddle with the southern kingdoms, or break down the barriers erected by the confederacy of Hamath and Damascus between Nineveh and the weaker principalities of Palestine. But now (B.C. 745) there came to the throne a king who, in Chaldæa, was known by the name of Pul, and in Assyria by the name of Tiglath-Pileser;[4] and being too formidable for any power to stay his path, he marched against Menahem. Already he was lord of the world from the Caspian to

---

[1] Hos. x. 14. This allusion is, however, uncertain. Shalmaneser III. is not elsewhere found abbreviated into Shalman. Some suppose him to be a Moabitish king, Salamannu, who was a vassal of Tiglath-Pileser. The LXX., Vulg., etc., identify him with the Zalmunna of Judg. viii. 18. Psalm lxxxiii. 11 renders the word *ex domo ejus qui judicavit Baal* (*i.e.*, Gideon). Beth-Arbel is either Arbela in Galilee, or Irbid, north-east of Pella.

[2] Nah. iii. 10.

[3] Isa. xiii. 16.

[4] The two predecessors of Tiglath-Pileser (*Tuklat-abal-isarra*) were Assurdayan and Assurnirari.

the Gulf of Persia; already he had subdued Babylonia, Elam, Media, Armenia, eastward—Mesopotamia and Syria westward. Who was Menahem, the petty usurper of a tenth-rate kingdom, that he should withstand his power or even retard his advance?

The cruel usurper was in no condition to resist him. The brand of Cain was on him and his kingdom. How could the weak, impoverished, harassed troops of Israel stand up in battle against those numberless serried ranks, or withstand their tremendous discipline? If the very name of Persia once struck terror into the brave Greeks before the spell of Persian ascendency was broken at Marathon, Thermopylæ, and Salamis, much more did the name of Assyria make the hearts of the wretched Israelites melt like water. They now for the first time saw those bearded warriors with their broad swords, their tremendous bows, their fierce, sensual faces, their thickset figures. In the language of the prophets we still hear the echo of the fears which they excited by their swift, unfaltering marches, their sleepless vigilance, their girded loins, stout sandals, and barbed arrows.[1]

"Their horses' hoofs," says Isaiah, "shall be like flint, and their wheels like a whirlwind: their roaring shall be like a lion, they shall roar like young lions; yea, they shall roar, and lay hold of the prey, and carry it away safe, and there shall be none to deliver. And they shall roar against them in that day like the roaring of the sea; and if one look unto the land, behold darkness and distress, and the light is darkened in the clouds thereof."

Ancient Assyria lay beneath the Snowy Mountains of Kurdistan; and its capital, Nineveh—near Mosul,

---

[1] Isa. v. 26-29.

Kouyunjik, and Neby-Junus—lay six hundred miles from the Gulf of Persia. The people spoke, as their descendants still speak, a dialect of Syriac, akin both grammatically and structurally to Hebrew. Assyria was constantly at war with Babylonia; but for the most part the kings of Assyria held Babylon in subjection, and Tiglath-Pileser was a king of the Chaldæans under the name Pul, as well as a king of Nineveh.

Menahem was warrior enough to know how hopeless it was to struggle against these trained forces. He was not even secure on his own throne. He thought it best to offer himself without resistance as a feudatory, if the Assyrian King would confirm his sovereignty. Tiglath-Pileser did not think Menahem worth more trouble, and was graciously pleased to accept by way of bribe a tribute of a thousand talents of silver, or about £125,000. This, however, as we learn from the *Eponym Canon*, was not all. Menahem had to pay a further tribute year by year. Later on, in 738, Shalmaneser mentions Minik-himmi (Menahem), as well as Rasunnu (Rezin), among his tributaries.

The Assyrian withdrew, and Menahem had to exact this vast sum of money from his miserable subjects. To tax the poor was hopeless. He found that there were some sixty thousand persons who might be reckoned among the wealthier farmers and proprietors,[1] and from them he at once exacted fifty shekels of silver (more than £3) apiece. Probably they thought that to pay the sum demanded was not too heavy a price for the retirement of these frightful Assyrians, whose forces Tiglath-Pileser did not withdraw until he had the money in hand. The event took place in 738, and Tiglath-Pileser continued to reign till 727. How bitterly

[1] Comp. Job xx. 15; Ruth ii. 1.

the burden of foreign tribute was felt appears from Hos. viii. 9, 10, which should perhaps be rendered, " They are gone up to Assyria like a wild ass alone by himself. Ephraim hath hired lovers. And they begin to be minished by reason of the burden of the king of princes." " The king of princes " was the haughty title usurped by Tiglath-Pileser, who said, " Are not my princes all of them kings ? " (Isa. x. 8).

All this was a fulfilment of what Hosea had foreseen :—

" Ephraim is oppressed, he is crushed in judgment, because he was content to walk after vanity. Therefore am I unto Ephraim as a moth, and to the house of Judah as rottenness. When Ephraim saw his sickness, and the house of Judah his wound, then went Ephraim to Assyria, and sent unto an avenging king :[1] yet could he not heal you, nor cure you of your wound. For I will be unto Ephraim as a lion, and as a young lion to the House of Judah : I, even I, will tear and go away ; I will take away, and none shall rescue him." The Assyrian was irresistible, because he was the destined instrument of the wrath of God. The " mixing with the heathens " was a sin, and Israel in cooing to Assyria was like a foolish dove ; but the day sometimes comes to doomed nations when no course can save them from the fate which they have provoked.[2]

---

[1] Hos. v. 11-13. Comp. x. 6: "It [Samaria] shall be carried to Assyria for a present unto King Jareb." Sayce (*Bab. and Orient. Records*, December 1887) thinks that Jareb may have been the original name of Sargon, and so too Neubauer, *Zeitschr. für Assyr.*, 1886. The Vulg. renders King Jareb *ad regem ultorem*, and so too Symmachus. Aquila and Theodotion have δικαζόμενον. It may be the name of an unknown king of Assyria, or of Pul, or of Sargon—R.V., margin, "a king that should contend."

[2] Hos. vii. 8-12.

Not long afterwards Menahem died, and he had sufficiently established his rule to be succeeded as a matter of course by his son Pekahiah.   But

"Revenge and wrong bring forth their kind;
The foul cubs like their parents are."

Samaria had fearful object-lessons in the apparently immediate success of murder and rebellion.   The prize looked near and splendid : the vengeance might be belated or might not come.   Of Pekahiah we are told absolutely nothing but that he reigned two years, with this stereotyped addition, that "he did that which was evil in the sight of Jehovah" by continuing the calf-worship.[1]   After this brief and uneventful reign, his captain Pekah got together fifty fierce Gileadites, and with the aid of two otherwise unknown friends, Argob and Arieh, murdered Pekahiah in his own harem.[2] Argob was probably so named from the district in Bashan, and Arieh was a fit name for a lion-faced Gadite (1 Chron. xii. 8).

The sacred historian troubles himself but little about these kings.   His annals of them are brief to extreme meagreness.   Like the prophet, he viewed them as God-abandoned phantoms of guilty royalty.

"They that cry unto me, My God, we, Israel, know thee.
Israel hath cast off that which is good :
The enemy shall pursue him.
They have set up kings, but not by Me ;
They have removed them, and I knew it not:
Of their silver and their gold have they made them idols,
That they may be cut off.
He hath cast off thy calf, O Samaria."

---

[1] Josephus says, τῇ τοῦ πατρὸς ἀκολουθήσας ὠμότητι.
[2] 2 Kings xv. 25, A.V.. "in the palace of the king's house" (armon), rather "fortress." For the character of the Gileadites see 1 Chron. xii. 8, xxvi. 31.

Probably Pekahiah was, as so often happens, the weak son of a vigorous father. The times could not tolerate incapable sovereigns; and the fact that Pekah not only maintained himself on the throne for twenty years,[1] but was able to take active steps of aggression against Jerusalem, seems to show that he was a man of some administrative capacity. If he had not achieved political and military importance, it would hardly have been worth while for a fierce and powerful king like Rezin, the last king of Syria, to form so close an alliance with him. Probably Rezin saw that his throne and his very existence were in danger, and Pekah wished with Rezin's aid to resist to the uttermost the encroachments of Assyria, and escape the burdensome tribute which Menahem had paid. Indeed, it may well be that Pekahiah's passive continuance of this tribute may have been distasteful to the people of the land, and that they condoned or even tacitly aided Pekah's rebellion in order to get rid of it, and to find protection in an abler monarch. It was the last, perhaps the only, chance for the kings of Syria and of Israel. As we hear no more of Hamath as a member of the alliance, we must suppose that it had now been reduced to impotence and vassalage by the all-powerful Assyrian. If, however, there was to be any over-

---

[1] The length of Pekah's reign is most doubtful. If the periods assigned to the reigns in the Northern and Southern Kingdoms be added together up to the Fall of Samaria in the sixth year of Hezekiah (2 Kings xviii. 9, 10), it will be found that the Southern chronology is twenty years longer than the Northern. G. Smith would alter the text, and make Jeroboam II. reign fifty-one years and Pekah thirty years; others invent an interregnum of eleven years between Jeroboam II. and Zachariah, and an anarchy of nine years before Hoshea's accession; others shorten Pekah's reign to *one* year.

balance to the colossal menace of Nineveh, it could only be by a large confederacy; and it may have been the refusal of Jotham to join that confederacy, on the death of his father Uzziah, which caused the joint invasion of Rezin and Pekah to force him to accept their alliance or to suppress him altogether. In that case they might have formed a close alliance with Egypt, and the forces of the united South might, they fancied, prove to be a match for the forces of the North.[1]

Whatever designs they may have formed against Jotham, or to whatever extent they may have annoyed him, it was not till the reign of his son Ahaz that they became formidable and ruinous. Of this we shall say more in recounting the reign of Ahaz. All that we need now remark is that their bold aggression on Judah became the cause of utter destruction to them both. They advanced against Ahaz, and overran his helpless country. It was their object to depose the descendant of David, and to crown in his place a certain unnamed "son of *Tabeal*," whom Ewald supposed to have been a Syrian, but whose name may possibly furnish a specimen of the later Jewish device of Gematria.[2]

It is not impossible that behind these events we may find the efforts and yearnings of a party which cared more for Israel's unity than for David's throne. Such a party may easily have sprung up during the splendid, prosperous reign of Jeroboam II. It has been conjectured by some that the election of Uzziah by the people—delayed, according to one reckoning, for twelve years—was in reality the triumph of the party which

---

[1] 2 Kings xv. 37.　　　[2] Vide *infra*.

felt an unquenchable allegiance to David's house. In
Deut. xxxiii. Reuben is put before Judah ; Jeshurun
(*i.e.*, Israel) is magnified far more than Judah ; and
some Northern shrine in Zebulon, as well as the Temple,
is celebrated as a sanctuary.[1] That there were men in
Jerusalem who preferred Rezin and Pekahiah to their
own king is clearly stated in Isaiah. He compares
them to those who prefer a turbid torrent to a soft,
sweet stream. " Because," he says, " this people
despise the waters of Shiloah that flow softly, and
take delight in Rezin and Remaliah's son ; now, therefore, the Lord bringeth upon them the waters of the
river, strong and many, even the King of Assyria, and
all his glory."[2] Isaiah seems to have had a contempt
for the whole attack. He told Ahaz not to fear for the
stumps of those two smoking firebrands Rezin, King
of Syria, and the Israelitish usurper, whom he only
condescends to call " Remaliah's son." He promises
the trembling Ahaz that, since he had faithlessly
refused a sign, God would give him a sign. The sign
was that the young woman who accompanied Isaiah—
perhaps his youthful wife—should bear a son, whose
name should be called Immanuel ; and that before the
child Immanuel—whose designation, " God with us,"
was an omen of the loftiest hope—should be of an age
to distinguish evil from good, the Northern land, which
Ahaz abhorred, should be forsaken of both her kings.

The prophecy came true in every particular. Rezin
and Pekah swept all before them, and besieged
Jerusalem ; but they wasted their time in vain before
the fortifications which Jotham had strengthened and

---

[1] Deut. xxxiii. 19: "They [Zebulon] shall call the peoples unto
the mountain : there shall they offer the sacrifices of righteousness."

[2] Isa. viii. 6, 7.

repaired. Obliged to raise the siege, Rezin carried his army southward, and indemnified himself by seizing Elath, by driving out the Judæan garrison, and replacing them with Syrians.[1] It was the last gleam of Syrian success, before the final overthrow of Damascus which prophecy had often and emphatically foretold.

Pekah also withdrew his forces—no doubt compelled to do so by the step which Ahaz took in his desperation. For now the King of Judah invoked the protection and invited the active interference of Tiglath-Pileser against his enemies—"to save him out of the hand of the King of Syria, and out of the hand of the King of Israel, who were risen up against him."

Rezin and Damascus first felt the might of the Assyrian's conquering arm. The account of his decisive conquest is preserved in the *Eponym Canon*, and the passages which refer to the defeat of the Syrians will be found in the First Appendix at the end of the volume. It appears from the monuments that Rezin (Rasannu) lost not only his kingdom, but his life.

It is the death-knell of Aramæan greatness, as Amos had foretold.

"Thus saith Jehovah :
For three transgressions of Damascus, and for four,
I will not turn away the punishment thereof ;
Because they have threshed Gilead with threshing instruments of
    iron :
But I will send a fire into the house of Hazael,
Which shall devour the palaces of Benhadad.
And I will break the bar of Damascus,[2]
And cut off him that sitteth [on the throne] in the Valley of Aven,[3]

---

[1] Perhaps we should read Edomites (2 Kings xvi. 6).
[2] The bar of its city gate.
[3] Bikath-Aven—"The cleft of Aven"—Cœle Syria, or Hollow

> And him that holdeth the sceptre from Beth-Eden : [1]
> And the people of Syria shall go into captivity unto Kir, [2]
> Saith Jehovah."

Rezin was slain—how we know not; very probably by one of the horrible methods of torture—by being flayed alive, or decapitated, or having his lips and nose cut off—which were practised by these demon-kings of Nineveh.

Nor did Pekah escape. Tiglath-Pileser advanced against the northern part of his dominions, and afflicted the land of Zebulon and Naphtali. Ijon; Abel-beth-Maachah, the city of Elisha; Zanoah, the ancient sanctuary of Kedesh-Naphtali, the home of the hero Barak; Hazor, the former capital of the Canaanitish king Jabin; Gilead; Galilee,—all submitted to him, apparently without striking a serious blow. He dealt with the miserable inhabitants in the way familiar to kings of Assyria. He deported them *en masse* into a strange country of which they did not understand the language, and in which they were reduced to hopeless subjection, while he supplied their places by aliens from various parts of his own dominions. There could be no securer method of reducing to paralysis all their national aspirations. Strangers in a strange land, they forgot their nationality, forgot their religion, forgot their language, forgot their traditions. Their sole resource was to plunge into material pursuits, and to melt away into indistinguishable obliteration among

---

Syria, still called by the Arabs El-Bukāa. Comp. Josh. xi. 17, xii. 7. Aven—or " Vanity "—is perhaps Heliopolis or Baalbek. Comp. Ezek. xxx. 17.

[1] Perhaps Beit el Jame, "House of Paradise"—about eight hours from Damascus (Porter, *Five Years in Syria*, i. 313).

[2] Kir, in Armenia—the land of their origin (Amos ix. 7).

the neighbouring heathen. It was the beginning of
the Northern Captivity—of the loss of the Ten Tribes.

As Tiglath-Pileser thus permanently subdued and
depopulated the land of the Northern Tribes, it is a
Jewish tradition that at this time he carried away the
golden "calf" from Dan among his spoils.[1] Scripture
does not record the fact, though in Hosea (viii. 5) there
may be an allusion to the fate of that at Bethel, whether
the right version be "He hath cast off thy calf, O
Samaria," or "Thy calf, O Samaria, hath cast thee
off."[2] "The workman made it," he continues; "therefore it is not God: for the calf of Samaria shall be
broken in pieces." And again (x. 5): "The people of
Samaria shall fear because of the heifer of the House of
Vanity: for the people thereof shall mourn over it, and
the *chemarim* [*i.e.*, the black-robed false priests thereof]
shall tremble for it, for the glory thereof, because it is
departed. It [the idol] shall also be carried to Assyria
for a present to King Combat."

For a time Pekah escaped; but unsuccess is fatal to
a murderous usurper, weakened by the loss and plunder
of dominions which he is unable to defend. Instead of
wasting time in the siege of a strong city like Samaria,
Tiglath-Pileser in all probability stirred up Hoshea, the

---

[1] But, after all, was there a golden calf at Dan? It is scarcely ever
alluded to, and the notion that there was one may have arisen (1) from
a corruption or mistaken rendering of the text in 1 Kings xii. 29, and
(2) from the existence there of the idolatrous ephod. See Klostermann, *ad loc.*; Isa. ix. 8–17.

[2] LXX., Ἀποτρίψαι τὸν μόσχον σοῦ, Σαμάρεια; Vulg., *Projectus est
vitulus tuus, Samaria.* Orelli renders it, "Abscheulich ist dein Kalb,
O Samaria." In Jer. xlvi. 15 we read (of Egypt), "Why is thy strong
one swept away?" where the true reading may be, "Hath Khaph [*i.e.*,
Apis], thy chosen one, fled?" LXX., Ἄπις ὁ μόσχος σοῦ, ὁ ἐκλεκτός. So
Amos had prophesied that the "god of Dan" and the "way of
Beersheba" should fall for evermore (Amos viii. 14).

son of Elah, to rise in conspiracy against his master and
slay him. For Pekah and Israel seem to have made
light of the Northern raid. They said in their pride
and stoutness of heart, "The bricks are fallen down,
but we will build with new stones : the sycomores are
cut down, but we will change them into cedars." Such
pretence of security was ill-timed and senseless, and
Isaiah denounced it. "Therefore," he said, "Jehovah
hath set up against Israel the adversaries of Rezin [*i.e.,*
the Assyrians], and hath stirred up his enemies ; the
Syrians on the east, and the Philistines on the west ;
and they have devoured Israel with open mouth. For
all this His anger is not turned away, but His hand is
stretched out still. Yet the people have not turned
unto Him that smote them, neither have they sought
the Lord of hosts. Therefore Jehovah hath cut off
from Israel palm-branch and rush in one day. The
elder and the honourable man, he is the head ; and the
prophet that speaketh lies, he is the tail. For they that
lead this people cause them to err, and they that are led
of them are swallowed up." [1]

The following verses furnish one of the numerous
pictures of the anarchy and abounding misery of these
evil days. "For wickedness burneth as the fire : it
devoureth the briers and thorns ; yea, it kindleth in the
thickets of the forest, and they roll upwards in thick
clouds of smoke. Through the wrath of the Lord of
hosts is the land burnt up ; the people also are the fuel
of fire : *no man spareth his brother.* And one shall
snatch on the right, and be hungry ; and he shall eat on
the left hand, and they shall not be satisfied : they shall
eat every man the flesh of his own arm : Manasseh,

---

[1] Isa. ix. 11-16. With this passage comp. 2 Kings xxiii. 5; Zeph.
i. 4; Hos. vii. 9, 10.

Ephraim; and Ephraim, Manasseh: and they together shall be against Judah. For all this His anger is not turned away, but His hand is stretched out still."

We are told in the Book of Kings that Pekah reigned for twenty years; but some of these later reigns must be shortened to suit the exigencies of known chronological data. It seems probable that he occupied the throne for a much shorter time.[1]

Such was the weakened, harassed, vassal kingdom—the gaunt spectre of itself—to the throne of which, after a period of anarchy and chaos, Hoshea, by conspiracy and murder, succeeded as the miserable feudatory of Assyria.

---

[1] Tiglath-Pileser says: " Pakaha, their king, I killed: Ausi [Hoshea] I placed over them. The distant land of Bit-Khumri [the "house of Omri"]—*the whole of its inhabitants*, with their goods—I carried away to Asshur" (B.C. 734). In this year he mentions Ahaz among his tributaries.

CHAPTER XXI

HOSHEA, AND THE FALL OF THE NORTHERN KINGDOM

B.C. 734—725

2 KINGS xvii. 1—41

"As for Samaria, her king is cut off as the foam upon the water."—Hos. x. 7.

AS a matter of convenience, we follow our English Bible in calling the prophet by the name Hosea, and the nineteenth, last, and best king of Israel Hoshea. The names, however, are identical (הושע), and mean "Salvation"—the name borne by Joshua also in his earlier days. In the irony of history the name of the last king of Ephraim was thus identical with that of her earliest and greatest hero, just as the last of Roman emperors bore the double name of the Founder of Rome and the Founder of the Empire—Romulus Augustulus. By a yet deeper irony of events the king in whose reign came the final precipitation of ruin wore the name which signified deliverance from it.

And more and more, as time went on, the prophet Hosea felt that he had no word of present hope or comfort for the king his namesake. It was the more brilliant lot of Isaiah, in the Southern Kingdom, to kindle the ardour of a generous courage. Like Tyrtæus, who roused the Spartans to feel their own greatness—

like Demosthenes, who hurled the might of Athens against Philip of Macedon—like Chatham, "bidding England be of good cheer, and hurl defiance at her foes"—like Pitt, pouring forth, in the days of the Napoleonic terror, "the indomitable language of courage and of hope,"—Isaiah was missioned to encourage Judah to despise first the mighty Syrian, and then the mightier Assyrian. Far different was the lot of Hosea, who could only be the denouncer of an inevitable doom. His sad function was like that of Phocion after Chæroneia, of Hannibal after Zama, of Thiers after Sedan: he had to utter the Cassandra-voices of prophecy, which his besotted and demented contemporaries—among whom the priests were the worst of all[1]—despised and flouted until the time for repentance had gone by for ever.

True it is that Hosea could not be content—what true heart could?—to breathe nothing but the language of reprobation and despair. Israel had been "yoked to his two transgressions,"[2] but Jehovah could not give up His love for His chosen people :—

"How shall I give thee up, Ephraim?
How shall I surrender thee, Israel?
How shall I make thee as Admah?
How shall I treat thee as Zeboim?
Mine heart is turned within Me;
I am wholly filled with compassion!

---

[1] Hos. iv. 4; v. 1, "Hear ye this, O priests . . . ye have been a snare on Mizpah," etc.; vi. 9, "The company of the priests murder by the way to Shechem."

[2] Hos. x. 10 (so. R.V., and in the main the versions after the Hebrew margin). LXX., ἐν τῷ παιδεύεσθαι αὐτοὺς ἐν ταῖς δύσιν ἀδικίαις αὐτῶν; Vulg., *cum corripientur propter duas iniquitates suas*"; A.V., "When they shall bind themselves in their two furrows." I believe that the "*two* iniquities" may mean *two* cherubs at Bethel. See x. 15: "So shall Bethel do unto you because of the evil of your evil"

> I will not execute the fierceness of Mine anger ;
> I will not again destroy Ephraim :
> For I am God, and not man.
> The Holy One in the midst of thee !
> I will not come to exterminate !
> They shall come after Jehovah as after a lion that roars !
> For he shall roar, and his sons shall come hurrying from the west,
> They shall come hurrying as a bird out of Egypt,
> And as a dove out of the land of Assyria;
> And I will cause them to dwell in their houses,
> > Saith Jehovah."[1]

Alas ! the gleam of alleviation was imaginary rather than actual. The prophet's wish was father to his thought. He had prophesied that Israel should be scattered in all lands (ix. 3, 12, 17, xiii. 3–16). This was true ; and it did not prove true, except in some higher ideal sense, that " Israel shall again dwell in his own land " (xiv. 4–7) in prosperity and joy.

The date of Hoshea's accession is uncertain, and we cannot tell in what sense we are to understand his reign as having lasted " nine years."[2] We have no grounds for accepting the statement of Josephus (*Antt.,* IX. xiii. 1), that Hoshea had been a friend of Pekah and plotted against him. Tiglath-Pileser expressly says that he himself slew Pekah and appointed Hoshea.[3] His must have been, at the best, a pitiful and humiliating reign. He owed his purely vassal sovereignty to Assyrian patronage. He probably did as well for Israel as was in his power. Singular to relate, he is the only one of all the kings of Israel of whom the historian has a word of commendation ; for while we

---

[1] Hos. xi. 8–11.

[2] 2 Kings xvii. 1 is inconsistent with xv. 30, 33, and it is wholly useless for our purpose to enter into complicated chronological hypotheses, every one of which may be erroneous.

[3] Schrader, *K. A. T.,* p. 255.

are told that "he did that which was evil in the sight of the Lord," it is added that it was "not as the kings of Israel that were before him." But we do not know wherein either his evil-doing or his superiority consisted. The Rabbis guess that he did not replace the golden calf at Dan which Tiglath-Pileser had taken away (Hos. x. 6); or that he did not prevent his subjects from going to Hezekiah's passover.[1] "It seems like a harsh jest," says Ewald, "that this Hoshea, who was better than all his predecessors, was to be the last king." But so it has often been in history. The vengeance of the French Revolution smote the innocent and harmless Louis XVI. and Marie Antoinette—not Louis XIV., or Louis XV. and Madame du Pompadour.

His patron Tiglath-Pileser ended his magnificent reign of conquest in 727, soon after he had seated Hoshea on the throne. The removal of his strong grasp on the helm caused immediate revolt. Phœnicia especially asserted her independence against Shalmaneser IV. He seems to have spent five years in an unavailing attempt to capture Island-Tyre. Meanwhile, the internal troubles which had harassed and weakened Egypt ceased, and a strong Ethiopian king named Sabaco established his rule over the whole country.[2]

---

[1] *Seder Olam*, xxii. 2; 2 Chron. xxx. 6–11.

[2] See Herod., ii. 137; called So (Heb., Sô or Seve) in 2 Kings xvii. 4. Perhaps Shebek, the founder of the twenty-fifth dynasty. LXX., Σηγώρ; Vulg., *Sua*; Manetho, *Sabachon*. In the *Eponym Canon* he is called an Egyptian general, *Sibakhi*, who helped Gaza against Assyria, and was defeated. The *ka* appended at the end of his name (Egyptian Shaba-ka) is thought by some to be the Cushite article. The race of the priest Hirhor died out with Piankhi, and the Ethiopians elected a noble named Kashta. Shabak was his son. He conquered Sais, and burnt his rival Bek-en-raut alive (B.C. 724). His dynasty ruled for fifty years; he was succeeded by Sevechus (Shabatok), and he by Tehrak (Tirhakah).

It was perhaps the hope that Phœnicia might hold out against the Assyrian, and that the Egyptian might protect Samaria, which kindled in the mind of Hoshea the delusive plan of freeing himself and his impoverished land from the grinding tribute imposed by Nineveh. While Shalmaneser [1] was trying to quell Tyre, Hoshea, having received promises of assistance from Sabaco, withheld the " presents "—the *minchah*, as the tribute is euphemistically called—which he had hitherto paid. Seeing the danger of a powerful coalition, Shalmaneser swept down on Samaria in 724. Possibly he defeated the army of Israel in the plain of Jezreel (Hos. i. 5), and got hold of the person of Hoshea. Josephus says that he " besieged him "; but the sacred historian only tells us that " he shut him up, and bound him in prison." Whether Hoshea was taken in battle, or betrayed by the Assyrian party in Samaria, or whether he went in person to see if he could pacify the ruthless conqueror, he henceforth disappears from history " like foam "—or like a chip or a bubble—" upon the water." We do not know whether he was put to death, but we infer from an allusion in Micah that he was subjected to the cruel indignities in which the Assyrians delighted; for the prophet says, " They shall smite the Judge of Israel with a rod upon the cheek." [2] Perhaps in the title " Judge " (Shophet, *suffes*) we may see a sign that Hoshea's royalty was little more than the shadow of a name.

Having thus got rid of the king, Shalmaneser proceeded to invest the capital. But Samaria was strongly fortified upon its hill, and the Jewish race has again

---

[1] His name means " Salmân, pardon." We have no monuments or inscriptions of this king; only an imperial weight.

[2] Mic. v. 1

and again shown—as it showed so conspicuously in the
final crisis of its destiny, when Jerusalem defied the
terrible armies of Rome—that with walls to protect
them they could pluck up a terrible courage and
endurance from despair. Strong as Assyria was, the
capital of Ephraim for three years resisted her beleaguering host and her crashing battering-rams. About
all the anguish which prevailed within the city, and the
wild vicissitudes of orgy and starvation, history is silent.
But prophecy tells us that the sorrows of a travailing
woman came upon the now kingless city. They
drank to the dregs the cup of fury.[1] The saddest
Northern prophet, "the Jeremiah of Israel," sings the
dirge of Israel's saddest king.[2]

> "I am become to them as a lion;
> As a leopard will I watch by the way;
> I will meet them as a bear bereaved of her whelps,
> And rend the caul of their heart,
> And there will I devour them like a lioness:
> The beast of the field shall tear them. . . .
> Where now is thy king, that he may save thee in all thy cities
> And thy judges, of whom thou saidst, 'Give me a king and
>   prince'?
> I give thee a king in Mine anger,
> And take him away in My wrath."

For three years Samaria held out. During the siege
Shalmaneser died, and was succeeded by Sargon, who—
though he vaguely talks of "the kings his ancestors,"
and says that he had been preceded by three hundred
and thirty Assyrian dynasts—never names his father,
and seems to have been a usurping general.[3]

---

[1] Hos. xiii. 13.

[2] Hos. xiii. 7-11. The prophecy is rhythmic, though not written in
actual poetry.

[3] Till the discovery of the Assyrian records, Sargon (Sharru-kenu,
'the faithful king') was but a name. The Jews knew but little of

Sabaco remained inactive, and basely deserted the miserable people which had relied on his protection. In this conduct Egypt was true to its historic character of untrustworthiness and inertness. Both in Israel and in Judah there were two political parties. One relied on the strength of Egypt; the other counselled submission to Assyria, or—in the hour when it became necessary to defy Assyria—confidence in God. Egypt was as frail a support as one of her own paper-reeds, which bent under the weight, and broke and ran into the hand of every one who leaned on it.

Sargon did not raze the city, and we see from the *Eponym Canon* that its inhabitants were still strong enough some years later to take part in a futile revolt. But we have one dreadful glimpse of the horrors which he inflicted upon it. They were the inevitable punish-

---

him. He is but once mentioned in Scripture (Isa. **xx.** 1), and was probably confused by some Jews with other kings. Yet he reigned sixteen years (722–705), and his records give the annals of fifteen campaigns. In 720 he crushed a confederacy headed by Yahubid of Hamath, and reduced that city to a "heap of ruins." He then advanced against Hanno, King of Gaza, who was in alliance with Sabaco, and defeated the combined forces of the Philistines and Egyptians at Raphia, half-way between Gaza and the Wady-el-Arish, "the torrent [*nachal*] of Egypt." Sargon was at the time too much occupied with other enemies to pursue his advantage over Egypt; for Armenia, Media, and other countries needed his attention. This encouraged Ashdod to rebel, and its king, Azuri, refused his tribute (see Isa. **xx.** 1). Sargon deposed him, and put his brother Ahimit in his place. Relying on Egyptian promises, Philistia joined Judah, Edom, and Moab in defying Assyria. They deposed Ahimit as an Assyrian nominee, and put Yaman in his place. Egypt, as usual, failed to help, and in 711 the Assyrian Turtan, or Commander-in-chief, took Ashdod after three years' resistance, and carried its people into captivity. The punishment of Egypt was reserved for the subsequent reigns of Esarhaddon (681–668) and Assurbanipal. See Driver's *Isaiah xlv.* (Isa. **xx.**). Isa. **xiv.** 29–32 is an ode of triumph for the Fall of Philistia.

ment of every conquered city which had dared to resist
the Assyrian arm.

> "Samaria shall bear her guilt,
> For she hath rebelled against her God.
> They shall fall by the sword:
> Their infants shall be dashed in pieces,
> And their women in child shall be ripped up."[1]

Sargon's own record of the matter on the tablets at
Khorsabad is: "I besieged, took, and occupied the city
of Samaria, and carried into captivity twenty-seven
thousand two hundred and eighty of its inhabitants.
I changed the former government of this country, and
placed over it lieutenants of my own. And Sebeh,
Sultan of Egypt, came to Raphia to fight against me.
They met me, and I routed them. Sebeh fled."[2] The
Assyrians were occupied in the unsuccessful siege of
Tyre between 720–715, during which years Sargon put
down Yahubid of Hamath, whose revolt had been aided
by Damascus and Samaria. In 710 he marched against
Ashdod (Isa. xx. 1). In 709 he defeated Merodach-
Baladan at Dur-Yakin, and reconquered Chaldæa,
deporting some of the population into Samaria. In
704, in the fifteenth year of his reign, he was assas-
sinated, after a career of victory. He inscribes on his
palace at Khorsabad a prayer to his god Assur, that,
after his toils and conquests, "I may be preserved for
the long years of a long life, for the happiness of my
body, for the satisfaction of my heart. May I accu-
mulate in this palace immense treasures, the booties of
all countries, the products of mountains and valleys."
Assur and the gods of Chaldæa were invoked in vain;

---

[1] Hos. xiii. 16.
[2] See De Hincks in *Journ. of Sacr. Lit.*, October 1858; Layard,
Nin. and Bab., i. 148.

the prayer was scattered to the winds, and the murderer's dagger was the comment on Sargon's happy anticipations of peace and splendour.

Israel fell unpitied by her southern neighbour, for Judah was still smarting under memories of the old contempt and injury of Joash ben-Jehoahaz, and the more recent wrongs inflicted by Pekah and Rezin. Isaiah exults over the fate of Samaria, while he points the moral of her fall to the drunken priests and prophets of Jerusalem. " Woe," he says, "to the crown of pride of the drunkards of Ephraim, and to the fading flower of his glorious beauty, which is on the head of the fat valley of them that are smitten down with wine ! Behold, the Lord hath a mighty and strong one [*i.e.*, the Assyrian] ; as a tempest of hail, a destroying storm, as a tempest of mighty water overflowing, shall he cast down to the earth with violence. The crown of pride, the drunkards of Ephraim, shall be trodden underfoot : and the fading flower of his glorious beauty, which is on the head of the fat valley, shall be as the first ripe fig before the summer ; which when he that looketh upon it seeth, while it is yet in his hand he eateth it up." [1] Israel had begun in hostility to Judah, and perished by it at last.

Such, then, was the end of the once brilliant kingdom of Israel—the kingdom which, even so late as the reign of Jeroboam II., seemed to have a great future before it. No one could have foreseen beforehand that, when, with the prophetic encouragement of Ahijah, Jeroboam I. established his sovereignty over the greater, richer, and more flourishing part of the land assigned to the sons of Jacob, the new kingdom should fall into utter ruin and destruction after only two and a half centuries

---

[1] Isa. xxviii. 1-4.

of existence, and its tribes melt away amid the surrounding nations, and sink into a mixed and semi-heathen
race without any further nationality or distinctive
history. It seemed far less probable that the mere
fragment of the Southern Kingdom, after retaining its
separate existence for more than one hundred and sixty
years longer than its more powerful brother, should
continue to endure as a nation till the end of time.
Such was the design of God's providence, and we
know no more. The Northern Kingdom had, up to
this time, produced the greatest and most numerous
prophets—Ahijah, Elijah, Elisha, Micaiah, Jonah,
Amos, Hosea, Nahum, and many more.[1] It had also
produced the loveliest and most enduring poetry in
the Song of Songs, the Song of Deborah, and other
contributions to the Books of Jashar, and of the Wars
of Jehovah. It had also brought into vigour the
earliest and best historic literature, the narratives of
the Elohist and the Jehovist. These immortal legacies
of the religious spirit of the Northern Kingdom were
incomparably superior in moral and enduring value to
the Levitic jejuneness of the Priestly Code, with its
hierarchic interests and ineffectual rules, which, in the
exaggerated supremacy attached to rites, proved to be
the final blight of an unspiritual Judaism. Israel had
also been superior in prowess and in deeds of war,
and in the days of Joash ben-Jehoahaz ben-Jehu had
barely conceded to Judah a right to separate existence.
More than all this, the apostasies of Judah, from the
days of Solomon downwards, were quite as heinous as
Jezebel's Baal-worship, and far more deadly than the
irregular but not at first idolatrous cultus of Bethel.

---

[1] 2 Kings xvii. 13, "by all the prophets, and all the *seers*" (*chôseh*).
Hävernick thinks that the *nebî'im* were such *officially*.

The prophets are careful to teach Judah that if she was spared it was not because of any good deservings.[1] Yet now the cedar was scathed and smitten down, and its boughs were rent and scattered; and the thistle had escaped the wild beast's tread!

In the former volume we glanced at some of the causes of this, and the blessings which resulted from it. The central and chiefest blessing was, first, the preservation of a purer form of monotheism, and a loftier ideal of religion—though only realised by a few in Judah—than had ever prevailed in the Northern Tribes; secondly, and above all, the development of that inspiring Messianic prophecy which was to be fulfilled seven centuries later, when He who was David's Son and David's Lord came to our lost race from the bosom of the Father, and brought life and immortality to light.

And it was the work purely of " God's unseen providence, by men nicknamed ' Chance,' " which, dealing with nations as the potter with his clay, chooses some to honour and some to dishonour. For, as all the prophets are anxious to remind the Judæan Kingdom, their success, the procrastination of their downfall, their restoration from captivity, were not due to any merits of their own. The Jews were and ever had been a stiff-necked nation; and though some of their kings had been faithful servants of Jehovah, yet many of them —like Rehoboam, and Ahaz, and Manasseh—exceeded in wickedness and inexcusable apostasy the least faithful of the worshippers at Gilgal and Bethel. They were plainly reminded of their nothingness: " And thou shalt speak and say before the Lord thy God,

---

[1] See Amos ii. 4, 5; Isa. xxviii. 15; Jer. xvi. 19, 20; Ezek. xx. 13-30, etc.

A Syrian ready to perish was my father, and he went down into Egypt, and sojourned there with a few, and became there a nation."[1] "Fear not, thou worm Jacob: I will help thee."[2]

But this was the end of the Ten Tribes. Nor must we say that Hosea's prediction of mercy was laughed to scorn by the irony of events, when he had given it as God's promise that—

> "I will not execute the fierceness of Mine anger,
> I will not again destroy Israel ;
> For I am God, and not man."[3]

The words mean that mercy is God's chiefest and most essential attribute ; and, after all, a nation is composed of families and individuals, and in political extinction there may have been many families and individuals in Israel, like that of Tobias, and like that of Anna, the prophetess of the tribe of Asher, who found, either in their far exile, or among the scattered Jews who still peopled the old territories, a peace which was impossible during the distracted anarchy and deepening corruption of the whole period which had elapsed since the founding of the house of Omri. In any case God knows and loves His own. The words,

> "I will not execute the fierceness of Mine anger ;
> For I am God, and not man,"

might stand for an epitome of much that is most precious in Holy Writ. God's orthodoxy is the truth ; and the truth remaineth, though man's orthodoxy exercises all its fury and all its baseness to overwhelm it. What hope has any man, even a St. Paul—what hope had even the Lord Himself—before the harsh,

---

[1] Deut. xxvi. 5.   [2] Isa. xli. 14.   [3] Hos. xi. 9.

self-interested tribunals of human judgment, or of that
purely external religionism which has always shown
itself more brutal and more blundering than secular
cruelty ? What chance has there been, humanly speaking, for God's best saints, prophets, and reformers, when
priests, popes, or inquisitors have been their judges ?
If God resembled those generations of unresisted eccle-
siastics, whose chief resort has been the syllogism of
violence, and whose main arguments have been the
torture-chamber and the stake, what hope could there
possibly be for the vast majority of mankind but those
endless torments by the terrors of which corrupt
Churches have forced their tyranny upon the crushed
liberties and the paralysed conscience of mankind ?
The Indian sage was right who said that " God can
only be truly described by the words No! No!"—
that is, by repudiating multitudes of the ignoble and
cruel basenesses which religious teachers have imagined
or invented respecting Him. Because God is God, and
not man—God, not a tyrant or an inquisitor—God,
with the great compassionate heart of unfathomable
tenderness,—therefore, in all who truly love Him,
perfect love casteth out fear, because fear hath torment.
Sin means ruin ; yet God is love.[1]

The historian of the Kings here digresses, in a manner
unusual to the Old Testament, to give us a most interesting glimpse of the fate of the conquered people,
and the origin of the race which was known to after-
ages by the name "Samaritan."

Sargon, when he had sacked the capital, carried out
the policy of deportation which had now been estab-

---

[1] See my *Minor Prophets*, 6-97.

lished by the Assyrian kings. He achieved the double
purpose of populating the capital and province of
Nineveh, while he reduced subject nations to inanition,
by sweeping away all the chief of the inhabitants from
conquered states, and settling them in his own more
immediate dominions. There they would be reduced
to impotence, and mingle with the races among whom
their lot would henceforth be cast. He therefore
"carried Israel away" into Assyria, and placed them
in Halah, north of Thapsacus, on the Euphrates, and
in Habor, the river of Gozan [1]—*i.e.*, on the river
in Northern Assyria which still bears the name of
Khabour, and flows into the Euphrates—and in the
cities of the Medes.[2] He replaced the old population
by Dinaites, Tarpelites, Apharsathchites, Susanchites,
Elamites, Dehavites, and Babylonians, after carrying
away the great bulk of the better-class population.[3]

After this the historian pauses to sum up and
emphasise once more the main lesson of his narrative.
It is that "righteousness exalteth a nation, and sin
is the reproach of any people." God had called His
son Israel out of Egypt, delivered His chosen from
Pharaoh, given them a pleasant land ; but "Israel had
sinned against Jehovah their God, and had feared
other gods, and walked in the statutes of the heathen."
They had failed therefore in fulfilling the very purpose

---

[1] Not as in A.V., " Habor, *by* the river of Gozan."

[2] 2 Kings xvii. 6. The LXX. has "rivers" and "mountains":
ἐν ᾿Αλαὲ καὶ ἐν ᾿Αβὼρ ποταμοῖς Γωζὰν καὶ ὄρη Μήδων. The river is not
Ezekiel's Chebar. These deportations *en masse* of a whole population,
with their women and children, their waggons and flocks, are depicted
on Sargon's series of tablets in his splendid palace at Khorsabad.

[3] Ezra iv. 10. "The great and noble Asnapper" of the passage
is either some Assyrian general, or a confusion of the name
Assurbanipal.

for which they had been set apart. They had been intended "to uplift among the nations the banner of righteousness" and the banner of the One True God. Instead of this, they were seduced by the heathen ritual of

"Gay religions full of pomp and gold."

They decked out alien institutions,[1] and alike in frequented and populous places—"from the tower of the watchmen to the fenced city"—set up *matstseboth* (A.V., "pillars") and *Asherim* on every high hill. The green trees became *obumbratrices scelerum*, the secret bowers of their iniquities. They burnt incense on the *bamoth*, and served idols, and wrought wickedness. Useless had been the voices of all the prophets and the seers. They went after vain things, and became vain. Beginning with the two "calves," they proceeded to lewd and orgiastic idolatries. Ahab and Jezebel seduced them into Tyrian Baal-worship. From the Assyrians they learnt and practised the adoration o the host of heaven.[2] From Moab and Ammon the) borrowed the abominable rites of Moloch, and used divination and enchantments by means of belomancy (Ezek. xxi. 21, 22) and necromancy, and sold them selves to do wickedness.

---

[1] 2 Kings xvii. 9. Heb., "covered"; A.V. and R.V., "did secretly, rather "perfidiously"; LXX., ἠμφιέσαντο λόγους ἀδίκους κατὰ κύριον Vulg., *Et offenderunt verbis non rectis dominum suum.*

[2] Star-worship is not mentioned in the Book of the Covenan (Exod. xx.–xxiii.) or the oldest sections of the Mosaic Law. It i first forbidden in Deut. iv. 19, xvii. 3, when contact with Syrian and Assyrians made it known (comp. Job xxxi. 26–28; Jer. viii. 2 xix. 13; Zeph. i. 5). The language of 2 Kings vii.–xxiii. frequently reflects the prohibitions of Deuteronomy (see Deut. xii. 2, 30, 31 iv. 19, v. 7, 8, xvi. 21, xviii. 10, xxxi. 16, etc.

Nor was this all. These idolatries, with their guilty ritualism, were not confined to Israel, but also

"Infected Zion's daughters with like heat,
Whose wanton passions in the sacred porch
Ezekiel saw, when, by the vision led,
His eye surveyed the dark idolatries
Of alienated Judah."

And thus, when Jehovah afflicted the seed of Israel and cast them out of His sight, Judah also had to feel the stroke of retribution.[1]

And it is idle to object that even if Israel had been faithful she must have inevitably perished before the superior might of Damascus, or Nineveh, or Babylon. How can we tell? It is not possible for us thus to write unwritten history, and there is absolutely nothing to show that the surmise is correct. In the days of David, of Uzziah, of Jeroboam II., Judah and Israel had shown what they could achieve. Had they been strong in faithfulness to Jehovah, and in the righteousness which that faith required, they would have shown an invincible strength amid the moral enervation of the surrounding people. They might have held their own by welding into one strong kingdom the whole of Palestine, including Philistia, Phœnicia, the Negeb, and the Trans-Jordanic region. They might have consolidated the sway which they at various times attained southwards, as far as the Red Sea port of Elath; northwards over Aram and Damascus, as far as the Hamath on the Orontes; eastwards to Thapsacus on the Euphrates; westward to the Isles of the Gentiles.

---

[1] In 2 Kings xvii. 11, for "they did wicked things," the LXX. has κοινωνοὺς (*i.e.*, *qedeshim*) ἐχάραξαν καὶ ἑταιρίδας (*qedeshôth*); *i.e.*, they had depraved *hieroduli* of both sexes. Comp. Hos. iv. 14; Gen. xxxviii. 21 (where the allusion is to one of the votaries of Asherah).

There is nothing improbable, still less impossible, in the view that, if the Israelites had truly served Jehovah and obeyed His laws, they might then have permanently established the monarchy which was ideally regarded as their inheritance, and which for brief and fitful periods they partially maintained. And such a monarchy, held together by warrior statesmen, strong and righteous, and above all secure in the blessing of God, would have been a thoroughly adequate counterpoise, not only to dilatory and distracted Egypt, which had long ceased to be aggressive, but even to brutal Assyria, which prevailed in no small measure because of the isolation and mutual dissension of these southern principalities.

But, as it was, "Assyria and Egypt—the two world-powers in the dawn of history, the two chief sources of ancient civilisation, the twin giant-empires which bounded the Israelite people on the right hand and on the left—were cruel neighbours, between whom the ill-fated nation was tossed to and fro in wanton sport like a shuttlecock. They were cruel friends before whom it must cringe in turns, praying sometimes for help, suing sometimes for very life—alternate scourges in the hand of the Divine wrath. Now it is the fly of Egypt, and now it is the bee of Assyria, whose ruthless swarms issue forth at the word of Jehovah, settling in the holes of the rocks, and upon all thorns, and upon all bushes, with deadly sting, fatal to man and beast, devastating the land far and wide. Holding the poor Israelite in their relentless embrace, they threatened ever and again to crush him by their grip. Like the fabled rocks which frowned over the narrow straits of the Bosporus, they would crash together and annihilate the helpless craft which the storms of destiny had placed at their mercy. Israel reeled under their successive blows. As was the beginning, so was the end. As the captivity of Egypt had been the cradle of the nation, so was the captivity of Assyria to be its tomb." [1]

In any case the principle of the historian remains unshaken. Sin is weakness; idolatry is folly and rebellion; uncleanness is decrepitude. St. Paul was not thinking of this ancient Philosophy of History when he wrote his Epistle to the Romans; yet the intense and masterly sketch which he gives of that moral corruption which brought about the long, slow, agonising dissolution of the beauty that was Greece, and the grandeur that was Rome, is one of its strongest justifications. His view only differs from the summary before us in the power of its eloquence and the profoundness of its psychologic insight. He says the same thing as the historian of the Kings, only in words of greater power and wider reach, when he writes: " For the wrath of God is revealed from heaven against all ungodliness and unrighteousness of men, who hold down the truth in unrighteousness. Knowing God, they glorified Him not as God, neither gave thanks; but became vain in their reasonings " ($\dot{\epsilon}\mu\alpha\tau\alpha\iota\dot{\omega}\theta\eta\sigma\alpha\nu$, the very word used in the LXX. in 2 Kings xvii. 15), "and their senseless heart was darkened. Professing themselves to be wise, they became fools" (words which might describe the expediency-policy of Jeroboam I., and its fatal consequences), "and changed the glory of the incorruptible God for the likeness of an image of corruptible man, and of birds, and four-footed beasts, and creeping things. For this cause God gave them up to passions of dishonour, and unto

---

[1] Bishop Lightfoot, *Sermons*, p. 267.

a reprobate mind, to do those things which are not fitting, being filled with all unrighteousness, wickedness, covetousness, maliciousness, full of envy, murder, strife, deceit, malignity,"—and so on, through a long catalogue of iniquities which are identical with those which we find so burningly denounced on the pages of the prophets of Israel and Judah.

Even a Machiavelli, cool and cynical and audacious as was his scepticism, could see and admit that faithfulness to religion is the secret of the happiness and prosperity of states.[1] An irreligious society tends inevitably and always to be a dissolute society ; and a " dissolute society is the most tragic spectacle which history has ever to present—a nest of disease, of jealousy, of dissensions, of ruin, and despair, whose last hope is to be washed off the world and disappear. Such societies must die sooner or later of their own gangrene, of their own corruption, because the infection of evil, spreading into unbounded selfishness, ever intensifying and reproducing passions which defeat their own aim, can never end in anything but moral dissolution." We need not look further than the collapse of France after the battle of Sedan, and the cause to which that collapse was attributed, not only by Christians, but by her own most worldly and sceptical writers, to see that the same causes ever issue and will issue in the same ruinous effects.

In order to complete the history of the Northern Kingdom, the historian here anticipates the order of time

---

[1] "La quale Religione se ne Principi della Republica Christiana si fusse mantenuta, secondo che dal dottore d'essa ne fu ordinato, sarebbero gli State e le Republiche Christiane più unite e più felici assai ch' elle non sono " (*Discorsi*, i. 12).

by telling us what happened to the mongrel population whom Sargon transplanted into central Ephraim in place of the old inhabitants.

The king, we are told, brought them from Babylon —which was at this time under the rule of Assyria; from Cuthah—by which seems to be meant some part of Mesopotamia near Babylon;[1] from Avva, or Ivah— probably the same as Ahavah or Hit, on the Euphrates, north-west of Babylon; from Sepharvaim, or Sippara, also on the Euphrates;[2] and from Hamath, on the Orontes, which had not long remained under Jeroboam II.[3] It must not be supposed that the whole population of Ephraim was deported; that was a physical impossibility. Although we are told in Assyrian annals that Sargon carried away with him so vast a number of captives, it is, of course, clear that the lowest and poorest part of the population was left.[4] We can imagine the wild confusion which arose when they found themselves compelled to share the dismantled palaces and abandoned estates of the wealthy with the horde of new colonists, whose language, in all probability, they but imperfectly understood. There must have been many a tumult, many a scene of horror, such as took place in the long antagonism of Normans

---

[1] 2 Kings xvii. 24. Comp. xviii. 34. Hence the later Jews comprehensively called the Samaritans Cuthites. Comp. 2 Kings xix. 13 Isa. xxxvii. 13.

[2] Heliopolis, Ptolemy, v. 18, § 7; Isa. xxxvi. 19. Here, according to the Chaldæan legends, Xisuthrus buried his tablets about the Creation, etc.

[3] From Ezra iv. 2 some infer that the main immigrants were introduced by Esarhaddon, who did not succeed till B.C. 681. He claims to have colonised Syria.

[4] So we see from 2 Kings xix. 13, which applies to the reign of Hezekiah.

and Saxons in England, before the immigrants and the relics of the former populace settled down to amalgamation and mutual tolerance.

Sargon is said to have carried away with him the golden calf or calves of Bethel, as Tiglath-Pileser is said by the Rabbis to have carried away that of Dan.[1] He also took away with him all the educated classes, and all the teachers of religion.[2] No one was left to instruct the ignorant inhabitants; and, as Hosea had prophesied, there was neither a sacrifice, nor a pillar, nor an ephod, and not even teraphim to which they could resort.[3] Naturally enough, the disunited dregs of an old and of a new population had no clear knowledge of religion. They "feared not Jehovah." The sparseness of inhabitants, with its consequent neglect of agriculture, caused the increase of wild beasts among them. There had always been lions and bears in "the swellings of Jordan,"[4] and in all the lonelier parts of the land; and to this day there are leopards in the woods of Carmel, and hyænas and jackals in many regions. Conscious of their miserable and godless condition, and afflicted by the lions, which they regarded as a sign of Jehovah's anger, the Ephraimites sent a message to the King of Assyria. They only claimed Jehovah as their local god, and complained that the new colonists had provoked the wrath of "the God of the land" by not knowing His "manner"—that

---

[1] See Appendix, "The Golden Calves."

[2] He uses the agency of "the great and noble Asnapper" (Ezra iv. 10) for the deportation (see Botta, 145; Layard, *Nin. and Bab.*, i. 148; Dr. Hincks, *Jour. of Sacr. Lit.*, October 1858), unless Asnapper be a confusion for Assurbanipal (Sardanapalus).

[3] Hos. iii. 4.

[4] See Jer. xlix. 19, l. 44; Prov. xxii. 13, etc.

is, the way in which He should be worshipped. The
consequence was that they were in danger of being
exterminated by lions. The kings of Assyria were
devoted worshippers of Assur and Merodach, but they
held the common belief of ancient polytheists that each
country had its own potent divinities. Sargon, therefore, gave orders that one of the priests of his captivity
should be sent back to Samaria, " to teach them the
manner of the god of the land." The priest selected
for the purpose returned, took up his residence at the
old shrine of Bethel, and "taught them how they
should fear Jehovah." His success was, however,
extremely limited, except among the former followers
of Jeroboam's dishonoured cult. The old religious
shrines still continued, and the immigrants used them
for the glorification of their former deities. Samaria,
therefore, witnessed the establishment of a singularly
hybrid form of religionism. The Babylonians worshipped
Succoth-Benoth,[1] perhaps Zirbanit, wife of Merodach
or Bel; the Cuthites worshipped Nergal, the Assyrian
war-god, the lion-god;[2] the Hittites, from Hamath,
worshipped Ashima or Esmûn, the god of air and
thunder, under the form of a goat;[3] the Avites preferred Nibhaz and Tartak, perhaps Saturn—unless
these names be Jewish jeers, implying that one of these

[1] Lit., "Daughter-huts" (Selden, *De Dis Syr.*, ii. 7), but probably
a transliteration. Zarpanit—"She who gives seed"—was Aphrodite
Pandemos (Mylitta—Herod., i. 199). The Rabbis—who only guess—
say she represented "the Clucking Hen"—*i.e.*, the Pleiades. There
does not seem to be any connection between Succoth and "Sakkuth,"
the various reading in Amos v. 26, which seems to be the Assyrian
Moloch.

[2] Said to be worshipped under the form of a cock.

[3] LXX., Ἐβλαζέρ. Jarchi says these deities were worshipped
under base animal forms—but it is more than doubtful.

deities had the head of a dog, and the other of an ass.[1]
More dreadful, if less ridiculous, was the worship
of the Sepharvites, who adored Adrammelech and
Anammelech, the sun-god under male and female forms,
to whom, as to Moloch, they burnt their children in the
fire. As for ministers, "they made unto them priests
from among themselves,[2] who offered sacrifices for them
in the shrines of the bamoth." Thus the whole mongrel
population "feared the Lord, and served their own
gods," as they continued to do in the days of the
annalist whose record the historian quotes. He ends
his interesting sketch with the words, that, in spite of
the Divine teaching, " these nations "—so he calls them,
and so completely does he refuse to them the dignity of
being Israel's children—feared the Lord, and served
their graven images, their children likewise, and their
children's children,—"as did their fathers, so do they
unto this day."[3]

The "unto this day" refers, no doubt, to the document from which the historian of the Kings was quoting
—perhaps about B.C. 560, in the third generation after
the fall of Samaria. A very brief glance will suffice to
indicate the future history of the Samaritans. We hear
but little of them between the present reference and
the days of Ezra and Nehemiah. By that time they
had purged themselves of these grosser idolatries, and
held themselves fit in all respects to co-operate with

---

[1] The Rabbis, from Exod. xxiii. 13 ; Josh. xxiii. 7, thought they
were bound to give scornful nicknames to heathen deities. Hence
such changes as Kir-Heres for Kir-Cheres, Beelzebub for Beelzebul,
Bethaven for Bethel, Bosheth for Baal, etc.

[2] Not as in A.V., "of the lowest of them," but "of all classes."
Comp. 1 Kings xii. 31.

[3] In 2 Kings xvii. 31–38 we again find repeated references to
Deuteronomy (iv. 23, v. 32, x. 20, etc.).

the returned exiles in the work of building the Temple. Such was not the opinion of the Jews. Ezra regarded them as "the adversaries of Judah and Israel."[1] The exiles rejected their overtures. In B.C. 409 Manasseh, a grandson of the high priest expelled by Nehemiah for an unlawful marriage with a daughter of Sanballat, of the Samaritan city of Beth-horon, built the schismatic temple on Mount Gerizim.[2] The relations of the Samaritans to the Jews became thenceforth deadly. In B.C. 175 they seconded the profane attempt of Antiochus Epiphanes to paganise the Jews, and in B.C. 130 John Hyrcanus, the Maccabee, destroyed their temple. They were accused of waylaying Jews on their way to the Feasts, and of polluting the Temple with dead bones.[3] They claimed Jewish descent (John iv. 12), but our Lord called them "aliens" (ἀλλογενής, Luke xvii. 18), and Josephus describes them as "residents from other nations" (μέτοικοι, ἀλλοεθνεῖς). They are now a rapidly dwindling community of fewer than a hundred souls—"the oldest and smallest sect in the world"—equally despised by Jews and Mohammedans. The Jews, as in the days of Christ, have no dealings with them. When Dr. Frankl, on his philanthropic visit to the Jews of the East, went to see their celebrated Pentateuch, and mentioned the fact to a Jewish lady—"What!" she exclaimed: "have you been among the worshippers of the pigeon? Take a

---

[1] Ezra iv. I. The actual word "Samaritans" occurs only once in the Old Testament, in 2 Kings xvii. 29.

[2] See Neh. xiii. 4-9, 28, 29; Jos., *Antt.*, XI. vii. 2. Josephus makes Manasseh a brother of the high priest Jaddua (B.C. 333).

[3] Jos., *Antt.*, IX. xiv. 3, XII. v. 5, XIII. ix. 1, XX. vi., XVIII. ii. 2. The bitterly hostile relations between Jews and Samaritans in the time of Christ are illustrated by Luke ix. 52-54.

purifying bath!" Regarding Gerizim as the place
which God had chosen (John iv. 20), they alone can
keep up the old tradition of the *sacrificial* passover.
For long centuries, since the Fall of Jerusalem, it is
only on Gerizim that the Paschal lambs and kids have
been actually slain and eaten, as they are to this day,
and will be, till, not long hence, the whole tribe
disappears.

CHAPTER XXII

THE REIGN OF AHAZ

B.C. 735—715

2 KINGS xvi. 1—20

> " Rimmon, whose delightful seat
> Was fair Damascus, on the fertile banks
> Of Abbana and Pharphar, lucid streams.
> He also against the House of God was bold:
> A leper once he lost, and gained a king—
> Ahaz, his sottish conqueror, whom he drew
> God's altar to disparage and displace
> For one of Syrian mode, whereon to burn
> His odious offerings, and adore the gods
> Whom he had vanquished."
>
> *Paradise Lost,* i. 467—476.

ACCORDING to our authorities, Ahaz ("Posses-sor")[1] began his reign of sixteen years at the age of twenty. Of the exactitude of these references we cannot be certain, because they also state (2 Kings xviii. 2) that Hezekiah was twenty-five years old when he began to reign, and this reduces us to the absurdity of supposing that Hezekiah was born when his father was only eleven years old.[2] We might infer from Isa. iii. 4 that Ahaz was not so old as twenty when he

---

[1] Probably a shortened form for Jehoahaz ("The Lord taketh hold"). He is called Jahuhazi in Tiglath-Pileser's inscription (Schrader, *Keilinschr.*, p. 163).

[2] For twenty-five it is not improbable that we should read fifteen.

succeeded Jotham; for there—in a terrible prophecy which can only refer to the beginning of this reign—we read, "And I will give children to be their princes, and babes shall rule over them"; or, as it should be perhaps rendered, "And with childishness, or wilfulness, shall they rule over them."

Whatever may have been the king's age, surely never king succeeded to a more distracted kingdom, or reigned over a more terrified people! If he could have had any choice in the matter, he might well have declined the fearful burden. Describing the state of things, the great prophet Isaiah, who now began his career, exclaims,—

"For, behold, the Lord, the Lord of hosts, doth take away from Jerusalem and from Judah stay and staff, the whole stay of bread, and the whole stay of water; the mighty man, and the man of war, the judge, and the prophet, and the diviner, and the elder; the captain of fifty, and the honourable man, and the counsellor, and the cunning charmer, and the skilful enchanter. And the people shall be oppressed every one by another, and every one by his neighbour: the child shall behave himself proudly against the elder, and the base against the honourable. Then a man shall take hold of his brother in the house of his father, saying, 'Thou hast clothing, be *thou our judge, and let this ruin be under thy hand*': in that day shall he lift his voice, saying, 'I will not be a builder-up; for in my house is neither bread nor clothing: ye shall not make me a ruler of the people.' For Jerusalem is ruined and Judah is fallen. The show of their countenance is against them; and they declare their sin as Sodom, and hide it not. As for My people, children are their oppressors, and women rule over them." [1]

_____

[1] Isa. iii. 1–12.

This is a frightful picture of famine—the dearth of intellect, the dearth of statesmen, of all genius, of all insight. It describes the prevalence of oppression and of ghastly destitution, accompanied by such utter despair that no one cared to exert himself for the arrest of the ruin which seemed imminent over that which was already no better than itself a ruin.

The Book of Isaiah is arranged in a most confused and unchronological manner, and it is probable that the first five chapters should be placed after the sixth, which describes the prophet's call in the year that King Uzziah died. They paint a picture of moral collapse. His first chapter is called by Ewald "the great arraignment," and by its references describes the awful period of alarm during the war of Syria and Ephraim against Judah. It might seem as if the combined host was even then in the country, or had only just retired from it; for we read,—

"Your country is desolate, your cities are burned with fire : your land, strangers devour it in your presence, and it is desolate, as overthrown by strangers. And the daughter of Zion is left as a booth in a wilderness, as a lodge in a garden of cucumbers, as a besieged city."

But even in the midst of this afflictive dispensation there were no signs of repentance. The children of Israel were rebels who despised the Holy One of Israel,—" Ah, sinful nation, a people laden with iniquity, a seed of evil-doers, children that deal corruptly!" (i. 7–9). They had all the externals of religion : they offered vain sacrifices, and kept a multitude of idle feasts, and offered many formal prayers ; but all this was but a cumbrance to Him who desired clean hands and a pure heart as conditions of forgiveness (10–20). What hope could there be for a city of murderers, who

loved bribes and perverted judgment (21–24)?   The
land was full of pride, full of idols, full of the luxury
of the rich amid the starvation of the poor (ii. 1–22).[1]
Women partook of the general corruption.   They
walked mincingly with stretched-forth necks and
wanton eyes,[2] thinking of nothing but their anklets,
and crescents, and bracelets, and mufflers, ear-drops,
head-tires, perfumes, mirrors, armlets, and nose-jewels :
therefore they should have sackcloth for stomachers,
ropes for girdles, and burning instead of beauty, and
only a remnant should escape (iii. 16–iv. 1).   Judah
was like a vineyard,—rich in advantages, blessed with
fondest care ; but when God looked for grapes, it only
brought forth wild grapes—a semblance, but only a
poisoned semblance, of the true vintage : therefore it
should be left neglected and rainless.   Woe to the
greedy land-grabbing, and drunkenness, and revelry
of the rich !   Woe to their mockery of God and their
devotion to vanity !   Woe to their insane pride and
wanton injustice !   Could they escape vengeance ?
No ! Jehovah had looked for judgment (*mishpat*), but
behold oppression (*mishpach*) ; for righteousness (*tse'da-
kah*), but behold a cry (*tse'akah*) (v. 1–24).[3]   They
might escape—they would escape—the Syrian and the
Ephraimite ; but behind these lay a more terrrible and

---

[1] In Isa. ii. 2–4 we find, as so often in the prophetic books in
their present too-often-haphazard arrangement, a glowing promise of
universal peace placed before unsparing denuciations.   The verses
are also found in Micah (iv. 1, 2), and it has been conjectured that in
both prophets they are a quotation from some older source—perhaps
from Jonah, son of Amittai.

[2] Heb., " deceiving with their eyes."

[3] Isa. v. 7.   The paronomasia of the original is striking.   Van Oort
renders it, " He looked for *reason*, but behold *treason*; and for *right*,
but behold *affright*."

a more portentous foe, even the Assyrian, the scourge
of God's wrath (25-30).

"It was told the house of David, saying, Syria is
confederate with Ephraim." Is it strange that in such
a condition of things the heart of Ahaz and of his
people "was moved as the trees of the wood are moved
with the wind"?

Such was the terrible crisis at which Isaiah began
his ministry. He was the son of Amoz,[1] who has
been (much too precariously) identified with a brother
of Amaziah. It is probable that he was a man of
distinguished, if not of princely, birth, and he exercised
a more powerful influence over the politics of his
country than any other prophet—not even excepting
Jeremiah.

---

[1] His name means "Jehovah saves," and is perhaps alluded to in
Isa. viii. 18. Amos ("One who bears a burden"), needless to say, is
a totally different name from that of Amoz ("Vigorous"), the father
of Isaiah.

CHAPTER XXIII

ISAIAH AND AHAZ

2 KINGS xvi

"Expediency is man's wisdom ; doing right is God's."
GEORGE MEREDITH.

ISAIAH was one of those men whom God provides for the need of kingdoms. He was not only a prophet, but a statesman, a reformer, a poet, a man of invincible faith and unequalled insight. If Ahaz had accepted his counsels and followed his moral guidance, the whole history of Judah might have been different.

But the position of things was indeed disastrous. Judah was attacked from every side. On the southeast the Edomites renewed their devastating raids, and swept off multitudes of captives, who were sold as slaves in the Western slave-markets. On the southwest the Philistines once more rose in revolt, and acquired permanent repossession of many parts of the Shephelah, mastering Beth-Shemesh, Ajalon, Gederoth. Shocho, Timnath, Gimzo, and all the adjacent districts, But this was nothing compared with the humiliation and destruction inflicted by Rezin and Pekah. They shut up Ahaz in Jerusalem ; and though they could not storm its almost impregnable defences, which had recently been fortified by Uzziah and Jotham, they were undisputed masters of the rest of the land, so

that Judah was "brought low and made naked."[1]
Rezin, indeed, weary of a tedious siege, swept southwards to Elath, on the gulf of Akabah, seized it, and
peopled it with an Edomite garrison, thereby destroying
the commerce in which Solomon and Jehoshaphat had
taken pride, and which Uzziah had recently re-established.   Having thus left an effectual annoyance to
Judah in his rear, he gave up the design of dethroning
Ahaz and substituting in his place "*the son of Tabeal*,"
who would have been a tool in the hands of the
confederate kings.   He seized, however, a multitude
of captives, and with them and with much booty he
returned to Damascus.   "The son of Tabeal"—a
name which occurs nowhere else— has been found very
puzzling.[2]   I believe it to be simply an instance of the
Rabbinic process of transposition, called *Themourah*.
Some identify it with Itibi'alu of an inscription of
Tiglath-Pileser.   Others suppose that he was a Syrian,
and that Tabeal stands for Tabrimnon.   But by the
application of Themourah (called the *Albam*) Tabeal
simply gives us " Remaliah," and is either a scornful
variation of the name of Pekah's father, or has arisen
from the watchword of a secret conspiracy.   Since in
the text of Jeremiah (li. 41, xxv. 26) (by *Atbash*,
another form of the secret transposition of letters of
which the generic name was *Gematria*) we read *Sheshach*
for Babel, the name Tabeal may have been dealt
with in a similar method.[3]   Pekah, according to the
Chronicler, inflicted far deadlier injuries than Rezin.   In
one day he slew one hundred and twenty thousand " sons

[1] 2 Chron. xxviii. 19.

[2] It may mean " God is good " (Tabeel).

[3] For further explanations I must refer to my paper on Rabbinic
Exegesis (*Expositor*, First Series, v. 373).

of valour," because they had forsaken Jehovah, God of their fathers. His general Zichri, a mighty Ephraimite, slew Maaseiah, the king's son ;[1] and Azrikam, the chancellor ; and Elkanah, "the second to the king." The army carried away two hundred thousand captives and much spoil to Samaria. But on their arrival, a prophet named Oded[2] reproved the Israelites for having massacred the Judæans "in a rage that reacheth to heaven." Aided by various princes, he succeeded in inducing the people to refuse to harbour the captives, and clothed, fed, and sent them back unharmed to Jericho, mounting the feeble on horses and asses. The story bears on the face of it the signs of enormous exaggeration.

In the crisis of their miseries, but just before the siege, Ahaz had gone outside the city walls "at the end of the conduit of the upper pool, in the causeway of the fuller's field," probably to look after the water-supply, which had always been a difficulty for Jerusalem, and on which depended her capacity to withstand a siege. Here he was met by the prophet Isaiah, who was leading by the hand the little son to whom he had given the name of "Shear-jashub" ("A remnant shall return"),[3] as a witness to the truth of the prophecy which he had heard on the occasion of his call,—

"And if there should yet be a tenth in it, this shall be again consumed ; yet as the terebinth and the oak, though cut down, have their stock remaining, even so a sacred seed shall be the stock thereof."[4]

---

[1] 2 Chron. xxviii. 7.

[2] Of Oded nothing else is known.

[3] Some, however, interpret the name "A remnant repents" (**LXX.,** ὁ καταλειφθεὶς Ἰασούβ ; Vulg., *Qui derelictus est Jaseb*).

[4] Isa. vi. 13.

The object of the prophet was to cheer up the fainting heart of the king, and to say to him first,—

" Take heed, and be quiet."

This mandate probably refers to rumours—which Isaiah must have heard—of the king's intention to follow the counsels of the party which urged him to seek foreign assistance. One of these parties advised him to throw himself into the arms of Egypt, and rely on her protection ; the other gave the more perilous counsel of invoking the aid of Assyria. Isaiah's mandate to the king and to the nation was to take neither step, but to trust in the Lord, and to repent of individual and national misdoing. He summed up his message in the rule,—

" In returning and rest shall ye be saved ; in quietness and confidence shall be your strength."

The advice was emphasised by a promise of the most decisive and encouraging kind. When all looked so helpless, the prophet was bidden to say,—

" Fear not, neither be faint-hearted, for these two stumps of smoking torches, for the fierce anger of Rezin with Syria, and of Remaliah's son. They have taken evil counsel against thee. But thus saith the Lord God, ' It shall not stand, neither shall it come to pass. For the head of Syria is only Rezin, and the head of Samaria is a mere Remaliah's son.' " [1]

And then, to confirm the lesson of confidence in God, the brief assurance,—

---

[1] The words " And within threescore and five years shall Ephraim be broken, that it be not a people " (Isa. vii. 8), are almost certainly an interpolation: for (1) the overthrow came within far less than sixty years; (2) the clause awkwardly breaks the context; (3) the " sixty years " is inconsistent with the promise (vii. 16) that it should be within very few years.

> "If ye will not confide,
> Surely ye shall not abide."

Convinced of the certainty of this immediate deliverance, Isaiah bade the king to ask for a sign from Jehovah, either in the height above, or in the depth beneath.

But the timid and hypocritical king was not so to be influenced. He had on his side " the scornful men, who ruled Judah"; the mocking priests, who sneered and jeered at Isaiah's teaching as repetitive and commonplace, and only fit for children ; and the princes and nobles, who formed the Court party, headed by Shebna the scribe. He probably looked on Isaiah as a mere unpractical faddist, an excited fanatic—all very well as a prophet, but not a man who ought to thrust himself into the plans of politicians. Ahaz had his own plans, and he had not the smallest intention of altering them in consequence of anything which Isaiah might say. He was far too timid and unfaithful to rely on anything so vague as Divine assurance. He was convinced that his only chance lay in the horses of Egypt or the fierce infantry of Assyria. So he said with sham piety, merely intended to put the prophet off, " I will not ask, neither will I tempt Jehovah."

That moment marks what may be called the birth-throe of Messianic prophecy in its most specific character. For then the prophet, after reproving the king for wearying Jehovah as well as His servants, adds, in words of far wider and deeper significance than their immediate bearing, that Jehovah Himself should give a sign ; for the maiden should conceive and bear a Son, and call His name Immanuel ("God with us"). The child should grow up in a time of scarcity ; for owing to the devastation of the land, he would only be able to be nurtured on curdled milk and honey. But before he had reached years of discretion—before he had arrived at the power of moral choice—the land whose two kings Ahaz abhorred should be a desert. Yet let not Ahaz exult too much in the immediate deliverance! Days of unexampled misery were at hand. Jehovah should hiss for the fly from the farthest canals of Egypt, and for the bee of Assyria, and they should settle in swarms in the valleys and pastures. Ahaz—he had not alluded to the design, but Isaiah knew it well—was about to hire a razor from beyond the Euphrates, but that razor should sweep away the hair and beard of Judah. Agriculture should languish, and the people should only be able to live in privation on whey and honey; and the vineyards should be full of briers and thorns, and should be mere places for hunting.[1]

This event, therefore, as Caspari says, stands at the turning-point of Old Testament History. It marks the beginning of that second period of the History of the Chosen People in which their hopes were granted as a counterpoise to their anguish and their humiliation. "It stood, therefore, at the point where a prospect offered itself to the eye of the prophet which reached out over the whole development of the people of God."

To all such prophecies Ahaz was utterly deaf: they did not for a moment induce him to swerve from his purpose. But to call still further attention to his promise as the Syrian Ephraimitish host pressed forward, Isaiah took a great piece of vellum, and inscribed on it, in the ordinary characters,—

"Speed-plunder-haste-spoil."

He put it up in some conspicuous place, before his own house or in the Temple, and took the priest Urijah and

---

[1] Isa. vii. 1-25.

Zechariah, the son of Jeberechiah, into his confidence as
faithful witnesses. He told them the explanation of his
sign, and they would satisfy the curiosity of the people
on the subject. It meant that in nine months' time his
wife should bear a son, and that he and his wife, the
prophetess, would call the boy's name "Speed-
plunder-haste-spoil," as a sign that before the child
was able to say "Father" or "Mother" Rezin and
Pekah should be extinguished. For the Assyrian
should speed to the plunder and haste to the spoil, and
the riches of Damascus and the spoil of Samaria should
be carried away by the King of Assyria. Since Judah
despised "the soft flowing waters of Shiloah,"[1] and
preferred Rezin and Pekah,[2] they should be deluged
by the Euphrates of Assyria, and Assyria's outspread
wings should overshadow thy land, O Immanuel (viii.
1–8). How vain, then, of the people to try and meet
the confederacy of Syria and Ephraim by new confederacy of Judah with Assyria! This, after all, is
Immanuel's land. God is with us. We have but to
fear God, we have but to be faithful to duty, and
Jehovah shall be our sanctuary, though He be a stum-
bling-block to many in Israel, and a snare to many in
Jerusalem.[3] This is God's teaching and God's testimony,
and Isaiah and his children are signs of it. For does
not Isaiah mean "Salvation of Jehovah"; and Shear-
jashub, "A remnant shall return"; and Maher-shalal-
hash-baz, "Swift-spoil-speedy-prey"; and Immanuel,

---

[1] Not improbably the water which afterwards flowed through Hezekiah's new tunnel between the Virgin's Tomb and the Pool of Siloam. It
is referred to in 2 Chron. xxxii. 3, 30 (Isa. xxii. 9–11). See Appendix II.

[2] This, if it be correct, can only mean that the son of Tabeal had
a party in Jerusalem; but Hitzig renders it "*dreadeth*," not "re-
joiceth in."

[3] The meaning is by no means clear.

" God is with us " ? What need, then, to seek wizards and necromancers ? Seek God; confide, abide ! [1] Trouble and darkness there should be ; but all was not utterly hopeless. Northern Israel had been bedimmed and afflicted ; but soon they should be exalted, and see light, and their yoke be broken as in the day of Midian, and the trampling boot and blood-stained mantle of the warrior shall be burned in the fire : for a Child is born, a Son is given unto us of David's line, who shall be a Mighty Deliverer, a Prince of Peace,—and Israel shall perish.

---

[1] See Driver, *Isaiah*, p. 34.

CHAPTER XXIV

THE APOSTASIES OF AHAZ

2 KINGS xvi. 1—18

"For when we in our wickedness grow hard,
Oh misery on't! the wise gods seal our eyes;
In our own filth drop our clear judgments; make us
Adore our errors; laugh at us while we strut
To our confusion."

AHAZ was indifferent to these prophecies because his heart was otherwise. It is clear from our authorities that this king had excited an unusually deep antipathy in the hearts of those later writers who judged religion not only from the earlier standpoint, but from the stern and inexorable requirements of the Deuteronomic and the Priestly Codes. The historian, adopting an unusual phrase, says that "he did not that which was right in the sight of the Lord, but he walked in the ways of the kings of Israel." He not only continued the high places, as the best of his predecessors had done, but he increased their popularity and importance by personally offering sacrifices and burning incense "on the hills and under every green tree." It is probable, too, that he introduced into Judah horses and chariots dedicated to the sun.[1] "He made

---

[1] See 2 Kings xxiii. 11, which shows that this was not an innovation of Manasseh's. They were common in Persia. See Q. Curtius, iii. 3.

molten images for the Baalim," says the Chronicler,
"and burnt incense in the valley of the son of
Himmon."

This last was his crowning atrocity: he actually
sanctioned the revolting worship of the abomination of
the children of Ammon, which Solomon had tolerated
on the mount of offence. "He made his son to pass
through the fire." The Chronicler expresses it still
more dreadfully by saying that "he *burnt his children*
in the fire."[1]

In the Valley of Ben-Hinnom, or of the Beni-Hinnom,
of which the name is perpetuated in Gehenna, the place
of torture for lost souls, there stood a frightful image
of the king—Moloch, Melek, Malcham. It represented
the sun-god, worshipped, not only as Baal under the
emblems of prolific nature, but, like the Egyptian
Typhon, as the emblem of the sun's scorching and
blighting force. It was perhaps a human figure with
the head of an ox. The arms of the brazen image
sloped downwards over a cistern, which was filled with
fuel; and when a human sacrifice was to be offered to
him, the child was probably first killed, and then placed
on these brazen arms as a gift to the idol. It rolled
down into the flaming tank, and was consumed amid
the strains of music. Recourse was only had to the

---

[1] 2 Kings xvii. 31; Ezek. xvi. 21, xxiii. 37, xxxiii. 6; Deut. xii. 31;
Jer. xix. 5. See 2 Chron. xxviii. 3; for "his son," בְּנוֹ, it uses בָּנָיו
"his sons," but perhaps generically. Moloch-worship may have been
stimulated by accounts of the Assyrian fire-god Adrammelech
(Movers, *Phöniz.*, ii. 101). On this sacrifice of children to Moloch,
which the Phœnicians referred back to the god El or Il, once King
of Byblos, who in a crisis of danger sacrificed his eldest son Icond,
see Plut., *De Superst.*, § 13; Diod. Sic., xx. 12–14; 2 Kings iii. 27,
xvi. 3, xxi. 6; Mic. vi. 7; Döllinger, *Judenthum u. Heidenthum* (E. T.),
i. 427–429.

most frightful form of human sacrifice—the burning of grown-up victims—in extremities of disaster, as when Mesha of Moab offered up his eldest son to Chemosh on the wall of Kir-Hareseth in the sight of his people and of the three invading armies. But the sacrifice of children was public, and perhaps annual. Hence Milton, following the learned researches of Selden in his Syntagma *De Dis Syriis*, writes :—

> "First, Moloch, horrid king, besmeared with blood
> Of human sacrifice, and parents' tears ;
> Though, for the noise of drums and timbrels loud,
> Their children's cries unheard that pass'd through fire
> To his grim idol. Him the Ammonite
> Worshipp'd in Rabba and her watery plain,
> In Argob and in Basan, to the stream
> Of utmost Arnon. Nor content with such
> Audacious neighbourhood, the wisest heart
> Of Solomon he led by fraud to build
> His temple right against the Temple of God
> On that opprobrious hill, and made his grove
> The pleasant Valley of Hinnom, Tophet thence
> And black Gehenna call'd, the type of hell."[1]

But it may be doubted whether Ahaz, in spite of his frightful position, or, in later days, the less excusable Manasseh, really destroyed the lives of their young sons.[2] The ancients had a notion that they could easily cheat their devil-deities. If a white ox of Clitumnus became unfitted for a victim to Jupiter of the Capitol by having on its body a few black spots, it

---

[1] This worship was to be punished by stoning (Lev. xviii. 21, xx. 2–5 ; Deut. xviii. 10). On the whole subject see Movers, *Phönis.*, 64 ; Jarchi *on Jer. vii.* 31 ; Euseb., *Præp. Ev.*, iv. 16.

[2] Josephus says that Ahaz made "a whole burnt-offering" of his son ; but his authority is very small (καὶ ἴδιον ὡλοκαύτωσεν παῖδα). Comp. Psalm cvi. 37.

was quite sufficient to make it pass with the *Di faciles*
by chalking the black spots over it.[1] If human victims
had to be thrown into the Tiber to Hercules, Numa
taught the people that little wickerwork images (*scirpea*)
would suit the purpose just as well.[2] Figures of dough
were sometimes offered instead of human beings on the
altar of Artemis of Tauris. Thus it became the custom,
it is believed, merely to throw or to pass children
through or over the flames, and conventionally to
regard them as having been sacrificed, though they
might escape the ordeal with little or no hurt. This
was called *februatio*, or "lustration by fire."[3] We may
hope that this device was adopted by the two Judæan
kings, and, if so, they did not add to their horrible
apostasy the crime of infanticide. If, however, Ahaz
was even to the smallest extent implicated in such foul
idolatries, it is not surprising that he was in no mood
to listen to Isaiah. What is profoundly surprising,
and is indeed a circumstance for which we cannot
account, is that no word of fierce indignation was
addressed to him on this account by Urijah, the high
priest, whom Isaiah seems to describe as faithful, or
by Zechariah, the son of Jeberechiah, or by Micah,
or by Isaiah, who feared man so little and God
so much.

The Assyrian party at the Court of Ahaz prevailed
over the Egyptian. Until the accession of the Ethiopian

---

[1] Ignorant Romanists have often cherished the same notions about
the saints. For centuries in Spain the people bought the old gowns
and cowls of the monks, and buried their dead in them, to deceive
St. Peter into the notion that they were Dominicans or Franciscans!
[2] See Ovid, *Fasti*, v. 659: "Scripea pro domino Tiberi jactatur
imago." They were also called *Argei*, *id.* 621 ; Varro, *L. L.*, vi. 3.
[3] Varro, *L. L.*, v. 3.

Sabaco[1] in 725, Egypt was indeed in so weak, harassed, and divided a condition under feeble native Pharaohs, that her help was obviously unavailable. The King of Judah, seeing no extrication from his calamities except in the way of worldly expediency, appealed to Tiglath-Pileser. In this he followed the precedent of his ancestor Asa, who had diverted the attack of Baasha by invoking the assistance of Syria. Ahaz sent to the Assyrian potentate the humble message, "I am thy servant and thy son : come up and save me from the Kings of Syria and Israel." If he had not faith to accept Isaiah's promises, what else could he do, when Syria, Israel, the Philistines, Edom, and Moab were all arrayed against him ? The ambassadors probably made their way, not without peril, along the east of Jordan, or else by sea from Joppa, and so inland. Whether they took with them the enormous bribe without which the appeal of the helpless king might have been in vain, or whether this was sent subsequently under Assyrian escort, we do not know. It was euphemistically described as "a present" or "a blessing," but must be regarded either as a tribute or a bribe.

Tiglath-Pileser II. saw his opportunity, and at once invaded Damascus. In B.C. 733 he failed, but the next year he entirely subjugated the kingdom, and put an end to the dynasty. Rezin was probably put to death with the horrible barbarities which were normal among the brutal Ninevites ; and as the Assyrians had no conception of colonisation or the wise government of dependencies, the Syrian popula-

---

[1] Herod., ii. 137. Egypt., *Sebek*; Heb., *So* (2 Kings xvii. 4), or perhaps *Seve*; Arab., *Shab'i*. Rawlinson, *Hist. of Anct. Egypt*, ii. 433-450.

tion was deported *en masse* to Elam and an unknown
Kir.[1] For a time Damascus was made "a ruinous
heap," and the cities of Aroer were the desolated lairs
of pasturing flocks. Israel, as we have seen, was
next overwhelmed by the same irremediable catastrophe,
none of her people being left except such as might be
compared to the mere gleanings of a vintage, and the
few berries on the topmost boughs of the olive tree.[2]

Tiglath-Pileser meant to make Ahaz feel his yoke.
He summoned him to do homage at Damascus, and
there Ahaz once more displayed his cosmopolitan
æstheticism at the expense of every pure tradition
of the religion of his fathers.

His visit to Damascus was no doubt compulsory.
His worldly policy, which looked so expedient, and
which—apart from the defiance which it involved to
the voice of God by His prophets—seemed to be so
pardonable, had for the time succeeded. Isaiah's
promises had been fulfilled to the letter. There was
nothing more to fear either from Rezin or from
Remaliah's son. Their kingdoms were a desolation.
In his own annals Tiglath-Pileser[3] does not exaggerate
his achievements.[4] He wrote as follows :—

"Rezin's warriors I captured, and with the sword I destroyed.
Of his charioteers and [his horsemen] the arms I broke:

---

[1] Kir (see Amos ix. 7) is omitted in the LXX. Elam is added in
Isa. xxii. 6. Tiglath-Pileser calls the king Rasunnu Sarimirisu—*i.e.*,
of Aram. See Smith, *Assyr. Discoveries*, p. 274; *Eponym Canon*, 68;
Schrader, *K. A. T.*, 152 ff. [2] Isa. xvii. 1-11.

[3] The name seems to be Tuklat-abal-isarra,—according to Oppert
worshipper of the son of the Zodiac—*i.e.*, of Nin or Hercules.
According to Polyhistor, he was a usurper who had been a vine-
dresser in the royal gardens. He never mentions his ancestry. But
see Schrader, *K. A. T.*, 217 ff., 240 ff., and in Riehm.

[4] *Eponym Canon*, p. 121, lines 1-15. On this fall of Damascus and
Samaria, see Isa. xvii

Their bow-bearing warriors, [their footmen] armed with spear
    and shield,
With my hand I captured them, and those that fought in their
    battle-line.
He to save his life fled away alone;
Like a deer [he ran], and entered into the great gate of his city.
His generals, whom I had taken alive, on crosses I hung;
His country I subdued;
Damascus, his city, I subdued, and like a caged bird I shut him in.
I cut down the unnumbered trees of his forest; I left not one.
Hadara, the palace of the father of Rezin of Syria, [I burnt].
The city of Samaria I besieged, I captured; eight hundred of its
    people and children I took;
Their oxen and their sheep I carried away.
I took five hundred and ninety-one cities;
Over sixteen districts of Syria like a flood I swept."

But the more complete destruction of Israel was due
to Shalmaneser IV., who says,—

"The city of Samaria I besieged, I took,
I carried away twenty-seven thousand two hundred of its inhabit-
    ants;
I seized fifty of their chariots.
I gave up to plunder the rest of their possessions.
I appointed officers over them;
I laid on them the tribute of the former king.
In their place I settled the men of conquered countries."

The immediate service to Judah looked immense.
The Assyrian might safely claim, and Ahaz might
truthfully confess, that the intervention of Tiglath-
Pileser had rescued him from the apparent imminence
of destruction. But the Assyrian kings served no one
for nothing. The price which had to be paid for
Tiglath-Pileser's intervention was vassalage and tribute.
Ahaz, or, as the Assyrians call him, Jehoahaz,[1] had

---

[1] Jahuhazi (Schrader, *Keilinschr.*, p. 263). He probably bore both
names; but, as in the case of Jeconiah, who is called Coniah, the
omission of the element " Jehovah " from his name may have been
intended as a mark of reprobation.

styled himself Tiglath-Pileser's "servant and his son,"
and the Assyrian chose to have substantial proof of
this parental suzerainty. The great king therefore
summoned the poor subject-potentate to Damascus,
where he was holding his victorious court.

So far Ahaz had no reason to complain of his
"dreadful patron"; and if he had returned when he
paid his homage, no immediate harm would have
happened. But during his visit he saw "the altar"
(*Heb.*) at the conquered city. Was it the altar of the
defeated Syrian god Rimmon? or did the Assyrian
persuade his willing vassal to sacrifice at the portable
altar of his god Assur? We may, perhaps, infer the
former from 2 Chron. xxviii. 23, where Ahaz says:
"Because the gods of the kings of Syria help them,
therefore will I sacrifice to them, that they may help
me." There is room to suspect some error here,
because Rezin had fallen, and Damascus was in ruins,
and Rimmon had conspicuously failed to help or to
avenge his votaries.[1] Ahaz admired the altar, to whatever god it had been erected; and unmindful, or
perhaps unconscious, that the altar of the Temple of
Jerusalem was declared in the Pentateuch to have been
divinely ordained—a fact to which the historian does not
himself refer—he sent to the head priest Urijah a pattern
of the altar which had struck his fancy at Damascus.
The subservient priest, without a murmur or a remonstrance, undertook to have a similar altar ready for
Ahaz in the Temple by the time of his return—a crime,
if crime it were, which the Chronicler conceals. " Never

---

[1] The remark may refer to some earlier period in the reign of Ahaz,
before the capture of Damascus. It is more probable that the altar
was used for some Assyrian deity, and the adoption of it may have
flattered Tiglath-Pileser.

any prince was so foully idolatrous," says Bishop Hall,
"as that he wanted a priest to second him.   A Urijah
is fit to humour an Ahaz.[1]   Greatness could never
command anything which some servile wits were not
ready both to applaud and justify."   Certainly we
should have hoped for more fidelity to ancient tradition
from a man who earned the approving word of Isaiah;
but it is only fair and just to admit that Urijah, in the
universal ignorance which prevailed about the codes
which were afterwards collected and published as the
total legislation of the wilderness, may have viewed his
obedience to the king's commands with very different
eyes from those by which it was regarded in the sixth
and fifth centuries before Christ.   He may have been
frankly unaware that he was guilty of an act which
would afterwards be denounced as an apostatising
enormity.[2]

When Ahaz returned, he was so much pleased with
his new plaything that he at once acted as priest at
his own new altar.   Without the least opposition from

---

[1] 2 Kings xvi. 11, which records the zealous subservience of Urijah,
is wanting in some MSS. of the LXX.   But that the altar was made,
and without his opposition, is clear from the narrative.   Asa (2 Chron.
xv. 8) had repaired Solomon's great altar; Hezekiah subsequently
cleansed it (*id.* xxix. 18); Manasseh rebuilt it (*Q'ri*).   The brass of
it ultimately went to Babylon (Jer. lii. 17-20).

[2] Bähr says : "It seems that Urijah, like his companion, was only
anxious for his revenues.   At any rate, his conduct is a sign of the
character and standing of the priests of that time.   They were
'dumb dogs who could not bark.'   They all followed their own ways,
every one for his own gain" (Isa. lvi. 10, 11).   "We have in this high
priest," says the *Würtemberg Summary*, "a specimen of those hypo-
crites and belly-servants who say, 'Whose bread I eat, his song
I sing'; who veer about with the wind, and seek to be pleasant to
all men ; who wish to hurt no one's feelings, but teach just what any
one wants to hear."

the priests—who had so sternly resisted Uzziah—he offered burnt-offerings and meat-offerings and drink-offerings, and sprinkled the blood of peace-offerings on his altar.[1]   Not content with this, he did not hesitate to order the removal of the huge brazen altar from the position, in front of the Temple porch, which it had held since the days of Solomon.   He did this in order that his own favourite altar might be in the line of vision from the court, and not be overshadowed by the old one, which he shifted from the place of honour to the north side.   He proceeded to call his own altar "the great altar," and ordered that the morning burnt-offering, and the evening *minchah*, and all the principal sacrifices should henceforth be offered upon it.[2]   He did not wholly supersede the old brazen altar, which, he said, "shall be for me to inquire by," or, as the Hebrew may perhaps mean, "it should await"—*i.e.*, "I will hereafter consider what to do with it."

Ahaz is charged with the additional crime of removing the ornamental festoons of bronze pomegranates from the lavers, and the brazen oxen from under the molten sea, which henceforth lay dishonoured, without its proper and splendid supports, on the pavement of the

---

[1] 1 Kings viii. 64; 2 Chron. iv. 1. In this and similar instances commentators, biassed by *a priori* considerations, have imagined that Ahaz did not in person offer sacrifices. But this is what the text says, and it was the custom of kings to regard themselves as invested with Divine attributes. Ahaz may have had this lesson impressed on his mind by his visit to Tiglath-Pileser. See Grätz, *Gesch. der Juden.*, ii. 150. Layard, *Nin. and Bab.*, 472 ff., gives us pictures of Assyrian kings ministering at their altars, which are of various shapes.

[2] 2 Kings xvi. 15. Vulg., *paratum erit ad voluntatem meam.* The LXX. followed another reading: ἔσται μοι εἰς τὸ πρωΐ. Grätz (ii. 150), for לְבַקֵּר, "to inquire," reads לְקָרֵב "to draw near to."

court.[1] He also took away the balustrade of the royal
"ascent" from the palace to the Temple, and made
a new entrance of a less gorgeous character than that
which, in the days of Solomon, the Queen of Sheba
had admired.[2]

No doubt these proceedings helped to heighten the
unpopularity of Ahaz. But what could he do? He
could, indeed, if he had had sufficient faith, have
"trusted in Jehovah," as Isaiah bade him do. But
he was under the terrific pressure of hostile circumstances, and, being a weak and timid man, felt himself
unable to resist the influence of the haughty politicians
and worldly priests by whom he was surrounded—men
who openly made Isaiah their scoff. When he invited
the interposition of Tiglath-Pileser,[3] all the other consequences of humiliation would naturally follow. He
probably disliked as much as any one to see the great
molten laver taken off the backs of the oxen which
showed the skill of the ancient Hiram, and did not
admire the despoiled aspect of the shrine of his capital.
But if the King of Assyria or his emissaries had (as
the historian implies) cast greedy eyes on these splendid
objects of antiquity, the poor vassal could not refuse
them. Better, he may have thought, that these material
ornaments should go to Nineveh than that he should

---

[1] 1 Kings vii. 23-39.

[2] 2 Kings xvi. 18. The allusions are obscure. R.V., "the covered
way"; A.V., "the covert for the Sabbath." See 2 Chron. ix. 4.
Here the Hebr. *Q'ri* has *Músak*, and the Vulg. *Musach Sabbati.* The
LXX. evidently did not understand it (καὶ τὸν θεμέλιον τῆς καθέδρας
ᾠκοδόμησεν). For "covert for the Sabbath," Geiger suggests "molten
images for the Shame" (Bosheth-Baal, by transposition of *Shabbath*).
Comp. 2 Chron. xxviii. 2.

[3] 2 Chron. xxviii. 20: "Tiglath-Pileser came unto him, and distressed him, but helped him not."

be forced to exact yet heavier burdens from an impoverished people.   His expedient is mentioned among
his crimes, yet no one blamed the pious Hezekiah
when, under similar circumstances, he acted in precisely the same manner.[1]

The Chronicler gives a darker aspect to his misdoings by saying that he cut to pieces the vessels of
the house of God, and made him altars in every corner
of Jerusalem, and *bamoth* to burn incense unto other
gods in every several city of Judah.   He says, further,
that he closed the great gates of the Temple; put an
end to the kindling of the lamps, the burning of incense,
and the daily offerings; and left the whole Temple to
fall into ruin and neglect.[2]   We know no more of him.
He lived through an epoch marked by the final crisis
in the existence of the kingdom of Israel.   Dark omens
of every kind were around him, and he seems to have
been too frivolous to see them.   If he plumed himself
on the removal of the two relentless invaders Rezin
and Pekah, he must have lived to feel that the terror
of Assyria had come appreciably nearer.   Tiglath-
Pileser had only helped Judah in furtherance of his
own designs, and his exactions came like a chronic
distress after the acuter crisis.   Nor was there any
improvement when he died in 727.   He was succeeded
by Shalmaneser IV., and Shalmaneser IV. by Sargon
in 722, the year of the fall of Samaria.   We know no
more of Ahaz.   The historian says that he was buried
with his fathers, and the Chronicler adds, as in the case

---

[1] 2 Kings xviii. 15, 16.

[2] In justice to Ahaz, we should observe that (1) in every instance
the later account multiplies and magnifies and gives a darker
colouring to his offences; (2) that neither Isaiah, Micah, nor any
other prophet has a word of reproach for such enormities in Ahaz.

of Uzziah and other kings, that he was not permitted
to rest in the sepulchres of the kings.[1] He had sown
the wind; his son Hezekiah had to reap the whirlwind.[2]

---

[1] It is a Jewish tradition that Hezekiah would not bury his father
Ahaz in a sarcophagus, but on a bier (*Pesachin*, f. 56, 1; *Sanhedrin*,
f. 47, 1; Grätz, *Gesch. d. Juden.*, ii. 224).

[2] His name, *Chizquiyyah*, is shortened from *Yechizquiyyahoo* (Isa.
i. 1; 2 Kings xx. 10; Hos. i. 1). It means "Jehovah's strength"
(*Gesen.*), or "Yah is might" (*Fürst*).

Probable Dates.

745. Accession of Tiglath-Pileser.

746. Death of Uzziah. Accession of Jotham. First vision of Isaiah (Isa. vi.).

735. Accession of Ahaz. Syro-Ephraimitish war.

734-732. Siege and capture of Damascus, and ravage of Northern Israel by Tiglath-Pileser. Visit of Ahaz to Damascus.

727. Accession of Shalmaneser IV.

722. Accession of Sargon. Capture of Samaria, and captivity of the Ten Tribes.

720. Defeat of Sabaco by Sargon at Raphia.

715 (?). Accession of Hezekiah.

711. Sargon captures Ashdod.

707. Sargon defeats Merodach-Baladan, and captures Babylon.

705. Murder of Sargon. Accession of Sennacherib.

701. Sennacherib besieges Ekron. Defeats Egypt at Altaqu. Invades Judah, and spares Hezekiah. Invades Egypt, and sends the Rabshakeh to Jerusalem. Disaster of Assyrians at Pelusium, and disappearance from before Jerusalem.

697. Death of Hezekiah. Accession of Manasseh.

681. Death of Sennacherib.

608. Battle of Megiddo. Death of Josiah.

607. Fall of Nineveh and Assyria. Triumph of Babylon.

605. Battle of Carchemish. Defeat of Pharaoh Necho by Nebuchadrezzar.

599. First deportation of Jews to Babylon by Nebuchadrezzar.

588. Destruction of Jerusalem. Second deportation.

538. Cyrus captures Babylon.

536. Decree of Cyrus. Return of Zerubbabel and the first Jewish exiles.

458. Return of Ezra.

CHAPTER XXV

HEZEKIAH

B.C. 715-686 [1]

2 KINGS xviii

"For Ezekias had done the thing that pleased the Lord, and was strong in the ways of David his father, as Esay the prophet, who was great and faithful in his vision, had commanded him."—ECCLUS. xlviii. 22.

THE reign of Hezekiah was epoch-making in many respects, but especially for its religious reformation, and the relations of Judah with Assyria and with Babylon. It is also most closely interwoven with the annals of Hebrew prophecy, and acquires unwonted lustre from the magnificent activity and impassioned eloquence of the great prophet Isaiah, who merits in many ways the title of "the Evangelical Prophet," and who was the greatest of the prophets of the Old Dispensation.

According to the notice in 2 Kings xviii. 2, Hezekiah was twenty-five years old when he began to reign in the third year of Hoshea of Israel. This, however, is practically impossible consistently with the dates that Ahaz reigned sixteen years and became king at the age of twenty, for it would then follow that Hezekiah was born when his father was a mere boy—

---

[1] The first of these dates is highly uncertain, as is the entire chronology of this reign. I follow Kittel.

and this, although Hezekiah does not seem to have been the eldest son ; for Ahaz had burnt "his son," and, according to the Chronicler, more than one son, to propitiate Moloch.   Probably Hezekiah was a boy of fifteen when he began to reign.   The chronology of his reign of twenty-nine years is, unhappily, much confused.

The historian of the Kings agrees with the Chronicler, and the son of Sirach, in pronouncing upon him a high eulogy, and making him equal even to David in faithfulness.   There is, however, much difference in the method of their descriptions of his doings.   The historian devotes but one verse to his reformation—which probably began early in his reign, though it occupied many years.   The Chronicler, on the other hand, in his three chapters manages to overlook, if not to suppress, the one incident of the reformation which is of the deepest interest.   It is exactly one of those suppressions which help to create the deep misgiving as to the historic exactness of this biassed and late historian.   It must be regarded as doubtful whether many of the Levitic details in which he revels are or are not intended to be literally historic.   Imaginative additions to literal history became common among the Jews after the Exile, and leaders of that day instinctively drew the line between moral homiletics and literal history.   It may be perfectly historical that, as the Chronicler says, Hezekiah opened and repaired the Temple ; gathered the priests and the Levites together, and made them cleanse themselves ; offered a solemn sacrifice ; reappointed the musical services ; and— though this can hardly have been till after the Fall of Samaria in 722—invited all the Israelites to a solemn, but in some respects irregular, passover of fourteen days.   It may be true also that he broke up the

idolatrous altars in Jerusalem, and tossed their *débris*
into the Kidron ; and (again after the deportation of
Israel) destroyed some of the *bamoth* in Israel as well
as in Judah.　If he reinstituted the courses of the
priests, the collection of tithes, and all else that he is
said to have done,[1] he accomplished quite as much as
was effected in the reign of his great-grandson Josiah.
But while the Chronicler dwells on all this at such
length, what induces him to omit the most significant
fact of all—the destruction of the brazen serpent ?

The historian tells us that Hezekiah " removed the
bamoth "—the chapels on the high places, with their
ephods and teraphim—whether dedicated to the worship
of Jehovah or profaned by alien idolatry.　That he did,
or attempted, something of this kind seems certain ; for
the Rabshakeh, if we regard his speech as historical
in its details, actually taunted him with impiety, and
threatened him with the wrath of Jehovah on this very
account.　Yet here we are at once met with the many
difficulties with which the history of Israel abounds,
and which remind us at every turn that we know much
less about the inner life and religious conditions of the
Hebrews than we might infer from a superficial study
of the historians who wrote so many centuries after the
events which they describe.　Over and over again their
incidental notices reveal a condition of society and
worship which violently collides with what seems to
be their general estimate.　Who, for instance, would
not infer from this notice that in Judah, at any rate,
the king's suppression of the " high places," and above
all of those which were idolatrous, had been tolerably
thorough ?　How much, then, are we amazed to find

---

[1] 2 Chron. xxxi. 2–21.

that Hezekiah had not effectually desecrated even the
old shrines which Solomon had erected to Ashtoreth,
Chemosh, and Milcom[1] " at the right hand of the mount
of corruption "—in other words, on one of the peaks
of the Mount of Olives, in full view of the walls of
Jerusalem and of the Temple Hill !

"And he brake the images," or, as the R.V. more
correctly renders it, "the pillars," the *matstseboth*.
Originally—that is, before the appearance of the Deuteronomic and the Priestly Codes—no objection seems to
have been felt to the erection of a *matstsebah*. Jacob
erected one of these *baitulia* or anointed stones at
Bethel, with every sign of Divine approval.[2] Moses
erected twelve round his altar at Sinai.[3] Joshua erected
them in Shechem and on Mount Ebal. Hosea, in one
passage (iii. 4), seems to mention pillars, ephods, and
teraphim as legitimate objects of desire. Whether they
have any relation to obelisks, and what is their exact
significance, is uncertain ; but they had become objects
of just suspicion in the universal tendency to idolatry,
and in the deepening conviction that the second com-
mandment required a far more rigid adherence than it
had hitherto received.

"And cut down the groves "—or rather the Asherim,
the wooden, and probably in some instances phallic,
emblems of the nature-goddess Asherah, the goddess of
fertility.[4] She is sometimes identified with Astarte,

---

[1] Josiah did this many years later (2 Kings xxiii. 13).

[2] Gen. **xxxv.** 14. See Spencer, *De legg. Hebr.*, i. 444; Bochart,
Canaan, ii. 2.

[3] Exod. **xxiv.** 4. Comp. Deut. vii. 5, xii. 3, xvi. 22; Lev. xxvi. 1;
2 Chron. **xiv.** 3, xxxi. 1; Jer. xliii. 13; Hos. **x.** 2; Mic. v. 13 (where
the A.V. often has " statue " or " image "). Comp. Clem. Alex., *Strom.,*
i. 24; Arnob., *c. Gent.,* i. 39.

[4] The rendering " grove " in the A.V. is borrowed from the ἄλσος

the goddess of the moon and of love ; but there is no
sufficient ground for the identification. Some, indeed,
doubt whether Asherah is the name of a goddess at all.
They suppose that the word only means a consecrated
pole or pillar, emblematic of the sacred tree.[1]

Then comes the startling addition, "And brake in
pieces the brazen serpent that Moses had made : *for
unto those days the children of Israel did burn incense to
it.*" This addition is all the more singular because the
Hebrew tense implies habitual worship. The story of
the brazen serpent of the wilderness is told in Num.
xxi. 9 ; but not an allusion to it occurs anywhere, till
now—some eight centuries later—we are told that up
to this time the children of Israel had been in the habit
of burning incense to it! Comparing Num. xxi. 4,
with xxxiii. 42, we find that the scene of the serpent-
plague of the Exodus was either Zalmonah ("the place
of the image ") or Punon, which Bochart connects with
Phainoi, a place mentioned as famous for copper-mines.[2]
Moses, for unknown reasons, chose it as an innocent
and potent symbol; but obviously in later days it
subserved, or was mingled with, the tendency to
ophiolatry, which has been fatally common in all ages

---

of the LXX., and the *lucus* of the Vulgate. On the connection of
the Asherah with the sacred tree of the Assyrian, see my article on
" Grove " in Smith's *Dict. of the Bible* ; and Fergusson, *Nineveh and
Persepolis Restored*, 299–304. On the worship of Asherah, see 1 Kings
xv. 13; 2 Kings xxi. 3–7, xxiii. 4 ; 2 Chron. xv. 16; Judg. iii. 5–7,
vi. 25, xviii. 18. Baudissin in *Herzog Realencykl., s.v.* We may well
be startled by the prevalence of idolatry in Jerusalem revealed in
Isa. x. 11, xxvii. 9, xxix. 11, xxx. 9, 22, etc.

[1] See Wellhausen, *Hist.*, 235; Stade, *Gesch. d. V. I.*, 460; W. R.
Smith, *Religion of the Semites*, 171 ; Cheyne, *Isaiah*, ii. 303; Renan,
Hist. du Peuple d'Israel, i. 230 (Prof. Driver, *Bibl. Dict.*, i. 258, 2nd
edition).

[2] *Hierozoicon*, ii. 3, § 13.

in many heathen lands. It is indeed most difficult to understand a state of things in which the children of Israel habitually *burned incense* to this venerable relic, nor can we imagine that this was done without the cognisance and connivance of the priests. Ewald makes the conjecture that the brazen *Saraph* had been left at Zalmonah, and was an occasional object of Israelite adoration in pilgrimage for the purpose. There is, however, nothing more extraordinary in the prevalence of serpent-worship among the Jews than in the fact that, " in the cities of Judah and the streets of Jerusalem, we " (the Jews), " and our fathers, our kings, and our princes, burnt incense unto the Queen of Heaven." [1] If this were the case, the serpent may have been brought to Jerusalem in the idolatrous reign of Ahaz. It shows an intensity of reforming zeal, and an inspired insight into the reality of things, that Hezekiah should not have hesitated to smash to pieces so interesting a relic of the oldest history of his people, rather than see it abused to idolatrous purposes. [2] Certainly, in conduct so heroic, and hatred of idolatry so strong, the Puritans might well find sufficient authority for removing from Westminster Abbey the images of the Virgin, which, in their opinion, had been worshipped, and before which lamps had been perpetually burned. If we can imagine an English king breaking to pieces the shrine of the Confessor in the Abbey, or a French king destroying the sacred

---

[1] Jer. xliv. **17.** In the collection of antiquities of Baron Ustinoff at Jaffa are five or six dragon-headed serpents, with ears of copper and hollow inside. They are ancient, and were perhaps used as talismanic copies of Nehushtan.

[2] If this was a genuine relic, it must have been nearly eight hundred years old. It is never mentioned elsewhere.

ampulla of Rheims or the *goupillon* of St. Eligius, on
the ground that many regarded them with superstitious
reverence, we may measure the effect produced by this
startling act of Puritan zeal on the part of Hezekiah.

"And he called it *Nehushtan.*" If this rendering—
in which our A.V. and R.V. follow the LXX. and the
Vulgate—be correct, Hezekiah justified the iconoclasm
by a brilliant play of words.[1] The Hebrew words for
"a serpent" (*nachash*) and for brass (*nechosheth*) are
closely akin to each other ; and the king showed his
just estimate of the relic which had been so shamefully
abused by contemptuously designating it—as it was in
itself and apart from its sacred historic associations—
"nehushtan," a thing of brass. The rendering, however, is uncertain, for the phrase may be impersonal—
"one" or "they" called it Nehushtan [2]—in which case
the assonance had lost any ironic connotation.[3]

For this act of purity of worship, and for other
reasons, the historian calls Hezekiah the best of all the
kings of Judah, superior alike to all his predecessors
and all his successors. He regarded him as coming up

---

[1] נְחֻשְׁתָּן, "a brazen thing." The king certainly showed a horror
of sacerdotal imposture and religious materialism. Yet Renan argues,
from Isa. x. 11, xxvii. 9, xxx. 9, 22, that he must have had a certain
amount of tolerance. See *Hist. du Peuple d'Israel*, iii. 30.

[2] 2 Kings xviii. 4. *Vayyikra* is like the English indefinite plural.
The impersonal rendering (as in other passages) is adopted in the
Targum of Jonathan, the Peshito, etc., and by Luther, Bunsen, Ewald,
and most moderns.

[3] This relic is still shown in the Church of St. Ambrose at Milan.
It used to be the popular notion that it would hiss at the end of the
world. The history of the Milan "relic" is that a Milanese envoy
to the court of the Emperor John Zimisces at Constantinople chose it
from the imperial treasures, being assured that it was made of the
same metal that Hezekiah had broken up (Sigonius, *Hist. Regn.
Ital.*, vii.). It is probably a symbol used by some ophite sect. See
Dean Plumptre, *Dict. of Bibl.*, *s.v.* "Serpent."

to the Deuteronomic ideal, and says that therefore "the Lord was with him, and he prospered whithersoever he went forth."

The date of this great reformation is rendered uncertain by the impossibility of ascertaining the exact order of Isaiah's prophecies. The most probable view is that it was gradual, and some of the king's most effective measures may not have been carried out till after the deliverance from Assyria. It is clear, however, that the wisdom of Hezekiah and his counsellors began from the first to uplift Judah from the degradation and decrepitude to which it had sunk under the reign of Ahaz. The boy-king found a wretched state of affairs at his accession. His father had bequeathed to him " an empty treasury, a ruined peasantry, an unprotected frontier, and a shattered army ";[1] but although he was still the vassal of Assyria, he reverted to the ideas of his great-grandfather Uzziah. He strengthened the city, and enabled it to stand a siege by improving the water-supply. Of these labours we have, in all probability, a most interesting confirmation in the inscription by Hezekiah's engineers, discovered in 1880, on the rocky walls of the subterranean tunnel (*siloh*) between the spring of Gihon and the Pool of Siloam.[2] He encouraged agriculture, the storage of

[1] 2 Kings xvi. 8; Driver, *Isaiah*, 68.

[2] The diverting of the water-courses enabled him to bring the water into the city by a subterranean tunnel. The Saracens took a similar precaution (Gul. Tyr., viii. 7). See Appendix II., where the inscription is given; and compare 2 Chron. xxxii. 30. Apparently it carried the water of Gihon to the south-east gate, where were the king's gardens. Ecclus. xlviii. 17: " Ezekias fortified his city, and brought in water into the midst thereof: he digged the hard rock with iron, and made wells for water." For "water" the MSS. read "Gog," a corruption probably for ἀγωγὸν, "a conduit" (Geiger) or " Gihon" (Fritzsche).

produce, and the proper tendance of flocks and herds, so that he acquired wealth which dimly reminded men of the days of Solomon.

There is little doubt that he early meditated revolt from Assyria; for renewed faithfulness to Jehovah had elevated the moral tone, and therefore the courage and hopefulness, of the whole people. The Forty-Sixth Psalm, whatever may be its date, expresses the invincible spirit of a nation which in its penitence and self-purification began to feel itself irresistible, and could sing :—

" God is our hope and strength,
A very present help in trouble.
Therefore will we not fear, though the earth be moved,
Though the hills be carried into the midst of the sea.
There is a river, the streams whereof make glad the city of God,
The Holy City where dwells the Most High.
God is in the midst of her; therefore shall she not be shaken :
God shall help her, and that right early.
Heathens raged and kingdoms trembled :
He lifted His voice—the earth melted away.
Jehovah of Hosts is with us ;
Elohim of Jacob is our refuge." [1]

It was no doubt the spirit of renewed confidence which led Hezekiah to undertake his one military enterprise—the chastisement of the long-troublesome Philistines. He was entirely successful. He not only won back the cities which his father had lost,[2] but he also dispossessed them of their own cities, even unto Gaza, which was their southernmost possession—" from the tower of the watchman to the fenced city." [3] There can be no doubt that this act involved an almost

---

[1] Psalm xlvi. 1–11.
[2] 2 Chron. xxviii. 18.
[3] 2 Kings xviii. 8 : comp. xvii. 9. Josephus says that he failed to take Gath (*Antt.*, IX. xiii. 3).

open defiance of the Assyrian King ; but if Hezekiah dreamed of independence, it was essential for him to be free from the raids and the menace of a neighbour so dangerous as Philistia, and so inveterately hostile. It is not improbable that he may have devoted to this war the money which would otherwise have gone to pay the tribute to Shalmaneser or Sargon, which had been continued since the date of the appeal of Ahaz to Tiglath-Pileser II. When Sargon applied for the tribute Hezekiah refused it, and even omitted to send the customary present.

It is clear that in this line of conduct the king was following the exhortations of Isaiah. It showed no small firmness of character that he was able to choose a decided course amid the chaos of contending counsels. Nothing but a most heroic courage could have enabled him, at any period of his reign, to defy that dark cloud of Assyrian war which ever loomed on the horizon, and from which but little sufficed to elicit the destructive lightning-flash.

There were three permanent parties in the Court of Hezekiah, each incessantly trying to sway the king to its own counsels, and each representing those counsels as indispensable to the happiness, and even to the existence, of the State.

I. There was the Assyrian party, urging with natural vehemence that the fierce northern king was as irresistible in power as he was terrible in vengeance. The fearful cruelties which had been committed at Beth-Arbel, the devastation and misery of the Trans-Jordanic tribes, the obliteration and deportation of the heavily afflicted districts of Zebulon, Naphtali, and the way of the sea in Galilee of the nations, the already inevitable and imminent destruction of Samaria and her

king and the whole Northern Kingdom, together with
that certain deportation of its inhabitants of which the
fatal policy had been established by Tiglath-Pileser,
would constitute weighty arguments against resistance.
Such considerations would appeal powerfully to the
panic of the despondent section of the community, which
was only actuated, as most men are, by considerations
of ordinary political expediency. The foul apparition
of the Ninevites, which for five centuries afflicted the
nations, is now only visible to us in the bas-reliefs and
inscriptions unearthed from their burnt palaces. There
they live before us in their own sculptures, with their
"thickset, sensual figures," and the expression of calm
and settled ferocity on their faces, exhibiting a frightful
nonchalance as they look on at the infliction of diaboli-
cal atrocities upon their vanquished enemies. But in the
eighth century before Christ they were visible to all the
eastern world in the exuberance of the most brutal
parts of the nature of man. Men had heard how, a
century earlier, Assurnazipal boasted that he had
"dyed the mountains of the Nairi with blood like
wool"; how he had flayed captive kings alive, and
dressed pillars with their skins; how he had walled
up others alive, or impaled them on stakes; how he
had burnt boys and girls alive, put out eyes, cut off
hands, feet, ears, and noses, pulled out the tongues of
his enemies, and "at the command of Assur his god"
had flung their limbs to vultures and eagles, to dogs
and bears. The Jews, too, must have realised with a
vividness which is to us impossible the cruel nature of
the usurper Sargon. He is represented on his monuments as putting out with his own hands the eyes of
his miserable captives; while, to prevent them from
flinching when the spear which he holds in his hand

is plunged into their eye-sockets, a hook is inserted through their nose and lips and held fast with a bridle. Can we not imagine the pathos with which this party would depict such horrors to the tremblers of Judah? Would they not bewail the fanaticism which led the prophets to seduce their king into the suicidal policy of defying such a power? To these men the sole path of national safety lay in continuing to be quiet vassals and faithful tributaries of these destroyers of cities and treaders-down of foes.

II. Then there was the Egyptian party, headed probably by the powerful Shebna, the chancellor.[1] His foreign name, the fact that his father is not mentioned, and the question of Isaiah—"What hast thou here? and whom hast thou here, that thou hast hewed thee out a sepulchre here?"—seem to indicate that he was by birth a foreigner, perhaps a Syrian.[2] The prophet, indignant at his powerful interference with domestic politics, threatens him, in words of tremendous energy, with exile and degradation.[3] He lost his place of chancellor, and we next find him in the inferior, though still honourable, office of secretary (*sopher*, 2 Kings xviii. 18), while Eliakim had been promoted to his vacant place (Isa. xxii. 21). Perhaps he may have afterwards repented, and the doom have been

---

[1] A.V., "treasurer" (*soken*; lit., "deputy" or "associate": Isa. xxii. 15). He was "over the household." The Egyptian alliance had for Judah, as Renan points out, some of the fascination that a Russian alliance has often had for troubled spirits in France (*Hist. du Peuple d'Israel*, iii. 12).

[2] Renan says that he may have been a Sebennyite, and his name Sebent.

[3] Isa. xxii. 17, 18: "Behold, the Lord shall sling and sling, and pack and pack, and toss and toss thee away like a ball into a distant land and there thou shalt die" (Stanley). The versions vary considerably.

lightened.[1] Circumstances at any rate reduced him from the scornful spirit which seems to have marked his earlier opposition to the prophetic counsels, and perhaps the powerful warning and menace of Isaiah may have exercised an influence on his mind.

III. The third party, if it could even be called a party, was that of Isaiah and a few of the faithful, aided no doubt by the influence of the prophecies of Micah. Their attitude to both the other parties was antagonistic.

i. As regards the Assyrian, they did not attempt to minimise the danger. They represented the peril from the kingdom of Nineveh as God's appointed scourge for the transgressions of Judah, as it had been for the transgressions of Israel.

Thus Micah sees in imagination the terrible march of the invader by Gath, Akko, Beth-le-Aphrah, Maroth, Lachish, and Adullam. He plays with bitter anguish on the name of each town as an omen of humiliation and ruin, and calls on Zion to make herself bald for the children of her delight, and to enlarge her baldness as the vultures, because they are gone into captivity.[2] He turns fiercely on the greedy grandees, the false prophets, the blood-stained princes, the hireling priests, the bribe-taking soothsayers, who were responsible for the guilt which should draw down the vengeance. He ends with the fearful prophecy—which struck a chill into men's hearts a century later, and had an important influence on Jewish history—"Therefore, because of you shall Zion be ploughed as a field,

---

[1] Isa. xxxvii. 2. There can be little doubt that there were not *two* Shebnas.

[2] Mic. i. 10–16. See the writer's *Minor Prophets* ("Men of the Bible" Series), pp. 130–133, for an explanation of this enigmatic prophecy.

and Jerusalem become ruins, and the hill of the Temple as heights in the wood ";—though there should be an ultimate deliverance from Migdal-Eder, and a remnant should be saved.[1]

Similar to Micah's, and possibly not uninfluenced by it, is Isaiah's imaginary picture of the march of Assyria, which must have been full of terror to the poor inhabitants of Jerusalem.[2]

> " He is come to Aiath !
> He is passed through Migron !
> At Michmash he layeth up his baggage!
> They are gone over the pass :
> 'Geba,' they cry, ' is our lodging.'
> Ramah trembleth :
> Gibeah of Saul is fled !
> Raise thy shrill cries, O daughter of Gallim !
> Hearken, O Laishah!   Answer her, O Anathoth!
> Madmenah is in wild flight (?).
> The inhabitants of Gebim gather their stuff to flee.
> This very day shall he halt at Nob.
> He shaketh his hand at the mount of the daughter of Zion,
> The hill of Jerusalem."

Yet Isaiah, and the little band of prophets, in spite of their perils, did *not* share the views of the Assyrian party or counsel submission.   On the contrary, even as they contemplate in imagination this terrific march of Sargon, they threaten Assyria.   The Assyrian might smite Judah, but God should smite the Assyrians.   He boasts that he will rifle the riches of the people as one robs the eggs of a trembling bird, which does not dare

---

[1] Jer. xxvi. 8–24.   He tells us that the prophecy was delivered in the reign of Hezekiah.   See my *Minor Prophets*, pp. 123-140.

[2] Isa. x. 28–32.   It would involve a cross-country route over several deep ravines—*e.g.*, the Wady Suweinit, near Michmash.   In 1 Sam. xiv. 2, Thenius, for " Migron," reads "the Precipice."   Some take Aiath for Ai, three miles south of Bethel.   Renan says (*Hist. du Peuple d'Israel*, iii.) : " Nom d'Anathoth, arrangé symboliquement."

to cheep or move the wing.[1] But Isaiah tells him
that he is but the axe boasting against the hewer, and
the wooden staff lifting itself up against its wielder.
Burning should be scattered over his glory. The
Lord of hosts should lop his boughs with terror, and
a mighty one should hew down the crashing forest of
his haughty Lebanon.

ii. Still more indignant were the true prophets
against those who trusted in an alliance with Egypt.
From first to last Isaiah warned Ahaz, and warned
Hezekiah, that no reliance was to be placed on Egyptian
promises—that Egypt was but like the reed of his own
Nile. He mocked the hopes placed on Egyptian intervention as being no less sure of disannulment than a
covenant with death and an agreement with Sheol.
This rebellious reliance on the shadow of Egypt was
but the weaving of an unrighteous web, and the adding
of sin to sin. It should lead to nothing but shame
and confusion, and the Jewish ambassadors to Zoan
and Egypt should only have to blush for a people
that could neither help nor profit. And then brand-
ing Egypt with the old insulting name of Rahab, or
" Blusterer," he says,—

> " Egypt helpeth in vain, and to no purpose.
> Therefore have I called her ' Rahab, that sitteth still.' "

Indolent braggart—that was the only designation which
she deserved ! Intrigue and braggadocio—smoke and
lukewarm water,—this was all which could be expected
from *her !*[2]

---

[1] Isa. x. 14. The metaphor of a bird's nest occurs more than once
in the boastful Assyrian records.

[2] Isa. xxx. 1–7. Rahab means " fierceness," " insolence." For the
various uses of the word, see Job xxvi. 12; Isa. li. 9, 10, 15;
Psalm lxxxix. 9, 10, lxxxvii. 4, 5.

Such teaching was eminently distasteful to the worldly politicians, who regarded faith in Jehovah's intervention as no better than ridiculous fanaticism, and forgot God's wisdom in the inflated self-satisfaction of their own. The priests—luxurious, drunken, scornful—were naturally with them. Men were fine and stylish, and in their religious criticisms could not express too lofty a contempt for any one who, like Isaiah, was too sincere to care for the mere polishing of phrases, and too much in earnest to shrink from reiteration. In their self-indulgent banquets these sleek, smug euphemists made themselves very merry over Isaiah's simplicity, reiteration, and directness of expression. With hiccoughing insolence they asked whether they were to be treated like weaned babes; and then wagging their heads, as their successors did at Christ upon the cross, they indulged themselves in a mimicry, which they regarded as witty, of Isaiah's style and manner. With him they said it is all,—

> "Tsav-la-tsav, tsav-la-tsav,
> Quav-la-quav, quav-la-quav,
> Z'eir sham, Z'eir sham!"—

which may be imitated thus:—With him it is always "Bit and bit, bid and bid, for-bid and for-bid, for*bid* and for*bid*, a lit-tle bit here, a lit-tle bit there." [1] Monosyllable is heaped on monosyllable; and no doubt the speakers tipsily adopted the tones of fond mothers addressing their babes and weanlings. Using the Hebrew words, one of these shameless roysterers would say, "*Tsav-la-tsav, tsav-la-tsav, quav-la-quav, quav-la-quav, Z'eir sham, Z'eir sham,*—that is how that

---

[1] See Dr. S. Cox (*Expositor*, i. 98–104) on Isa. xxviii. 7–13.

simpleton Isaiah speaks." And then doubtless a
drunken laugh would go round the table, and half a
dozen of them would be saying thus, " *Tsav-la-tsav,
tsav-la-tsav,*" at once. They derided Isaiah just as the
philosophers of Athens derided St. Paul—as a mere *sper-
mologos,* "a seed-pecker ! "[1] or "picker-up of learning's
crumbs." Is all this petty monosyllabism fit teaching
for persons like us ? Are we to be taught by copy-
books ? Do we need the censorship of this Old
Morality ?

On whom, full of the fire of God, Isaiah turned, and
told these scornful tipsters, who lorded it over God's
heritage in Jerusalam, that, since they disdained his
stammerings, God would teach them by men of strange
lips and alien tongue. They might mimic the style of
the Assyrians also if they liked; but they should fall
backward, and be broken, and snared, and taken.[2]

It must not be forgotten that the struggle of the
prophets against these parties was far more severe than
we might suppose. The politicians of expediency had
supporters among the leading princes. The priests—
whom the prophets so constantly and sternly denounce
—adhered to them ; and, as usual, the women were all
of the priestly party (comp. Isa. xxxii. 9–20). The
king, indeed, was inclined to side with his prophet, but
the king was terribly overshadowed by a powerful and
worldly aristocracy, of which the influence was almost
always on the side of luxury, idolatry, and oppression.

iii. But what had Isaiah to offer in the place of the
policy of these worldly and sacerdotal advisers of the
king ? It was the simple command " Trust in the Lord."
It was the threefold message " God is high ; God is

---

[1] Acts xvii. 18.   [2] Isa. xxviii. 7–22.

near ; God is Love."[1]   Had he not told Ahaz not to fear
the "stumps of two smouldering torches," when Rezin
and Pekah seemed awfully dangerous to Judah ?   So
he tells them now that, though their sins had necessitated the rushing stroke of Assyrian judgment, Zion
should not be utterly destroyed.   In Isaiah "the calmness requisite for sagacity rose from faith."   Mr. Bagehot
might have appealed to Isaiah's whole policy in illustration of what he has so well described as the military
and political benefits of religion.   Monotheism is of
advantage to men not only "by reason of the high
concentration of steady feeling which it produces.
but also for the mental calmness and sagacity which
surely springs from a pure and vivid conviction that
the Lord reigneth."[2]   Isaiah's whole conviction might
have been summed up in the name of the king himself:
"Jehovah maketh strong."

King Hezekiah, apparently not a man of much personal force, though of sincere piety, was naturally
distracted by the counsels of these three parties : and
who can judge him severely if, beset with such terrific
dangers, he occasionally wavered, now to one side, now
to the other ?   On the whole, it is clear that he was
wise and faithful, and deserves the high eulogy that
his faith failed not.   Naturally he had not within his
soul that burning light of inspiration which made Isaiah
so sure that, even though clouds and darkness might
lower on every side, God was an eternal Sun, which
flamed for ever in the zenith, even when not visible
to any eye save that of Faith.

---

[1] Professor Smith, *Isaiah*, i. 12.
[2] Bagehot, *Physics and Politics*, p. 73 ; Smith, *Isaiah*, 109.

CHAPTER XXVI

HEZEKIAH'S SICKNESS, AND THE EMBASSY FROM BABYLON

2 KINGS xx. 1—19

"Thou hast loved me out of the pit of nothingness."—ISA. xxxviii. 17 (A.V., margin).

> "See the shadow of the dial
> In the lot of every one
> Marks the passing of the trial,
> Proves the presence of the Sun."
>
> E. B. BROWNING.

IN the chaos of uncertainties which surrounds the chronology of King Hezekiah's reign, it is impossible to fix a precise date to the sickness which almost brought him to the grave. It has, however, been conjectured by some Assyriologists that the story of this episode has been displaced, because it seemed to break the continuity of the narrative of the Assyrian invasion ; and that, though it is placed in the Book of Kings after the deliverance from Sennacherib, it really followed the earlier incursion of Sargon. This is rendered more probable by Isaiah's promise (2 Kings xx. 6), "I will deliver thee and this city out of the hand of the King of Assyria," and by the fact that Hezekiah still possessed such numerous and splendid treasures to display to the ambassadors of Merodach-Baladan. This could hardly have been the case after he had been forced to pay a fine to the King of Assyria of all the silver that was found in the house of the Lord, and in the treasures of the king's house, to cut off the gold from the doors and pillars of the Temple, and even to send as captives to Nineveh some of his wives, and of the eunuchs of his palace.[1] The date "in those days" (2 Kings xx. 1) is vague and elastic, and may apply to any time before or after the great invasion.

He was sick unto death. The only indication which we have of the nature of his illness is that it took the form of a carbuncle or imposthume,[2] which could be locally treated, but which, in days of very imperfect therapeutic knowledge, might easily end in death, especially if it were on the back of the neck. The conjecture of Witsius and others that it was a form of the plague which they suppose to have caused the disaster to the Assyrian army has nothing whatever to recommend it.

Seeing the fatal character of his illness, Isaiah came to the king with the dark message, "Set thine house in order; for thou shalt die, and not live."

The message is interesting as furnishing yet another proof that even the most positive announcements of the prophets were, and were always meant to be, to some extent hypothetical and dependent on unexpressed conditions. This was the case with the famous prophecy of Micah that Zion should be ploughed down into a heap of ruins. It was never fulfilled; yet the prophet lost none of his authority, for it was well understood

---

[1] One of the first to point out the *necessary* rearrangement of the events of Hezekiah's reign was Dr. Hincks, in his paper on "A Rectification of Chronology which the newly discovered Apis-stélès render necessary" (*Journ. of Sacred Lit.*, October 1858). See my article on Hezekiah, Smith, *Dict. of the Bible*, 2nd ed., ii. 1251.

[2] Heb., *sh'chin*; LXX., ἕλκος; Vulg., *ulcus*.

that the doom which would otherwise have been carried out had been averted by timely penitence.

But the message of Isaiah fell with terrible anguish on the heart of the suffering king. He had hoped for a better fate. He had begun a great religious reformation. He had uplifted his people, at least in part, out of the moral slough into which they had fallen in the days of his predecessor. He had inspired into his threatened capital something of his own faith and courage. Surely he, if any man, might claim the old promises which Jehovah in His loving-kindness and truth had sworn to his father David and his father Abraham, that he being delivered out of the hand of his enemies should serve God without fear, walking in holiness and righteousness before Him all the days of his life. He was but a young man still—perhaps not yet thirty years old ; further, not only would he leave behind him an unfinished work, but he was childless,[1] and therefore it seemed as if with him would end the direct line of the house of David, heir to so many precious promises. He has left us—it is preserved in the Book of Isaiah—the poem which he wrote on his recovery, but which enshrines the emotion of his agonising anticipations[2] :—

"I said, In the noontide of my days I shall go into the gates of
    Sheol.
I am deprived of the residue of my years.
I said, I shall not see Yah, Yah, in the land of the living,
I shall behold no man more, when I am among them that cease
    to be.

---

[1] The Rabbis even make his sickness the punishment for his having neglected to secure an heir. He pleads that he foresaw the wickedness of his son. Isaiah tells him not to try to forestall God (*Berachoth*, f. 10, 1).

[2] Isa. xxxviii. 10-20.

> Mine habitation is removed, and is carried away from me like a
> shepherd's tent.
> Like a weaver I have rolled up my life ; he will cut me from the
> thrum.
>
> .   .   .   .   .   .
>
> Like a swallow or a crane, so did I chatter ;
> I did mourn as a dove ; mine eyes fail with looking upward.
> O Lord, I am oppressed ; be Thou my surety."

We must remember, as we contemplate his utter prostration of soul, that he was not blessed, as we are, with the sure and certain hope of the resurrection to eternal life. All was dim and dark to him in the shadowy world of *eidola* beyond the grave, and many a century was to elapse before Christ brought life and immortality to light. To enter Sheol meant to Hezekiah to pass beyond the cheerful sunshine of earth and the felt presence of God. No more worship, no more gladness there !

> " For Sheol cannot praise Thee, Death cannot celebrate Thee;
> They that go down into the pit cannot hope for Thy truth."

On every ground, therefore, the feelings of Hezekiah, had he not been a worshipper of God, might have been like those of Mycerinus, and, like that legendary Egyptian king, he might have cursed God before he died.

> " My father loved injustice, and lived long;
> I loved the good he scorned and hated wrong—
> The gods declare my recompense to-day.
> I looked for life more lasting, rule more high;
> And when six years are measured, lo, I die !
> Yet surely, O my people, did I ween
> Man's justice from the all-just gods was given,
> A light that from some upper point did beam,
> Some better archetype whose seat was heaven:
> A light that, shining from the blest abodes,
> Did shadow somewhat of the life of gods."

The indignation of Mycerinus often finds an echo on

Pagan tombstones, as in the famous epitaph on the grave of the girl Procope :—

> "I, Procope, lift up my hands against the gods,
> Who took me hence undeserving,
> Aged nineteen years."

It was far otherwise with Hezekiah. There was anguish in his heart, but no rebellion or defiance. He wept sore; he turned his face to the wall and wept;[1] but as he wept he also prayed, and said,—

"O Lord, remember now how I have walked before Thee in truth, and with a perfect heart, and have done that which is good in Thy sight."

Isaiah, after delivering his dark message, and doubtless adding to it such words of human consolation as were possible—if under such circumstances any were possible—had left the king's chamber. On every ground his feelings must have been almost as overwhelmed with sorrow as those of the king. Hezekiah was personally his friend, and the hope of his nation. Doubtless the prophet's prayers rose as fervently and as effectually as those of Luther, which snatched his friend Melanchthon back from the very gates of death. By the time that he had reached the middle of the court,[2] he felt borne in upon him, by that Divine

---

[1] Comp. 1 Kings xxi. 4 (Ahab).

[2] 2 Kings xx. 4. The *Q'ri* or "read" text is, as here rendered, *chatsee* (comp. 1 Kings vii. 8), and is followed by the LXX. (ἐν τῇ αὐλῇ τῇ μέσῃ), by the Vulgate (*mediam partem atrii*), and by the A.V. The R.V., which adopts the Kethib or written text, *ha'ir*, renders it "the middle part of the city." If this be the true reading, it would mean that Isaiah had gone some distance from the palace, and was now perhaps in the Valley between the Upper and the Lower City. But it seems not improbable that (1) "the steps of Ahaz" would be in the royal court, and (2) the answer of God, like the mercy of Christ to the suffering, may have come promptly as an echo to the appealing cry.

intuition which constituted his prophetic call, the certainty that God would withdraw the immediate doom which he had been commissioned to announce. It has been conjectured by some that the conviction was deepened in his mind by observing on the steps of Ahaz one of those remarkable but rare effects of refraction—or, as some have conjectured, of a solar eclipse, involving an obscuration of the upper limb of the sun—which had seemed to take the advancing shadow ten steps backwards; and that this was to him a sign from heaven of the promise of God and the prolongation of the king's life. Awestruck and glad, he hastened back into the presence of the dying king with the life-giving message that God had heard his prayer, and seen his tears, and would add fifteen years to his life, and would defend him, and deliver him and Jerusalem out of the hand of the King of Assyria. And this should be the sign to him from Jehovah—Jehovah would bring again the shadow ten steps up the stairs of Ahaz. To this sign—if it was visible from the chamber-window—he called the attention of the astonished king.[1]

We here naturally follow the narrative of Isaiah himself, as more authoritative than that of the historian of the Kings as to details in which they differ.[2] Not only is it quite in accordance with all that we know of history that slight variations should occur in the

---

[1] The LXX. calls "the stairs" ἀναβαθμοὺς τοῦ οἴκου τοῦ πατρός σου, and so, too, Josephus (*Antt.*, X. ii. 1). The Targum calls them "an hour-stone." Symmachus has, στρέψω τὴν σκίαν τῶν γραμμῶν ἣ κατέβη ἐν ὡρολογίῳ Ἀχάς.

[2] It should, however, be observed that on the question of priority critics are divided. Grotius, Vitringa, Paulus, Drechsler, etc., thought that the account in the Book of Isaiah is the original; De Wette, Maurer, Koster, Winer, Driver, etc., regard that account as a later abbreviation, perhaps from a common source.

traditions of long-past times, but the text of the Book
of Kings suggests some difficulty.   There we read that
Hezekiah asked Isaiah what should be the sign of the
promise—not mentioned in Isaiah—that he should go
up to the House of the Lord the third day.   Isaiah
then asked him whether the sign should be that the
shadow should advance ten steps, or recede ten steps.
But there is no interrogation in the Hebrew, which
rather means, "The shadow hath advanced ten steps
. . . if it shall recede ten steps ?" or if we insert the
interrogation in the first clause, "Hath the shadow
advanced ten steps?"[1]   The king's natural answer to
so strange an alternative would be that for the shadow
to advance ten steps was nothing; whereas its retro-
gression would be a sign indeed.   Then Isaiah cried
unto Jehovah, and the shadow went backward.   In
the obvious divergence of details we naturally follow
Isaiah himself; and if it be a true and understood rule
of all theology, "*Miracula non sunt multiplicanda præter
necessitatem,*" the miracle in this case—in the oppor-
tuneness of its occurrence, and the issues which it
inspired—was none the less a miracle because it was
carried out in direct accordance with God's unseen,
perpetual, miraculous Providence, which none but
unbelievers will nickname Chance.   That we are here
dealing with an historic incident is certain ; and they
who see and acknowledge God in all history find no
difficulty at all in seeing His dealings with men in
striking interpositions.   But these, by the analogy of
His whole Divine economy, would naturally be carried
out in accordance with natural laws.

The words rendered "the sun-dial of Anaz" mean
no more than "the steps [*ma'aloth*] of Ahaz."   Ahaz

---

[1] See Professor Lumby, *ad loc.*

evidently was a king of æsthetic tastes, who was fond of introducing foreign novelties and curiosities into Jerusalem.[1]   Steps, with a staff on the top of them as a gnomon, to serve as sun-dials had been invented at Babylon, and Ahaz may probably have become acquainted with their form and use when he paid his visit to Tiglath-Pileser at Damascus.   No one could blame him—it was indeed a meritorious act—to introduce to his people so useful an invention.   The word " hour " first occurs in Dan. iii. 6, and it was doubtless from Babylon that the Hebrews borrowed the division of days into hours.   This is the earliest instance in the Bible of the mention of any instrument to measure time.   That the recession of the shadow could be caused by refraction is certain, for it has been observed in modern days.   Thus, as is mentioned by Rosen-müller, on March 27th, 1703, Père Romauld, prior of the monastery at Metz, noticed that the shadow on his dial deviated an hour and a half, owing to refraction in the higher regions of the atmosphere.[2]   Or again, according to Mr. Bosanquet, the same effect might have been produced by the darkening shadow of an eclipse.   But while he appealed to Divine indications the great prophet did not neglect natural remedies.   He ordered that a cake of figs should be laid on the imposthume. It was a recognised and an efficient remedy, still recommended, centuries later, by Dioscorides, by Pliny, and by St. Jerome.   By God's blessing on man's therapeutic care, the king was speedily rescued from the gates of death.   Constantly in Scripture what we call the miraculous and what we call the providential are mingled together.   To those who regard the

---

[1] There is an exactly similar sun-dial not far from Delhi.
[2] *Journ. of Asiatic Soc.*, xv. 286–293.

providential as a constant miracle, the question of the miraculous becomes subordinate.[1]

With intense joy and gratitude the king hailed the respite which God had granted him. In fifteen years much might be done, much might be hoped for. All this he acknowledged with deep feeling in the song which he wrote on his recovery.

> "I shall go as in solemn procession [2] all my years because of the bitterness of my soul.
> O Lord, by these things men live,
> And wholly therein is the life of my spirit.
> Behold, it was for my peace that I had great bitterness;
> But Thou hast loved my soul from the pit of nothingness:
> For Thou hast cast all my sins behind Thy back.
>
> .   .   .   .
>
> The Lord is ready to save me ;
> Therefore will we sing my songs to the stringed instruments
> All the days of our life in the house of the Lord."[3]

"The wonder done in the land" was, according to the Chronicler, one of the grounds for the embassy which, after his recovery, Hezekiah received from Merodach-Baladan, the patriot prince of Babylon. The other ostensible object of the embassy was to send letters and a present in congratulation for the king's restoration to health. But the real object lay deeper, out of sight. It was to secure a southern alliance for Babylon against the incessant tyranny of Nineveh.

---

[1] Figs have a recognised use for imposthumes. See Dioscorides and Pliny quoted in Celsius, *Hierobot.*, ii. 373. In the passage of *Berachoth* quoted above, Hezekiah in his sickness asks Isaiah to give him his daughter in marriage, that he may have an heir. Isaiah replies that the decree of his death is irrevocable. The king bids Isaiah depart, and says (quoting Job xiii. 15) that a man must not despair, even if a sword is laid on his neck.

[2] Comp. Psalm xlii. 4.

[3] Isa. xxxviii. 10-20.

Merodach Baladan is mentioned in the inscriptions of Sargon.[1] He is described as " Merodach-Baladan, son of Baladan, King of Sumîr and Accad, king of the four countries, and conqueror of all his enemies." There had been long struggles, lasting indeed for centuries, between the city on the Euphrates and the city on the Tigris. Sometimes one, sometimes the other, had been victorious. Babylon—on the monuments Kur-Dunyash —had its original Accadian name of Ca-dinirra, which, like its Semitic equivalent Bal-el, means "Gate of God." Kalah (Larissa and Birs Nimroud) had been built by Shalmaneser I. before B.C. 1300. His son conquered Babylon, but not permanently ; for in some later raid the Babylonians got possession of his signet-ring, with its proud inscription, " Conqueror of Kur-Dunyash," and it was not recovered by the Assyrians till six centuries later, when it fell into the hands of Sennacherib. About 1150 Nebuchadrezzar I. of Babylon thrice invaded Assyria, but there was again peace and alliance in 1100. Merodach-Baladan I. reigned before 900. The king who now sought the friendship of Hezekiah was the second of the name. He seized or recovered the throne of Babylon in 721, after the

---

[1] The Babylonian form of his name is Marduk-habal-iddi-na—*i.e.*, " Merodach gave a son." He is the Mardokempados of the *Ptolemaic Canon*, and the second fragment of his reign (six months) is mentioned by Polyhistor (*ap.* Euseb.). Josephus calls him Baladan (*Antt.*, X. ii. 2). He was originally the prince of the Chaldæan *Bit Yakim.* Sargon calls him " Merodach-Baladan, the foe, the perverse, who, contrary to the will of the great gods, ruled as king at Babylon." He displaced him for a time by " Belibus, the son of a wise man, whom one had reared like a little dog " (as we might say "like a tame cat") "in my palace " (Schrader, ii. 32). In the Assyrian records he is often called (by mistake ?) "the son of Yakim." For the adventures of the Babylonian hero, see Schrader, *K. A. T.*, 213 ff., 224 ff., 227, and in Riehm, *Handwörterbuch*, ii. 982.

death of Shalmaneser, perhaps because Sargon was a
usurper of dubious descent. He helped the Elamites
against Assyria. Sargon was compelled to retreat to
Assyria, but returned in 712, and drove Merodach-
Baladan to flight. He was captured and taken to
Assyria. But on the murder of Sargon in 705, he
again managed to seize the throne of Babylon, killed
the viceroy who had been set up, and became king
for six months. After this, Sennacherib invaded his
country, defeated him, and drove him once more to
flight. He was perhaps killed by his successor.

Whether his overtures to Hezekiah took place before
his defeat by Sargon, or after his escape, is uncertain.
In either case he doubtless sent a splendid embassy,
for Babylon was far-famed for its golden magnificence
as "the glory of kingdoms" and "the beauty of the
Chaldees' excellency."[1] At that time the Jews knew
but little of the far-off city which was destined to
be so closely interwoven with their future fortunes,
as it was mingled with their oldest and dimmest traditions.[2] Apart from the magnificence of the presents
brought to him, it was not unnatural that Hezekiah
should regard this embassy with intense satisfaction.
It was flattering to the power of his little kingdom that
its alliance should be sought by the far-off and powerful
capital on the great river;[3] it was still more encouraging
to know that the frightful Nineveh had a strong enemy
not far from her own frontier. Merodach-Baladan's ambassadors would be sure to inform Hezekiah that their
lord had flung off the authority of Sargon, had kept
him at bay for many years, and was still the undisputed

---

[1] Isa. xiv. 4, xiii. 19.
[2] Gen. x. 10, 11, xi. 1-9.
[3] Jos., *Antt.*, X. ii. 2: Σύμμαχόν τε αὐτὸν εἶναι παρεκάλει καὶ φίλον.

king of the dominions snatched from the common enemy.
It might have seemed reasonable that Hezekiah, for his
part, should desire to leave the most favourable impression of his wealth and power on the mind of his
distant and magnificent ally. He "hearkened unto"
the ambassadors, or, more properly, "he was glad of
them" (R.V.),[1] and "showed them all the house of his
spicery and other treasures, his precious unguents, his
armoury, his bullion, plate, and the whole resources
of his kingdom." The Chronicler regards this as
ingratitude to God. He says that "Hezekiah rendered
not again according unto the benefits done unto him;
for his heart was lifted up: therefore there was wrath
upon him, and upon Judah and Jerusalem." It is a
severe judgment of later times, and the historian of
the Kings pronounces no such censure. Nevertheless,
he records the stern sentence pronounced by Isaiah.
The prophet had seen through the secret diplomacy
of the Babylonian ambassadors, and knew that the real
object of their mission was to induce his king to revolt
against Assyria in reliance on an arm of flesh. He
came to ask Hezekiah whose these men were, whence
they came, and what they had said. The king told
him who they were, and how he had received them;
but he did not think it wise to reveal their secret
proposals. If Isaiah had so vehemently reproved all
negotiations with Egypt, there was little probability
that he would sanction the overtures of Babylon. He
saw in Hezekiah's conduct a vein of ostentatious
elation, a swerving from theocratic faith; and with
remarkable prophetic insight convinced the king of the
error and impolicy of his proceedings, by announcing
that the final and, in fact, irrevocable captivity of Judah

---

[1] 2 Kings xx. 13. LXX., ἐχάρη.

would ultimately come, not from Nineveh, the fierce enemy, whose cloud of war was lurid on the horizon, but from Babylon, the apparently weaker friend, who was now making overtures of amity. With what heartrending grief must the king have heard the doom that the display of his treasures would prove to be in the future an incentive to the cupidity of the kings of Babylon, and that they would sweep away all those precious things to the banks of the Euphrates with such final overthrow that even the descendants of David should be sunk to the infinite degradation of being eunuchs in the palace of the King of Babylon.[1] The doom seems to have been fulfilled in part in the reign of Hezekiah's son, and more fearfully in the days of his great-grandchildren.[2]

The king's pride was humbled to the dust. In the spirit of Job—"The Lord gave, and the Lord hath taken away ; blessed be the name of the Lord"[3]—he resigned himself without a murmur to the will of Heaven, and exclaimed that all which God did must be well done. At least God granted him a respite. Peace and truth would be in his own days ; for that let him be thankful. They were words of humble resignation, uttered by one who had learnt to believe that whatever God decreed was just and right.

It would be unjust to measure the feelings of those far centuries by those of our own day, and there was none of the gross selfishness in the words of Hezekiah which led Nero to quote the line—

"When I am dead, let earth be mixed with fire";

or which led Louis XIV. to say—

"Après moi le déluge."

---

[1] See Dan. i. 6.   [2] 2 Chron. xxxiii. 11.   [3] Job i. 21.

We may perhaps trace in his exclamation something of the fatalism which gives a touch of apathy to the submissiveness of the Oriental. Some, too, have imagined that his distress was tinged by a gleam of happiness at the implicit promise that he should have a son. His wife's name was Hephzibah ("My delight is in her)," and within two years she brought forth the firstborn son, whose career, indeed, was dark and evil, but who became in due time an ancestor of the promised Messiah. The name "Manasseh" given him by his parents recalled the child born to Joseph in the land of his exile who had caused him to forget his sorrows.[1] Hezekiah had the spirit which says, —

> "That which Thou blessest is most good,
>   And unblest good is ill;
> And all is right which seems most wrong,
>   So it be Thy sweet will."

---

[1] Manasseh seems to mean "one who forgets." See Gen. xli. 51. It was the name of the husband of Judith (Judith viii. 2), and is found in Ezra x. 30, 33.

CHAPTER XXVII

HEZEKIAH AND ASSYRIA

B.C. 701

2 KINGS xviii. 13—xix. 37

'Αλλ' ὁ σοφώτατος βασιλεὺς οὐχ ὅπλα ταῖς ἐκείνων βλασφημίαις, ἀλλὰ προσευχὴν καὶ δάκρυα καὶ σάκκον ἀντέταξεν.—THEODORET.

> " When, sudden—how think ye the end ?
> Did I say 'without friend'?
> Say rather from marge to blue marge
> The whole sky grew his targe,
> With the sun's self for visible boss,
> While an Arm ran across
> Which the earth heaved beneath like a breast,
> Where the wretch was safe pressed."
>
> BROWNING.

ALTHOUGH during a few memorable scenes the relations of Judah with Assyria in the reign of Hezekiah leap into fierce light, many previous details are unfortunately left in the deepest obscurity—an obscurity all the more impenetrable from the lack of certain dates. It will perhaps help to simplify our conceptions if we first sketch what is known of Assyria from the cuneiform inscriptions, and then fill up the sketch of those scenes which are more minutely delineated in the Book of Kings and in the prophecies of Isaiah.

Sargon—perhaps a successful general of royal blood, though he never calls himself the son of any one [1]—

---

[1] One legend of his birth resembles the finding of Moses in the bulrushes.

seems to have usurped the throne on the death of
Shalmaneser IV., during the siege of Samaria in B.C.
722. He took Samaria, deported its inhabitants, and
repeopled it from the Assyrian dominions. "In their
place," he says, in his tablets in the halls of his palace
at Khorsabad, "I settled the men of countries conquered [by my hand]."[1] In 720 he suppressed a
futile attempt at revolt, headed by a pretender named
Yahubid, in Hamath, which he reduced to "a heap of
ruins." For some years after this he was occupied
mainly on his northern frontiers, but he tells us that
until 711 tribute continued to come in from Judah and
Philistia. Meanwhile, these terrified and oppressed
feudatories, writhing under the remorseless dominion
of Nineveh, naturally began to listen to the intrigues
of Egypt, whose interest it was to create a bulwark
between herself and the invasion of the armies which
were the abhorrence of the world. Under the influence
of Sabaco, which gave new strength and unity to Egypt,
she succeeded in seducing Ashdod from its allegiance to
Sargon. Sargon at once deposed Azuri, King of Ashdod, and put his brother Ahimit in his place. The
Ashdodites soon after deposed Ahimit, and elected
in his place Jaman, who was in alliance with Sabaco.[2]
This revolt was evidently favoured by Judah, Edom,
and Moab; for Sargon says that they, as well as the
people of Philistia, "were speaking treason." The
rebellion was crushed by Sargon's promptitude.[3] He
tells his own tale thus :—

"In the wrath of my heart I did not divide my army,
and I did not diminish the ranks, but I marched against

---

[1] Schrader, *K. A. T.*, pp. 272–274; *Records of the Past*, vii. 28.

[2] Smith, *Eponym Canon*, p. 130.

[3] See Prof. Smith, *Isaiah*, p. 198.

Ashdod with my warriors, who did not separate themselves from the traces of my sandals. I besieged, I
took Ashdod and Gunt-Asdodim. I then re-established
these towns. I placed [in them] the people whom my
arms had conquered, I put over them my lieutenant as
governor. I regarded them as Assyrians, and they
practised obedience."[1]

Sargon does not, however, seem to have conducted
this campaign in person; for we read in Isa. xx. 1
that he sent his Turtan—*i.e.*, his commander-in-chief,[2]
whose name seems to have been Zir-bâni—to Ashdod,
who fought against it and took it. The wretched
Philistines had put their trust in Sabaco. " The
people," says Sargon, " and their evil chiefs sent their
presents to Pharaoh, King of Egypt, a prince who could
not save them, and besought his alliance." Isaiah had
for three years been indicating how vain this policy was
by one of those acted parables which so powerfully
affect the Eastern mind. He had, by the word of the
Lord, stripped the shoes from off his feet and the upper
robe of sackcloth from his loins, and walked, " naked
and barefoot, for a sign and portent against Egypt and
Ethiopia," to indicate that even thus should the people
of Egypt and Ethiopia be carried away as captives,
naked and barefoot, by the kings of Assyria. Egypt
was the boast of one party at Jerusalem, and Ethiopia,
which had now become master of Egypt under Sabaco,
was their expectation ; but Isaiah's public self-humilia-

---

[1] *Records of the Past*, vii. 40. Sargon's words are, " The people of
Philistia, Judah, Edom, and Moab were speaking treason. The people
and their evil chiefs, to fight against me, unto *Pharaoh, the King of
Egypt, a monarch who could not save them*, their presents carried,
and besought his alliance " (G. Smith, *Assyrian Discoveries*, 290).

[2] On the monuments called *Turtanu*, " Holder of power." See
Schrader in Riehm, *s.v.*

tion showed how utterly their hopes should come to nought.[1] Before the outbreak at Ashdod, Sargon had suppressed a revolt of Hanun, or Hanno, King of Gaza, and Egypt and Assyria first met face to face at Raphia (about B.C. 720), where Sabaco fought in person with an Egyptian contingent, at a spot half-way between Gaza and the "river of Egypt."[2] Sabaco, whom Sargon calls "the Sultan of Egypt" (Siltannu Muzri), had been defeated, and fled precipitately, but Sargon was not then sufficiently free from other complications to advance to the Nile. The hoarded vengeance of Assyria was inflicted upon Egypt nearly a century later by Esarhaddon and Assurbanipal.

In the two suppressions of revolt at Ashdod, Sargon or his Turtan must have come perilously near Jerusalem, and perhaps he may have inflicted sufficient damage to admit of the boast that he had "conquered" Judæa. If so, his military vanity made him guilty of an exaggeration.

Far more serious to Sargon was the revolt of Merodach-Baladan, King of Chaldæa. Babylon had always been a rival of Nineveh in the competition for worldwide dominion, and for twelve years, as Sargon says, Merodach-Baladan had been "sending ambassadors"[3]—

---

[1] Raphia, or Ropeh, is on the borders of the desert. Asia beat Africa in every encounter—at Raphia, at Altaqu, at Carchemish. The impression of the seal of Shabak, attached to his capitulations with Sargon, was found at Nineveh by Sir A. H. Layard, and is now in the British Museum. Shabak died in 712. His son Shabatoh succeeded him in Egypt, and his nephew (?) Tirhakah in Ethiopia. Sabaco's name assumes many forms (LXX., Σηγώρ; Herod., ii. 137; Σαβακώς; Vulg., Sua). The Egyptians called him Shaba(ka).

[2] Isa. xx. 1–6.

[3] Lenormant, *Les Premières Civilisations*, ii. 203; *Records of the Past*, vii. 41–46.

to Hezekiah among others—in the patient effort to consolidate a formidable league.   Elam and Media were with him ; and at a solemn banquet, for which they had " spread the carpets," [1] and eaten and drank, the cry had risen, " Arise, ye princes ! anoint the shield. ' Standing in ideal vision on his watch-tower, Isaiah saw the sweeping rush of the Assyrian troops on their horses and camels on their way to Babylon.   What should come of it ?   The answer is in the words, " Fallen, fallen is Babylon, and all the images of her gods he [Sargon] hath broken to the ground."   Alas ! there is no hope from Babylon or its embassy !   Would that Isaiah could have held out a hope !   But no, " O my threshed one, son of my threshing-floor, that which I have heard from the Lord of hosts, the God of Israel, that have I declared unto you." [2]   And so it came to pass.   The brave Babylonian was defeated.   In 709 Sargon occupied his palace, took Dur-yakin, to which he had fled for refuge, and made himself Lord Paramount as far as the Persian Gulf.   It was his last great enterprise.   He built and adorned his palaces, and looked forward to long years of peace and splendour ; but in 705 the dagger-thrust of an assassin—a malcontent of the town of Kullum—found its way to his heart ; and Sennacherib reigned in his stead.

Sennacherib—Sin-ahi-irba (" Sin, the moon-god, has

---

[1] Isa. **xxi.** 6, A.V., " Watch in the watch-tower."   Hitzig, Cheyne, " They spread the carpets."   Much in this short oracle (xxi. 1-10) is obscure.   Isaiah seems, in denouncing the fate of Babylon, to mourn for the ruin of the smaller states of which it was the prelude (G. Smith, *Soc. of Bibl. Arch.*, ii. 320 · Kleinert, *Stud. u. Krit.*, 1877 W. R. Smith in *Enc. Brit.*, *s.v.* " Isaiah ").

[2] Isa. **xxi.** 10—*i.e.*, " My people threshed and trodden "; LXX., ὁ καταλελειμμένος καὶ οἱ ὀδυνώμενοι ; *Records of the Past*, vii. 47.

multiplied brothers ") [1]—was one of the haughtiest, most splendid, and most powerful of all the kings of Assyria, though the petty state of Judah, relying on her God, defied and flouted him. The son of a mighty conqueror, at the head of a magnificent army, he regarded himself as the undisputed lord of the world.[2] Born in the purple, and bred up as crown prince, his primary characteristic was an overweening pride and arrogance, which shows itself in all his inscriptions. He calls himself "the Great King, the Powerful King, the King of the Assyrians, of the nations of the four regions, the diligent ruler, the favourite of the Great Gods, the observer of sworn faith, the guardian of law, the establisher of monuments, the noble hero, the strong warrior, the first of kings, the punisher of unbelievers, the destroyer of wicked men." [3] He was mighty both in war and peace. His warlike glories are attested by Herodotus, by Polyhistor, by Abydenus, by Demetrius, and by his own annals. His peaceful triumphs are attested by the great palace which he erected at Nineveh, and the magnificent series of sculptured slabs with which he adorned it ; by his canals and aqueducts, his gateways and embankments, his Bavian sculpture, and his *stêlê* at the Nahr-el-Kelb. He was a worthy suc-

---

[1] Herod., Σαναχάριβos; Jos., Σεναχήριβos. See Appendix I. Sin was the moon-god ; Merodach, the planet Jupiter ; Adar, Saturn ; Ishtai, Venus ; Nebo, Mercury ; Nergal, Mars (Schrader, ii. 117).

[2] Sargon seems to have been murdered in the palace of unparalleled splendour which he built at Dur-Sharrukin ("The City of Sargon "). It took him five years to build it with armies of workmen. Its halls, opened by Botta, were the first Assyrian halls ever entered by a modern's foot. It is strange that this greatest of Assyrian kings is only mentioned once in the Bible (Isa. xx. 1). We owe to Assyriology his restoration to his proper place in the annals of mankind. See Ragozin, *Assyria*, 247–254.

[3] Rawlinson, *Ancient Monarchies*, ii. 178.

cessor of his father Sargon, and of the second Tiglath-Pileser—active in his military enterprises, indefatigable, persevering, full of resource.[1]

On one of his bas-reliefs we see this magnificent potentate seated on his throne, holding two arrows in his right hand, while his left grasps the bow. A rich bracelet clasps each of his brawny arms. On his head is the jewelled pyramidal crown of Assyria, with its embroidered lappets. His dark locks stream down over his shoulders, and the long, curled beard flows over his breast. His strongly marked, sensual features wear an aspect of unearthly haughtiness. He is clad in superbly broidered robes, and his throne is covered with rich tapestries, and bas-reliefs of Assyrians or captives, who, like the Greek caryatides, uphold its divisions with their heads and arms.

Yet all this glory faded into darkness, and all this colossal pride crumbled into dust. Sennacherib not only died, like his father, by murder, but by the murderous hands of his own sons, and after the shattering of all his immense pretensions—a defeated and dishonoured man.

One of his invasions of Judæa occupies a large part of the Scripture narrative.[2] It was the fourth time of that terrible contact between the great world-power which symbolised all that was tyrannic and idolatrous, and the insignificant tribe which God had chosen for His own inheritance.

---

[1] Canon Rawlinson, *Kings of Israel and Judah*, 187.

[2] On his own monuments this campaign, except its final catastrophe, is narrated in four sections : (1) The subjugation of Phœnicia, and of Philistine towns ; (2) the conquest of King Zidka of Askelon ; (3) the defeat of Ekron, the restoration of their vassal king Padi to his throne, and the defeat of Egypt at Altaqu ; (4) the expedition against Jerusalem (Schrader, E. Tr., i. 298). See Appendix I.

In the reign of Ahaz, about B.C. 732, Judah had come into collision with Tiglath-Pileser II.

Under Shalmaneser IV. and Sargon, the Northern Kingdom had ceased to exist in 722.

Under Sargon, Judah had been harassed and humbled, and had witnessed the suppression of the Philistian revolt, and of the defeat of the powerful Sabaco at Raphia about 720.

Now came the fourth and most overwhelming calamity. If the patriots of Jerusalem had placed any hopes in the disappearance of the ferocious Sargon, they must speedily have recognised that he had left behind him a no less terrible successor.

Sennacherib reigned apparently twenty-four years (B.C. 705-681). On his accession he placed a brother, whose name is unknown, on the vice-regal throne of Babylon, and contented himself with the title of King of the Assyrians. This brother was speedily dethroned by a usurper named Hagisa, who only reigned thirty days, and was then slain by the indefatigable Merodach-Baladan, who held the throne for six months. He was driven out by Belibus, who had been trained "like a little dog" in the palace of Nineveh,[1] but was now made King of Sumîr and Accad—*i.e.*, of Babylonia. Sennacherib entered the palace of Babylon and carried off the wife of Merodach and endless spoil in triumph, while Merodach fled into the land of Guzumman, and (like the Duke of Monmouth) hid himself "among the marshes and reeds," where the Assyrians searched for him for five days, but found no trace of him. After three years (702-699) Belibus proved faithless, and

---

[1] This allusion is said to be the only instance of humour—"*grim humour*, or it would not be Assyrian"—which occurs in the Assyrian annals.

Sennacherib made his son Assur-nadin-sum viceroy of Babylon.

His second campaign was against the Medes in Northern Elam.

His third (701) was against the Khatti (the Hittites) —*i.e.*, against Phœnicia and Palestine.[1] He drove King Luli from Sidon "by the mere terror of the splendour of my sovereignty," and placed Tubalu (*i.e.*, Ithbaal) in his place, and subdued into tributary districts Arpad, Byblos, Ashdod, Ammon, Moab, and Edom, suppressing at the same time a very abortive rising in Samaria. " All these brought rich presents and kissed my feet." He also subdued Zidka, King of Askelon, from whom he took Beth-Dagon, Joppa, and other towns. Padî, the King of Ekron, was a faithful vassal of Assyria ; he was therefore deposed by the revolting Ekronites, and sent in chains into the safe custody of Hezekiah, who "imprisoned him in darkness." The rebel states all relied on the Egyptians and Ethiopians. Sennacherib fought against Egyptians and Ethiopians, "in reliance upon Assur my God," at Altaqu (B.C. 701), and claims to have defeated them, and carried off the sons and charioteers of the King of Egypt, and the charioteers of the kings of Ethiopia.[2] He then tells us that he punished Altaqu and Timnath.[3] He impaled the rebels of Ekron on stakes all round the city. He restored Padî, and made him a vassal. "Hezekiah [Chazaqiahu] of Judah, who had not submitted to my yoke, the terror of

---

[1] Schrader, pp. 234-279. The account of the memorable campaign is narrated in duplicate on the Taylor Cylinder in the British Museum, and on the Bull Inscription at Kouyunjik.

[2] Sennacherib calls Tirhakah's army "a host that no man could number"; but it was defeated by the better discipline, the heavier armour, and the superior physical strength of the Assyrians.

[3] See Josh. xix. 43.

the splendour of my sovereignty overwhelmed. Himself as a bird in a cage, in the midst of Jerusalem, his royal city, I shut up. The Arabians and his dependants, whom he had introduced for the defence of Jerusalem, his royal city, together with thirty talents of gold, eight hundred of silver, bullion, precious stones, ivory couches and thrones, an abundant treasure, with his daughters, his harem, and his attendants, I caused to be brought after me to Nineveh. He sent his envoy to pay tribute and render homage." At the same time, he overran Judæa, took forty-six fenced cities and many smaller towns, "with laying down of walls, hewing about, and trampling down," and carried off more than two hundred thousand captives with their spoil. Part of Hezekiah's domains was divided among three Philistine vassals who had remained faithful to Assyria.

It was in the midst of this terrible crisis that Hezekiah had sent to Sennacherib at Lachish his offer of submission, saying, "I have offended; return from me; that which thou puttest upon me I will bear."[1] The spoiling of the palace and Temple was rendered necessary to raise the vast mulct which the Assyrian King required.[2]

It is at Lachish—now Um-Lakis, a fortified hill in the Shephelah, south of Jerusalem, between Gaza and Eleutheropolis—that we catch another personal glimpse of the mighty oppressor. We see him depicted, on his triumphal tablets, in the palace-chambers of Kouyunjik,

---

[1] This very phrase "I imposed on them" is found on Sennacherib's monument (Schrader, ii. 1). The references, when not otherwise specified, are to Whitehouse's English translation.

[2] In 2 Kings xviii. 16 the word "pillars" or "doorposts" is uncertain. LXX., ἐστηριγμένα; Vulg., *laminas auri.*

engaged in the siege ; for the town offered a determined resistance,[1] and required all the energies and all the trained heroism of his forces. We see him next, carefully painted, seated on his royal throne in magnificent apparel, with his tiara and bracelets, receiving the spoils and captives of the city. The inscription says : "Sennacherib, the mighty king, the king of the country of Assyria, sitting on the throne of judgment at the entrance of the city of Lakisha. I give permission for its slaughter." He certainly implied that he took the city, but a doubt is thrown on this by 2 Chron. xxxii. 1, which only says that " he *thought* to win these cities " ; and the historian says (2 Kings xix. 8) that he " departed from Lachish." Lachish was evidently a very strong city, and it is so depicted in the palace-tablets at Kouyunjik. It had been fortified by Rehoboam, and had furnished a refuge to the wretched Amaziah.[2]

If Judah and Jerusalem had listened to the messages of Isaiah,[3] they might have been saved the humiliating affliction which seemed to have plunged the brief sun of their prosperity into seas of blood. He had warned

---

[1] 2 Chron. xxxii. 9. He had to besiege it " with all his power." He seems to have thought it even more important than Jerusalem, for he superintended the siege in person (Layard, *Nineveh and Babylon,* 150; *Monuments of Nineveh,* 2nd series, pl. 21). The ruined Tel of Umm-el-Lakis lies between the Wady Simsim and the Wady-el-Ahsy (Riehm).

[2] See 2 Chron. xi. 9, xxv. 27; Jer. xxxiv. 7. The allusion to this city in Micah (i. 13) is obscure: "O thou inhabitant of Lachish [swift steed], bind the chariot to the swift steed: she is the beginning of sin to the daughter of Zion: for the transgressions of Israel were found in thee." This seems to imply that some form of idolatry had come from Israel to Lachish, and from Lachish to Jerusalem. In Sennacherib's picture of the city, foreign worship is represented as going on in it (Layard, *Monuments of Nineveh,* Pls. 21 and 24; Rawlinson, *Herodotus,* i. 477).

[3] Isa. xxix., xxx., xxxi.

them incessantly and in vain. He had foretold their
present desolation, in which Zion should be like a
woman seated on the ground, wailing in her despair.
He had taught them that formalism was no religion,
and that external rites did not win Jehovah's approval.
He had told them how foolish it was to put trust in the
shadow of Egypt, and had not shrunk from revealing
the fearful consequences which should follow the setting
up of their own false wisdom against the wisdom of
Jehovah. Yet, intermingled with pictures of suffering,
and threats of a harvestless year, designed to punish
the vanity and display of their women, and the intimation—never actually fulfilled—that even the palace and
Temple should become " the joy of wild asses, a pasture
of flocks," he constantly implies that the disaster
would be followed by a mysterious, divine, complete
deliverance, and ultimately by a Messianic reign of joy
and peace. Night is at hand, he said, and darkness;
but after the darkness will come a brighter dawn.

CHAPTER XXVIII

THE GREAT DELIVERANCE

B.C. 701

2 KINGS xix. 1—37

"There brake He the lightnings of the bow, the shield, the sword,
and the battle."—PSALM lxxvi. 3.

"ᾠδὴ πρὸς τὸν Ἀσσύριον."—LXX.

"And the might of the Gentile, unsmote by the sword,
Hath melted like snow at the glance of the Lord."

BYRON.

"Vuolsi cosi colà dove si puote
Cio che si vuole: e più non dimandare."

DANTE.

"Through love, through hope, through faith's transcendent dower,
We feel that we are greater than we know."

WORDSWORTH.

"God shall help her, and that when the morning dawns."—
PSALM xlvi. 5.

IN spite of the humble submission of Hezekiah, it is
a surprise to learn from Isaiah that Sennacherib—
after he had accepted the huge fine and fixed the
tribute, and departed to subdue Lachish—broke his
covenant.[1] He sent his three chief officers—the Turtan,
or commander-in-chief, whose name seems to have been
Belemurani;[2] the Rabsaris, or chief eunuch;[3] and the

---

[1] Isa. xxxiii. 8.   [2] Isa. xx. 1.
[3] Jer. xxxix 3. The meaning of the name is not certain. *Saris*,
in Hebrew, is "eunuch"; but the word is not known in Assyrian
records, and we should expect *Rabsarisim*, as in Dan. i. 3.

Rabshakeh, or chief captain[1]—from Lachish to Hezekiah, with a command of absolute, unconditional surrender, to be followed by deportation. By this conduct Sennacherib violated his own boast that he was "a keeper of treaties." Yet it is not difficult to conjecture the reason for his change of plan. He had found it no easy matter to subdue even the very minor fortress of Lachish; how unwise, then, would it be for him to leave in his rear an uncaptured city so well fortified as Jerusalem! He was advancing towards Egypt. It was obviously a strategic error to spare on his route a hostile and almost impregnable stronghold as a nucleus for the plans of his enemies. Moreover, he had heard rumours that Tirhakah, the third and last Ethiopian king of Egypt, was advancing against him, and it was most important to prevent any junction between his forces and those of Hezekiah.[2] He could not come in person to Jerusalem, for the siege of Lachish was on his hands; but he detached from his army a large contingent under his Turtan, to win the Jews by seductive promises, or to subdue Jerusalem by force. Once more, therefore, the Holy City saw beneath her often-captured walls the vast beleaguering host, and "governors and rulers clothed most gorgeously, horsemen riding upon horses, all of them desirable young men." Isaiah describes to us how the people crowded to the house-tops, half dead with fear, weeping and

---

[1] Rabsak perhaps means *chief officer* or vizier, and is Hebraised into Rabshakeh. Prof. G. A. Smith (*Isaiah*, p. 345) calls him "Sennacherib's Bismarck." Rabshakeh, usually rendered "chief cupbearer," is an Aramaised form of Rabsak (great chief); but we know of no chief cupbearer at the Assyrian court (Schrader, *K. A. T.*, 199 f.).

[2] From an Apis-stélè he seems to have reigned twenty-six years (B.C. 694–668?).

despairing, and crying to the hills to cover them, and
bereft of their rulers, who had been bound by the
archers of the enemy in their attempt to escape.   They
gazed on the quiver-bearing warriors of Elam in their
chariots, and the serried ranks of the shields of Kir,
and the cavalry round the gates.   And he tells us how,
as so often occurs at moments of mad hopelessness,
many who ought to have been crying to God in sackcloth and ashes, gave themselves up, on the contrary,
to riot and revelry, eating flesh, and drinking wine,
and saying : " Let us eat and drink ; for to-morrow we
die."[1]   The king alone had shown patience, calmness,
and active foresight ; and he alone, by his energy and
faith, had restored some confidence to the spirits of his
fainting people.

Although the city had been refortified by the king,
and supplied with water, the hearts of the inhabitants
must have sunk within them when they saw the
Assyrian army investing the walls, and when the three
commissioners—taking their station " by the conduit of
the upper pool which is in the highway of the fuller's
field "—summoned the king to hear the ultimatum of
Sennacherib.

The king did not in person obey the summons ; but
he, too, sent out his three chief officers.   They were
Eliakim, the son of Hilkiah, who, as the chamberlain
(*al-hab-baîth*), was a great prince (*nagîd*) ; Shebna, who
had been degraded, perhaps at the instance of Isaiah,
from the higher post, and was now secretary (*sopher*) ;
and Joah, son of Asaph, the chronicler (*mazkîr*), to
whom we probably owe the minute report of the
memorable scene.   No doubt they went forth in the
pomp of office—Eliakim with his robe, and girdle, and

---

[1] Isa..xxii. 1-13.

key.[1] The Rabshakeh proved himself, indeed, "an affluent orator," and evinced such familiarity with the religious politics of Judah and Jerusalem, that this, in conjunction with his perfect mastery of Hebrew, gives colour to the belief that he was an apostate Jew. He began by challenging the idle confidence of Hezekiah, and his vain words[2] that he had counsel and strength for the war. Upon what did he rely? On the broken and dangerous bulrush of Egypt?[3] It would but pierce his hand! On Jehovah? But Hezekiah had forfeited his protection by sweeping away His *bamoth* and His altars! Why, let Hezekiah make a wager;[4] and if Sennacherib furnished him with two thousand horses, he would be unable to find riders for them! How, then, could he drive back even the lowest of the Assyrian captains? And was not Jehovah on their side? It was He who had bidden them destroy Jerusalem!

That last bold assertion, appealing as it did to all that was erroneous and abject in the minds of the superstitious, and backed, as it was, by the undeniable force of the envoy's argument, smote so bitterly on the ear of Hezekiah's courtiers, that they feared it would render negotiation impossible. They humbly entreated the orator to speak to "his servants" in the Aramaic language of Assyria, which they understood,[5] and not in Hebrew, which was the language of all the Jews who stood in crowds on the walls. Surely this was

---

[1] Eliakim. See Isa. xxii. 21, 22.

[2] "Vain words"; lit., "a word of the lips." LXX., λόγοι χειλέων.

[3] Comp. Isa. xxx. 1–7 ; Ezek. xxix. 6. It seems to be an over-refinement to suppose that Sennacherib refers to the divisions between Egypt and Ethiopia.

[4] 2 Kings xviii. 23, A.V.: "Let Hezekiah give pledges."

[5] Heb., *Arâmith.*

a diplomatic embassy to their king, not an incitement
to popular sedition?

The answer of the Rabshakeh was truly Assyrian
in its utterly brutal and ruthless coarseness. Taking
up his position directly in front of the wall,[1] and
ostentatiously addressing the multitude, he ignored
the representatives of Hezekiah. Who were they?
asked he. His master had not sent him to speak to
them, or to their poor little puppet of a king, but to the
people on the wall, the foul garbage of whose sufferings
of thirst and famine they should share.[2] And to all
the multitude the great king's[3] message was:—Do not
be deceived. Hezekiah cannot save you. Jehovah
will not save you. Come to terms with me, and give
me hostages and pledges and a present, and then live
in happy peace and plenty until I come and deport you
to a land as fair and fruitful as this. How should
Jehovah deliver them? Had any of the gods of the
nations delivered them out of the hands of the King of
Assyria? "Where are the gods of Hamath, and of
Arpad? Where are the gods of Sepharvaim, Hena,
and Ivvah? Have the gods of Samaria delivered
Samaria out of my hand, that Jehovah should deliver
Jerusalem out of my hand?"[4]

It was a very powerful oration, but the orator must
have been a little disconcerted to find that it was
listened to in absolute silence. He had disgracefully

---

[1] 2 Kings xviii. 28, where *stood* should be rendered *came forward*.

[2] The coarse expression is softened down by the Chronicler
(2 Chron. xxxii. 18).

[3] The kings of Assyria usually called themselves "great king,
mighty king, king of the multitude, king of the land Assur."

[4] Every one must notice the glaring inconsistency between this
defiance of Jehovah and the previous claim to the possession of His
sanction. On Hamath, Arpad, etc., see Schrader, ii. 7-10.

violated the comity of international intercourse by appealing to subjects against their lawful king ; yet from the starving people there came not a murmur of reply. Faithful to the behest of their king in the midst of their misery and terror, they answered not a word. Agamemnon is silent before the coarse jeers of Thersites. " The sulphurous flash dies in its own smoke, only leaving a hateful stench behind it !" And in this attitude of the people there was something very sublime and very instructive. Dumb, stricken, starving, the wretched Jews did not answer the envoy's taunts or menaces, because they would not. They were not even in those extremities to be seduced from their allegiance to the king whom they honoured, though the speaker had contemptuously ignored his existence. And though the Rabshakeh had cut them to the heart with his specious appeals and braggart vaunts, yet "this clever, self-confident, persuasive personage, with two languages on his tongue, and an army at his back," could not shake the confidence in God, which, however unreasonable it might seem, had been elevated into a conviction by their king and their prophet. The Rabsak had tried to seduce the people into rebellion, but he had failed.[1] They were ready to die for Hezekiah with the fidelity of despair. The mirage of sensual comfort in exiled servitude should not tempt them from the scorched wilderness from which they could still cry out for the living God.

Yet the Assyrian's words had struck home into the hearts of his greatest hearers, and therefore how much more into those of the ignorant multitudes ! Eliakim

---

[1] Isa. xxxiii. 8: "He hath broken the covenant, he hath despised the cities, he regardeth no man."

and Shebna and Joah came to Hezekiah with their clothes rent, and told him the words of the Rabshakeh. And when the king heard it, when he found that even his submission had been utterly in vain, he too rent his clothes, and put on sackcloth,[1] and went into the only place where he could hope to find comfort, even into the house of the Lord, which he had cleansed and restored to beauty, although afterwards he had been driven to despoil it. Needing an earthly counsellor, he sent Eliakim and Shebna and the elders of the priests to Isaiah. They were to tell him the outcome of this day of trouble, rebuke, and contumely; and since the Rabshakeh had insulted and despised Jehovah, they were to urge the prophet to make his appeal to Him, and to pray for the remnant which the Assyrians had left.[2]

The answer of Isaiah was a dauntless defiance. If others were in despair, he was not in the least dismayed. "Be not afraid"—such was his message—"of the mere words with which the boastful boys of the King of Assyria have blasphemed Me.[3] Behold, I will put a spirit in him, and he shall hear a rumour,[4] and shall return to his own land; and I will cause him to fall by the sword in his own land."

Much crestfallen at the total and unexpected failure of the embassy, and of his own heart-shaking appeals, the Rabshakeh returned. But meanwhile Sennacherib had taken Lachish, and marched to Libnah (Tel-es-

---

[1] 1 Kings xx. 32; 2 Kings vi. 30.

[2] Sennacherib had already carried off vast numbers. See Isa. xxiv. 1-12; Demetrius *ap.* Clem. Alex., *Strom.*, i. 403.

[3] Isaiah's phrase, *na'ari melek*, "lads of the king," is contemptuous. LXX., παιδάρια.

[4] Heb., *ruach*; LXX., δίδωμι ἐν αὐτῷ πνεῦμα. Theodoret calls this "spirit" *cowardice* (τὴν δειλίαν οἶμαι δηλοῦν).

Safîa), which he was now besieging.[1] There it was
that he heard the "rumour" of which Isaiah had
spoken—the report, namely, that Tirhakah, the third
king of the Ethiopian dynasty of Pharaohs,[2] was
advancing in person to meet him.   This was B.C. 701,
and it is perhaps only by anticipation that Tirhakah
is called "King" of Ethiopia.   He was only the general
and representative of his father Shabatok, if (as some
think) he did not succeed to the throne till 698.

It was impossible for Sennacherib under these circumstances to return northwards to Jerusalem, of which
the siege would inevitably occupy some time.   But
he sent a menacing letter,[3] reminding Hezekiah that
neither king nor god had ever yet saved any city from
the hands of the Assyrian destroyers.   Where were
the kings, he asked again, of Hamath, Arpad, Sepharvaim, Hena, Ivvah?   What had the gods of Gozan,
Haran, Rezeph, and the children of Eden in Telassar
done to save their countries from Sennacherib's ancestors, when they had laid them under the ban ?[4]

---

[1] Libnah means "whiteness."   Dean Stanley (*S. and P.*, 207, 258)
identifies it with a white-faced hill, the Blanchegarde of the Cru-
saders.

[2] The dates usually given are Sabaco, B.C. 725–712; Shabatok,
712–698; Tirhakah, 698–672.   Manetho, Τάραχος; Strabo, Τερáκων, ὁ
Αἰθιώψ.   He was third king of the twenty-fifth dynasty, and the
greatest of the Egyptian sovereigns who came from Ethiopia.   He
reigned gloriously for many years.   We see his figure at Medinet
Abou, smiting ten captive princes with an iron mace; but he was
finally defeated by Esarhaddon, and in 668 by Assurbanipal at
Karbanit (Canopus).   He is called by his conqueror "Tar-ku-u, King
of Egypt and Cush" (Schrader, *K. A. T.*, 336 ff.).

[3] Heb., *Sepharim*; Vulg., *litteræ*; 2 Chron. xxxii. 17.   The more
ordinary term for a letter is *iggereth*.

[4] 2 Kings xix. 12 (Heb.); Ezek. xxvii. 23.   On these places see
Schrader, ii. 11, 12.   It had been indeed Sennacherib's work "to

Again the pious king found comfort in God's Temple.
Taking with him the scornful and blasphemous letter,
he spread it out before Jehovah in the Temple with
childlike simplicity, that Jehovah might read its insults
and be moved by this dumb appeal.[1]   Then both he
and Isaiah cried mightily to God, "who sitteth above
the cherubim," admitting the truth of what Sennacherib
had said, and that the kings of Assyria had destroyed
the nations, and burnt their vain gods in the fire
But of what significance was that?   Those were but
gods of wood and stone, the works of men's hands.[2]
But Jehovah was the One, the True, the Living God.
Would He not manifest among the nations His eternal
supremacy ?

And as the king prayed the word of Jehovah
came to Isaiah, and he sent to Hezekiah this glorious
message about Sennacherib :—

"The virgin, the daughter of Zion, hath despised
thee, and laughed thee to scorn.   The daughter of
Jerusalem hath shaken her head at thee."[3]

---

reduce fenced cities to ruinous heaps." He boasts on the Bellino
Cylinder, "Their smaller towns without number I overthrew, and
reduced them to heaps of rubbish" (*Records of the Past*, i. 27).

[1] "It is a prayer without words, a prayer in action, which then
passes into a spoken prayer" (Delitzsch).

[2] The Assyrians are sometimes represented in their monuments
as hewing idols to pieces in honour of their god Assur (Botta,
Monum., pl. 140).

[3] LXX., κινεῖν τὴν κεφαλήν, "a gesture of scorn" (Psalm xxii. 7,
cix. 25; Lam. ii. 15).   With the vaunts of Sennacherib compare
Claudian, *De bell. Geth.*, 526–532.

> "Cum cesserit omnis
> Obsequiis natura meis ?   Subsidere nostris
> Sub pedibus montes, *arescere vidimus amnes* • • •
> Fregi Alpes, *galeis Padum victricibus hausi.*"
> > KEIL, *ad loc.*

The blasphemies, the vaunts, the menacing self-con‹ fidence of Sennacherib, were his surest condemnation. Did he count God a cypher? It was to God alone that he owed the fearful power which had made the nations like grass upon the housetops, like blasted corn, before him. And because God knew his rage and tumult, God would treat him as Sargon his father had treated conquered kings:—

"I will put My hook in thy nose, and My bridle in thy lips.[1] And I will turn thee back by the way by which thou camest." He had thought to conquer Egypt:[2] instead of that he should be driven back in confusion to Assyria.

It was but a plainer enunciation of the truths which Isaiah had again and again intimated in enigma and parable. It was the fearless security of Judah's lion; the safety of the rock amid the deluge; the safety of the poor brood under the wings of the Divine protection from "the great Birds'-nester of the world"; the crashing downfall of the lopped Lebanonian cedar, while the green shoot and tender branch out of the withered stump of Jesse should take root downward and bear fruit upward.[3]

And the sign was given to Hezekiah that this should be so.[4] This year there should be no harvest, except

---

[1] Comp. 2 Chron. xxxiii. 11 (Heb.); Psalm xxxix. 1; Isa. xxx. 28; Ezek. xxxviii. 4, xxix. 4. The Assyrians drove a ring through the lower lip, the Babylonians through the nose. See Rawlinson, *Ancient Monarchies*, ii. 314, iii. 436.

[2] 2 Kings xix. 33. "The river of Egypt" (*Nachal-ha-Mizraim*) is the Wady-el-Arish.

[3] Isa. x. 33, 34, xi. 1, xiv. 8; Stanley, *Lectures*, ii. 410.

[4] אוֹת. A sign "is a thing, an event, or an action intended as a pledge of the Divine certainty of another. Sometimes it is a miracle (Gen. iv. 15, Heb.), or a permanent symbol (Isa. viii. 18, xx. 3, xxxvii. 30; Jer. xliv. 29)" (Delitzsch).

such as was spontaneous; for in the stress of Assyrian invasion sowing and reaping had been impossible. The next year the harvest should only be from this accidental produce. But in the third year, secure at last, they should sow and reap, and plant vineyards and eat the fruit thereof.[1] And though but a remnant of the people was left out of the recent captivity, they should grow and flourish, and Jerusalem should see the besieging host of Assyria no more for ever; for Jehovah would defend the city for His own sake, and for His servant David's sake.

Thereafter occurred the great deliverance.[2] In some way—we know not and never shall know how—by a blast of the simoom, or sudden outburst of plague, or furious panic, or sudden assault, or by some other calamity,[3] the host of Assyria was smitten in the camp, and one hundred and eighty-five thousand, including their chief leaders, perished. The historian, in a manner habitual to pious Semitic writers, attributes the devastation to the direct action of "the angel of the Lord";[4] but as Dr. Johnson said long ago, "We are certainly not to suppose that the angel went about

---

[1] The first year they should eat *saphiach* (LXX., αὐτόματα; Vulg., *quæ repereris*); the second year, *sachish* (LXX., τὰ ἀνατέλλοντα; Vulg, *quæ sponte nascuntur*).

[2] 2 Kings xix. 35: "It came to pass that night." Isaiah only has "then"; Josephus, κατὰ τὴν πρώτην τῆς πολιορκίας νύκτα. Menochius understands it "*in celebri illa nocte.*" The LXX. omits "that," and simply says "in the night" (νυκτός). Comp. Psalm xlvi. 5 (Heb.); Isa. xvii. 14.

[3] Josephus, followed by many moderns, and even by Keil, suggests a plague. The malaria of the Pelusiotic marshes easily breeds pestilence. The "*maleak Jehovah*" is "the destroyer" (*mashchith*) (Exod. xii. 23; 2 Sam. xxiv. 16. Comp. Justin., xix. 11; Diod. Sic., xix. 434.

[4] Comp. 2 Sam. xxiv. 15, 16.

with a sword in his hand, striking them one by one, but that some powerful natural agent was employed."[1]

The Forty-Sixth Psalm is generally regarded as the *Te Deum* sung in the Temple over this deliverance, and its opening words, "God is our refuge and strength," are inscribed over the cathedral of St. Sophia at Constantinople.

It is usually supposed that this overwhelming disaster happened to the host of Assyria *before Jerusalem.* This, however, is not stated; and as the capture of Lachish was an urgent necessity, it is probable that the Turtan led back the forces which had accompanied him, and took them afterwards to Libnah.[2] Yet, since Libnah was but ten miles from Jerusalem, the Jews could not feel safe for a day until the mighty news came that the

> "Angel of God spread his wings on the blast,
> And breathed in the face of the foe as he passed,
> And the eyes of the sleepers waxed heavy and chill,
> And their breasts but once heaved, and for ever grew still."

When the catastrophe which had happened to the main army and the flight of Sennacherib became known, the scattered forces would melt away.

All the Assyrians who escaped were now hurrying back[3] to Nineveh with their foiled king. Sennacherib

---

[1] The Babyl. Talmud and some Targums, followed by Vitringa, etc., attribute to it storms of lightning; Prideaux, Heine, and Faber, to the simoom; R. José, Ussher, etc., to a nocturnal attack of Tirhakah.

[2] It is, however, perfectly possible that a contingent was left on guard. "Where is the [past] terror? Where is he that rated the tribute? Where is he that received it?" (Isa. xxxiii. 18). "At the noise of the tumult the people flee" (Isa. xxxiii. 3); "At Thy rebuke, O God of Jacob, both chariot and horse are cast into a dead sleep" (Psalm lxxvi. 6). Comp. Psalm xlviii. 4–6.

[3] This is the meaning of "he departed, and went, and returned."

seems to have occupied himself in the north, except so far as he was forced to fight fiercely against his own rebel subjects.   He never recovered this complete humiliation.   He never again came southwards.   He survived the catastrophe for seventeen or twenty years,[1] and fought five or six campaigns ; but at the end of that period, while he was worshipping in the house of Nisroch or Assarac (Assur), his god,[2] he was murdered by his two sons Adrammelech (Adar-malik—" Adar is king") and Sharezer (Nergal-sarussar—"Nergal protect the king "),[3] who envied him his throne.   They escaped into the land of Ararat, but were defeated and killed by their younger brother Esarhaddon (Assur-âkh-iddin —" Assur bestowed a ' brother ' ") at the battle of Hani-Rabbat, on the Upper Euphrates.   He succeeded Sennacherib, and ultimately avenged on Egypt his father's overwhelming disaster.   He is perhaps the " cruel lord " of Isa. xix. 4, and it is not unnatural that he should have prevailed against his parricidal brothers, for we are told that in a previous battle at Melitene he had shown such prowess that the troops then and there proclaimed him King of Assyria with shouts of " This is our king."[4]   He reigned from B.C.

---

[1] Not, only fifty-five days, as we read in Tobit i. 21.

[2] Jos., *Antt.*, X. i. 5: " In his own temple to Araskê"; LXX., Ἀσαράχ ; Isa. xxxvii. 38.   One guess connects the word with Nesher, " the eagle-god," often seen on the Assyrian bas-reliefs.   Lenormant calls him " the god of human destiny."

[3] Alex. Polyhistor *ap.* Euseb., i. 27 ; Kimchi *ad* 2 Kings xix. 37. Buxtorf (*Bibl. Rabbinic.*) says that Sennacherib entered the temple to ask his counsellors why Jehovah favoured Israel.   Being told that it was because of Abraham's willingness to offer Isaac, he said, "Then I will offer my two sons."   Rashi adds that they slew him to save their own lives.   (See Schenkel and Riehm, *s.v.* " Sanherib " —both articles by Schrader).

[4] See Schrader in Riehm's *Handwörterbuch, s.vv.* " Sanherib,"

681–668, and in his reign Assyria culminated before her last decline.[1]   He was the builder of the temple at Nimrûd, and erected thirty other temples.   Babylon and Nineveh were both his capitals,[2] and he had previously been viceroy of the former.

The glorious deliverance in which the faith and courage of the King of Judah had had their share naturally increased the prosperity and prestige of Hezekiah, and lifted the authority of Isaiah to an unprecedented height.   Hezekiah probably did not long survive the uplifting of this dark cloud, but during the remainder of his life "he was magnified in the sight of all nations."[3]   When he died, all Judah and Jerusalem did him honour, and gave him a splendid burial. Apparently the old tombs of the kings—the catacomb constructed by David and Solomon—had in the course of two and a half centuries become full, so that he had to be buried "in the ascent of the sepulchres," perhaps some niche higher than the other graves of the catacomb, which was henceforth disused for the burial of the kings of Judah.   We have had occasion to observe the many particulars in which his reign was memorable, and to his other services must be added the literary activity to which we owe the collection and editing, by his scribes, of the Proverbs of Solomon.   His reign had practically witnessed the institution of the faithful

---

"Asarhaddon."   Esarhaddon, judging from what is called "Sennacherib's will," in which the king leaves him splendid presents, seems to have been a favourite of his father (*Records of the Past*, i. 136).   He says that on hearing of his father's murder, " I was wrathful as a lion, and my soul raged within me, and I lifted my hands to the great gods to assume the sovereignty of my father's house."   See Appendix I.

[1] The Book of Tobit (i. 21) calls him Sarchedonas.

[2] 2 Chron. xxxiii. 11.

[3] 2 Chron. xxxii. 23.

Jewish Church under the influence of his great prophetic guide.[1]

The question whether the portent of the destruction of the Assyrian was identical with that related by Herodotus has never been finally answered. Herodotus places the scene of the disaster at Pelusium,[2] and tells this story :—Sennacherib, King of the Arabs and Assyrians, invaded Egypt. Its king, Sethos, of the Tanite dynasty, in despair entered the temple of his god Pthah (or Vulcan), and wept.[3] The god appeared to him with promises of deliverance, and Sethos marched to meet Sennacherib with an army of poor artisans, since he was a priest, and the caste of warriors was ill-affected to him. In the night the god Pthah sent hosts of field-mice, which gnawed the quivers, bow-strings, and shield-straps of the Assyrians, who consequently fled, and were massacred. An image of the priest-king with a mouse in his hand stood in the temple of Pthah, and on its pedestal the inscription, which might also point the moral of the Biblical narrative, 'Ἐς ἐμέ τις ὀρεῶν εὐσεβὴς ἔστω ("Let him who looks on me be pious "). Josephus seems so far to accept this version that he refers to Herodotus, and says that Sennacherib's failure was the result of a frustration in Egypt.[4] The *mouse* in the hand of the statue probably originated the details of the legend ; but according to Horapollion it was the hieroglyphic

---

[1] Wellhausen, p. 116.

[2] Herod., ii. 14. "Sin" (Tanis ?), Ezek. xxx. 15. It lay in the midst of morasses, and some attribute the catastrophe to the malaria.

[3] The deliverance is really connected with Tirhakah, whose deeds are recorded in a temple at Medinet Habou, but the jealousy of the Memphites attributed it to the piety of Sethos. See G. W. Wilkinson, *Ancient Egyptians*, i. 141 ; Rawlinson, *Herodotus*, i. 394.

[4] *Antt.*, X. i. 1-5.

sign of destruction by plague.[1]   Bähr says that it was
also the symbol of Mars.   Readers of Homer will
remember the title Apollo *Smintheus* ("the destroyer of
mice"), and the story that mice were worshipped in the
Troas because they gnawed the bow-strings of the
enemy.

But whatever may have been the mode of the retribution, or the scene in which it took place, it is certainly
historical.   The outlines of the narrative in the sacred
historian are identical with those in the Assyrian
records.   The annals of Sennacherib tell us the four
initial stages of the great campaign in the conquest of
Phœnicia, of Askelon, and of Ekron, the defeat of the
Egyptians at Altaqu, and the earlier hostilities against
Hezekiah.   The Book of Kings concentrates our attention on the details of the close of the invasion.   On
this point, whether from accident, or because Sennacherib did not choose to register his own calamity,
and the frustration of the gods of whose protection he
boasted, the Assyrian records are silent.   Baffled con-
querors rarely dwell on their own disasters.   It is not
in the despatches of Napoleon that we shall find the
true story of his abandonment of Syria, of the defeats
of his forces in Spain, or of his retreat from Moscow.[2]

The great lesson of the whole story is the reward
and the triumph of indomitable faith.   Faith may still
burn with a steady flame when the difficulties around
it seem insuperable, when all refutation of the attacks

---

[1] Comp. 1 Sam. v., vi., where, after a plague, the Philistines sent an
expiation of five golden mice.

[2] We may add that even the Chronicler drops a veil over Sennacherib's actual capture of fortresses in Judah ("he *thought* to win
them for himself," 2 Chron. xxxii. 1: comp. 2 Kings xviii. 13;
Isa. xxxvi. 1).

of its enemies seems to be impossible, when Hope itself has sunk into white ashes in which scarcely a gleam of heat remains. Isaiah had nothing to rely upon ; he had no argument wherewith to furnish Hezekiah beyond the bare and apparently unmeaning promise, " Jehovah is our Judge ; Jehovah is our Lawgiver ; Jehovah is our King. He will save us." It was a magnificent vindication of his inspired conviction, when all turned out—not indeed in minute details, but in every essential fact—exactly as he had prophesied from the first. Even in B.C. 740 he had declared that the sins of Judah deserved and would receive condign punishment, though a remnant should be saved.[1] That the retribution would come from some foreign enemy—Assyria or Egypt, or both—he felt sure. Jehovah would hiss for the fly in the uttermost canals of Egypt, and for the bee that is in the land of Assyria, and both should swarm in the crevices of the rocks, and over the pastures.[2] Later on in 732, in the reign of Ahaz, he pointed to Assyria,[3] as the destined scourge, and he realised this still more clearly in 725 and 721, when Shalmaneser and Sargon were tearing Samaria to pieces.[4] Contrary, indeed, to his expectation, the Assyrians did not then destroy Jerusalem, or even formally besiege it. The revolt from Assyria, the reliance on Egypt, did not for a moment blind his judgment or alter his conviction ; and in 701 it came true when Sennacherib was on the march for Palestine.[5] Yet he never wavered in the apparently impossible conclusion, that, in spite of all, in spite even of his own darker prophecies (xxxii. 14), Jerusalem shall in some Divine

---

[1] Isa. vi. 11–13.
[2] Isa. v. 26–30.
[3] Isa. vii. 18.
[4] Isa. viii., xxviii. 1-15, x. 28–34.
[5] Isa. xiv. 29–32, xxix., xxx.

manner be saved.[1] The deliverance would be, as he
declared from first to last, the work of Jehovah, not the
work of man,[2] and because of it Sennacherib would
return to his own land and perish there.[3] The details
might be dim and wavering; the result was certain.
Isaiah was no thaumaturge, no peeping wizard, no mut-
tering necromancer, no monthly prognosticator.[4] He
was a prophet—that is, an inspired moral and spiritual
teacher who was able to foresee and to foretell, not in
their details, but in their broad outlines, the events yet
future, because he was enabled to read them by the eye
of faith ere they had yet occurred. His faith convinced
him that predictions founded on eternal principles have
all the certainty of a law, and that God's dealings with
men and nations in the future can be seen in the light
of experience derived from the history of the past.
Courage, zeal, unquenchable hope, indomitable resolution, spring from that perfect confidence in God which
is the natural reward of innocence and faithfulness.
Isaiah trusted in God, and he knew that they who put
their trust in Him can never be confounded.

No event produced a deeper impression on the minds
of the Jews, though that impression was soon afterwards, for a time, obliterated. Naturally, it elevated
the authority of Isaiah into unquestioned pre-eminence
during the reign of Hezekiah. It has left its echo, not
only in his own triumphant pæans, but also in the Forty-
Sixth Psalm, which the Septuagint calls " An ode to the
Assyrian," and perhaps also in the Seventy-Fifth and

---

[1] Isa. i. 19, 20.

[2] Isa. x. 33, xxix. 5–8, xxx. 20–26, 30–33.

[3] Isa. xxxviii. 6. See for this paragraph an admirable chapter in
Prof. Smith's *Isaiah*, pp. 368–374.

[4] Isa. xlvii. 13.

Seventy-Sixth Psalms.   In the minds of all faithful
Israelites it established for ever the conviction that God
had chosen Judah for Himself, and Israel for His own
possession ; that God was in the midst of Zion, and
she should not be confounded : " God shall help her, and
that right early."   And it contains a noble and inspiring
lesson for all time.   " It is not without reason," says
Dean Stanley, " that in the Churches of Moscow the
exultation over the fall of Sennacherib is still read on
the anniversary of the retreat of the French from
Russia, or that Arnold, in his lectures on Modern
History, in the impressive passage in which he dwells
on that great catastrophe, declared that for the memorable night of the frost in which twenty thousand horses
perished, and the strength of the French army was
utterly broken, he knew of no language so well fitted
to describe it as the words in which Isaiah described the advance and destruction of the hosts of
Sennacherib." [1]

They had been brought face to face, the two kings—
Sennacherib and Hezekiah.   One was the impious
boaster who relied on his own strength, and on the
mighty host which dried up rivers with their trampling
march—the worldling who thought to lord it over the
affrighted globe ; the other was the poor kinglet of the
Chosen People, with his one city and his enfeebled
people, and his dominion not so large as one of the
smallest English counties.   But " one with God is
irresistible," " one with God is always in a majority."
The poor, weak prince triumphs over the terrific conqueror, because he trusts in Him to whom world-
desolating tyrants are but as the small dust of the

---

[1] Stanley, *Lectures*, ii. 531.

balance, and who "taketh up the isles as a very little thing."[1]

As Assyria now vanishes almost entirely from the history of the Chosen People, we may here recall with delight one large and loving prophecy, to show that the Hebrews were sometimes uplifted by the power of inspiration above the narrowness of a bigoted and exclusive spirit.   Desperately as Israel had suffered, both from Egypt and Assyria, Isaiah could still utter the glowing Messianic Prophecy which included the Gentiles in the privileges of the Golden Age to come. He foretold that—

"In that day shall Israel be the third with Egypt and Assyria, as a blessing in the midst of the land : whom the Lord of hosts shall bless, saying, Blessed be Egypt My people, and Assyria the work of My hands, and Israel Mine inheritance."[2]

"That strain I heard was of a higher mood!"

King Hezekiah can have no finer panegyric than that of the son of Sirach : "Even the kings of Judah failed, for they forsook the law of the Most High : all except David, and Ezekias, and Josias failed."[3]

---

[1] Isa. xl. 15.   [2] Isa. xix. 24, 25.   [3] Ecclus. xlix. 4.

CHAPTER XXIX

MANASSEH

B.C. 686—641

2 KINGS xxi. 1—16

" Shall the throne of wickedness have fellowship with Thee,
That frameth mischief by statute ?
They gather themselves in troops against the soul of the righteous,
And condemn the innocent blood."—PSALM xciv. 20, 21.

"Though the mills of God grind slowly, yet they grind exceeding
small ;
Though with patience long He waiteth, with exactness grinds
He all."

MANASSEH was born after Hezekiah's recovery from his terrible illness. He was but twelve years old when he began to reign. Of his mother Hephzibah we know nothing, nor of the Zechariah who was her father ; but perhaps Isaiah in one passage (lxii. 4) may refer to her name, " My delight is in her." [1] The son of Hezekiah and Hephzibah was the worst of all the kings of Judah, and had the longest reign.

The tender age of Manasseh when he came to the throne may perhaps account for the fact that the

---

[1] One legend says that Hephzibah was a daughter of Isaiah. Not so Josephus (*Antt.*, X. iii. 1).

351

"forgetfulness" which his name implied[1] was not a forgetting of other sorrows, but of all that was noble and righteous in the attempted reformation which had been the main religious work of his father's life.   In Judah, as in England, a king was not supposed to be of age until he was eighteen.[2]   For six years Manasseh must have been to a great extent under the influence of his regents and counsellors.

There always existed in Jerusalem, even in the best times, a heathenising party, and it was, unfortunately, composed of princes and aristocrats who could bring strong influence to bear upon the king.[3]   They did not deny Jehovah, but they did not recognise Him as the sole or the supreme God of heaven and earth.   To them He was the local deity of Israel and Judah.   But there were other gods, the gods of the nations, and their aim always was to recognise the existence of these deities and to pay homage to their power.   If their favour could not be purchased except by their immediate votaries, at least their anger might be averted.   These politicians advocated a fatal and incongruous syncretism, or at least an unlimited tolerance for heathen idols, for which they could, unhappily, quote the precepts and example of the Wise King, Solomon. If any one questioned their views as a dangerous idolatry, and an insult to

> "Jehovah thundering out of Zion, throned
> Between the cherubim,"

---

[1] See Gen. xli. 51.   His name may have referred to the new union between the Northern and Southern Kingdoms.   Comp. 2 Chron. xxx. 6, xxxi. 1.

[2] 2 Chron. xxxiv. 1-3.

[3] See Zeph. i. 8.   Comp. 2 Chron. xxiv. 17; Isa. xxviii. 14; Jer. v. 5, etc.

they had but to point from the walls of Jerusalem to
the confronting summit of Olivet, where still remained
the shrines which the son of David had erected three
centuries earlier to Chemosh, and Milcom, and Ashtoreth, who, since his day, had always found, even
in Jerusalem, some worshippers, open or secret, to
acknowledge their divinity.

And these worldlings, in their tolerance for the
intolerable, could always appeal to two powerful
instincts of man's fallen nature—sensuality and fear—
"lust hard by hate." There was something in the
worship of Baal-Peor and of Moloch which appealed to
the undying ape and tiger in the unregenerate human
heart.

The true worship of Jehovah is exactly that form
of religion which man finds it least easy to render to
Him—the religion of pure morality. Services, rites,
functions, look like religious diligence, and readily secure
a reverent outward devotion. Even self-maceration,
fasts, and flagellation are a cheap way of escaping the
"endless torments" which always loom so hugely in
terrifying superstition.

Such superstitions are children of the fear and faithlessness which hath torment. They are the corruptions
with which every form of false religion, and with which
also a corrupt and perverted Christianity, are always
tainted. And they demand the easy expiation of physical
ritual. But all the best and most spiritual teachers of
Scripture—alike the Hebrew Prophets and the Christian
Apostles—are at one with the Lord Christ in perpetual
insistence on the truth that "mercy is better than
sacrifice," and that true religion consists in that good
mind and good life which are the sole proof of genuine
sincerity.

23

If Jehovah would but be contented with gifts, men would gladly offer Him thousands of rams and tens of thousands of rivers of oil. But the prophets taught that He was above all mean bribes, and that such offerings never could be anything to One whose were all the beasts of the forests and the cattle upon a thousand hills. It was not easy, then, to bribe such a God, or to make Him a respecter of persons.

How easy, again, would it be, if He would even accept human sacrifices! A child was but a child. How easy to kill a child, and place it in the brazen arms which sloped over the fiery cistern! Moloch and Chemosh were supremely to be won by such holocausts; and surely Moloch and Chemosh must be lords of power! But here again the prophets of Jehovah stepped in, and said that it was of no avail with the High, the Holy, the Merciful, to give even our first-born for our transgressions, or the fruit of the body for the sin of the soul.

Asceticism, then—occasional fasting, severe self-deprivations—surely the gods would accept these? And they were as nothing compared to the burden of sin and the agony of conscience! Baal and Asherah could command agonised devotees, and could approve of them. By Jehovah and His prophets such bodily service is discouraged and forbidden.

Pleasure, then?—the consecration of the natural impulses, the devotion in religious cultus of the passions and appetites of the flesh—why should that be so abhorrent to Jehovah? Other deities exulted in licentiousness. Was not the temple of Astarte full of her women-worshippers and of her eunuchs? Was there no fascination in the voluptuous allurements, the orgiastic dances, the stolen waters, the bread eaten in secret, when not only was the conscience lulled by the removal therefrom of all sense of guilt and degradation, but such orgies were even crowned with merit, as part of an acceptable worship ? After all, there was "a fascination of corruption" in these idols of gold and jewels, of lust and blood !

How stern, how cold, how bare, by comparison, was the moral law which only said, "Thou shalt not," and emphasised its prohibition with the unalterable sanctions, "This do, and thou shalt live"; "Do it not, and thou shalt die"! What could they make of a religion which was so eloquently silent as to the meritoriousness of ritual ?

And how chill and simple and dreary was that which —according to Micah—Jehovah had shown to be good, and which He required of every man,—which was nothing more than to do justly, and to love mercy, and to walk humbly with God !

And what right had the prophets—so asked these apostates—to lord it over God's heritage in this way ? Solomon was the greatest king of Israel and Judah ; and Solomon had never been so exclusive in his religionism, though he had built the Temple of the Lord ; nor Rehoboam ; nor the great Phœnician Queen Athaliah ; nor the cultivated and æsthetic Ahaz ; nor, in the kingdom of Israel, the lordly warrior Ahab ; nor the splendid and long-lived victor Jeroboam II. Had not Manasseh plenty of examples of religious syncretism, to which he might appeal in the joy of his youthful age ?

Not impossibly there lay in the background another reason why the young king might be inclined to listen to these evil counsellors. Micah may still have been living ; but of Isaiah we hear no more. Probably he was dead. It is not recorded that he delivered any prophecy during the reign of Manasseh, nor is it certain that he outlived the former king. Tradition, indeed, in later days, asserted that he had confronted Manasseh, and been doomed to death; that he had taken refuge in a cedar tree, and in that cedar had been sawn asunder; but the tradition is wholly without a vestige of authority. One of Micah's sternest oracles was perhaps uttered in the days of Manasseh.[1] But Micah was only a provincial prophet of Moresheth-Gath. He never moved in the midst of princes as Isaiah had done, or possessed a tithe of the authority which had rested for so many years on the shoulders of his mighty contemporary.

Moreover—so the heathen party might suggest— had not Isaiah's prophecies been falsified by the result? Had he not distinctly promised and pledged his credit to two things? and had not both turned out to be unworthy of reliance?

i. Surely he had prophesied the utter downfall of the Assyrians. And it was true that after his disaster on the confines of Egypt, Sennacherib had fled in haste to Nineveh, and his occupations with rebels on his own frontiers had left Judah unmolested, and he had been murdered by his sons. But, on the other hand, in no sense of the word had Assyria fallen. On the contrary, she had never been more powerful. Not one of his predecessors had seemed more irresistible than Esarhaddon. He was undisputed king of Babylon and of Nineveh. There would be no more embassies from Merodach-Baladan, or any revolted viceroy! And rumour would early begin to narrate that Esarhaddon had not forgotten the catastrophe at Pelusium, but

---

[1] Mic. vii. 1-20.

intended to avenge it, and to teach Egypt the forgotten
lessons of Raphia (B.C. 720) and Altaqu (B.C. 701).

ii. And as for Judah, where was the golden Messianic
age which Isaiah had promised ?   Where did they see
the Divine Prince whom he had foretold, or the lion
lying down with the lamb, and the child laying his
hand on the cockatrice's den ?

All this, they would argue, had greatly shaken
Isaiah's prophetic authority.   Judah was a mere vassal
—safe only in so far as she remained a vassal, and did
not join Tyre or any other rebellious power, but abode
safe under the shadow of Assyria's mighty wings.

Was it not, then, as well to look facts in the face ?
to accept things as they were ?   And—so they would
argue, with false plausibility—since the triumph, after
all, had remained with the gods of the nations, might
it not be as well to dethrone Jehovah from His exclusive dominion, and at least to propitiate the potent and
less-exacting deities, the charming *Di faciles* who smiled
at lewd aberrations, and even flung over them the
glamour of devotion ?

With these bolder renegades would be the whole
body of the priests of the *bamoth*.   Those old sanctuaries had been repressed by Hezekiah without any
compensation ; for in those days life-interests were
little, or not at all, regarded.   Multitudes of priests and
Levites must have been flung out of employment and
reduced to poverty by the recent religious revolution.
It is not likely that they bore without a murmur the
obliteration of forms of worship sanctioned by immemorial custom, or that they made no efforts to procure
the re-establishment of what the people loved.

Thus a vast weight of evil influence was brought to
bear upon the boy-king ; and it was also the more

powerful because repeated indications exist that, while the king was nominally a despot, and was surrounded with external observance, the real control of affairs was, to a large extent, in the hands of an aristocracy of priests and princes, except when the king was a man of great personal force.

Manasseh went over to these retrogressionists heart and soul, and he contentedly remained a tributary of Assyria. Even when Esarhaddon's forces marched to the chastisement of Egypt, he felt secure in his allegiance to the dominant tyrant of Babylon and Nineveh, whose interest it would be not to disturb a faithful subject.

There followed a reaction, an absolute rebound from the old monotheistic strictness and righteousness. The nation emancipated itself from the moral law as with a shout of relief, and plunged into superstition and licentiousness. The reign of Manasseh resembled at once the recrudescence of Popery in the reign of Mary Tudor, with its rekindling of the fires of Smithfield, and the foul orgies of debauchery at the Restoration of 1660, when human nature, loving degraded licence better than strenuous liberty, flung away the noble freedom of Puritanism for the loathly mysteries of Cotytto. The age of Manasseh resembled that of Charles II., in the famous description of Lord Macaulay. " Then came days never to be recalled without a blush, the days of servitude without loyalty, and sensuality without love, of dwarfish talents and gigantic vices, the paradise of cold hearts and narrow minds, the golden age of the coward, the bigot, and the slave. In every high place worship was paid to Belial and Moloch, and England propitiated these obscene and cruel idols with the blood of her best and bravest children." Sensuous intoxication is in all cases closely connected with

fiendish cruelty, and the introducer of voluptuous
idolatries naturally became the first persecutor of the
true religion.

1. The first step of the king, and probably the one
which the people welcomed most, was the restoration
of the chapelries under the trees and on the hills, which,
more strenuously than any of his predecessors, Hezekiah
had at least attempted to put down. For this step
Manasseh might have pleaded the sanction of ages
to which the Book of Deuteronomy had either been
wholly unknown, or during which its laws had become
as utterly forgotten as though they had never existed.
To many worshippers these old shrines had become
extremely precious. They felt it to be either an actual
impossibility, or at the best intolerably burdensome, to
make their way by long, dreary, and difficult journeys
to Jerusalem, when they desired to pay the most
ordinary rites of worship. They knew no reason, and
had never known of any reason, why Jehovah should
be worshipped in one Temple only. All their religious
instincts led them the other way. They could point to
the example of all the highly honoured saints who had
worshipped God at Gilgal, Shechem, Bethel, Hebron,
Beersheba, Kedesh, Gibeah, and many another shrine ;
and of all the saintly kings who had not dreamt of
interfering with such free worship. Why should
Jerusalem monopolise all sanctity ? It might be a
politic view for kings to maintain, and highly profitable
for priests to establish ; but none of their great prophets,
not even the princely Isaiah, had said one syllable
against the innocent high places of Jehovah. In those
days there were no synagogues. The extinction of the
high places doubtless seemed to many of the people an
extinction of religion in daily life, and they were more

than half disposed to agree with the Rabshakeh that Jehovah was offended by what they regarded as a burdensome, unwise, and sweeping innovation.—If it be necessary to answer arguments which might have seemed natural, against a custom which might have seemed innocent, it must suffice to say that it was the chief mission of Israel to keep alive among the nations of the world the knowledge of the One True God, and that, amid the constant temptations to accept the gods of the heathen as they were adored in groves and on high places, the faith of Israel could no longer be kept pure except by the Deuteronomic institution of one central and exclusive shrine.

2. But Manasseh did far worse than rehabilitate the worship at the high places which his father had discouraged. " He reared up altars for Baal, and made an Asherah, as did Ahab, King of Israel." This was the first bad element of the new cosmopolitan eclecticism. It involved the acceptance of the Phœnician nature-worship with its manifold abominations. The people had grown familiar with it under Athaliah (2 Kings xi. 18), and under Ahaz (2 Chron. xxviii. 2) ; but Manasseh, as we infer from the account given of Josiah's reformation, had gone further than either. He had actually ventured to introduce the image of Baal into the Temple, and to set up the Asherah-pillar in front of it (2 Kings xxiii. 4). Worse even than this, he had

---

[1] LXX., τῇ Βαάλ. The feminine, however, does not imply that Baal was here worshipped as a female deity, but is probably due to the fact that later Jews always avoided using the *names* of idols (from a misapprehension or too literal view of Exod. xxiii. 13), and therefore called Baal *Bosheth* ("shame"), which is feminine. Hence the names Mephibosheth, Jerubbesheth, Ishbosheth. In Suidas (*s.v.* Μανασσῆς) he is charged with having set up in the Temple "a four-faced image of Zeus."

erected in the very Temple (*id.* 7) houses devoted to the execrable *Qedeshim* (Vulg., *effeminati*), in which also the women wove broidered hangings to adorn the shrines of the idol image, as in the worship of the Assyrian Mylitta.[1] He, at the same time, displaced the altar and removed the Ark. To the latter circumstances is perhaps due the Rabbinic legend that Hezekiah hid the Ark till the coming of the Messiah.

3. To this Phœnician worship he added Sabaism, the worship of the stars, "all the host of heaven, whom he served." This was an entirely new phase of idolatry, unknown to the Hebrews till they came in contact with Assyria.[2] It came rapidly into vogue, and exercised over their imaginations the spell of a seductive novelty, as we see from the strong testimony of the prophet Jeremiah.[3] This is why it is so emphatically forbidden in the Book of Deuteronomy.[4] The king built altars to the stars of the Zodiac (*Mazzaroth*), both in the outer court of the Temple, and in the court of the priests, and on these altars incense or victims were continually burned. He also introduced or encouraged the introduction into the Temple precincts of the horses and chariots dedicated to the sun.[5]

When we read of the actual invasion of the Temple-precincts in this as in preceding and subsequent reigns,

---

[1] For בָּתִּים, in 2 Kings xxiii. 7, the LXX. read χεττίμ (?). Grätz, (*Gesch. d. Juden.*, ii. 277) suggests בְּגָדִים, "broidered robes." Ezek. xvi. 16. See Herod., i. 199; Strabo, xvi. 1058; Luc., *De Deâ. Syr.*, § 6; Libanius, *Opp.*, xi. 456, 557; *Ep. of Jeremy*, 43; Döllinger, *Judenthum u. Heidenthum*, i. 431; Rawlinson, *Phœnicia*, 431.

[2] 2 Chron. xxxiii. 3; 2 Kings xxiii. 5. Movers, *Rel. d. Phönis.*, i. 65 "In all the books of the Old Testament written before the Assyrian period no trace of star-worship is to be found." 2 Kings xvii. 16.

[3] Jer. vii. 18, viii. 2, xix. 13; Zeph. i. 5.

[4] See Deut. iv. 19, xvii. 3.

[5] 2 Kings xxiii. 11, 12.

we cannot but ask, Were these atrocities committed with the sanction or with the connivance of the priests? We are not told.   Yet how can it have been otherwise? If the high priest Azariah could muster eighty priests to oppose King Uzziah, when he merely wished to burn incense in the Temple, as Solomon had done before him, and as Ahaz did after him—if Jehoiada could, according to the Chronicler, muster a perfect army of priests and Levites to dethrone Athaliah, and could so stir up the people that they rose *en masse* to tear down the temple of Baal, and slay Mattan, his high priest,—how was it possible for Manasseh to perpetrate these flagrant acts of idolatrous apostasy, if the priests were all ranged in opposition to his power? Was their authority suddenly paralysed?   Did their influence with the people shrivel into nothing when Hezekiah had been carried to his tomb?   Or did these priests follow ·the easy and profitable course which they seem to have followed throughout the whole history of the kings without an exception?—did they simply answer the kings according to their idols?

4. Another, and the most hideous, element of the new mixture of cults was the reintroduction of the ancient Canaanite worship of Moloch with its human sacrifices. Manasseh, like Ahaz, made his son—or, according to the Chronicler and the Septuagint, "his sons"—pass through the fire to this grim Ammonite idol in Tophet of the Valley of Hinnom, so as to leave no chance untried.   And herein he was far more inexcusable than his grandfather; for Ahaz had at least been driven by desperate extremity to this last expedient, but Manasseh was living, if not in prosperity, at least in unbroken peace.   Moreover, he not only did this himself, but did his utmost to make a popular institution of children-

sacrifice, so that many practised it in the dreadful
valley and amid the rocks outside Jerusalem.[1]

5. Even this did not suffice him.　To these Assyrian,
Phœnician, and Canaanite elements of idolatry he
added Babylonian novelties.　He practised augury, and
used enchantments, and he dealt with familiar spirits
and wizards, as though without Egyptian necromancy
and Mesopotamian shamanism his eclectic worship
would be incomplete.[2]

6. Thus "he wrought much wickedness in the sight
of the Lord to provoke Him to anger."　He placed a
graven image of his Asherah inside the Temple, and
utterly profaned the sacred house, and seduced his
people "to do more evil than did the nations whom
the Lord destroyed before the children of Israel."

Whatever was the conduct of the priests, the
prophets were not silent.　They denounced Manasseh
for having done worse than even the ancient Amorites,
and declared that, in consequence of his crimes, God
would bring upon Jerusalem such evil as would cause
both the ears of him that heard it to tingle ; [3] that he
would stretch over Jerusalem for ruin the line and the
level of Ahab ; [4] that He would cast off even the remnant,
and deliver them to their enemies ; that He would wipe
out Jerusalem "as a man wipeth a dish, wiping and
turning it upside down."[5]

---

[1] See Jer. vii. 31, 32, xix. 2-6, xxxii. 35 ; Psalm cvi. 37, 38.

[2] Ewald infers from Isa. lvii. 5-9 ; Jer. ii. 5-13, that he actually
sought for all foreign kinds of worship, in order to introduce them.

[3] I Sam. iii. 11 ; Jer. xix. 3.

[4] Comp. Isa. xxxiv. 11 ; Lam. ii. 8.

[5] 2 Kings xxi. 13.　LXX., ἀλάβαστρος, *al.* πυξίον.　The Vulgate also
takes it to mean the obliteration of writing on a tablet : "Delebo
Jerusalem sicut deleri solent tabulæ ; et ducam crebrius stylum
super faciem ejus."

The finest oracles of Micah (vi. 1–vii. 7) were probably uttered in the reign of Manasseh, and give the simplest and purest expression to the supremacy of morality as the one true end and test of religion. Micah is as indifferent as the Decalogue to all claims of rites, ceremonies, and outward worship. " Jehovah demands nothing for Himself; all that He asks is for man : this is the fundamental law of the theocracy."

The apostasies of the king and the denunciation of the prophets thus came into fierce collision, and led naturally to persecution and bloodshed. Perhaps in Mic. vii. 1–7 we catch the echoes of the Reign of Terror. The king resorted to violence, using, no doubt, the tyrant's devilish plea of necessity. He made blood run like water in the streets of Jerusalem from end to end,[1] and, in the exaggerated phrase of Josephus, was *daily* slaying the prophets.[2] It was during this persecution, according to Rabbinic tradition, that Isaiah received the martyr's crown.[3]

And no miracles were wrought to save the martyrs. Elijah and Elisha had been surrounded with a blaze of miracles, but in Judah no prophet arose who could so wield the power of Heaven.

At this point the narrative of the historian about Manasseh ends. If he shared the current opinion of his day, which connected individual and national pros-

---

[1] 2 Kings xxi. 16; Heb., "from mouth to mouth "; LXX., στόμα εἰς στόμα ; Vulg., *donec impleret Jerusalem usque ad os.* Comp. 2 Kings x. 21.

[2] *Antt.*, X. iii. 1 : " He butchered alike all the just among the Hebrews." To this reign of terror some refer Psalm xii. 1 ; Isa. lvii. 1–4.

[3] This (as I have said) cannot be regarded as certain. Isaiah began to prophesy in the year that King Uzziah died, sixty years before Manasseh. It is a Jewish Haggadah. See Gesen on Isa. i., p. 9, and the Apocryphal "Ascension of Isaiah."

perity with well-doing, and regarded length of days as a
sign of the favour of Heaven, while, on the other hand,
misfortune and misery invariably resulted from the
wrath of Jehovah, he could not have been otherwise
than surprised, and perhaps even pained, to have to
relate that Manasseh reigned fifty-five years. Not
only was his reign longer than that of any other king
of Israel or Judah; not only did he attain a greater
age than any of them; but, further, no calamity seems
to have marked his rule. A contented and protected
vassal of Esarhaddon, secure from his attacks, and
also unmolested by the weakened and subjugated
nations around him, he would seem, in the story of the
Kings, to have enjoyed an enviable external lot, and to
have presided over a people who were happy, in that,
during his rule, they had no history. But whatever
the writer may have felt, he tells us no more, and lets
us see Manasseh sink peacefully into his grave "in the
garden of his own house, in the garden of Uzza,"
and leave to his son Amon a peaceful realm and an
undisputed crown. Such a career would undoubtedly
perplex and confound all the preconceived opinions of
Jewish orthodoxy. The prosperity of Manasseh would
have presented as great a problem to them as the
miseries of Job. They looked to temporal prosperity
as the reward of righteousness, and to acute misery as
the retribution of apostasy and sin. They had little
or no conception of a future which should redress the
balance of apparent earthly inequalities. Alike the
sight of Manasseh's long reign and Josiah's undeserved
death in battle would give a powerful shock to their
fixed convictions.

Far different is the end of the story in the Book of
Chronicles   The records of Esarhaddon tell us that

in 680 he made an expedition into Palestine to restore the shaken influence of his father,[1] and about 647 he mentions among his submissive tributaries the kings of Tyre, Edom, Moab, Gaza, Ekron, Askelon, Gebal, Ammon, Ashdod, and Manasseh, King of Judah ("Minasi-sar-Yahudi"), as well as ten princes of Cyprus. Whether the King of Judah rebelled later on, and intrigued with Tirhakah, we do not know; but in 2 Chron. xxxiii, 11 we read that Esarhaddon sent his generals to Jerusalem, took Manasseh by stratagem, drove rings through his lips, bound him in chains, and brought him to Babylon, where Esarhaddon was holding his court.[2] We find from the *Eponym Canon* that Tyre revolted from Assyria in the tenth year of Esarhaddon, and Manasseh may have been drawn away to join in the revolt; or he may have joined Shamash-shum-ukîn, the Viceroy of Babylon, in his revolt against his brother Assurbanipal. As a rule, the lot of a conquered vassal at the Assyrian Court was horrible, and in his utter misery Manasseh repented, humbled himself, and prayed. His prayer was heard. The despots of Nineveh were capricious alike in their

---

[1] Esarhaddon reigned only eight years, till 668, and then resigned in favour of his son Assurbanipal. In his reign Psammetichus recovered Egypt, and put an end to the Dodecarchy. In the reign of his successor, Assuredililani, Assyria began to decline (647–625).

[2] Comp. Isa. xxxix. 6; Jos., *Antt.*, X. iii. 2. The phrase "among the thorns" means "*with rings*" (comp. Isa. xxx. 28, xxxvii. 29; Ezek. xxxviii. 4; Amos iv. 2). Assurbanipal says similarly that he seized Necho, "bound him with bonds and iron chains, hands and feet," but afterwards allowed him to return to Egypt (Schrader, ii. 59).

[3] Late and worthless Haggadoth, echoed by still later writers (Suidas and Syncellus), say he was kept in a brazen cage, fed on bran bread dipped in vinegar, etc. See *Apost. Const.*, ii. 22: "And the Lord hearkened to his voice, and there became about him a flame of fire, and all the irons about him melted." John Damasc., *Parall.*,

insults and in their favours, and Esarhaddon not only
pardoned Manasseh, but sent him back to Jerusalem,[1]
thinking that he would be more useful to him there than
in a Babylonian dungeon. After this reprieve he lived
like a penitent and a patriot. Esarhaddon was preparing
for his expedition against Tirhakah, and would not attack
a king who was now bound to him by gratitude as well
as fear. But the times were very troublous. Manasseh
prepared for eventualities by building an outer wall on
the west of the city of David, unto Gihon in the Valley,
by surrounding Ophel with a high wall, and by garri-
soning the fenced cities.[2] All this was necessary and
patriotic work, considering that Judah might be attacked
by other enemies as well as the Assyrians. She was
like a grain of corn amid the grinding mills of the
nations. Media and Lydia were rising into strong
kingdoms. Babylon was becoming daily more formidable. Dim rumours reached the East of movements
among vast hosts of Cimmerian and Scythian barbarians.
Jerusalem had no human strength for war. She could
only rely upon her battlements, on the natural strength
of her position, and on the protection of her God.
Almost in the last year of Manasseh, the powerful
Psammetichus I., king of a now united Egypt, made an
assault on Ashdod; but he did not venture on the
difficult task of besieging Jerusalem.

The religious reformation of Manasseh attested the

---

ii. 15, quotes from Julius Africanus, that while Manasseh was saying
a psalm his iron bonds burst, and he escaped. See *Speaker's Commentary*, on Apocrypha, ii. 363.

[1] Such pardon from a king of Assyria was rare, but not unparalleled.
Pharaoh Necho I. was taken in chains to Nineveh, and afterwards set
free (Schrader, *K. A. T.*, p. 371).

[2] See 2 Chron. xxvii. 3. The "fish gate" was, perhaps, a weak
point (Zeph. i. 10).

sincerity of his amendment. He flung out the Asherah from the Temple, put away the strange gods, destroyed the altars, burnt sacrifices to God, and used all his power to restore the worship of Jehovah. He did not, however, destroy the high places. For this story the Chronicler refers to "the words of Chozai,"[1] according to the present text, which some suppose to have meant "the story of the Seers." He also refers to a prayer of Manasseh, which cannot of course be the Greek forgery of the second or third century which goes by that name in the Apocrypha.[2] His repentance doubtless secured his own salvation. "Whoso saith 'Manasseh hath no part in the world to come,'" said Rabbi Johanan, " discourageth the penitent " ;—but the partial reformation was too late to save his land.

Is this a literal history, or an edifying Haggadah? The non-historical character of the story is maintained by De Wette, Graf, Nöldeke, and many others. Both views have been taken. This we can, at any rate, assert—that there seems to be nothing in the story which is inconsistent with probability. The Chronicler may have derived it from genuine documents or traditions, though it is difficult to account for the silence of the elder and more trustworthy historian. Nor is it only his silence for which we have to account ; it is the continuance of his positive statements. It would

---

[1] 2 Chron. xxxiii. 19. Heb., *dibhri Chozai*; A.V., "the story of the Seers"; R.V., "in the history of Hozai"; LXX., ἐπὶ τῶν λόγωι τῶν οὐρανιῶν; Vulg., *in sermonibus Hozai*. The elements of doubt suggested by the name "Babylon," and by the liberation of Manasseh, have been removed by further knowledge. See Budge, *Hist. of Esarhaddon*, p. 78; Schrader, *K. A. T.*, 369 ff.

[2] Since the Council of Trent this prayer has been relegated to the end of the Vulgate with 3, 4, Esdras. Verse 8 (the supposed sinlessness of the Patriarchs) at once shows it to be a mere composition.

be, in any case, a strange conception of history which, after narrating a man's crimes, omitted alike the retribution which befell him on account of them, the heartfelt penitence for the sake of which they were forgiven, and the seriously earnest endeavour to undo at least something of the evil which he had done.   Not only does the historian make these omissions, but in no subsequent allusion to Manasseh does he so much as indicate that he is aware of his amendment.[1]   He says that Amon "did evil in the sight of the Lord, as his father Manasseh did."[2]   He speaks of the altars to the hosts of heaven which Manasseh had made in the two courts of the Temple as still standing in the reign of Josiah, though the Chronicler tells us that Manasseh had cast them all out of the city.[3]   He says that, notwithstanding all that Josiah did, "the Lord turned not from the fierceness of His great wrath, because of all the provocations that Manasseh had provoked Him withal,"[4] and that on this account God cast off Jerusalem.   Never, even by the most distant allusions, does he refer to Manasseh's captivity, his prayer, his penitence, or his counter-efforts.   Had he been aware of these, his silence would have been neither generous nor just. Nay, he even leaves apparent facts at conflict with the Chronicler's story, for he makes Josiah do all that the Chronicler tells us that Manasseh himself had done in the removal of his worst abominations.

Even now we have not exhausted the historic difficulties which surround the repentance of Manasseh. During his reign Jeremiah received his call, and while still a young boy began his work.   Neither he, nor Zephaniah, nor Habakkuk drop the slightest hint that

---

[1] 2 Kings xxiii. 12.   [3] 2 Chron. xxxiii. 15.
[2] 2 Kings xxi. 20.   [4] 2 Kings xxiii. 26.

24

the wicked, idolatrous king had ever turned over a new leaf. Jeremiah's silence is specially difficult to account for. He, too, records Jehovah's final and irrevocable decree, that He would give up Judah to death, to exile, and to famine, to the sword to slay, to the dogs to tear, to the fowls of the heaven and the beasts of the earth to devour and to destroy.[1] And the cause of the pitiless doom pronounced by a Judge weary of repenting is " because of Manasseh, the son of Hezekiah, King of Judah, for that which he did in Jerusalem." [2]

The judgment was not long delayed.

It was the vast movement of the Scythians in Media and Western Asia, and the rumours of it, which gave to Manasseh and Amon such respite as they had ; and even this respite was full of misery and fear.[3]

---

[1] Jer. xv. 1–9.

[2] The later Jews certainly took no account of his repentance. His name was execrated (see the substitution of Manasseh for Moses in Judg. xviii. 30), and he was denied all part in the world to come. The Apocryphal " Prayer of Manasses" has no authority, though it is interesting (Butler, *Analogy*, pt. ii., ch. v.).

[3] In estimating the Chronicler's story, we cannot wholly forget the fact that a number of Haggadic legends clustered thickly round the name of Manasseh in the literature of the later Jews. He is charged with incest, with the murder of Isaiah, the distortion of Scripture, etc., and is represented as having got to heaven, not by real repentance, but by challenging God on His superiority to idols. The Targum, after 2 Chron. xxxiii. 11, adds, "And the Chaldees made a copper mule, and pierced it all over with little holes, and put him therein. And when he was in straits, he cried in vain to all his idols. Then he prayed to Jehovah and humbled himself; but the angels shut every window and lattice of heaven, that his prayer might not enter. But forthwith the pity of the Lord of the world rolled forth, and He made an aperture in heaven, and the mule burst asunder, and the Spirit breathed on him, and he forsook all his idols." " No books," says Dr. Neubauer, "are more subject to additions and various adaptations than popular histories." See Mr. Ball's commentary (*Speaker's Commentary*, ii. 309, and *Sanhedrin*, f. 99, 2 ; 101, 1 ; 103, 2).

AMON[1]

B.C. 641—639

2 KINGS xxi. 19—26

THE brief reign of Amon is only a sort of unimportant and miserable annex to that of his father. As he was twenty-two years old when he began to reign, he must have witnessed the repentance and reforming zeal of his father, if, in spite of all difficulties, we assume that narrative to be historical. In that case, however, the young man was wholly untouched by the latter phase of Manasseh's life, and flung himself headlong into the career of the king's earlier idolatries. "He walked in all the way that his father walked in, and served the idols that his father served, and worshipped them"— which was the more extraordinary if Manasseh's last acts had been to dethrone and destroy these strange gods. He even "multiplied trespass," so that in his son's reign we find every form of abomination as triumphant as though Manasseh had never attempted to check the tide of evil. We know nothing more of Amon. Apparently he only reigned two years.[2] He is the only Jewish king who bears the name of a foreign—an Egyptian—deity.

For pictures of the state of things in this reign we may look to the prophets Zephaniah and Jeremiah, and they are forced to use the darkest colours.

---

[1] The name Amon is unusual. Some identify it with the name of the Egyptian sun-god (Nah. iii. 8). If so, we see yet another element of Manasseh's syncretism, and (as some fancy) an attempt to open relations with Psammetichus of Egypt. But perhaps the name may be Hebrew for "Architect" (1 Kings xxii. 26; Neh. vii. 59).

[2] 2 Kings xxi. 19. The LXX. reads "twelve years," but not so Josephus (*Antt.*, X. iv. 1), or 2 Chron. xxxiii. 21.

This is Zephaniah's picture :—

> " Woe to her that is rebellious and polluted, to the oppressing city !
> She obeyed not the voice ; she received not instruction ;
> She trusted not in the Lord ; she drew not near to her God.
> Her princes in the midst of her are roaring lions ;
> Her judges are evening wolves ; they gnaw not the bones on the
>   morrow.
> Her prophets are light and treacherous persons :
> Her priests have profaned the sanctuary, they have done violence
>   to the law." [1]

He tells us that Baal and his black-robed *chemarim* [2] are still prevalent—that men worshipped on their house-tops the host of heaven, and swore by " Moloch their king." Therefore would God search Jerusalem with candles, and would visit the men who had sunk, like thick wine on the lees, and who said in their infidel hearts, " Jehovah will not do good, neither will He do evil." He is an Epicurean God, a cypher, a *fainéant*. " Men make all kinds of fine calculations," says Luther, " but the Lord God says to them, ' For whom, then, do you hold Me ? For a cypher ? Do I sit here in vain, and to no purpose ? You shall know that I will turn their accounts about finely, and make them all false reckonings.' "

Not less dark is the view of Jeremiah. [3] Like Diogenes in Athens, Jeremiah in vain searches Jerusalem for a faithful man. Among the poor he finds brutish obstinacy, among the rich insolent defiance.

---

[1] Zeph. iii. 1–11. Comp. i. 4.

[2] *Chemarim*, 2 Kings xxiii. 5 ; Hos. x. 5. The root in Syriac means "to be sad," but Kimchi derives it from a root "to be black." The Vulgate renders it *æditui* and *aruspices*.

[3] We are told in the titles of their books that both these prophets prophesied in the days of Josiah ; but such pictures can only apply to the earliest years of his reign.

They were like fed horses in the morning—lecherous
and unruly.   They are slanderers, adulterers, cor-
rupters, murderers.   They worship Baal and strange
gods.   "They set a trap, they catch men.   As a cage
is full of birds, so are their houses full of deceit.   They
are waxen fat, they shine; yea, they overpass in deeds of
wickedness."[1]   "An astonishment and horror is done
in the land; the prophets prophesy falsely, and the
priests bear rule by their means; and My people love
to have it so: and what will ye do in the end thereof?"[2]

"From the least of them even unto the greatest of
them every one is given to covetousness; and from
the prophet even unto the priest every one dealeth
falsely.   They have treated also the hurt of My people
lightly, saying, 'Peace, peace,' when there is no peace.
Were they ashamed when they had committed abominations?   Nay, they were not at all ashamed, neither
could they blush : therefore shall they fall among them
that fall."[3]

The wretched reign ended wretchedly.   Amon met
the fate of Amaziah and of Joash.   He was murdered
by conspirators—by some of his own courtiers—in his
own palace.   He was not the victim of any general
rebellion.   The people of the land were apparently
content with the existent idolatry, which left them free
for lives of lust and luxury, of greed and gain.   They
resented the disorder introduced by an intrigue of
eunuchs or court officials.   They rose and slew the
whole band of conspirators.   Amon was buried with
his father in the new burial-place of the Kings in the
garden of Uzza, and the people placed his son Josiah
—a child of eight years old—upon the throne.

---

[1] See Jer. v., vi., vii., *passim.*   [3] Jer. vi. 13-15.
[2] Jer. v. 30, 31.

CHAPTER XXX

JOSIAH

B.C. 639—608[1]

2 KINGS xxii., xxiii

"Τὴν δὲ φύσιν αὐτὸς ἄριστος ὑπῆρχε καὶ πρὸς ἀρετὴν εὖ γεγονώς."—
Jos., *Antt.*, X. iv. 1.

"In outline dim and vast
Their fearful shadows cast
The giant forms of Empires, on their way
To ruin : one by one
They tower, and they are gone."

KEBLE.

IF we are to understand the reign of Josiah as a
whole, we must preface it by some allusion to the
great epoch-marking circumstances of his age, which
explain the references of contemporary prophets, and
which, in great measure, determined the foreign policy
of the pious king.

The three memorable events of this brief epoch
were, (I.) the movement of the Scythians, (II.) the rise
of Babylon, and (III.) the humiliation of Nineveh,
followed by her total destruction.

I. Many of Jeremiah's earlier prophecies belong to
this period, and we see that both he and Zephaniah
—who was probably a great-great-grandson of King

[1] Kamphausen (*Die Chronologie der hebräischer Könige*) makes
Josiah suceed to the throne in 638.

Hezekiah himself,[1] and prophesied in this reign[2]—are greatly occupied with a danger from the North which seems to threaten universal ruin.

So overwhelming is the peril that Zephaniah begins with the tremendously sweeping menace, "*I will utterly consume all things off the earth,* saith the Lord."

Then the curse rushes down specifically upon Judah and Jerusalem; and the state of things which the prophet describes shows that, if Josiah began himself to seek the Lord at eight years old, he did not take—and was, perhaps, unable to take—any active steps towards the extinction of idolatry till he was old enough to hold in his own hand the reins of power.

For Zephaniah denounces the wrath of Jehovah on three classes of idolaters—viz., (1) the remnant of Baal-worshippers with their *chemarim,* or unlawful priests, and the syncretising priests (*kohanim*) of Jehovah, who combine His worship with that of the stars, to whom they burn incense upon the housetops; (2) the waverers, who swear at once by Jehovah and by Malcham, their king; and (3) the open despisers and apostates. For all these the day of Jehovah is near; He has prepared them for sacrifice, and the sacrificers are at hand.[3] Gaza, Ashdod, Askelon, Ekron, the Cherethites,

---

[1] Otherwise his genealogy would not be mentioned for four generations (Hitzig).

[2] Zeph. i. 1. Jeremiah also was highly connected. He was a priest, and his father Hilkiah may be the high priest who found the book; "for his uncle Shallum, father of his cousin Hanameel, was the husband of Huldah the prophetess (2 Kings xxii. 14; Jer. xxxii. 7). The fact that Jeremiah's property was at Anathoth, where lived the descendants of Ithamar (1 Kings ii. 26), whereas Hilkiah was of the family of Eleazar (1 Chron. vi. 4-13), does not seem fatal to the view that his father was the high priest.

[3] Zeph. ii. 4-7.

Canaan, Philistia, are all threatened by the same impending ruin, as well as Moab and Ammon, who shall lose their lands. Ethiopia, too, and Assyria shall be smitten, and Nineveh shall become so complete a desolation that "pelicans and hedgehogs shall bivouac upon her chapiters, the owl shall hoot in her windows, and the crow croak upon the threshold, 'Crushed! desolated!' and all that pass by shall hiss and wag their hands."[1]

The pictures of the state of society drawn by Jeremiah do not, as we have seen, differ from those drawn by his contemporary.[2] Jeremiah, too, writing perhaps before Josiah's reformation, complains that God's people have forsaken the fountains of living water, to hew out for themselves broken cisterns. He complains of empty formalism in the place of true righteousness, and even goes so far as to say that backsliding Israel has shown herself more righteous than treacherous Judah (iii. 1–11). He, too, prophesies speedy and terrific chastisement. Let Judah gather herself into fenced cities, and save her goods by flight, for God is bringing evil from the North, and a great destruction.[3]

"The lion is come up from his thicket, and the destroyer of the nations is on his way; he is gone forth from his place to make thy land desolate; and thy cities shall be laid waste, without an inhabitant. Behold, he cometh as clouds, and his chariots shall be as the whirlwind." Besiegers come from a far country, and give out their voice against the cities of Judah.

---

[1] Zeph. ii. 12–15.

[2] Jer. ii. 1–35. Considering the very great part played by Jeremiah for nearly half a century of the last history of Judah, the non-mention of his name in the Book of Kings is a circumstance far from easy to explain.

[3] Jer. iv. 6, A.V., "retire, stay not." Comp. Isa. x. 24–31.

The heart of the kings shall perish, and the heart of the princes ; and the priests shall be astonished, and the prophets shall wonder.

"For thus hath the Lord said, The whole land shall be desolate ; yet will I not make a full end "—and, "O Jerusalem, wash thine heart from wickedness, that thou mayest be saved!"[1]

"I will bring a nation upon you from far, O House of Israel, saith the Lord : it is a mighty nation, it is an ancient nation, a nation whose language "—unlike that of the Assyrians—"thou knowest not, neither understandest what they say. Their quiver is an open sepulchre, they are all mighty men. They shall batter thy fenced cities, in which thou trustest with weapons of war."[2]

"O ye children of Benjamin, save your goods by flight : for evil is imminent from the North, and a great destruction. Behold, a people cometh from the North Country, and a great nation shall be raised from the farthest part of the earth. They lay hold on bow and spear ; they are cruel, and have no mercy ; their voice roareth like the sea ; and they ride upon horses, set in array as men for war against thee, O daughter of Zion. We have heard the fame thereof : our hands wax feeble."[3]

And the judgment is close at hand. The early blossoming bud of the almond tree is the type of its imminence. The seething caldron, with its front turned from the North, typifies an invasion which shall soon boil over and flood the land.[4]

---

[1] Jer. iv. 7–27.

[2] Jer. v. 15–17.

[3] Jer. vi. 1, 22, 23, 24.

[4] The almond tree (*shâqâd*) "seems to be awake (*shâqâd*), what-soever trees are still sleeping in the torpor of winter" (Tristram *Nat. Hist. of the Bible*, 332 ; Jer. i. 11–14).

What was the fierce people thus vaguely indicated as coming from the North? The foes indicated in these passages are not the long-familiar Assyrians, but the Scythians and Cimmerians.[1]

As yet the Hebrews had only heard of them by dim and distant rumour. When Ezekiel prophesied they were still an object of terror, but he foresees their defeat and annihilation. They should be gathered into the confines of Israel, but only for their destruction.[2] The prophet is bidden to set his face towards Gog, of the land of Magog, the Prince of Rosh,[3] Meshech, and Tubal, and prophesy against him that God would turn him about, and put hooks in his jaws, and drive forth all his army of bucklered and sworded horsemen, the hordes of the uttermost part of the North. They should come like a storm upon the mountains of Israel, and spoil the defenceless villages; but they should come simply for their own destruction by blood and by pestilence. God should smite their bows out of their left hands, and their arrows out of the right, and the ravenous birds of Israel should feed upon the carcases of their warriors. There should be endless

---

[1] The name Kimmerii (on the Assyrian inscriptions Gimirrai) is connected with Gomer. The Persians call them Sakai or Scyths. The nomad Scyths had driven the Kimmerii from the Dniester while Psammetichus was King of Egypt. For allusions to this see Jer. vi. 22 *seq.*, viii. 16, ix. 10. The first notice of them is in an inscription of Esarhaddon, B.C. 677, who says that he defeated "Tiushpa, *the Gimirrai, a roving warrior,* whose own country was remote." Zephaniah and Jeremiah were certainly thinking of the Scythians (Eichhorn, Hitzig, Ewald; and more recently Kuenen, *Onderzoek,* ii. 123; Wellhausen, *Skizzen,* 150). In B.C. 626 they could not have consciously had the Chaldæans in view, though, twenty-three years later, Jeremiah may have had.

[2] See Ezek. xxxviii., xxxix.

Ezek. xxxviii. 2. So Gesenius, Hävernick, etc., and R.V.

bonfires of all the instruments of war, and the place of their burial should be called "the valley of the multitude of Gog."

Much of this is doubtless an ideal picture, and Ezekiel may be thinking of the fall of the Chaldæans. But the terms he uses remind us of the dim Northern nomads, and the names Rosh and Meshech in juxtaposition involuntarily recall those of Russia and Moscow.[1]

Our chief historical authority respecting this influx of Northern barbarians is Herodotus.[2] He tells us that the nomad Scythians, apparently a Turanian race, who may have been subjected to the pressure of population, swarmed over the Caucasus, dispossessed the Cimmerians (Gomer), and settled themselves in Saccasene, a province of Northern Armenia. From this province the Scythians gained the name of the Saquî. The name of Gog seems to be taken from Gugu, a Scythian prince, who was taken captive by Assurbanipal from the land of the Saquî.[3] Magog is perhaps Mat-gugu, "land of Gog." These rude, coarse warriors, like the hordes of Attila, or Zenghis Khan, or Tamerlane—who were descended from them—magne-

---

[1] The form in the Vulgate and the Alexandrian MS. of the LXX. is Mosech; in the Assyrian inscription, Muski. As far back as 1120 Tiglath-Pileser I. had overrun Tubal (the Tublai, Tabareni) and Moschi, between the Black Sea and the Taurus. They were neither Aryans nor Semites. In Gen. x. 2; 1 Chron. i. 5, Gog, Magog, Meshech, and Gomer are sons of Japheth. They are referred to in Rev. xx. 8.

[2] Herod., i. 74, 103-106, iv. 1-22, vii. 64; Pliny, *H. N.*, v. 16; Jos., *Antt.*, I. vi. 1; Syncellus, *Chronogl.*, i. 405.

[3] Sayce, *Ethnology of the Bible*; *Records of the Past*, ix. 40; Schrader, *K. A. T.*, 159. Some identify Gog with Gyges, King of Lydia, who was killed in battle *against* the Scythians, but whose name stood for a geographical symbol of Asia Minor, sometimes called Lud. It is said that in 665 Gyges (Gugu) sent two Scythian chiefs as a present to Nineveh.

tised the imagination of civilised people, as the Huns did in the fourth century.[1]   They overthrew the kingdom of Urartis (Armenia), and drove the all-but exterminated remnant of the Moschi and Tabali to the mountain-fortresses by the Black Sea, turning them, as it were, into a nation of ghosts in Sheol.[2]   Then they burst like a thunder-cloud on Mesopotamia, desolating the villages with their arrow-flights, but too unskilled to take fenced towns.   They swept down the Shephelah of Palestine, and plundered the rich temple of Aphrodite (Astarte Ourania) at Askelon, thereby incurring the curse of the goddess in the form of a strange disease. But on the borders of Egypt they were diplomatically met by Psammetichus (d. 611) with gifts and prayers. Judah seems only to have suffered indirectly from this invasion.   The main army of Scyths poured down the maritime plain, and there was no sufficient booty to tempt any but their straggling bands to the barren hills of Judah.[3]   It was the report of this over-flooding from the North which probably evoked the alarming prophecies of Zephaniah and Jeremiah, though they found their clearer fulfilment in the invasion of the Chaldees.

---

[1] Hence, in 2 Macc. iv. 47, 3 Macc. vii. 5, Scythian is used with the modern connotation of "Barbarian."

[2] Ezek. xxxii. 26, 27 ; Cheyne, *Jeremiah* ("Men of the Bible") p. 31.

[3] *Expositor*, 2nd series, iv 263 ; Cheyne, *Jeremiah*, 31.   Hitzig and Ewald (erroneously?) refer Psalms lv., lix., to these events, and it seems also to be an error to suppose that the later name of Bethshan —Scythopolis—has anything to do with this incursion.   Like the names of Pella, Philadelphia, etc., it is later than the age of Alexander the Great.   See 2 Macc. xii. 30 ; Jos., *B. J.*, II. xviii., *Vit.* vi. Perhaps Scythopolis is a corruption of Sikytopolis, the city of Sikkuth ; or Scythian may merely stand for "Barbarian," as in 3 Macc. vii. 5 ; Col. iii. 11 (Cheyne, *l.c.*).

II. This rush of wild nomads averted for a time the fate of Nineveh.

The Medes, an Aryan people, had settled south of the Caspian, B.C. 790 ; and in the same century one of these tribes—the Persians—had settled south-east of Elam the northern coast of the Persian Gulf. Cyaxares founded the Median Empire, and attacked Nineveh. The Scythian invasion forced him to abandon the siege, and the Scythians burnt the Assyrian palace and plundered the ruins. But Cyaxares succeeded in intoxicating and murdering the Scythian leaders at a banquet, and bribed the army to withdraw. Then Cyaxares, with the aid of the Babylonians under Nabopolassar their rebel viceroy, besieged and took Nineveh—probably about B.C. 608—while its last king and his captains were revelling at a banquet.[1]

The fall of Nineveh was not astonishing. The empire had long been "slowly bleeding to death" in consequence of its incessant wars. The city deemed itself impregnable behind walls a hundred feet high, on which three chariots could drive abreast, and mantled with twelve hundred towers ; but she perished, and all the nations—whom she had known how to crush, but had with "her stupid and cruel tyranny" never known how to govern—shouted for joy. That joy finds its triumphant expression in more than one of the prophets, but specially in the vivid pæan of Nahum. His date is approximately fixed at about B.C. 660, by his reference to the atrocities inflicted by Assurbanipal on the Egyptian city of No-Amon. "Art thou [Nineveh] better," he asks, "than No-Amon, that was situate among the canals, that had the water round about her,

---

whose rampart was the Nile, and her wall was the waters ? Yet she went into captivity ! Her young children were dashed to pieces at the head of all the streets : they cast lots for her honourable men, and all her great men were bound in chains. Thou also shalt be drunken : thou shalt faint away, thou shalt seek a stronghold because of the enemy."[1]

All the details of her fall are dim ; but Nineveh was, in the language of the prophets, swept with the besom of destruction. Her ruins became stones of emptiness, and the line of confusion was stretched over her. Nahum ends with the cry,—

> " There is no assuaging of thy hurt; thy wound is grievous :
> All that hear the bruit of this, clap the hands over thee :
> For upon whom hath thy wickedness not passed continually ? "

In truth, Assyria, the ferocious foe of Israel, of Judah, and all the world, vanished suddenly, like a dream when one awaketh ;[2] and those who passed over its ruins, like Xenophon and his Ten Thousand in B.C. 401, knew not what they were.[3] Her very name had become forgotten in two centuries. *" Etiam periere ruinæ ! "* The burnt relics and cracked tablets of her former splendour began to be revealed to the world once more in 1842, and it is only during the last quarter of a century that the fragments of her history have been laboriously deciphered.

III. Such were the events witnessed in their germs or in their completion by the contemporaries of Josiah and the prophets who adorned his reign. It was during

---

[1] Nah. iii. 8–11.
[2] Strabo, xvi. 1, 3 : ἠφανίσθη παοαχρῆμα.
[3] Xen., *Anab.*, III. iv. 7.

this period, also, that the power to whom the ultimate ruin and capitivity of Jerusalem was due sprang into formidable proportions. The ultimate scourge of God to the guilty people and the guilty city was not to be the Assyrian, nor the Scythian, nor the Egyptian, nor any of the old Canaanite or Semitic foes of Israel, nor the Phœnician, nor the Philistine. With all these she had long contended, and held her own. It was before the Chaldee that she was doomed to fall, and the Chaldee was a new phenomenon of which the existence had hardly been recognised as a danger till the warning prophecy of Isaiah to Hezekiah after the embassy of the rebel viceroy Merodach-Baladan.[1]

It is to Habakkuk, in prophecies written very shortly after the death of Josiah, that we must look for the impression of terror caused by the Chaldees.

Nabopolassar,[2] sent by the successor of Assurbanipal to quell a Chaldæan revolt, seized the viceroyalty of Babylon, and joined Cyaxares in the overthrow of Nineveh. From that time Babylon became greater and more terrible than Nineveh, whose power it inherited. Habakkuk (ii. 1–19) paints the rapacity, the selfishness, the inflated ambition, the cruelty, the drunkenness, the idolatry of the Chaldæans. He calls them (i. 5–11) a rough and restless nation, frightful and terrible, whose horsemen were swifter than leopards, fiercer than evening wolves, flying to gorge on prey like the vultures, mocking at kings and princes, and flinging dust over strongholds. Nor has he the least comfort in looking on their resistless fury, except the deeply

---

[1] Chaldees, Kardim, Kasdim, Kurds.
[2] Nabu-pal-ussur, "Nebo protect the son" B.C. 625–7. Jos., *Antt.* X. xi. 1: comp. *Ap.,* i. 19.

significant oracle—an oracle which contains the secret of their ultimate doom—

"Behold, his soul is puffed up ; it is not upright in him:
But the righteous man shall live by his fidelity."

The prophet places absolute reliance on the general principle that "pride and violence dig their own grave."[1]

---

[1] Newman, *Hebrew Monarchy*, p. 315.

CHAPTER XXXI

JOSIAH'S REFORMATION

2 KINGS xxii. 8—20, xxiii. 1—25

"And the works of Josias were upright before his Lord with a heart full of godliness."—I ESDRAS i. 23.

"From Zion shall go forth the Law, and the Word of the Lord from Jerusalem."—ISA. ii. 3.

IT is from the Prophets—Zephaniah, Jeremiah, Nahum, Habakkuk, Ezekiel—that we catch almost our sole glimpses of the vast world-movements of the nations which must have loomed large on the minds of the King of Judah and of all earnest politicians in that day. As they did not directly affect the destiny of Judah till the end of the reign, they do not interest the historian of the Kings or the later Chronicler. The things which rendered the reign memorable in their eyes were chiefly two—the finding of "the Book of the Law" in the House of the Lord, and the consequent religious reformation.

It is with the first of these two events that we must deal in the present chapter.

Josiah began to reign as a child of eight, and it may be that the emphatic and honourable mention of his mother—Jedidah (" Beloved "), daughter of Adaiah of Boscath—may be due to the fact that he owed to her training that early proclivity to faithfulness which earns for him the unique testimony, that he not only " walked

385   25

in the way of David his father," but that "he turned
not aside to the right hand or to the left."

At first, of course, as a mere child, he could take no
very active steps. The Chronicler says that at sixteen
he began to show his devotion, and at twenty set
himself the task of purging Judah and Jerusalem from
the taint of idols. Things were in a bad condition, as
we see from the bitter complaints and denunciations
of Zephaniah and Jeremiah. Idolatry of the worst
description was still openly tolerated. But Josiah was
supported by a band of able and faithful advisers.
Shaphan, grandfather of the unhappy Gedaliah—afterwards the Chaldæan viceroy over conquered Judah—
was scribe; Hilkiah, the son of Shallum and the
ancestor of Ezra, was the high priest.[1] By them the
king was assisted, first in the obliteration of the prevalent emblems of idolatry, and then in the purification
of the Temple. Two centuries and a half had elapsed
since it had been last repaired by Joash, and it must
have needed serious restoration during long years of
neglect in the reigns of Ahaz, of Manasseh, and of
Amon. Subscriptions were collected from the people
by "the keepers of the door," and were freely entrusted
to the workmen and their overseers, who employed them
faithfully in the objects for which they were designed.[2]

The repairs led to an event of momentous influence
on all future time. During the cleansing of the Temple
Hilkiah came to Shaphan, and said, "I have found the
Book of the Law in the House of the Lord." Perhaps

---

[1] 2 Kings xxiii. 4. We have here the first mention of "the second
priest" (if, with Grätz, we read *Cohen mishneh*, as in 2 Kings xxv.
18; Jer. lii. 24). In later days he was called "the Sagan." At this
time he probably acted as "Captain of the Temple" (Grätz, ii. 319).

[2] Comp. 2 Kings xii. 15, where we find the same remark.

the copy of the book had been placed by some priest's hand beside the Ark, and had been discovered during the removal of the rubbish which neglect had there accumulated. Shaphan read the book; and when next he had to see the king to tell him about the progress of the repairs, he said to him, " Hilkiah the priest hath handed me a book." Josiah bade him read some of it aloud. It is evident that he read the curses contained in Deut. xxviii. They horrified the pious monarch; for all that they contained, and the laws to which they were appended, were wholly new to him. He might well be amazed that a code so solemn, and purporting to have emanated from Moses, should, in spite of maledictions so fearful, have become an absolute dead letter. In deep alarm he sent the priest, the scribe Shaphan, with his son Ahikam, and Abdon, the son of Micaiah, and Asahiah, a court official, to inquire of Jehovah, whose great anger could not but be kindled against king and people by the obliteration and nullity of His law. They consulted Huldah, the only prophetess mentioned in the Old Testament, except Miriam and Deborah.[1] She was the wife of Shallum and keeper of the priests' robes,[2] and she lived in the suburbs of the city.[3] Her answer was an uncompromising menace. All the curses which the king had

---

[1] Exod. xv. 20; Judg. iv. 4; Isa. viii. 3. " The prophetess " seems to mean "prophet's wife." Noadiah was a false prophetess.

[2] Exod. xxviii. 2, etc.

[3] 2 Kings xxii. 14. Heb., *mishneh*, lit. "second"; A.V., " the college "; R.V., "the second quarter." Perhaps it means " the lower city " (Neh. xi. 9; Zeph. i. 10). It puzzled the LXX.: ἐν τῇ μασενᾷ. Vulg., *in secunda.* Jerome says, " *Haud dubium quin urbis partem significet quæ interiori muro vallabatur.*" Comp. Zeph. i. 10, " an howling from the *second* " (*i.e.*, quarter of the city); Neh. xi. 9, where, for " *second over the city* " (A. and R.V.), read " over the second part of the city."

heard against the place and people should be pitilessly fulfilled,—only, as the king had showed a tender heart, and had humbled himself before Jehovah, he should go to his own grave in peace.[1]

Thereupon the king summoned to the Temple a great assembly of priests, prophets, and all the people, and, standing by the pillar (or "on the platform ")[2] in the entrance of the inner court, read "all the words of the Book of the Covenant which had been found in the House of the Lord " in their ears, and joined with them in " the covenant " to obey the hitherto unknown or totally forgotten laws which were inculcated in the newly discovered volume.

Immediate action followed. The priests were ordered to bring out of the Temple all the vessels made for Baal, for the Asherah, and for the host of heaven; they were burnt outside Jerusalem in the Valley of Kedron, and their ashes taken to Bethel.[3] The *chemarim* of the high places were suppressed, as well as all other idolatrous priests who burnt incense to the signs of the Zodiac, the Hyades, and the heavenly bodies.[4] The Asherah itself was taken out of the

---

[1] Another reading is "in Jerusalem," which gets over an historic difficulty.

[2] Comp. 2 Kings xi. 14; LXX., ἐπὶ τοῦ στύλου; Heb., *al-ha-ammud*; Vulg., *super gradum*.

[3] 2 Kings xxiii. 4; for "in the fields of Kedron " one version has ἐν τῷ ἐμπυρισμῷ τοῦ χειμάῤῥου, "in the burning-place of the wady,"— perhaps reading *bemisrephoth* for *bishedamoth*, and alluding to lime-kilns in the wady. It is surprising that they should carry the ashes "to Bethel." Thenius suggests the reading בֵּית־אָֽוֶל, "place of execution" (lit., "house of nothingness ").

[4] Hos. x. 5; Zeph. i. 4 (the only other places where the word occurs). The *delevit* of the Vulgate (2 Kings xxiii. 5) only means that he put them down, and the κατέκαυσε of the LXX. should be κατέπαυσε.

Temple, and it is truly amazing that we should find it there so late in Josiah's reign. He burnt it in the Kedron, stamped it to powder, and scattered the powder "on the graves of the common people." The Chronicler says "on the graves of them that had sacrificed" to the idols [1];—but this is an inexplicable statement, since it is (as Professor Lumby says) very improbable that idolaters had a separate burial-place. It is equally shocking, and to us incomprehensible, to read that the houses of the degraded *Qedeshim* still stood, not "by the Temple" (A.V.), but "*in* the Temple," [2] and that in these houses, or chambers, the women still "wove embroideries [3] for the Asherah." What was Hilkiah doing? If the priests of the *high places* were so guilty from Geba to Beersheba, did no responsibility attach to the high priest and other priests of the Temple who permitted the existence of these enormities, not only in the *bamoth* at the city gates,[4] but in the very courts of the mountain of the Lord's House? If the priests of the immemorial shrines were degraded from their prerogatives, and were not allowed to come up to the altar of Jehovah in Jerusalem, by what law of justice were they to be regarded as so immeasurably inferior to the highest members of their own order, who, for years together, had permitted the worship of a wooden phallic emblem, and the existence of the worst heathen abominations within the very Temple

---

[1] Comp. Jer. ii. 23, where the LXX. has ἐν τῷ πολυανδρίῳ. In 2 Chron. xxxiv. 4, perhaps the true reading is, not *Beni-ha-'âm*, but *Beni-hinnom*—which would mean that he scattered the dust in the gehenna of Jerusalem. Comp. 1 Kings xv. 13.

[2] For these Galli, see Seneca, *De Vit. Beat.*, 27; Pliny, *H. N.*, xi. 49.

[3] Heb., *bathim*, lit. "tents" or "houses"; Vulg., *quasi domunculas*

[4] In 2 Kings xxiii. 8, Geiger would read "the high places of the satyrs" (שְׂעִירִים).

of the Lord ?   Every honest reader must admit that
there are inexplicable difficulties and uncertainties in
these ancient histories, and that our knowledge of the
exact circumstances—especially in all that regards the
priests and Levites, who, in the Chronicles, are their
own ecclesiastical historians—must remain extremely
imperfect.

And what can be meant by the clause that the
degraded priests of the old high places, though they
were not allowed to serve at the great altar, yet "did
eat of the *unleavened bread* among their brethren"?
Unleavened bread was only eaten at the Passover ; and
when there *was* a Passover, was eaten by all alike.
Perhaps the reading for "unleavened bread" should
be (priestly) "portions"—a reading found by Geiger
in an old manuscript.

Continuing his work, Josiah defiled Tophet ;[1] took
away the horses given by the kings of Judah to the
sun, which were stabled beside the chamber of the
eunuch Nathan-Melech in the precincts ;[2] and burnt the
sun-chariots in the fire.   He removed the altars to the
stars on the roof of the upper chamber of Ahaz,[3] and
ground them to powder.   He also destroyed those of
his grandfather Manasseh in the two Temple courts—
which we supposed to have been removed by Manasseh
in his repentance—and threw the dust into the Kedron.
He defiled the idolatrous shrines reared by Solomon
to the deities of Sidon, Ammon, and Moloch, broke the
pillars, cut down the Asherim, and filled their places

---

[1] Usually derived (as by Selden and Milton) from *toph*, "drum,"
but perhaps from *tuph* (to *spit* in sign of abhorrence).

[2] *Parvar*—perhaps "open portico."   Renan connects the word
with the Greek περίβολος.   On horses dedicated to the sun, see Xen.
Cyrop., viii. 3, 5, 12 ; *Anab.*, iv. 5.

[3] See Zeph. i. 5 ; Jer. xix. 13, xxxii. 29.

with dead men's bones.[1]   Travelling northwards, he
burnt, destroyed, and stamped to powder the altars and
the Asherim at Bethel, and burnt upon the altars
the remains found in the sepulchres,[2] only leaving
undisturbed the remains of the old prophet from
Judah, and of the prophet of Samaria.[3]   He then
destroyed the other Samaritan shrines, exercising an
undisputed authority over the Northern Kingdom.   The
mixed inhabitants did not interfere with his proceedings;
and in the declining fortunes of Nineveh, the Assyrian
viceroy—if there was one—did not dispute his authority.
Lastly, in accordance with the fierce injunction of
Deut. xvii. 2–5, "he slew all the priests of the high
places" on their own altars, burnt men's bones upon
them, and returned to Jerusalem.

It is very difficult, with the milder notions which
we have learnt from the spirit of the Gospel, to look
with approval on the recrudescence of the Elijah-spirit
displayed by the last proceeding.   But many centuries
were to elapse, even under the Gospel Dispensation,
before men learnt the sacred principle of the early
Christians that "violence is hateful to God."   Josiah
must be judged by a more lenient judgment, and he
was obeying a mandate found in the new Book of
the Law.   But the question arises whether the fierce

---

[1] 2 Kings xxiii. 13: "The Mount of Corruption"; Vulg., *Mons
offensionis*; LXX., τοῦ ὄρους τοῦ Μοσθάθ.   Some conjecture that
Maschith may be a derisive change for some word which meant
"anointing" (from being the *Oil* Mountain, *Har ham-mischchah*).

[2] In burning the bones of the dead, he violated all Jewish feeling.
Amos (ii. 1) had severely rebuked this form of revenge and insult
even in the case of the heathen King of Moab.   Bones defiled the
touch (Num. xix. 16; Herod., iv. 73).   Josiah's question at Bethel
was, "What *pillar* is that?" (*tsiyun*).   LXX., σκόπελον.   Comp. Gen.
xxxv. 20.

[3] 1 Kings xiii. 29–31.

commands of Deuteronomy were ever intended to be taken *au pied de la lettre*. May not Deut. xiii. 6–18 have been intended to express in a concrete but ideal form the spirit of execration to be entertained towards idolatry? Perhaps in thinking so we are only guilty of an anachronism, and are applying to the seventh century before Christ the feelings of the nineteenth century after Christ.

After this Josiah ordered the people to keep a Deuteronomic Passover, such as we are told—and as all the circumstances prove—had not been kept from the days of the Judges. The Chronicler revels in the details of this Passover, and tells us that Josiah gave the people thirty thousand lambs and kids, and three thousand bullocks; and his priests gave two thousand six hundred small cattle, and three hundred oxen; and the chief of the Levites gave the Levites five thousand small cattle, and five hundred oxen. He goes on to describe the slaying, sprinkling of blood, flaying, roasting, boiling in pots, pans, and caldrons, and attention paid to the burnt-offerings and the fat;[1] but neither the historians nor the chroniclers, either here or anywhere else, say one word about the Day of Atonement, or seem aware of its existence. It belongs to the Post-Exilic Priestly Code, and is not alluded to in the Book of Deuteronomy.

Continuing his task, he put away them that had familiar spirits (*oboth*), and the wizards, and the *teraphim*, with a zeal shown by no king before or after him; but Jehovah "turned not from the fierceness of His anger, because of all the provocations which Manasseh had provoked Him withal." Evil, alas! is more diffusive, and in some senses more permanent, than good, because of the perverted bias of human nature. Judah and

---

[1] 2 Chron. xxxv. 1–19.

Jerusalem had been radically corrupted by the apostate
son of Hezekiah, and it may be that the sudden and
high-handed reformation enforced by his grandson depended too exclusively on the external impulse given
to it by the king to produce deep effects in the hearts
of the people. Certain it is that even Jeremiah — though
he was closely connected with the finders of the book,
had perhaps been present when the solemn league
and covenant was taken in the Temple, and lived
through the reformation in which he probably took a
considerable part—was profoundly dissatisfied with the
results. It is sad and singular that such should have
been the case ; for in the first flush of the new enthusiasm he had written, "Cursed be the man that heareth
not the words of this covenant, which I commanded
your fathers in the day that I brought them forth out
of the land of Egypt, saying, 'Obey My voice.'"[1] Nay,
it has been inferred that he was even an itinerant
preacher of the newly found law ; for he writes : "And
the Lord said unto me, 'Proclaim all these words in the
cities of Judah, and in the streets of Jerusalem, saying,
Hear ye the words of this covenant, and do them.'"[2]

The style of Deuteronomy, as is well known, shows
remarkable affinities with the style of Jeremiah. Yet
it is clear that after the death of Josiah the prophet

---

[1] Jer. xi. 3, 4. Since, in this part of my subject, I make frequent
reference to the prophecies of Jeremiah which are indispensable to
the right understanding of the history, I may here say that modern
critics (Cheyne and others) arrange them as follows :—

In the reign of *Josiah,* Jer. ii. 1–iii. 5, iii. 6–vi. 30, vii. 1–ix. 25, **xi.** 1–17.

In the reign of *Jehoiakim,* xxvi. 2–6, xlvi. 2–12, xxv., **xxxv.,** and
possibly xvi. 1, xviii. 19–27, xiv., xv., xviii., xi. 18–xii. 17.

In the reign of *Jehoiachin,* x. 17–23, xiii.

In the reign of *Zedekiah,* xxii.–xxiv., xxvii.–xxix. 1–11 (?), lii.

In the *Exile,* xxxix.–xliv.

[2] See Cheyne, *Jeremiah,* p. 56, *id.* 6.

became utterly disillusioned with the outcome of the whole movement. It proved itself to be at once evanescent and unreal. The people would not give up their beloved local shrines.[1] The law, as Habakkuk says (i. 4), became torpid; judgment went not forth to victory; the wicked compassed about the righteous, and judgment was perverted. It was easy to obey the external regulations of Deuteronomy; it was far more difficult to be true to its noble moral precepts. The reformation of Josiah, so violent and radical, proved to be only skin-deep; and Jeremiah, with bitter disappointment, found it to be so. External decency might be improved, but rites and forms are nothing to Him who searcheth the heart.[2] There was, in fact, an inherent danger in the place assumed by the newly discovered book. "Since it was regarded as a State authority, there early arose a kind of book-science, with its pedantic pride and erroneous learned endeavours to interpret and apply the Scriptures. At the same time there arose also a new kind of hypocrisy and idolatry of the letter, through the new protection which the State gave to the religion of the book acknowledged by the law. Thus scholastic wisdom came into conflict with genuine prophecy."[3]

How entirely the improvement of outward worship failed to improve men's hearts the prophet testifies.[4] "The sin of Judah," he says, "is written with a pen of

---

[1] Canon Cheyne shows that even Mohammed could not persuade the Qurashites wholly to give up their black stone at the Kaaba, and their dolmens and sacred trees (*id.* 103). He left the *auçab*, or sacrificial stones (*matstseboth*), though he warns his followers against them (*Quran*, v. 92).

[2] Jer. xvii. 9–11.

[3] Ewald, *The Prophets*, iii. 63, 64.

[4] Jer. xvii. 1–4.

iron, and with the point of a diamond : it is graven
upon the tablets of their hearts, and upon the horns of
their altars, and their Asherim by the green trees [1] upon
the high hills. O My mountain in the field, I will
cause thee to serve thine enemies in the land thou
knowest not : for ye have kindled a fire in Mine
eyes, which shall burn for ever." While Josiah lived
this apostasy was secret ; but as soon as he died the
people " turned again to folly," [2] and committed all the
old idolatries except the worship of Moloch. There
arose a danger lest even the moderate ritualism of
Deuteronomy should be perverted and exaggerated
into mere formality. In the energy of his indignation
against this abuse, Jeremiah has to uplift his voice
against any trust even in the most decided injunctions
of this newly discovered law. He was " a second Amos
upon a higher platform." The Deuteronomic Law did
not as yet exhibit the concentrated sacerdotalism and
ritualism which mark the Priestly Code, to which it is
far superior in every way. It is still prophetic in its
tone. It places social interests above rubrics of worship.
It expresses the fundamental religious thought " that
Jehovah is in no sense inaccessible ; that He can be
approached immediately by all, and without sacerdotal
intervention ; that He asks nothing for Himself, but
asks it as a religious duty that man should render

---

[1] The Qurashites and other heathen Arabs accounted holy a large
green tree, and every year had a sacrifice in its honour. "On the
way to Hunain we called to God's Messenger (Mohammed) that he
should appoint for us such trees. But he was terrified, and said,
'Lord God, Lord God ! Ye speak even as the Israelites . . . ye are
still in ignorance,—thus are heathen enslaved ' " (Vakīdi, *Book of the
Campaigns of God's Messenger*, quoted by Cheyne, *Jeremiah*, p. 103,
from Wellhausen).

[2] Psalm lxxxv. 8.

unto man what is right; that His Will lies not in any known height, but in the moral sphere which is known and understood by all."[1] The book ordained certain sacrifices; yet Jeremiah says with startling emphasis, "To what purpose cometh there to Me frankincense from Sheba, and the sweet calamus from a far country? Your burnt-offerings are not acceptable, nor your sacrifices pleasant unto Me."[2] Therefore He bids them, "Put your burnt-offerings to your sacrifices, and eat them as flesh"—*i.e.*, "Throw all your offerings into a mass, and eat them at your pleasure (regardless of sacerdotal rules): they have neither any inherent sanctity nor any secondary importance from the characters of the offerers."[3] And in a still more remarkable passage, "*For I spake not unto your fathers, nor commanded them in the day that I brought them out of the land of Egypt, concerning burnt-offerings and sacrifices: but this thing I commanded them, saying, 'Obey My voice.'"[4]

Nay, in the most emphatic ordinances of Deuteronomy he found that the people had created a new peril. They were putting a particularistic trust in Jehovah, as though He were a respecter of persons, and they His favourites. They fancied, as in the days of Micah, that it was enough for them to claim His name, and

---

[1] Deut. xxx. 11–14. See Wellhausen, p. 165.

[2] Jer. vi. 20. The passages of Jeremiah which seem of a different spirit may have been added by later hands—*e.g.*, xxxiii. 18, which is not in the LXX.

[3] Jer. vii. 21; Ewald; and Cheyne, *l.c.* 120. So the Jews seem to have understood it, for they appoint this passage to be read on the *Haphtara* after the *Parashah* about sacrifices from Leviticus.

[4] Jer. vii. 22, 23. This alone would show that Jeremiah did not (as earlier critics thought) *write* "Deteronomy," in spite of the numerous close resemblances in phraseology. Thus, Jeremiah often denounces the priests (i. 18, ii. 8–26, iv. 9, v. 31, viii. 1, xiii. 13, xxxii. 32). Cheyne, p. 82.

bribe Him with sacrifices.[1] Above all, they boasted of
and relied upon the possession of His Temple, and
placed their trust on the punctual observance of
external ceremonies. All these sources of vain confidence it was the duty of Jeremiah rudely to shatter
to pieces. Standing at the gates of the Lord's House,
he cried : "Trust ye not in lying words, saying, 'The
Temple of the Lord ! the Temple of the Lord ! the
Temple of the Lord, are these !' Behold, ye trust in
lying words, that cannot profit. Will ye steal, murder,
commit adultery, swear falsely, burn incense unto Baal,
and walk after other gods ; and come and stand before
Me in this house, whereupon My name is called, and
say, 'We are delivered,' that ye may do all these
abominations ? Is this house become a den of robbers
in your eyes ? But go ye now to My place which was
in Shiloh, where I caused My name to dwell at the
first, and see what I did to it for the wickedness of
My people. I will do unto this house as I have done
to Shiloh ; and I will cast you out of My sight, as I have
cast out the whole house of Ephraim." [2]—Yet all hope
was not extinguished for ever. The Scythian might
disappear ; the Babylonian might come in his place ;
but one day there should be a new covenant of pardon
and restitution ; and as had been promised in Deuteronomy, "*all* should know Jehovah, from the least to
the greatest."

At last he even prophesies the entire future annul-
ment of the solemn covenant made on the basis of
Deuteronomy, and says that Jehovah will make a new
covenant with His people, not according to the covenant which He made with their fathers.[3] And in his

---

[1] Mic. iii. 11.

[2] Jer. vii. 4, 8–15.

[3] Jer. xxxi. 31, 32.

final estimate of King Josiah after his death, he does not so much as mention his reformation, his iconoclasm, his sweeping zeal, or his enforcement of the Deuteronomic Law, but only says to Jehoiakim :—

" ' Did not thy father eat and drink, and do judgment and justice ?—then it was well with him. He judged the cause of the poor and needy; then it was well. *Was not this to know Me ?' saith the Lord.*" [1]

Whether because its methods were too violent, or because it only affected the surface of men's lives, or because the people were not really ripe for it, or because no reformation can ever succeed which is enforced by autocracy, not spread by persuasion and conviction, it is certain that the first glamour of Josiah's movement ended in disillusionment. A religion violently imposed from without as a state-religion naturally tends to hypocrisy and externalism. What Jehovah required was, not a changed method of worship, but a changed heart; and this the reformation of Josiah did not produce. It has often been so in human history. Failure seems to be written on many of the most laudable human efforts. Nevertheless, truth ultimately prevails. Isaiah was murdered, and Urijah, and Jeremiah. Savonarola was burnt, and Huss, and many a martyr more; but the might of priestcraft was at last crippled, to be revived, we hope, no more, either by open violence or secret apostasy.

"Then to side with Truth is noble, when we share her wretched crust,
Ere her cause bring fame and profit, and 'tis prosperous to be just;
Then it is the brave man chooses, while the coward stands aside,
Doubting in his abject spirit till his Lord is crucified,
And the multitude make virtue of the faith they have denied."

[1] Jer. xxii. 15, 16.

NOTE TO CHAPTER XXXI.

"Jehovah is our Lawgiver."—ISA. xxxiii. 22.

WHAT was the Book of the Law which Hilkiah found in the Temple?

The great majority of eminent modern critics have now come to the conclusion that it was the kernel of the Book of Deuteronomy. Nor is this in any sense a mere modern notion. It occurs as far back as St. Jerome (*Adv. Jovin.*, i. 5) and St. Chrysostom (*Hom. in Matt.*, ix., p. 135, B. See W. Rob. Smith, p. 258).

It is no part of my immediate duty to argue this question, but I may state that the arguments for this conclusion are partly historical, partly literary, and partly depend on internal evidence.

I. As regards the *literary* argument, it is maintained that—

1. The full, rounded, rhetorical style of Deuteronomy, so widely different from the extreme dryness of other parts of the Torah, could not have been as yet developed in the days of Moses, and required the slow training of centuries for its perfection. It is a new phenomenon, and differs widely from earlier prophetic writings, such as those of Amos and Hosea.

2. The style and language of the Deuteronomist are so marked, that they can scarcely escape an intelligent reader of the English Version. Riehm enumerates sixty-four characteristic words or phrases. Their significance lies in the fact that they express obvious ideas, and are not names for special objects, which force a writer to use peculiar words. The style closely resembles in many phrases and particulars the style of Jeremiah, and of him alone among the prophets. "Even supposing that no historic text," it has been said, "taught us that the articles of Smalkald were the work of Luther, we should still have the right to affirm that these articles closely resemble the ideas of Luther, and could hardly have been published without his cognisance."

II. As regards *historical* evidence, we observe that—

1. No author earlier than Josiah shows any acquaintance with Deuteronomy : after that date, proofs of such knowledge abound.

2. The Book of Deuteronomy insisted with reiterated emphasis on the centralisation of worship. All its ordinances are framed with a view to promote this end. But we have seen that there

is not a trace of any belief that local shrines were prohibited earlier than the reign of Hezekiah, who certainly would have defended his boldness by appeal to a written law if he had known of such as existing.

III. As regards *internal* evidence, we see that—

1. Many passages and injunctions of the Book of Deuteronomy differ entirely from those found in the old Book of the Covenant which forms the most ancient nucleus of Exodus (Exod. xx. 22–xxiii. 33).

2. Even the most conservative English critics—even those who, with any pretence to competent knowledge, argue against the more advanced conclusions of the Higher Criticism—cannot help admitting that at least three codes, which in many, and in some fundamental, respects differ widely from each other, and which make no reference to each other, are found in our present Pentateuch—viz., that of the Book of the Covenant, that of the Deuteronomist (D.), and that of the Priestly writer (P.). All three may contain elements as old as the days of Moses; but most critics (with scarcely an exception in Germany) now believe that the Deuteronomic Code, in its present form, is not earlier than the date of Josiah's reformation (*circ.* B.C. 621); and the Priestly Codex (whatever older documents may exist in it) not older, in its present form, than about the time of Ezra (B.C. 444). Dillmann, Kittel, and in his later days Delitzsch, have been of necessity compelled to give up the views that, in their present form, D. and P. are as ancient as the days of Moses. The last German critic who held that Moses wrote our present Pentateuch was Keil (*d.* 1888). Canon Cheyne argues for the late date of this misnamed "Deuteronomy," on the grounds that the authors (1) used documents manifestly later than Moses; (2) alluded to events which only occurred long after Moses; and (3) expressed ideas which, in the age of Moses, are not psychologically possible.

The Book of Deuteronomy consists mainly of an historical introduction, probably added later (i. 1–5); Moses' *first* discourse (i. 6—iv. 40); Moses' *second* discourse (iv. 44-xxvi.); a section marked specially by blessings and curses (xxvii.-xxix.); a *third* discourse of Moses (xxix. 2-xxx. 20); his farewell (xxxi. 1–13); his song (xxxi. 14-xxxii. 47); conclusion, narrating his blessing and death (xxxii. 48-xxxiv. 12).

I have no space here to enter fully into the arguments which seem decisive as to the date of the main part of Deuteronomy. Those who desire to see them must study Colenso, *The Pentateuch*, pt. iii.; Reuss, *Hist. Sainte et la Loi*, i. 154-211; W. Robertson Smith, *Old Test. in the Jewish Church*, lect. xvi.; Kuenen, *The Hexateuch*, E. T., 1886; Kittel, *Gesch. d. Hebräer*, pp. 43-59; Cheyne, *Jeremiah*, pp. 48-86; S. R. Driver, *s.v.* "Deuteronomy" (Smith's *Dict. of the Bible*, new ed.); W. Aldis Wright, *The Documents of the Hexateuch*, pp. lvii.-lxxix. The name "Deuteronomy" (or "second law") arises from the mistaken rendering of the LXX. and Vulgate in Deut. xvii. 18.

CHAPTER XXXII

THE DEATH OF JOSIAH

B.C. 608

2 Kings xxiii. 29, 30

"Howl, O fir tree ; for the cedar is fallen."—Zech. xi. 2.

JOSIAH survived by thirteen years the reformation and covenant which are the chief events of his reign. He lived in prosperity and peace. He did justice and judgment ; the poor and needy flourished under his royal protection ; and it was well with him. It seemed as if the Deuteronomic blessings on faithfulness to its law were about to be abundantly fulfilled, when "the azure calm of heaven" was suddenly shattered, and "down came the thunderbolt." The great and victorious Assurbanipal of Assyria had died, and left his power to weaker successors. Meanwhile, Egypt was growing in power and splendour under Pharaoh Necho II. (B.C. 612–596), the sixth king of the twenty-fifth or Saitic dynasty. He nearly anticipated M. de Lesseps in making the Suez Canal,[1] and perhaps actually anticipated Vasco de Gama in rounding the Cabo Tormentoso, or Cape of Good Hope, in a three years' voyage. He was fired by the ambitious dream

---

[1] He was forced to desist by a fearful mortality among the labourers.

of succeeding the Assyrians as the chief power in the world, or at any rate of seizing part of the dominions which they had conquered.[1]   Accordingly, in B.C. 608, he went up against the King of Assyria to the river Euphrates.   The Chronicler says that his destination was Carchemish, on the Euphrates, and some have conjectured that the vague phrase "against the King of Assyria" is incorrect, and that, as Josephus states, he was really marching against the Medes and Babylonians after the fall of Nineveh.[2]

With this expedition Josiah was not greatly concerned.   He may have begun his reign as the vassal of Assurbanipal; but if so, it is probable that he had long since ceased to pay tribute to a power which was tottering to its fall under the attacks of Scythians and Babylonians.   He had availed himself of the disorganisation of the Assyrian power to re-establish some, at least, of the old authority of the House of David over the Northern Kingdom, and perhaps he only undertook the desperate expedient of withstanding the northward march of the Egyptian host under the notion that either on the march or on his return the Pharaoh intended to subjugate Palestine to Egypt.

Pharaoh Necho II., among his other achievements, had created a powerful fleet,[3] and it is nearly certain that he did not advance along the coast of Palestine, but made his way by sea to Acco or Dor.[4]   Here he received the news that Josiah meant to block his path

---

[1] *Circ.* B.C. 611–605.   Herod., ii. 158, 159, iv. 42.   Psamatik, the father of Necho, was perhaps a Lybian.   He established his sway over all Egypt displacing the Assyrians.

[2] *Antt.*, X. v. 1.

Herod., ii. 158.   His father Psamatik had left him an adequate army of natives and mercenaries.

[4] Herodotus says of his ships: Αἱ μὲν ἐπὶ τῇ βορηίῃ θαλάσσῃ ἐποιήθησαν.

at Megiddo, on the plain of Jezreel. **Th**at plain has been the great and only possible battle-field of Palestine, from the revolt in which Barak destroyed the host of Jabin,[1] to that in which Tryphon met Jonathan the Maccabee,[2] and Kleber in 1799 defeated twenty-five thousand Turks with three thousand French.

The Chronicler here adds a very remarkable incident.[3] Necho, like Joash of Israel in former days, did not care to fight with the poor little King of Judah—or at any rate did not wish to do so at present, when he was on his way to the greater encounter. He therefore sent an embassy to Josiah, saying, "What have I to do with thee, King of Judah? I come not against thee this day, but against the house wherewith I have war.[4] For God [Elohim] commanded me [in a dream] to make haste.[5] Forbear, then, from meddling with God, who is with me, that He destroy thee not."

The conjecture "in a dream" is not unlikely, nor is it in disaccord with other events in the annals of the Pharaohs and the Sargonidæ of Assyria.[6] We may indeed be surprised that an Egyptian Pharaoh should profess to deliver to a Jewish king the messages of Elohim, though we have seen something like this in the case of the Rabshakeh.[7] The variation in 1 Esdras i. 26–28 is curious and interesting. We are there told

---

[1] Judg. iv. 23; 1 Sam. xxix. 1–11; 1 Kings xx. 26; 2 Kings xxiii. 29; 2 Chron. xxxv. 22; Rev. xvi. 16 (Armageddon). Herodotus confuses it with Migdol (Μάγδολον).

[2] 1 Macc. xii. 49; Jos., *Antt.*, XIII. vi. 2.

[3] 2 Chron. xxxv. 20–22.

[4] According to 1 Esdras i. 25–32, "for upon Euphrates is my war."

[5] Klostermann, in 2 Chron. xxxv. 21, reads *bachalôm*, "in a dream," instead of "to make haste."

[6] Gen. xli. 1; Herod., ii. 188; *Records of the Past*, ix. 52.

[7] 2 Kings xviii. 25.

that the message was sent to Josiah, not only by Pharaoh Necho, who had sent to say "The Lord is with me hastening me forward : depart from me, and be not against the Lord," but also by "the prophet Jeremy." Josephus frankly ascribes the error of Josiah to destiny, as though he had been infatuated by the dementation which the Greeks attributed to Atè.[1]

This, however, is not likely; for it is clear that Jeremiah, though not mentioned in the Book of Kings, must have had a strong influence over the mind of Josiah, whom he loved, whose views he shared, in whose religious revolution he had taken part. Further, we do not read of any warning recorded by the prophet himself; and had he uttered one, it would certainly have been mentioned, when he committed his prophecies to writing twenty-three years after their commencement. A warning of which the neglect had led to fatal issues would have been so decisive a confirmation of Jeremiah's prophetic insight that it could not have been passed over in silence.

Indeed, Jeremiah may have shared the conviction which, founded on imperfect generalisation, perhaps dazzled the unfortunate king to his ruin. Josiah had accepted the Book of Deuteronomy with the whole strength of his belief, and the Book of Deuteronomy had proclaimed to Israel as the reward of faithfulness this promise: "And it shall come to pass that Jehovah, thy God, shall set thee on high above all the nations of the earth. . . . Jehovah shall cause thine enemies which rise up against thee to be smitten before thy face : they shall come out against thee one way, and flee before thee seven ways."[2] In the strength of that

---

[1] *Antt.*, X. v. 1: Τῆς πεπρωμένης οἶμαι εἰς τοῦτ' αὐτόν παρορμησάσης.

[2] Deut. xxviii. 1-8.

promise, Josiah was perhaps saying to himself, in the language of the Psalms, that Jehovah could not fail to save His anointed, and dash His enemies to pieces under His feet ;[1] in the language, perhaps, of later days, that the sound of a shaken leaf should chase them, and they should flee when none pursued.[2]

Alas ! such passages do not apply invariably to our wordly fortunes ! God's promises are general. The individual must be considered apart from the universal in the region of spiritual and eternal blessings. In the affairs of earth the wicked often seem to be in prosperity, while the righteous are overwhelmed by all God's waves and storms. Further, Josiah evidently received a warning—a warning which professed to come, and really came, from God[3]—whether uttered by Pharaoh or by Jeremiah. And in this instance Josiah had sought war ; he had not been forced into it. It was not for him to go out of his way to champion the cause either of cruel Assyria or vaunting Babylon.

The result was entire disenchantment. No more disheartening and disastrous calamity could have happened to the kingdom, which had just begun to struggle out of the slough of idolatry and humiliation.

Heedless of the message he had received, strong in mistaken hopes, Josiah opposed his poor, weak forces to the powerful host of renovated Egypt. The result was instantaneous ruin.[4] Judah was defeated and scattered without a blow,—Necho came, saw, conquered. Josiah, according to the present record of the Chronicles,

---

[1] Psalm xx. 6, xviii. 29–50.
[2] Lev. xxvi. 36.
[3] 2 Chron. xxxv. 22 : "hearkened not *to the words of Necho from the mouth of God.*"
[4] "When he had *seen* him." Comp. 2 Kings xiv. 8.

like Ahab, "disguised himself"[1] and went into the
battle; and as he drove from rank to rank an Egyptian
archer drew a bow at a venture, and smote him while
he was putting his forces in array. The arrow-point
brought conviction too late. Josiah saw his error; he
knew that his own death involved the rout of his army.
He sounded a retreat, and said to his servants, "Bear
me away to my travelling chariot, for I am sore
wounded."[2] He died at Megiddo, where his ancestor
Ahaziah had died before him from the arrow-wounds
of Jehu's pursuers. His servants carried him in a
chariot dead from Megiddo. The famous plain of
Esdraelon had already witnessed two great victories—
that of Barak over Sisera, and that of Gideon over the
Midianites; and one deplorable defeat—that of Saul by
the Philistines. It was now darkened by a catastrophe
even more sad.[3]

When that chariot, accompanied by its wailing escort,
entered the gates of Jerusalem, with the routed army
of Judah behind it, the feeling of the people must have
resembled that of the Athenians when the news reached
them that Lysander had destroyed their whole fleet
at Ægospotami, and the long wail went thrilling up
through that sleepless night from the Peiræus all along
the Makra Teichè to the Parthenon and the Acropolis.
And there followed such a mourning as the land had
never known before. It had begun at Megiddo and
Hadadrimmon, leaving the sad memory of its hopeless

---

[1] 1 Esdras i. 25; and LXX., "firmly resolved," "strengthened himself," as in 2 Chron. xxv. 11.

[2] Jos., *Antt.*, X. v. 1; and 2 Chron. xxxv. 23; 1 Esdras i. 30.

[3] The fortunes of the Jews again prevailed in this plain in the days of Holofernes (Judith vii. 3); but they were defeated there by Placidus (Jos., *B. J.*, IV. i. 8).

intensity. It was renewed at Jerusalem when they buried the king in his own sepulchre. "The land mourned, every family apart; the family of the House of David apart, and their wives apart; the family of the House of Nathan apart, and their wives apart; the family of the House of Levi apart, and their wives apart; the family of Shimei apart, and their wives apart; all the families that remained, every family apart, and their wives apart."[1] "And all Judah and Jerusalem mourned for Josiah. And Jeremiah lamented for Josiah: and all the singing men and the singing women spake of Josiah in their lamentations unto this day, and they were made an institution in Israel: and, behold, they are written in the Lamentations."[2] Not even for heroic David, or royal Solomon, or pious Asa, or prosperous Jehoshaphat had there been so loud a dirge.

But, alas! there was cause for far deeper sorrow than the loss of a prince, however able, however beloved. The dead was dead. Natural sorrow for the bereavement of the people would soon be healed by time, but behind the passing affliction lay a great fear and a great reaction.

A great fear,—for now a southern foe was added to the northern. Jeremiah and other prophets had warned Israel of the peril from the North. When the Scythian wave "rolled shoreward, struck and was dissipated,"

---

[1] Zech. xii. 11–13 (comp. Jer. xxii. 10, 18). No such place as Hadadrimmon is known, though there is a Rummâne not far from Megiddo. Jerome (*Comm. in Zach.*) identifies it with a place which he calls Maximianopolis. Wellhausen (*Skizzen*, 192) thinks that the mourning is compared to some wail over the god Hadadrimmon, like the wailing for Tammuz. Jonathan and Jarchi say that Hadadrimmon was the son of Tabrimmon, who opposed Ahab at Ramoth-Gilead.

[2] 2 Chron. xxxv. 24, 25. Jeremiah's elegy has probably perished. It would have been most interesting had it been preserved. Lam. iv. is too vague to have been this lost poem.

when the source of Assyrian terror seemed to be drying up, worldlings may have felt inclined to laugh at Jeremiah. But now it was evident that, sooner or later, the Chaldæans would be as formidable as their predecessors, and out of the serpent's egg was breaking forth a cockatrice. The uncalled-for attempt of Josiah to bar the path of the new and mighty Pharaoh had also added Egypt to the list of formidable enemies. For the present the Pharaoh had passed on to the Euphrates; but whether he returned victorious or defeated, his troops could not but be a source of danger to the little kingdom, which would henceforth be help-less between the overwhelming forces of its foes.

If such were the fears of the timid and the pessimistic, still deeper was the disheartenment of the faithful. Josiah had been the most obedient, the most religious, of all the kings of Judah from childhood upwards. Where, then, were Jehovah's old loving-kindnesses which He sware unto David in His truth? Had God forgotten to be gracious? Had He hidden away His mercy in displeasure? Where were the blessings of the newly discovered Book of the Law, if the curse fell on its most earnest votary? Where was Huldah's promise that he should be gathered to his fathers in peace, if he was carried back dead from the field of fruitless battle? There can be little doubt that the apparent blight which had fallen on unavailing righteousness hastened the reaction of the subsequent reigns. Many might be inclined to cry out with even Jeremiah in his moments of overwhelming despondency, "Ah, Lord God! surely Thou hast greatly deceived this people and Jerusalem, saying, 'Ye shall have peace'; whereas the sword reacheth unto the soul."[1]   "O Lord,

---

[1] Jer. iv. 10.

Thou has deceived me, and I was deceived: Thou art stronger than I, and hast prevailed: I am a derision daily, every one mocketh me. Whenever I speak, I must shout, I must cry violence and spoil; for the word of the Lord is made a reproach unto me, and a derision, daily."[1]

But man judges partially and judges amiss. God's ways are not as man's ways. God sees the whole; He sees the future; He sees things as they are. Through defeat, through captivity, through multiform affliction, lay the path to the final deliverance of the nation from the grosser forms of idolatry. When they wept as they remembered Zion, when they took down their harps from the willows by the water-courses of Babylon to sing the Lord's song in a strange land, they turned again—and at last with their whole heart—to God their Saviour, who had done so great things for them;—until the grey secret lingering in the East was brightened by the Morning Star, and there was revealed to the world a True Israel, and a New Jerusalem, wherein the Lord should be King for evermore.

---

[1] Jer. xx. 7, 8.

CHAPTER XXXIII

JEHOAHAZ

B.C. 608

2 KINGS xxiii. 31—33

"I went by, and, lo! he was gone: I sought him, but his place could nowhere be found."—PSALM xxxvii. 36.

IT was under the disastrous circumstances which attended his father's death at Megiddo that Jehoahaz began to reign. There is some confusion about the four sons of Josiah, whom the Chronicler calls Johanan, Jehoiakim, Zedekiah, and Shallum.[1] From Jer. xxii. 11, it appears that Jehoahaz was the royal name taken on his anointing by Shallum, the third son.[2] If so, he cannot be identified with Johanan, the firstborn, as in the margin of our version. Further, it appears from our historians that Jehoahaz was twenty-three at his succession, and was therefore younger than Jehoiakim who (three months later) succeeded him at the age of

---

[1] Chron. iii. 15.

[2] He is named "fourth," but he was older than his brothers Jehoiakim and Zedekiah (2 Kings xxiii. 31, xxiv. 18). The genealogy is as follows:—

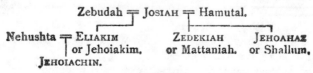

Zebudah ⊤ JOSIAH ⊤ Hamutal.

Nehushta ⊤ ELIAKIM   ZEDEKIAH   JEHOAHAZ
    or Jehoiakim.   or Mattaniah.   or Shallum.
JEHOIACHIN.

411

twenty-five. Jehoahaz was the own brother of Zedekiah, Jehoiakim being his half-brother by another mother (Zebudah).

We do not know for what reason he was preferred by "the people of the land" to his elder brother Eliakim or Jehoiakim. It was probably because they regarded him as a prince of eminent courage and ability. The high hopes which the nation conceived of him may be seen in the pathetic elegy of Ezek. xix. :—

"Moreover take thou up a lamentation for the princes of Israel, and
    say,—
What was thy mother ? A lioness !
Amidst lions she couched,
In the midst of the young lions she nourished her whelps.
She brought up one of her whelps: he became a young lion ;
He learned to catch the prey ; he devoured men.
The nations heard of him ;
In their pit was he taken,[1]
And they brought him with hooks into the land of Egypt."[2]

We see, too, that he was to an eminent degree the darling of the nation in the still more plaintive wail of Jeremiah which will be quoted later.

The fact that Shallum solemnly changed his name to Jehoahaz ("Jehovah taketh hold"),[3] and that the people of the land not only "made him king in his father's stead," but also "anointed him," points to a disputed succession.[4] High hopes were conceived of

---

[1] An allusion to the Syrian mode of hunting the lion by driving it with cries into a concealed pit (Tristram, *Nat. Hist. of the Bible*, 118; Cheyne, 140).

[2] Ezek. xix. 1–4.

[3] The name Shallum means "recompense." It may have been regarded as ill-omened, since the King of Israel who bore this rare name had only reigned a month.

[4] The Talmud says that kings were only anointed in special cases (*Keritoth* f. 5, 2; Grätz, ii. 328).

him ; but he hardly had a chance of fulfilling them, for he was only permitted to reign three months. What were the events of those months we do not know. Jehoahaz must have disappointed any hopes which may have been formed of him by the religious party ; for dear as he was to them, the historians record of him that " he did that which was evil in the sight of the Lord, according to all that his fathers had done," although they specify no particular offence. The same sad verdict is passed on all his four successors ; but Josephus says even more emphatically of Jehoahaz that he was impious and impure.[1]

He must have shown some activity in other respects, or else Ezekiel would hardly have said that " the nations heard of him," and that " he learned to catch the prey ; he devoured men." Over all his deeds, whatever they may have been, " the iniquity of oblivion has blindly scattered her poppy," and he fell a victim to the great world-movements of those troublous times.

For Pharaoh, after his defeat of Josiah at Megiddo, proceeded to make himself master of Syria and Palestine. He took Cadytis, which Herodotus calls "a large city of Syria,"[2] and which—since it cannot here mean Gaza, as in Herod., iii. 5—has been identified by some with Kadesh. Thence he marched to Carchemish, on the right bank of the Euphrates,[3] none venturing to check him, till " once more, after the lapse of nine centuries, Egyptian garrisons looked down on that historic stream."[4] On his return he stopped at Riblah, on the

---

[1] Jos., *Antt.*, X. v. 2 : Ἀσεβὴς καὶ μιαρὸς τὸν τρόπον.

[2] Herod., ii. 159.

[3] Mr. G. Smith identifies Carchemish with Jerablûs.

[4] Cheyne, *Jeremiah*, p. 127.

Orontes,[1] to consolidate his Syrian conquests; and there he learnt that, without consulting him, the people of Jerusalem had made Jehoahaz their king. Perhaps he heard enough of the warlike prowess of Jehoahaz to make him resent this act of independence. After his three months' campaign he sent for Jehoahaz to Riblah, and the unhappy prince had no choice but to obey. Possibly the Egyptian party in Jerusalem, headed by his disappointed elder brother Eliakim, may have intrigued against him with Pharaoh Necho. When he reached Riblah, he was unceremoniously deposed; and though we may hope that the expression of Ezekiel, that "they brought him with *hooks* into the land of Egypt," belongs to the metaphor of the captured lion's whelp, it is certain that he was taken to the banks of the Nile as a fettered captive, never to return. How long his miserable life was protracted, or how he was treated in Egypt, we do not know. The sun of the young prince went down in darkness while it was yet day. No king of Judah before him had died in prison and in exile, and the calamity smote heavily the heart of his people. Egypt was not to escape—shortly thereafter—the doom of violence and pride; but whether the young Jewish king had died meanwhile of a broken heart, or whether he dragged on to hoar hairs his maimed life, or whether he was murdered in his dungeon, no man knew. One thing only was clear to the sad prophet—that he would never return.

"Weep ye not for the dead, neither bemoan him:

---

[1] Comp. 2 Kings xxv. 20, 21. The old Hittite capital of Riblah was a convenient halting-place on the road between Babylon and Jerusalem. It was on the northernmost boundary of Palestine towards Damascus (Amos vi. 14).

but weep ye sore for him that is gone away: for he shall return no more, nor see his native country. For thus saith Jehovah concerning Shallum, the son of Josiah, King of Judah, which reigned instead of Josiah his father, which went forth out of this place: 'He shall not return thither any more: but in the place whither they have led him captive there shall he die, and he shall see this land no more.'"[1]

To show his absolute power over Judah and Jerusalem, Pharaoh Necho not only deposed and fettered their king, but put the whole land under a yearly tribute of one hundred talents of silver (about £40,000) and a talent of gold (about £4,000).[2]

Even this comparatively small sum was a heavy burden for so greatly afflicted and impoverished a country, and Pharaoh further imposed on them a vassal to see that it was duly extorted. This was Eliakim, the eldest living son of Josiah. There was nothing left to plunder in the Temple or the palace, and therefore the exaction had to be borne by the taxed and suffering people.

---

[1] Jer. xxii. 10-12.

[2] 2 Chron. xxxvi. 3; 1 Esdras i. 36. The smallness of the tribute proves the impoverishment of the land. Sennacherib demanded from Hezekiah three hundred talents of silver, and thirty of gold; and Menahem paid one thousand talents of silver to Tiglath-Pileser.

CHAPTER XXXIV

JEHOIAKIM

B.C. 608—597

2 KINGS xxiii. 36—xxiv. 7

"But those things that are recorded of him, and of his uncleanness and impiety, are written in the Chronicles of the Kings."—
1 ESDRAS i. 42.

"When Jehoiakim succeeded to the throne, he said, 'My predecessors knew not how to provoke God.'"—*Sanhedrin*, f. 103, 2

"There is no strange handwriting on the wall,
Through all the midnight hum no threatening call,
Nor on the marble floor the stealthy fall
Of fatal footsteps. All is safe.—Thou fool,
The avenging deities are shod with wool!"

W. ALLEN BUTLER.

ELIAKIM succeeded to the throne at the age of
twenty-five under very unenviable circumstances—
as a nominal king, a helpless nominee and tributary
of the Pharaoh. He seems to have been thoroughly
distasteful to the people; and if we may judge from the
fact that Ezekiel frankly ignores him and passes from
Jehoahaz to Jehoachin, he was regarded as a tax-
gathering usurper nominated by an alien tyrant. For
after speaking of Jehoahaz, Ezekiel says,—

"Now when she [Judah] saw that she had waited [for the
restoration of Jehoahaz], and her hope was lost,

416

> Then she took another of her whelps;[1]
> A young lion she made him.
> He went up and down among the lions;
> He became a young lion."[2]

The historian says that Necho turned the name of Eliakim ("God will establish") to Jehoiakim ("Jehovah will establish"); but by this can hardly be meant more than that he sanctioned the change of El into Jehovah on Eliakim's installation upon the throne.

Jehoiakim is condemned in the same terms as all the other sons of Josiah. His misdoings are far more definitely recorded in the Prophets, who furnish us with details which are passed over by the historians. Some of his sins may have been due to the influence of his wife Nehushta, who was a daughter of Elnathan of Achbor, one of the princes of the heathen party. It was this Elnathan whom the king chose as a fitting ambassador to demand the extradition of the prophet Urijah from Egypt. One of the crimes with which Jehoiakim is charged is the building for himself of a sumptuous palace, and thus vainly trying to emulate the splendours of Assyrian, Babylonian, and Egyptian kings. In itself the act would not have been more wicked than it was in Solomon, whose architectural parade is dwelt upon with enthusiasm. But the circumstances were now wholly different. Solomon was at that time in all his glory, the possessor of boundless wealth, the ruler of an immense and united territory, the head of a powerful and prosperous people, the successor of an unconquered hero who had gone to his grave in peace; Jehoiakim,

---

[1] Not Jehoiakim, but Jehoiachin, as the sequel shows.

[2] Ezek. xix. 5-9. The allusions to Jehoiakim by Jeremiah are numerous, and all unfavourable (xxii. 13-19, xxvi. 20-23, xxxvi. 20-31, etc.).

on the other hand, had succeeded a father who had died in defeat on the field of battle, and a brother who was hopelessly pining in an Egyptian prison. The Tribes had been carried into captivity by Assyria; the nation was beaten, oppressed, and poor; the king himself possessed but a shadow of royalty. In such a condition of things it would have been his glory to maintain a watchful and strenuous activity, and to devote himself in simplicity and self-denial to the good of his people. It showed a perverted and sensuous mind to insult the misery of his subjects at such a time by feeble attempts to rival heathen potentates in costly æstheticism. But this was not all; he carried out his ignoble selfishness at the cost of oppression and wrong.[1]

It is possible that the prophet Habakkuk alludes to him in the words:—

"Woe to him that getteth an evil gain for his house, that he may set his nest on high, that he may be delivered from the hand of evil![2] Thou hast consulted shame to thy house by cutting off many peoples, and hast sinned against thy soul. For the stone shall cry out of the wall, and the beam out of the timber shall answer it."[3]

The thought of the Jewish king's selfish expensiveness may have crossed the mind of Habakkuk, though the taunt is addressed directly to the Chaldæans, and especially to Nebuchadrezzar, who was at that time revelling in the beautifying of Babylon, and especially

---

[1] Josephus (*Antt.*, X. v. 2) is very severe on this king. He says that "he was unjust in disposition, an evil-doer, neither pious towards God nor just towards men."

[2] Perhaps an allusion to a sort of fortified palace on Ophel.

[3] Hab. ii. 9-11.

of his own royal palace. On the other hand, the rebuke, or rather the denunciation, uttered by Jeremiah against the king for this line of conduct, and for the forced labour which it required, is terribly direct.

> " ' Woe unto him that buildeth his house by unrighteousness,
> And his chambers by wrong;
> That useth his neighbour's service without wages,
> And giveth him not his hire;
> That saith, " I will build me a wide house and spacious chambers,"
> And cutteth out windows;
> And it is ceiled with cedar, and painted with vermilion.
> Shalt thou reign because thou viest with the cedar ?[1]
> Did not thy father eat and drink, and do judgment and justice ?
> Then it was well with him !
> Was not this to know Me ? ' saith the Lord.
> ' But thine heart is not but for thy dishonest gain,
> And for to shed innocent blood,
> And for oppression and for violence to do it.' "[2]

Then follows the stern message of doom which we shall quote hereafter. The king's bad example stimulated or perhaps emulated similar folly and want of patriotism on the part of his nobles. They were shepherds who destroyed and scattered the sheep of Jehovah's pastures. But vain was their imagined security, and their ostentation. The judgment was imminent.[3]

"O inhabitress of Lebanon, that makest thy nest in the cedars," exclaims the prophet in bitter mockery, " how greatly wilt thou groan when pangs come upon thee, the pain as of a woman in travail ! "[4]

---

[1] The text is perhaps corrupt. Two MSS. of the LXX. read "because thou viest *with Ahab*," and the Vatican MSS. has "*with Ahaz.*" Cheyne adopts the former reading.

[2] Jer. xxii. 13-17.

[3] Jer. xxiii. 1.

[4] Jer. xxii. 23.

But Jehoiakim's offences were deadlier than this.
The Chronicler speaks of "the abominations which he
did"; and some have therefore supposed that the evil
state of things described by Jeremiah (xix.) refers to
this reign. If so, he plunged into the idolatry which
caused Judah to be shivered like a potter's vessel.
Certainly he sinned grievously against God in the
person of His prophets.

Jeremiah was not the only prophet who disdained
the easy and traitorous popularity which was to be won
by prophesying "peace, peace," when there was no
peace. He had for his contemporary another messenger
of God, no less boldly explicit than himself—Urijah,
the son of Shemaiah of Kirjath-Jearim. Jeremiah had
as yet only prophesied in his humble native village
of Anathoth; he had not been called upon to face
"the swellings" or "the pride of Jordan."[1] Urijah had
been in the fuller glare of publicity in the capital, and
his bold declaration that Jerusalem should fall before
Nebuchadrezzar and the Chaldæans had excited such
a fury of indignation that he escaped into Egypt for his
life. Surely this should have appeased the rulers, even
if they chose to pay no attention to the Divine menace.
For the prophets were recognised deliverers of the
messages of Jehovah; and with scarcely an exception,
even in the most wicked reigns, their persons had been
regarded as sacrosanct. But Jehoiakim would not let
Urijah escape. He sent an embassy to Necho, headed
by his father-in-law Elnathan, son of Achbor, requesting
his extradition. Urijah had been dragged back from
Egypt, and, to the horror of the people, the king had
slain him with the sword, and flung his body into the

graves of the common people.[1] What made this conduct more monstrous was the precedent of Micah the
Morasthite.   He, in the days of Hezekiah, had prophesied,—

> "Zion shall be ploughed as a field,
>   And Jerusalem shall become heaps,
>   And the Mountain of the House as the wooded heights."[2]

Yet so far from putting him to death, or even stirring
a finger against him, the pious king had only been
moved to repentance by the Divine threatenings.   Thus
the blood of the first martyr-prophet, if we except the
case of Zechariah, had been shed by the son of Judah's
most pious king.   Jeremiah himself only narrowly
escaped martyrdom.   The precedent of Micah helped
to save him, though it had not saved Urijah.   He was
far more powerfully protected by the patronage of the
princes and the people.   Standing in the Temple court,
he had declared that, unless the nation repented, that
house should be like Shiloh, and the city a curse to
all the nations of the earth.   Maddened by such words
of bold rebuke, the priests and the prophets and the
people had threatened him with death.   But the princes
took his part, and some of the people came over to
them.   His most powerful protector was Ahikam, the
son of Shaphan, a member of a family of the utmost
distinction.

Meanwhile, we must follow for a time the outward
fortunes of the king and of the world.

Necho, after his successful advance, had retired to

---

[1] Jer. xxvi. 20-23. So far as I am aware, Bunsen stands alone in
identifying Urijah with the "Zechariah" who wrote Zech. xii.-xiv.
Others refer Zech. xii. 10 to the murder of Urijah.

[2] Jer. xxvi. 18.

Egypt, and Jehoiakim continued to be for three years his obsequious servant. An event of tremendous importance for the world changed the entire fortunes of Egypt and of Judah. Nineveh fell with a crash which terrified the nations. We might apply to her the language which Isaiah applies to her successor, Babylon :—

" Sheol from beneath is moved for thee to meet thee at thy coming : it stirreth up the shades for thee, even the Rephaim of the earth; it hath raised up from their thrones all the kings of the nations. All they shall answer and say unto thee, ' Art thou also become weak as we ? art thou become like unto us ? ' . . . All the kings of the nations, all of them, sleep in glory, every one in his own house. But thou art cast forth away from thy sepulchre like an abominable branch, as the raiment of those that are slain, that are thrust through with the sword, that go down to the stones of the pit. . . . They that see thee shall narrowly look upon thee . . . and say, ' Is this the man that made the earth to tremble ? that did shake kingdoms ? that made the world as a wilderness, and overthrew the cities thereof ? that let not loose his prisoners to their home ? ' " [1]

Yes, Assyria had fallen like some mighty cedar in Libanus, and the nations gazed without pity and with exultation on his torn and scattered branches.

And coincident with the fate of Nineveh had been the rise of the Chaldæan power.

Nabupalussur [2] had been a general of one of the last Assyrian kings, and had been sent by him with an army to quell a Babylonian revolt. Instead of this, he seized the city and made himself king. When the

---

[1] Isa. xiv., *passim.*
[2] Nabu-pal-ussur, " Nebo protect the son."

final overthrow and obliteration of Nineveh had secured
his power, he sent his brave and brilliant son Nebuchadrezzar [1] (B.C. 605) to secure the provinces which he had
wrested from Assyria, and especially to regain possession of Carchemish, which commanded the river.

Necho marched to protect his conquests, and at
Carchemish the hostile forces encountered each other
in a tremendous battle,—immemorial Egypt under the
representative of its age-long Pharaohs; Babylon, with
her independence of yesterday, under a prince hitherto
unknown, whose name was to become one of the
most famous in the world.   The result is described by
Jeremiah (xlvi. 1–12).   Egypt was hopelessly defeated.
Her splendidly arrayed warriors were panic-stricken
and routed; her chief heroes were dashed to pieces
by the heavy maces of the Babylonians, or fled without
so much as looking back.   The scene was one of
" Magor-missabib "—terror on every side.[2]   Pharaoh's
host came up like the Nile in flood with its Ethiopian
hoplites and Asiatic archers; but they were driven
back.   The daughter of Egypt received a wound which
no balm of Gilead could cure.   The nations heard of
her shame, and the prophet pronounced her further
chastisement by the hands of Nebuchadrezzar.

---

[1] Nabu-kudur-ussur, "Nebo protect the crown" (Schrader, ii. 48),
or "the youth" (Oppert).   The portrait of Nebuchadrezzar—this is
the proper spelling, as generally in Jeremiah—is preserved for us on
a black cameo which he presented to the god Merodach.   It is now
in the Berlin Museum, and shows strong but not cruel or ignoble
characteristics.   It is copied in Riehm's *Handwörterbuch*, ii. 1067.
The Jews, as they were fond of doing to their enemies, made insulting puns on his name.   Thus in the *Vayyikra Rabba* (Wünsche, *Bibl.
Rabb.*) the Three Children are represented as saying to him, "You
are Neboo-cad-netser: bark [*nabach*] like a dog; swell like a water-
jar [*kad*], and chirp like a cricket [*tsertser*],"—in allusion to his madness.

[2] Jer. xlvi. 5 (vi. 25).

Then, in the fourth year of Jehoiakim, the young Babylonian conqueror swept down upon Syria and Palestine like a bounding leopard, like an avenging eagle (Hab. i. 7, 8). Jehoiakim had no choice but to change his vassalhood to Necho for a vassalage to Nebuchadrezzar.[1] He might have suffered severe consequences, but tidings came to the young Chaldæan that his father had ended his reign of twenty-one years and was dead. For fear lest disturbances might arise in his capital, he at once dashed home across the desert with some light troops by way of Tadmor, while he told his general to follow him home through Syria by the longer route. He seems, however, to have carried away with him some captives, among whom were Daniel, Ananias, Azarias, and Misael,[2] destined hereafter for such memorable fortunes. Jehoiakim himself was thrown into fetters to be carried into Babylon; but the conqueror changed his mind, and probably thought that it would be safer for the present to accept his pledges and assurances, and leave him as his viceroy. "He took an oath of him," says Ezekiel (xvii. 13); "he took also the mighty of the land."[3]

For three years this frivolous egotist who occupied the throne of Judah remained faithful to his covenant with the King of Babylon, but at the end of that time he rebelled. In this rebellion he was again deluded by the glamour of Egypt, and reliance on the empty promise of "horses and much people." Ezekiel openly

---

[1] Jos., *Antt.*, X. xi.; Berosus, p. 11. The Chronicler and Josephus show some confusion, caused by the similarity of the names Jehoiakim and Jehoiachin.

[2] Dan. i. 6.

[3] We might infer from Ezek. xvii. 12 that Nebuchadrezzar actually took Jehoiakim with him to Babylon.

disapproved of this policy,[1] and reproached the king for his faithlessness to his oath. Jeremiah went further, and declared in the plainest language that "Nebuchadrezzar would certainly come up and destroy this land, and cause to cease from thence both man and beast."[2]

Nearer and nearer the danger came. At first the King of Babylon was too busy to do more than send against the Jewish rebel marauding bands of Chaldæans, who acted in concert with the hereditary depredators of Judah—Syrians, Moabites, and Ammonites. But the prophet knew that the danger would not end there, believing that God would yet "remove Judah out of His sight" for the unforgiven sins of Manasseh and the innocent blood with which he had filled Jerusalem.[3] At last Nebuchadrezzar had time to turn closer attention to the affairs of Judah, and this became necessary because of the revolt of Tyre under its King Ithobalus. In the stress of the peril Jehoiakim proclaimed a fast and a day of humiliation in the Temple. Jeremiah was at this time "shut up"—either in hiding, or in some sort of custody. As he could not go and preach in person, he dictated his prophecy to Baruch, who wrote it on a scroll, and went in the prophet's place to read it in the Lord's House to the people there assembled from Jerusalem and all Judah in the chamber of Gemariah, the son of Shaphan, in the inner court, by the new gate.[4] Gemariah was the brother of Ahikam, the protector of the prophet.

No one was more painfully alarmed by Jeremiah's prophecy than Micaiah, the son of Gemariah, and he

---

[1] Ezek. xvii. 15.
[2] Jer. xxxvi. 29, xxv. 9, xxvi. 6.
[3] 2 Kings xxiv. 2-4.
[4] Grätz thinks that Jeremiah's roll was substantially Jer. xxv.

thought it his duty to go and tell his father and the
other princes what he had heard.   They were assembled in the scribe's chamber, and sent a courtier
of Ethiopian race—Jehudi, the son of Cushi—bidding
him to bring the scroll with him, and to come to them.[1]

Baruch was a person of distinction.   He was the
brother of Seraiah, who is called in our A.V. "a quiet
prince," and in the margin "prince of Menucha" or
"chief chamberlain," literally "master of the resting-
place"; and he was the grandson of Maaseiah, "the
governor" of the city.[2]   The office imposed on him by
Jeremiah was so perilous and painful that it nearly
broke his heart.   He exclaimed to Jeremiah, "Woe is
me now! the Lord hath added grief to my sorrow.   I
am weary with my sighing, and I find no rest."   The
answer which the prophet was commissioned to give
him was very remarkable.   It confirmed the terrible
doom on his native land, but added, "'And seekest thou
great things for thyself? Seek them not. For, behold,
I will bring evil upon all flesh,' saith the Lord: 'but thy
life will I give unto thee for a prey in all places whither
thou goest.'"[3]

Baruch obeyed the summons of the princes, and at
their request sat down with them and read the scroll
in their ears.   When they had heard the portentous
prophecy, they turned shuddering to one another, and
said, "We must tell the king of all these words."
They asked Baruch how he had written them, and he
said he had taken them down at the prophet's dictation.
Then, knowing the storm which would burst over the

---

[1] Jos., *Antt.*, IX. ix. 1.

[2] Jer. li. 59.   Ewald, Hitzig, and others take the title to mean
'quartermaster" (2 Chron. xxxiv. 8).

[3] Jer. xlv. 1-5.

bold offenders, they said, "Go, hide thee, thou and Jeremiah, and let no man know where ye be."

Not daring to imperil the awful document, they laid it up in the chamber of Elishama, the scribe, but went to the king and told him its contents. He sent Jehudi to fetch it, and to read it in their hearing. Jehoiakim and the illustrious company were seated in the winter-chamber; for it was October, and a fire was burning in the brazier, where Jehoiakim sat warming himself in the chilly weather.

As he listened, he was filled not only with fury, but with contempt. Such a message might well have caused him and his worst counsellors to rend their clothes; but instead of this they adopted a tone of defiance. By the time that Jehudi had read three or four columns, Jehoiakim snatched the scribe's knife which hung at his girdle, and began to cut up the scroll, with the intention of burning it. Seeing his purpose, Gemariah, Elnathan, and Seraiah entreated him not to destroy it. But he would not listen. He flung the fragments into the brazier, and they were consumed. He ordered his son Jerahmeel,[1] with Seraiah and Shelemiah, to seize both Baruch and Jeremiah, and bring them before him for punishment. Doubtless they would have suffered the fate of Urijah, but "the Lord hid them." There were enough persons of power on their side to render their hiding-place secure.

But the king's impious indifference, so far from making any difference in the things that were, only brought down upon his guilt a fearful doom. Truth

---

[1] Zeph. i. 8; 1 Kings xxii. 26; Jer. xxxvi. 26, A.V., "The son of Hammelech." Comp. xxxviii. 6. *Hammelech* may be a proper name, or a prince of the blood-royal may be intended.

cannot be cut to pieces, or burnt, or mechanically
suppressed.

> "Truth, crushed to earth, shall rise again;
> The eternal years of God are hers:
> But error, vanquished, writhes in pain,
> And dies amid her worshippers."

All the former denunciations, and new ones added
to them, were rewritten by Jeremiah and his faithful
friend in their hiding-place, and among them these
words [1]:—

"Thus saith the Lord of Jehoiakim, King of Judah,
'He shall have none to sit upon the throne of David;
and his dead body shall be cast out in the day to the
heat, and in the night to the frost.'"

A frightful drought added to the misery of this reign,
but failed to bring the wretched king to his senses.
Jeremiah describes it [2]:—

"Judah mourneth, and the gates thereof languish;
they bow down mourning unto the ground; and the cry
of Jerusalem is gone up. And the nobles send their
menials to the waters: they come to the pits, and find
no water; they return with their vessels empty; they
are ashamed and confounded, and cover their heads,
because of the ground which is chapped, for that no
rain hath been in the land. . . . Yea, the hind also in
the field calveth, and forsaketh her young, because
there is no grass. And the wild asses stand on the

---

[1] "The 'Book,' now as afterwards, was to be the death-blow of the
old regal, aristocratic, sacerdotal exclusiveness. The 'Scribe,' now
first rising into importance in the person of Baruch to supply the
defects of the living Prophet, was, as the printing-press in later ages
handing on the words of truth, which else might have irretrievably
perished" (Stanley).

[2] Cheyne, *Jeremiah*, p. 149; Jer. xiv. 1–xv. 9.

bare heights, they pant for air like jackals; their eyes fail, because there is no herbage."

Even this affliction, so vividly and pathetically described, failed to waken any repentance. And then the doom fell. Nebuchadrezzar advanced in person against Jerusalem.[1] Even the hardy nomad Rechabites had to fly before the Chaldæans, and to take refuge in the cities which they hated. The sacred historian tells us nothing as to the manner of the death of Jehoiakim, only saying that he "slept with his fathers": his narrative of this period is exceedingly meagre. Josephus says that Nebuchadrezzar slew him and the flower of the citizens, and sent three thousand captives to Babylon.[2] Some imagine that he was killed by the Babylonians in a raid outside the walls of Jerusalem, or "murdered by his own people, and his body thrown for a time outside the walls." If so, the Babylonians did not war with the dead. His remains, after this "burial of an ass,"[3] may have been finally suffered to rest in a tomb. The Septuagint says (2 Chron. xxxvi. 8) that he was buried "in Ganosan," by which may be meant the sepulchre of Manasseh in the garden of Uzza.[4] Not

---

[1] Nebuchadrezzar occupies a larger space in the Bible than any heathen king, being spoken of in 2 Kings, 2 Chronicles, Ezra, Nehemiah, Jeremiah, Ezekiel, and Daniel.

[2] For further details of Jehoiakim see 1 Esdras i. 38 : " He bound Joakim and the nobles; *but Zaraces* his brother he apprehended, and brought him out of Egypt." The allusion is entirely obscure, and probably arises from some corruption of the text. The literal rendering is : " And *Joakim* bound the nobles; but Zaraces his brother he apprehended, and brought him out of Egypt." Zaraces might be a corruption for Zedekiah, who was Jehoiakim's half-brother. Some think that Zaraces is a corruption for Urijah, and "his brother" a clerical error.

[3] Jer. xxxvi. 30, xxii. 19.

[4] LXX., καὶ ἐκοιμήθη Ἰωακεὶμ ἐν Γανοζὰν μετὰ τῶν πατέρων ἑαυτοῦ.

for him was the wailing cry "*Hoî, adon!   Hoî, hodo!*"
("Ah, Lord!   Ah, his glory!").

"The memory of the wicked shall rot."   Certainly
this was the case with Jehoiakim.   The Chronicler
mysteriously alludes to "his abominations which he
did, *and that which was found in him.*"[1]   The Rabbis,
interpreting this after their manner, say that "the thing
found" was the name of the demon Codonazor, to whom
he had sold himself, which after his death was discovered
legibly written in Hebrew letters on his skin.   "Rabbi
Johanan and Rabbi Eleazar debated what was meant
by 'that which was found on him.'   One said that he
tattooed the name of an idol upon his body (אמתו), and
the other said that he had tatooed the name of the
god Recreon."[2]

---

[1] 2 Chron. xxxvi. 8.

[2] *Sanhedrin,* f. 104, 2.   For another allusion see *id.* 49, 1; Hershon,
Treasures of the Talmud, p. 232.

CHAPTER XXXV

JEHOIACHIN

B.C. 597

2 KINGS xxiv. 8—16

"There are times when ancient truths become modern falsehoods, when the signs of God's dispensations are made so clear by the course of natural events as to supersede the revelations of even their most sacred past."—STANLEY, *Lectures*, ii. 521.

JEHOIACHIN—"Jehovah maketh steadfast"—who is also called Jeconiah, and—perhaps with intentional slight—Coniah, succeeded, at the age of eighteen, to the miserable and distracted heritage of the throne of Judah. The "eight years old" of the Chronicler must be a clerical error, for he had a harem. He only reigned for three months; and the historian pronounces over him, as over all the four kings of the House of Josiah, the stereotyped condemnation of evil-doing. Was there anything in the manner in which Josiah had trained his family which could account for their unsatisfactoriness? In Jehoiachin's case we do not know what his transgressions were, but perhaps his mother's influence rendered him as little favourable to the prophetic party as his brother Jehoiakim had been. For the *Gebirah* was Nehushta, the daughter of Elnathan of Jerusalem. Her name means apparently "Brass," and nothing can be deduced from it; but her father Elnathan was (as we

431

have seen) the envoy who, by order of Jehoiakim, had dragged back from Egypt the martyr-prophet Urijah.[1]

Brief as was his reign of three months and ten days[2] —a hundred days, like that of his unhappy uncle Jehoahaz—he is largely alluded to by the contemporary prophets.

Indignant at the sins and apostasies of Judah, and convinced that her retribution was nigh at hand, Jeremiah took with him an earthen pot to the Valley of Hinnom, and there shivered it to pieces at Tophet in the presence of certain elders of the people and of the priests, explaining that his symbolic action indicated the destruction of Jerusalem.   On hearing the tenor of these prophecies, the priest Pashur, who was officer of the Temple, smote Jeremiah in the face, and put him in the stocks in a prominent place by the Temple gate.[3] Jeremiah in return prophesied that Pashur and all his family should be carried into captivity, so that his name should be changed from Pashur to Magor-Missabib, "Terror on every side."

Against the king himself he pronounced the doom : "'As I live,' saith the Lord, 'though Coniah, the son of Jehoiakim, King of Judah, were the signet on My right hand, yet will I pluck thee thence; and I will give thee into the hands of them that seek thy life, . . . even into the hand of Nebuchadrezzar. . . . And I will hurl thee, and thy mother that bare thee, into another

---

[1] Jer. xxvi. 22.

[2] 2 Chron. xxxvi. 9.

[3] Jer. xx. 2.   There seem to have been special "stocks" and "collars" in the Temple, reserved, by order of the priest Jehoiada, for those whom the priests regarded as unruly prophets (Jer. xxix. 26).

country ;[1] . . . and there shall ye die.' . . . Is this man
Coniah a despised broken piece of work? is he a
vessel wherein is no pleasure? wherefore are they
hurled, he and his seed, and cast into a land which
they know not? O land, land, land! hear the word
of the Lord. Thus saith the Lord, 'Write ye this
man childless, a man that shall not prosper in his
days : for no man of his seed shall prosper, sitting
upon the throne of David, or ruling any more in
Judah.'"

Yet there must have been something in Jeconiah
which impressed favourably the minds of men. Brief
as was his reign, his memory was never forgotten. We
learn from the *Mishna* that one of the gates of Jerusalem
—probably that by which he left the city—for ever
bore his name.[2] Josephus says that his captivity
was annually commemorated. Jeremiah writes in the
Lamentations :—

"Our pursuers are swifter than the eagles of heaven :
they have pursued us upon the mountains, they have
laid wait for us in the wilderness. The breath of our
nostrils, the anointed of the Lord, was taken in their
pits, of whom we said, 'Under his shadow we shall live
among the heathen.'"

Ezekiel compares him to a young lion :—

"He went up and down among the lions, he became
a young lion, and learned to catch the prey. And he
knew their palaces, and laid waste their cities ; and the
land was desolate, and the fulness thereof, by the
noise of his roaring. Then the nations set against him

---

[1] Jer. xxii. 24–30. The captivity of the queen-mother struck
men's imaginations (Jer. xxix. 2).

[2] *Middoth*, ii. 6, quoted by Cheyne, p. 163; Jos., *B.J.*, VI. ii. 1,
Comp. Ezek. i, 2.

on every side from the provinces, and spread their net over him : he was taken in their pit. And they put him in ward in hooks, and brought him to the King of Babylon : they brought him into holds, that his voice should no more be heard upon the mountains of Israel." [1]

A prince of whom a contemporary prophet could thus write was obviously no *fainéant*. Indeed, the energetic measures which Nebuchadrezzar adopted against him may have been due to the fact that he had endeavoured to rouse his discouraged people. But what could he do against such a power as that of the Chaldæans ? Nebuchadrezzar sent his generals against Jerusalem ; and when it was ripe for capture, advanced in person to take possession of it. Resistance had become hopeless; there lay no chance in anything but that complete submission which might possibly avert the worst effects of the destruction of the city. Accordingly, Jeconiah, accompanied by his mother, his court, his princes, and his officers, went out in procession, and threw themselves on the mercy of the King of Babylon. Nebuchadrezzar was far less brutal than the Sargons and Assurbanipals of Assyria ; but Judah had twice revolted, and the defection of Tyre showed him that the affairs of Palestine could no longer be neglected. He thoroughly despoiled the Temple and the palace, and carried the spoils to Babylon, as Isaiah had forewarned Hezekiah should be the case. [2] That he might further weaken and

---

[1] Ezek. xix. 6–9. The special allusions are no longer certain.

[2] 2 Kings xx. 17. The expression "*he cut to pieces* all the vessels of gold which Solomon had made" is hardly consistent with Ezra i. 7–11, unless we understand the word in a loose sense.

humiliate the city, he stripped it of its king, its royal
house, its court, its nobles, its soldiers, even its craftsmen and smiths, and carried ten thousand eight hundred
and thirty-two captives to Babylon (Jos., *Antt.*, X.
vii. 1), among whom was the prophet Ezekiel. He
naturally spared Jeremiah, who regarded him as "the
sword of Jehovah" (Jer. xlvii. 6), and as "Jehovah's
servant, to do His pleasure" (Jer. xxv. 9, xxvii. 6,
xliii. 10). On the whole, Nebuchadrezzar is not treated
with abhorrence by the Jews. There was something
in his character which inspired respect ; and the Jews
deal with him leniently, both in their records and
generally in their traditions. "Nebuchadnezzar," we
read in the Talmud (*Taanith*, f. 18, 2), "was a worthy
king, and deserved that a miracle should be performed
through him."

From the allusion of Ezekiel we might infer that
Jehoiachin was violent and self-willed ; but Josephus
speaks of his kindness and gentleness.[1] Was he, as
Jeremiah had prophesied, literally "childless"?[2] It is
true that in 1 Chron. iii. 17, 18, eight sons are ascribed to him, and among them Shealtiel, in whom the
royal line was continued. But it is far from certain
that these sons were not the sons of his brother Neri,
of the House of Nathan,[3] and it seems that they were
only adopted by the unhappy captive. The Book of
Baruch describes him weeping by the Euphrates.[4] But

---

[1] He says that he nobly gave himself up to save the city (*Antt.*,
X. vii. 1). His captivity was made an era from which to date Ezek.
i. 2, viii. 1, xxiv. 1, xxvi. 1, etc. Comp. Susannah 1-4.

[2] Jer. xxii. 30, *'ariri*. His "son" Assir (1 Chron. iii. 17) may have
been made an eunuch (Isa. xxxix. 7).

Luke iii. 27, 31 ; Matt. i. 12.

[4] Baruch i. 3, 4.

if we may trust the story of Susannah, his outward fortunes were peaceful, and he was allowed to live in his own house and gardens in peace, and in a certain degree of splendour.[1]

---

[1] The favourable notice of Nebuchadrezzar in *Taanith* (quoted above) is not found in *Berachoth*, f. 57, 2, where he is called "the wicked." There are many wild legends about him. In *Nedarim* (f. 65, 2), R. Yitzchak says: "May melted gold be poured into the mouth of the wicked Nebuchadrezzar! Had not an angel struck him on the mouth, he would have outshone all David's songs and praises." With reference to Isa. xxii. 1, 2, the Rabbis say that Jeconiah went to the Temple roof, and flung up the keys into the air, when Nebuchadrezzar required them: "a hand took them, and they were seen no more" (*Shekalim*, vi. 5). In *Nedarim* (f. 65, 2) we are told that Zedekiah's rebellion consisted in divulging, contrary to his oath, that he had seen Nebuchadrezzar eating a live hare (Hershon, *Treasures of the Talmud*).

CHAPTER XXXVI

ZEDEKIAH, THE LAST KING OF JUDAH

B.C. 597—586

2 KINGS xxiv. 18—xxv. 7

"Quand ce grand Dieu a choisi quelqu'un pour être l'instrument de ses desseins rien n'arrête le cours, où il enchaine, où il aveugle, où il dompte tout ce qui est capable de résistance."

BOSSUET, *Oraison funèbre de Henriette Marie.*

WHEN Jehoiachin was carried captive to Babylon, never to return, his uncle Mattaniah ("Jehovah's gift"), the third son of Josiah, was put by Nebuchadrezzar in his place. In solemn ratification of the new king's authority, the Babylonian conqueror sanctioned the change of his name to Zedekiah ("Jehovah's righteousness").[1] He was twenty-one at his accession, and he reigned eleven years.

"Behold," writes Ezekiel, "the King of Babylon came to Jerusalem, and took the king thereof, and the princes thereof, and brought them to him to Babylon; and he took of the seed royal" (*i.e.*, Zedekiah), "*and made a covenant with him; he also brought him under an oath : and took away the mighty of the land, that the kingdom might be base, that it might not lift itself up, but that by keeping of his covenant it might stand.*"[2]

---

[1] Comp. Jer. xxiii. 6 : Jehovah-Tsidkenu.

[2] Ezek. xvii. 12–14.

Perhaps by this covenant Zechariah meant to emphasise the meaning of his name, and to show that he would reign in righteousness.

The prophet at the beginning of the chapter describes Nebuchadrezzar and Jehoiachin in " a riddle."

" A great eagle," he says, "with great wings and long pinions, full of feathers, which had divers colours, came unto Lebanon, and took the top of the cedar" (Jehoiachin): " he cropped off the topmost of the young twigs thereof, and carried it into a land of traffic; he set it in a city of merchants. He took also of the seed of the land" (Zedekiah), "and planted it in a fruitful soil; he placed it beside great waters, he set it as a willow tree. And it grew, and became a spreading vine of low stature, whose branches turned towards him, and the roots thereof were under him: so it became a vine, and brought forth branches, and shot forth sprigs."[1]

The words refer to the first three years of Zedekiah's reign, and they imply, consistently with the views of the prophets, that, if the weak king had been content with the lowly eminence to which God had called him, and if he had kept his oath and covenant with Babylon, all might yet have been well with him and his land. At first it seemed likely to be so; for Zedekiah wished to be faithful to Jehovah. He made a covenant with all the people to set free their Hebrew slaves. Alas! it was very shortlived. Self-sacrifice cost something, and the princes soon took back the discarded bond-servants.[2] What made this conduct the more shocking was that their covenant to obey the law had been made in the most solemn manner by " cutting a calf in twain, and passing between the severed halves."[3] But the

---

[1] Ezek. xvii. 1–6.   [2] Jer. xxxiv. 8–11.
[3] Jer. xxxiv. 19. Comp. Gen. xv. 17.

weak king was perfectly powerless in the hands of his tyrannous aristocracy.[1]

The exiles in Babylon were now the best and most important section of the nation. Jeremiah compares them to good figs; while the remnant at Jerusalem were bad and withered. He and Ezekiel raised their voices, as in strophe and antistrophe, for the teaching alike of the exiles and of the remnant left at Jerusalem, for whom the exiles were bidden to entreat God in prayer. Zedekiah himself made at least one journey northward, either voluntarily or under summons, to renew his oath and reassure Nebuchadrezzar of his fidelity.[2] He was accompanied by Seraiah, the brother of Baruch, who was privately entrusted by Jeremiah with a prophecy of the fall of Babylon, which he was to fling into the midst of the Euphrates.[3]

The last King of Judah seems to have been weak rather than wicked. He was a reed shaken by the wind. He yielded to the influence of the last person who argued with him; and he seems to have dreaded above all things the personal ridicule, danger, and opposition which it was his duty to have defied. Yet we cannot withhold from him our deep sympathy; for he was born in terrible times—to witness the death-throes of his country's agony, and to share in them. It was no longer a question of independence, but only of the choice of servitudes. Judah was like a silly and trembling sheep between two huge beasts of prey.[4]

---

[1] This is strikingly shown by his piteous remark to them in Jer. xxxviii. 5.

[2] He first sent two of Jeremiah's friends, Elasah and Gemariah, the son of Shaphan.

[3] Some critics have doubted the authenticity of Jer. li., lii.

[4] 2 Chron. xxxvi. 14-21 · Stanley, ii. 528; Milman, i. 394.

Only thus can we account for the strange apostasies —" the abominations of the heathen "—with which he permitted the Temple to be polluted ; and for the ill-treatment which he allowed to be inflicted on Jeremiah and other prophets, to whom in his heart he felt inclined to listen.

What these abominations were we read with amazement in the eighth chapter of Ezekiel. The prophet is carried in vision to Jerusalem, and there he sees the Asherah—" the image which provoketh to jealousy "—which had so often been erected and destroyed and re-erected. Then through a secret door he sees creeping things, and abominable beasts, and the idol-blocks of the House of Israel pourtrayed upon the wall, while several elders of Israel stood before them and adored, with censers in their hands—among whom he must specially have grieved to see Jaazaneiah, the son of Shaphan,[1] flattering himself, as did his followers, that in that dark chamber Jehovah saw them not. Next at the northern gate he sees Zion's daughters weeping for Tammuz, or Adonis. Once more, in the inner court of the Temple, between the porch and the altar, he sees about twenty-five men with their backs to the altar, and their faces to the east ; and they worshipped the sun towards the east ; and, lo ! they put the vine branch to their nose,[2] Were not these crimes sufficient to evoke the wrath of Jehovah, and to alienate His ear from prayers offered by such polluted worshippers ? Egypt, Assyria, Syria, Chaldæa,

---

[1] Shaphan's other sons, Gemariah, Ahikam, Elasah, and his grandson Gedaliah, were friends of Jeremiah.

[2] Ezek. viii. 17. The allusion seems to be to a custom like that of the Parsees, who hold a branch of tamarisk or pomegranate twigs (called *barsom*) before their mouths when they adore the sacred fire. Strabo, xv. 732; Spiegel, *Zendavesta*, ii., p. lxviii; *Eran: Alterthumsk.*, iii. 571 (Orelli, *ad loc.*). Lightfoot explains it, " add fuel to their wrath."

all contributed their idolatrous elements to the detestable syncretism ; and the king and the priests ignored, permitted, or connived at it.[1]   This must surely be answered for.   How could it have been otherwise ?   The king and the priests were the official guardians of the Temple, and these aberrations could not have gone on without their cognisance.   There was another party of sheer formalists, headed by men like the priest Pashur, who thought to make talismans of rites and shibboleths, but had no sincerity of heart-religion.[2]   To these, too, Jeremiah was utterly opposed.   In his opinion Josiah's reformation had failed.   Neither Ark, nor Temple, nor sacrifice were anything in the world to him in comparison with true religion.   All the prophets with scarcely one exception are anti-ritualists ; but none more decidedly so than the prophet-priest. His name is associated in tradition with the hiding of the Ark, and a belief in its ultimate restoration ; yet to Jeremiah, apart from the moral and spiritual truths of which it was the material symbol, the Ark was no better than a wooden chest.   His message from Jehovah is, " I will give you pastors according to My heart, . . . and they shall say no more, ' The Ark of the Covenant of the Lord ' : neither shall it come to mind ; neither shall they remember it ; neither shall they miss it ; neither shall it be made any more."[3]

Doom followed the guilt and folly of king, priests, and people.   If political wisdom were insufficient to show Zedekiah that the necessities of the case were an indication of God's will, he had the warnings of the prophets constantly ringing in his ears, and the assur-

---

[1] Ezek. xvi. 15–34.
[2] Jer. vii. 4, 21–28, viii. 8, xxiii. 31–33, xxxi. 33, 34.
[3] Jer. iii. 15, 16.

ance that he must remain faithful to Nebuchadrezzar. But he was in fear of his own princes and courtiers. A combined embassy reached him from the kings of Edom, Ammon, Moab, Tyre and Sidon, urging him to join in a league against Babylon.[1] This embassy was supported by a powerful party in Jerusalem. Their solicitations were rendered more plausible by the recent accession (B.C. 590) of the young and vigorous Pharaoh Hophrah—the Apries of Herodotus [2]—to the throne of Egypt, and by the recrudescence of that incurable disease of Hebrew politics, a confidence in the idle promises of Egypt to supply the confederacy with men and horses.[3] In vain did Jeremiah and Ezekiel uplift their warning voices. The blind confidence of the king and of the nobles was sustained by the flattering visions and promises of false prophets, prominent among whom was a certain Hananiah, the son of Azur, of Gibeon, "the prophet."[4] To indicate the futility of the contemplated rebellion, Jeremiah had made "thongs and poles" with yokes, and had sent them to the kings, whose embassy had reached Jerusalem, with a message of the most emphatic distinctness, that Nebuchadrezzar was God's appointed servant, and that they must serve him till God's own appointed time. If they obeyed this intimation, they would be left undisturbed in their own lands; if they disobeyed it, they would be scourged into absolute submission by the sword, the famine, and the pestilence. Jeremiah delivered the same oracle to his own king.[5]

---

[1] Jer. xxvii. 3.   [2] Herod., ii. 161.

[3] Psammis, the son of Necho, only reigned six years; Hophrah (B.C. 594) was his son.

[4] The LXX. calls him "the false prophet."

[5] Jer. xxvii. 1-8, 12-18. On vv. 16-22 see the LXX.

The warning was rendered unavailing by the conduct of Hananiah. He prophesied that within two full years God would break the yoke of the King of Babylon; and that the captive Jeconiah, and the nobles, and the vessels of the House of the Lord would be brought back. Jeremiah, by way of an acted parable, had worn round his neck one of his own yokes. Hananiah, in the Temple, snatched it off, broke it to pieces, and said, "So will I break the yoke of Nebuchadrezzar from the neck of all nations within the space of two full years." [1]

We can imagine the delight, the applause, the enthusiasm with which the assembled people listened to these bold predictions. Hananiah argued with them, so to speak, in shorthand, for he appealed to their desires and to their prejudices. It is always the tendency of nations to say to their prophets, " Say not unto us hard things: speak smooth things; prophesy deceits."

Against Hananiah personally there seems to have been no charge, except that in listening to the lying spirit of his own desires he could not hear the true message of God. But he did not stand alone.[2] Among the children of the captivity, his promises were echoed by two downright false prophets, Ahab and Zedekiah, the son of Maaseiah, who prophesied lies in God's name. They were men of evil life, and a fearful fate overtook them. Their words against Babylon came to the ears of Nebuchadrezzar, and they were "roasted in the fire," so that the horror of their end passed into

---

[1] Here (Jer. xxviii. 11, and in xxxiv. 1, xxxix. 5) the name is written "Nebuchadnezzar"; everywhere else in Jeremiah it is "Nebuchadrezzar."

[2] Part of his dispute with Jeremiah turned on the recovery or non-recovery of the Temple vessels. Zedekiah is said to have given a set of silver vessels to replace the old ones (Baruch i. 8).

a proverb and a curse.[1] Truly God fed these false prophets with wormwood, and gave them poisonous water to drink.[2]

After the action of Hananiah, Jeremiah went home stricken and ashamed: apparently he never again uttered a public discourse in the Temple. It took him by surprise; and he was for the moment, perhaps, daunted by the plausive echo of the multitude to the lying prophet. But when he got home the answer of Jehovah came: "Go and tell Hananiah, Thou hast broken the yokes of wood; but thou hast made for them yokes of iron. I have put a yoke of iron on the necks of all these nations, that they may serve Nebuchadrezzar. Hear now, Hananiah, The Lord hath not sent thee: thou makest this people to trust in a lie. Behold, this year thou shalt die, because thou hast spoken revolt against the Lord. What hath the chaff to do with the wheat? saith the Lord."[3]

Two months after Hananiah lay dead, and men's minds were filled with fear. They saw that God's word was indeed as a fire to burn, and as a hammer to dash in pieces.[4] But meanwhile Zedekiah had been over-persuaded to take the course which the true prophets had forbidden. Misled by the false prophets and mincing prophetesses whom Ezekiel denounced,[5] who daubed men's walls with whitened plaster, he had sent an embassy to Pharaoh Hophrah, asking for an army of infantry and cavalry to support his rebellion from Assyria.[6] In the eyes of Jeremiah and Ezekiel the crime did not only consist in defying the exhortations of those whom Zedekiah knew to be Jehovah's

---

[1] Jer. xxix. 21–23.
[2] Jer. xxiii. 9–32.
[3] Jer. xxviii. 13–16, xxiii. 28.
[4] Jer. xxiii. 29.
[5] Ezek. xiii. 1–23.
[6] Ezek. xvii. 25.

accredited messengers. In mitigation of this offence
he might have pleaded the extreme difficulty of dis-
criminating the truth amid the ceaseless babble of false
pretenders.[1] But, on the other hand, he had broken
the solemn oath which he had taken to Nebuchadrezzar
in the name of God, and the sacred covenant which he
seems to have twice ratified with him.[2] This it was
which raised the indignation of the faithful, and led
Ezekiel to prophesy :—

"Shall he prosper ?
Shall he escape that doeth such things ?
Or shall he break the covenant and be believed ?
'As I live,' saith the Lord God, 'surely in the place where the king
   dwelleth that made him king,
Whose oath he despised and whose covenant he broke,
Even with him in the midst of Babylon, shall he die.'"[3]

Sad close for a dynasty which had now lasted for
nearly five centuries !

As for Pharaoh, he too was an eagle, as Nebuchadrezzar was—a great eagle with great wings and many
feathers, but not so great. The trailing vine of Judah
bent her roots towards him, but it should wither in
the furrows when the east wind touched it.[4]

The result of Zedekiah's alliance with Egypt was
the intermission of his yearly tribute to Assyria ; and
at last, in the ninth year of Zedekiah, Nebuchadrezzar
was aroused to put down this Palestinian revolt, supported as it was by the vague magnificence of Egypt.

---

[1] Josephus rightly attributes the unfortunate career of Zedekiah to
the weakness with which he listened to evil counsellors, and to the
insolent multitude.

[2] 2 Chron. xxxvi. 13 ; Jer. lii. 3.

[3] Ezek. xvii. 15, 16, 18, 19.

[4] Ezek. xvii. 7-10.

Jeremiah had said, "Pharaoh, the King of Egypt, is but a noise [or desolation]: he hath passed the time appointed."[1]

This was about the year 589. In 598 Nebuchadrezzar had carried Jehoachin into captivity, and ever since then some of his forces had been engaged in the vain effort to capture Tyre, which still, after a ten years' siege, drew its supplies from the sea, and remained impregnable on her island rock. He did not choose to raise this long-continued siege by diverting the troops to beleaguer so strong a fortress as Jerusalem, and therefore he came in person from Babylon.

In Ezek. xxi. 20–24 we have a singular and vivid glimpse of his march. On his way he came to a spot where two roads branched off before him. One led to Rabbath, the capital of Ammon, on the east of Jordan; the other to Jerusalem, on the west. Which road should he take? Personally, it was a matter of indifference; so he threw the burden of responsibility upon his gods by leaving the decision to the result of belomancy.[2] Taking in his hand a sheaf of brightened arrows, he held them upright, and decided to take the route indicated by the fall of the greater number of arrows. He confirmed his uncertainty by consulting teraphim, and by hepatoscopy—i.e., by examining the liver of slain victims. Rabbath and the Ammonites were not to be spared, but it was upon the covenant-breaking king and city that the first vengeance was

---

[1] Jer. xlvi. 17.

[2] Another form of belomancy is still commonly practised among the Arabs. Three arrows are placed in a vessel: on one of them is written, "My God permits me"; on another, "My God forbids me"; the third is blank. They are then shaken, and the decision is guided by the one which falls out first. Comp. Homer, *Iliad*, iii. 316; *Speaker's Commentary, ad loc.*

to fall.[1] And this is what the prophet has to say to
Zedekiah :—

"And thou, O deadly-wounded wicked one, the
prince of Israel, whose day is come in the time of the
iniquity of the end ; thus saith the Lord God, 'Remove
the mitre, and take off the crown. This shall be not
thus. Exalt the low, and abase that which is high.
An overthrow, overthrow, overthrow, will I make it :
this also shall be no more, until He come whose right
it is : and I will give it Him."[2]

So (B.C. 587) Jerusalem was delivered over to siege,
even as Ezekiel had sketched upon a tile.[3] It was to
be assailed in the old Assyrian manner—as we see it
represented in the British Museum bas-relief, where
Sennacherib is portrayed in the act of besieging
Lachish—with forts, mounds, and battering-rams ; and
Ezekiel had also been bidden to put up an iron plate
between him and his pictured city, to represent the
mantelet from behind which the archers shot.

In this dread crisis Zedekiah sent Zephaniah, the son
of Maaseiah, the priest, and Jehucal, to Jeremiah, en-
treating his prayers for the city,[4] for he had not yet
been put in prison. Doubtless he prayed, and at first
it looked as if deliverance would come. Pharaoh
Hophrah put in motion the Egyptian army with its
Carian mercenaries and Soudanese negroes, and Nebuchadrezzar was sufficiently alarmed to raise the siege
and go to meet the Egyptians. The hopes of the
people probably rose high, though multitudes seized

---

[1] Ezek. xxi. 28-32.

[2] An allusion to the restoration of Jeconiah or his descendants, and
to the far-off Messiah, meek and lowly.

[3] Ezek. iv. 1-3.

[4] Jer. xxxvii. 3.

the opportunity to fly to the mountains.[1] The circumstances closely resembled those under which Sennacherib had raised the siege of Jerusalem to go to meet Tirhakah the Ethiopian; and perhaps there were some, and the king among them, who looked that such a wonder might be vouchsafed to him through the prayers of Jeremiah as had been vouchsafed to Hezekiah through the prayers of Isaiah. Not for a moment did Jeremiah encourage these vain hopes. To Zephaniah, as to an earlier deputation from the king, when he sent Pashur with him to inquire of the prophet, Jeremiah returned a remorseless answer. It is too late. Pharaoh shall be defeated; even if the Chaldæan army were smitten, its wounded soldiers would suffice to besiege and burn Jerusalem, and take into captivity the miserable inhabitants after they had suffered the worst horrors of a besieged city.[2]

---

[1] Ezek. vii. 16.

[2] Jer. xxi. 1–10, xxxvii. 1–17. Josephus says that Pharaoh was defeated (*Antt.*, X vii. 3). Jeremiah merely says that he and his army returned to their own land.

CHAPTER XXXVII

JEREMIAH AND HIS PROPHECIES

JER. i. 1—v. 31

"Count me o'er earth's chosen heroes—they were souls that stood
  alone,
While the men they agonised for hurled the contumelious stone ;
Stood serene, and down the future saw the golden beam incline
To the side of perfect justice, mastered by their faith divine,
By one man's plain truth to manhood and to God's supreme
  design."   LOWELL.

TRULY Jeremiah was a prophet of evil. The king
   might have addressed him in the words with
which Agamemnon reproaches Kalchas.[1]

"Augur accursed ! denouncing mischief still :
  Prophet of plagues, for ever boding ill !
  Still must that tongue some wounding message bring,
  And still thy priestly pride provoke thy king."

Never was there a sadder man.[2] Like Phocion, he
believed in the enemies of his country more than he
believed in his own people. He saw "Too late"
written upon everything. He saw himself all but universally execrated as a coward, as a traitor, as one who
weakened the nerves and damped the courage of those

---

[1] Homer, *Iliad*, i. 106–109.
[2] But it must not be forgotten that Jer. xxxi. 1–34 is so hopeful
that it has been called "the Gospel before Christ."

who were fighting against fearful odds for their wives and children, the ashes of their fathers, their altars, and their hearths. It had become his fixed conviction that any prophets—and there were a multitude of them—who prophesied peace were false prophets, and *ipso facto* proved themselves conspirators against the true well-being of the land.[1] In point of fact, Jeremiah lived to witness the death-struggle of the idea of religion in its predominantly national character (vii. 8–16, vi. 8). "The continuity of the national faith refused to be bound up with the continuance of the nation. When the nation is dissolved into individual elements, the continuity and ultimate victory of the true faith depends on the relations of Jehovah to individual souls out of which the nation shall be bound up."[2]

And now a sad misfortune happened to Jeremiah. His home was not at Jerusalem, but at Anathoth, though he had long been driven from his native village by the murderous plots of his own kindred, and of those who had been infuriated by his incessant prophecies of doom. When the Chaldæans retired from Jerusalem to encounter Pharaoh, he left the distressed city for the land of Benjamin, "to receive his portion from thence in the midst of the people"—apparently, for the sense is doubtful, to claim his dues of maintenance as a priest. But at the city gate he was arrested by Irijah, the son of Shelemiah, the captain of the watch, who charged him with the intention of deserting to the Chaldæans. Jeremiah pronounced the charge to be a lie; but Irijah took him before the princes, who hated him, and consigned him to dreary and dangerous imprisonment in

---

[1] Jer. vi. 14, viii. 11 ; Ezek. xiii. 10.
[2] W. R. Smith, "Prophets" (*Enc. Brit.*).

the house of Jonathan the scribe. In the vaults of this "house of the pit" he continued many days.[1] The king sympathised with him : he would gladly have delivered him, if he could, from the rage of the princes; but he did not dare.[2]

Meanwhile, the siege went on, and the people never forgot the anguish of despair with which they waited the reinvestiture of the city. Ever since that day it has been kept as a fast—the fast of Tebeth. Zedekiah, yearning for some advice, or comfort—if comfort were to be had—from the only man whom he really trusted, sent for Jeremiah to the palace, and asked him in despicable secrecy, "Is there any word from the Lord ? " The answer was the old one : "Yes! Thou shalt be delivered into the hands of the King of Babylon." Jeremiah gave it without quailing, but seized the opportunity to ask on what plea he was imprisoned. Was he not a prophet ? Had he not prophesied the return of the Chaldæan host ? Where now were all the prophets who had prophesied peace ? Would not the king at least save him from the detestable prison in which he was dying by inches ?

The king heard his petition, and he was removed to a better prison in the court of the watch, where he received his daily piece of bread out of the bakers' street until all the bread in the city was spent.

For now utter famine came upon the wretched Jews, to add to the horrors and accidents of the siege. If

---

[1] Jer. xxxvii. 11-15.

[2] Jer. xxxviii. 5. The Jewish aristocracy consisted, says Grätz, of three classes: the *beni hammelech*, or "king's sons"—*i.e.*, princes of the blood-royal; the *roshi aboth*, "heads of the fathers," or *zekenim*, "elders"; and the *abhodi hammelech*, "king's servants," or "courtiers" (ii. 446).

we would know what that famine was in its appalling
intensity, we must turn to the Book of Lamentations.
Those elegies, so unutterably plaintive, may not be by
the prophet himself, but only by his school; but they
show us what was the frightful condition of the people
of Jerusalem before and during the last six months of
the siege.   " The sword of the wilderness "—the roving
and plundering Bedouin—made it impossible to get out
of the city in any direction.   Things were as dreadfully
hopeless as they had been in Samaria when it was
besieged by Benhadad.[1]   Hunger and thirst reduce
human nature to its most animal conditions.   They
obliterate the merest elements of morality.   They make
men like beasts, and reveal the ferocity which is never
quite dead in any but the purest and loftiest souls.
They arouse the least human instincts of the aboriginal
animal.   The day came when there was no more bread
left in Jerusalem.[2]   The fair and ruddy Nazarites, who
had been purer than snow, whiter than milk, more
ruddy than corals, lovely as sapphires, became like
withered boughs,[3] and even their friends did not recognise them in those ghastly and emaciated figures which
crept about the streets.   The daughters of Zion, more
cruel in their hunger than the very jackals, lost the
instincts of pity and motherhood.   Mothers and fathers
devoured their own little unweaned children.[4]   There
was parricide as well as infanticide in the horrible
houses.   They seemed to plead that none could blame
them, since the lives of many had become an intolerable
anguish, and no man had bread for his little ones, and

---

[1] Lam. v. 4.
[2] Jer. xxxvii. 21, xxxviii. 9, lii. 6.
[3] Lam. iv. 7, 8.
[4] Lam. iv. 10, ii. 20; Ezek. v. 10; Baruch ii. 3.

their tongues cleaved to the roof of their mouth. All that happened six centuries later, during the siege of Jerusalem by Titus, happened now. Then Martha, the daughter of Nicodemus ben-Gorion, once a lady of enormous wealth, was seen picking the grains of corn from the offal of the streets; now the women who had fed delicately and been brought up in scarlet were seen sitting desolate on heaps of dung.[1] And Jehovah did not raise His hand to save His guilty and dying people. It was too late!

And as is always the case in such extremities, there were men who stood defiant and selfish amid the universal misery. Murder, oppression, and luxury continued to prevail. The godless nobles did not intermit the building of their luxurious houses, asserting to themselves and others that, after all, the final catastrophe was not near at hand. The sudden death of one of them—Pelatiah, the son of Benaiah—while Ezekiel was prophesying, terrified the prophet so much that he flung himself on his face and cried with a loud voice, "Ah, Lord God! wilt Thou make a full end of the remnant of Israel?" But on the others this death by the visitation of God seems to have produced no effect; and the glory of God left the city, borne away upon its cherubim-chariot.[2]

Even under the stress of these dreadful circumstances the Jews held out with that desperate tenacity which has often been shown by nations fighting behind strong walls for their very existence, but by no nation more decidedly than by the Jews. And if the rebel-party, and the lying prophets who had brought the city to this pass, still entertained any hopes either of

---

[1] Lam. iv. 5. See Stanley, *Lectures*, ii. 470.   [2] Ezek. xi. 23.

a diversion caused by Pharaoh Hophrah, or of some miraculous deliverance such as that which had saved the city from Sennacherib years earlier, it is not unnatural that they should have regarded Jeremiah with positive fury. For he still continued to prophesy the captivity. What specially angered them was his message to the people that all who remained in Jerusalem should die by the sword, the famine, and the pestilence, but that those who deserted to the Chaldæans should live. It was on the ground of his having said this that they had imprisoned him as a deserter; and when Pashur and his son Gedaliah heard that he was still saying this, they and the other princes entreated Zedekiah to put him to death as a pernicious traitor, who weakened the hands of the patriot soldiers. Jeremiah was not guilty of the lack of patriotism with which they charged him. The day of independence had passed for ever, and Babylon, not Egypt, was the appointed suzerain. The counselling of submission— as many a victorious chieftain has been forced at last to counsel it, from the days of Hannibal to those of Thiers—is often the true and the only possible patriotism in doomed and decadent nations. Zedekiah timidly abandoned the prophet to the rage of his enemies; but being afraid to murder him openly as Urijah had been murdered, they flung him into a well in the dungeon of Malchiah, the king's son. Into the mire of this pit he sank up to the arms, and there they purposely left him to starve and rot.[1] But if no Israelite pitied him, his condition moved the compassion of Ebed-Melech, an Ethiopian, one of the king's eunuch-chamberlains. He hurried to the king in a storm of

---

[1] This may possibly be alluded to in Psalm lxix. 2.

pity and indignation. He found him sitting, as a king should do, at the post of danger in the gate of Benjamin ; for Zedekiah was not a physical, though he was a moral, coward. Ebed-Melech told the king that Jeremiah was dying of starvation, and Zedekiah bade him take three [1] men with him and rescue the dying man. The faithful Ethiopian hurried to a cellar under the treasury, took with him some old, worn fragments of robes, and, letting them down by cords, called to Jeremiah to put them under his arm-pits. He did so, and they drew him up into the light of day, though he still remained in prison.

It seems to have been at this time that, in spite of his grim vaticination of immediate retribution, Jeremiah showed his serene confidence in the ultimate future by accepting the proposal of his cousin Hanameel to buy some of the paternal fields at Anathoth, though at that very moment they were in the hands of the Chaldæans. Such an act publicly performed must have caused some consolation to the besieged, just as did the courage of the Roman senator who gave a good price for the estate outside the walls of Rome on which Hannibal was actually encamped.

Then Zedekiah once more secretly sent for him, and implored him to tell the unvarnished truth. " If I do," said the prophet, " will you not kill me ? and will you in any case hearken to me ? " Zedekiah swore not to betray him to his enemies ; and Jeremiah told him that, even at that eleventh hour, if he would go out and make submission to the Babylonians, the city should not be burnt, and he should save the lives of himself and of his family. Zedekiah believed him, but pleaded that

---

[1] Jer. xxxviii. 10, A.V., " thirty."

he was afraid of the mockery of the deserters to whom he might be delivered. Jeremiah assured him that he should not be so delivered, and that, if he refused to obey, nothing remained for the city, and for him and his wives and children, but final ruin. The king was too weak to follow what he must now have felt to be the last chance which God had opened out for him. He could only " attain to half-believe." He entrusted the result to chance, with miserable vacillation of purpose ; and the door of hope was closed upon him. His one desire was to conceal the interview ; and if it came to the ears of the princes—of whom he was shamefully afraid—he begged Jeremiah to say that he had only entreated the king not to send him back to die in Jonathan's prison.

As he had suspected, it became known that Jeremiah had been summoned to an interview with the king. They questioned the prophet in prison. He told them the story which the king had suggested to him, and the truth remained undiscovered. For this deflection from exact truth it is tolerably certain that, in the state of men's consciences upon the subject of veracity in those days, the prophet's moral sense did not for a moment reproach him. He remained in his prison, guarded probably by the faithful Ebed-Melech, until Jerusalem was taken.

Let us pity the dreadful plight of Zedekiah, aggravated as it was by his weak temperament. " He stands at the head of a people determined to defend itself, but is himself without either hope or courage."[1]

---

[1] Van Oort, iv. 52.

CHAPTER XXXVIII

THE FALL OF JERUSALEM

b.c. 586

2 Kings xxv. 1—21

"In that day will I make Jerusalem a burdensome stone for all
nations."—Zech. xii. 3.
"An end is come, the end is come; it awaketh against thee: behold
the end is come."—Ezek. vii. 6.

> " Behold yon sterile spot
> Where now the wandering Arab's tent
> Flaps in the desert blast;
> There once old Salem's haughty fane
> Reared high to heaven its thousand golden domes,
> And in the blushing face of day
> Exposed its shameful glory."
>
> Shelley.

AFTER the siege had lasted for a year and a half,
all but one day, at midnight the besiegers made
a breach in the northern city wall.[1] It was a day of
terrible remembrance, and throughout the exile it was
observed as a solemn fast.[2]

Nebuchadrezzar was no longer in person before the

---

[1] Jos., *Antt.*, X. viii. 2 ; 2 Chron. xxxii. 5, xxxiii. 14. First and
last, the siege seems to have lasted one year, five months, and twenty-
seven days.

[2] Zech. viii. 19.

walls. He had other war-like operations and other sieges on hand—the sieges of Tyre, Asekah, and Lachish—as well as Jerusalem. He had therefore established his headquarters at Lachish, and did not superintend the final operations against the city.[1] But now that all had become practically hopeless, and the capture of the rest of Jerusalem was only a matter of a few days more, Zedekiah and his few best surviving princes and soldiers fled by night through the opposite quarter of the city. There was a little unwatched postern between two walls near the king's garden, and through this he and his escort fled, hoping to reach the Arabah, and make good his escape, perhaps to the Wady-el-Arish, which he could reach in five hours, through the wilds beyond the Jordan.[2] The heads of the king and his followers were muffled, and they carried on their shoulders their choicest possessions.[3] But he was betrayed by some of the mean deserters,[4] and pursued by the Chaldæans. His movements were doubtless impeded by the presence of his harem and his children. His little band of warriors could offer no resistance, and fled in all directions. Zedekiah, his family, and his attendants were taken prisoners, and carried to Riblah

---

[1] The inscriptions of Nebuchadrezzar which have been as yet deciphered speak of his sumptuous buildings and of his worship of the gods rather than of his conquests. See *Records of the Past*, vii. 69–78.

[2] Robinson, *Bibl. Res.*, ii. 536. Some suppose that "the king's garden" was near the mouth of the Tyropœon Valley.

[3] Ezek. xii. 12. Perhaps the gate alluded to is the fountain gate of Neh. iii. 15. Ezekiel seems to speak of "digging through the wall." Robinson says that a trace of the outermost wall still exists in the rude pathway which crosses the mouth of the Tyropœon on a mound hard by the old mulberry tree which marks the traditional site of Isaiah's martyrdom.

[4] Jos., *Antt.*, X. viii. 2.

to appear before the mighty conqueror.[1] Nebuchadrezzar showed no pity towards one whom he had
elevated to the throne, and who had violated his most
solemn assurances by intriguing with his enemies.
He brought him to trial, and doomed him to witness
with his own eyes the massacre of his two sons and
of his attendants. After he had endured this anguish,
worse than death, his eyes were put out, and, bound
in double fetters,[2] he was sent to Babylon, where he
ended his miserable days. To blind a king deprived
him of all hope of recovering the throne, and was
therefore in ancient days a common punishment.[3]
The LXX. adds that he was sent by the Babylonians
to grind a mill—εἰς οἰκίον μυλῶνος. This is probably
a reminiscence of the blinded Samson. But thus were
fulfilled with startling literalness two prophecies which
might well have seemed to be contradictory.[4] For
Jeremiah had said (xxxiv. 3),—

"Thine eyes shall behold the eyes of the King of
Babylon, and he shall speak with thee mouth to mouth,
and thou shalt go to Babylon."

Whereas Ezekiel had said (xii. 13),—

---

[1] Traces of his presence are found in inscriptions in the Wady of
the Dog near Beyrout, and in Wady Brissa. See Sayce, *Proceedings
of the Bibl. Arch. Soc.*, November 1881.

[2] 2 Kings xxv. 7. See Layard, *Nineveh*, ii. 376.

[3] The blinding was sometimes done by passing a red-hot rod of
silver or brass over the open eyes; sometimes by plucking out the
eyes (Jer. lii. 11, Vulg. *oculos eruit*; 2 Kings xxv. 7, *effodit*). See a
hideous illustration of a yet more brutal process in Botta (*Monum. de
Nineve*, Pl. cxviii.), where Sargon with his own hand is thrusting
a lance into the eyes of a captive prince, whose head is kept steady by
a bridle fastened to a hook through his lips. See also Judg. xvi. 21 ;
Xen., *Anab.*, i. 9, § 13; Procopius, *Bel. Pers.*, i. 1; Ammianus, xxvii.
12 ; Rawlinson, *Ancient Monarchies*, i. 307.

[4] Jos., *Antt.*, X. viii. 2, 3.

"I will bring him to Babylon, the land of the Chaldæans; yet shall he not see it, though he shall die there."

Henceforth Zedekiah was forgotten, and his place knew him no more. We can only hope that in his blindness and solitude he was happier than he had been on the throne of Judah, and that before death came to end his miseries he found peace with God.

The conqueror did not come to spoil the city. He left that task to three great officers,—Nebuzaradan, the captain of the guard, or chief executioner;[1] Nebushasban, the Rabsaris, or chief of the eunuchs; and Nergalshareser, the Rabmag, or chief of the magicians. They took their station by the Middle Gate, and first gave up the city to pillage and massacre. No horror was spared.[2] The sepulchres were rifled for treasure; the young Levites were slain in the house of their Sanctuary; women were violated; maidens and hoary-headed men were slain. "Princes were hanged up by the hand, and the faces of elders were dishonoured; priest and prophet were slain in the Sanctuary of the Lord,"[3] till the blood flowed like red wine from the winepress over the desecrated floor.[4] The guilty city

---

[1] Nebur-zir-iddina, "Nebo bestowed seed." Jer. xxxix. 9, 13, is in some way corrupt. Ezekiel (ix. 2), however, and Josephus (*Antt.*, X. viii. 2) mention *six* officers. Nebuzaradan was "chief of the executioners" (Gen. xxxvii. 36; I Kings ii. 25, 35, 46).

[2] Psalm lxxix. 2, 3.

[3] 2 Chron. xxxvi. 17; Lam. ii. 21, v. 11, 12.

[4] To the reminiscences of these scenes are partly due the Talmudic legend about the blood of Zechariah, the son of Jehoiada, bubbling up to demand vengeance. Nebudchadrezzar slew a holocaust of human victims to appease the shade of the wrathful prophet, until the king himself was terrified, and asked if he wished his whole people to be slaughtered. Then the blood ceased to bubble.

drank at the hand of God the dregs of the cup of His fury.[1] It was the final vengeance. "The punishment of thine iniquity is accomplished, O daughter of Zion. He will no more carry thee away into captivity."[2] And, meanwhile, the little Bedouin principalities were full of savage exultation at the fate of their hereditary foe.[3] This was felt by the Jews as a culmination of their misery, that they became a derision to their enemies. The callous insults hurled at them by the neighbouring tribes in their hour of shame awoke that implacable wrath against Gebal and Ammon and Amalek which finds its echo in the Prophets and in the Psalms.[4]

After this the devoted capital was given up to destruction. The Temple was plundered. All that remained of its often-rifled splendours was carried away, such as the ancient pillars Jachin and Boaz, the masterpieces of Hiram's art, the caldron, the brazen sea, and all the vessels of gold, of silver, and of brass. Then the walls of the city were dismantled and broken down. The Temple, and the palace, and all the houses of the princes were committed to the flames. As for the principal remaining inhabitants, Seraiah the chief priest, perhaps the grandson of Hilkiah and the grandfather of Ezra, Zephaniah the second priest, the three Levitic doorkeepers, the secretary of war, five of the greatest nobles who "saw the king's face,"[5] and sixty of the common people who had been marked out for special punishment, were taken to Riblah, and there

---

[1] See Rawlinson, *Kings of Israel and Judah*, p. 236.
[2] Lam. iv. 22.
[3] Psalm lxxix. 1.
[4] Obad. 14–16; Psalm cxxxvii. 7; 1 Esdras iv. 45.
[5] Comp. Esther i. 14.

massacred by order of Nebuchadrezzar.[1] With these
Nebuchadrezzar took away as his prisoners a multitude
of the wealthier inhabitants, leaving behind him but
the humblest artisans.   As the craftsmen and smiths
had been deported,[2] these poor people busied themselves
in agriculture, as vine-dressers and husbandmen.   The
existing estates were divided among them ; and being
few in number, they found the amplest sustenance in
treasures of wheat and barley, and oil and honey, and
summer fruits, which they kept concealed for safety,
as the fellaheen of Palestine do to this day.[3]

According to the historic chapters added to the
prophecies of Jeremiah, the whole number of captives
carried away from Jerusalem by Nebuchadrezzar in
the seventh, the eighteenth, and the twenty-third years
of his reign were 4,600.[4]   The completeness of the
desolation might well have caused the heart-rending
outcry of Psalm lxxix. : " O God, the heathen are
come into Thine inheritance ; Thy holy Temple have
they defiled ; they have made Jerusalem a heap of
stones.   The dead bodies of Thy servants have they
given to be meat unto the fowls of heaven, and the
flesh of Thy saints unto the beasts of the land.   Their
blood have they shed like water round about Jerusalem ;
and there was no man to bury them."

Among the remnant of the people was Jeremiah.
Nebuzaradan had received from his king the strictest

---

[1] On these personages see 1 Chron. vi. 13, 14; 2 Kings xxii. 4 ;
Ezra vii. 1 ; Jer. xxi. 1, xxxvii. 3, etc.

[2] Nebuchadrezzar had no doubt needed them for his great buildings
at Babylon, and their deportation would render more difficult any
attempt to refortify Jerusalem.

[3] Jer. xli. 8, xl. 12.

[4] Jer. lii. 28–30. In his seventh year, 3,023 ; in his eighteenth, 832
in his thirty-third, 745 = 4,600.

injunctions to treat him honourably; for he had heard
from the deserters that he had always opposed the
rebellion, and had prophesied the issue of the siege.
He was indeed sent in manacles to Ramah;[1] but there
Nebuchadrezzar gave him free choice to do exactly as
he liked—either to accompany him to Babylon, where
he should be well treated and cared for, or to return to
Jerusalem, and live where he liked.   This was his desire.
Nebuchadrezzar therefore dismissed him with food and
a present;[2] and he returned.   The LXX. and Vulgate
represent him as sitting weeping over the ruins of
Jerusalem, and tradition says that he sought for his
lamentations a cave still existing near the Damascus
Gate.   Of this Scripture knows nothing.   But the
melancholy prophet was only reserved for further
tragedies.   He had lived one of the most afflicted of
human lives.   A man of tender heart and shrinking
disposition, he had been called to set his face like a flint
against kings, and nobles, and mobs.   Worse than this,
being himself a prophet and priest, naturally led to
sympathise with both, he was the doomed antagonist
of both—victim of "one of the strongest of human
passions, the hatred of priests against a priest who
attacks his own order, the hatred of prophets against
a prophet who ventures to have a voice and a will of his
own."   Even his own family had plotted against his
life at humble Anathoth;[3] and when he retreated to
Jerusalem, he found himself at the centre of the storm.

---

[1] Ramah was but five miles from Jerusalem, and at first Jeremiah
may not have been identified (Jer. xl. 1-6).

[2] The present, if accepted, could only be regarded, under the circumstances, as part of the necessity of life.   It does not fall under
the head of the presents often offered to prophets (1 Sam. ix. 7;
2 Kings iv. 42; Mic. iii. 5, 11; Amos vii. 12).

[3] Jer. xi. 19-21, xii. 6.

Now perhaps he hoped for a gleam of sunset peace. But his hopes were disappointed. He had to tread the path of anguish and hatred to the bitter end, as he had trodden it for nearly fifty years of the troubled life which had followed his call in early boyhood.

"But, in the case of Jerusalem," says Dean Stanley, "both its first and second destruction have the peculiar interest of involving the dissolution of a religious dispensation, combined with the agony of an expiring nation, such as no other people has survived, and, by surviving, carried on the living recollection, first of one, and then of the other, for centuries after the first shock was over."[1]

---

[1] Stanley, *Lectures*, ii. 515.

CHAPTER XXXIX

GEDALIAH

B.C. 586

2 KINGS xxv. 22—30

"Vedi che son un che piango."—DANTE, *Inferno*

" No, rather steel thy melting heart
To act the martyr's sternest part,
To watch with firm, unshrinking eye
Thy darling visions as they die,
Till all bright hopes and hues of day
Have faded into twilight grey."

KEBLE.

IN deciding that he would not accompany Nebuchadrezzar to Babylon, Jeremiah made the choice of
duty. In Chaldæa he would have lived at ease, in plenty,
in security, amid universal respect. He might have
helped his younger contemporary Ezekiel in his struggle
to keep the exiles in Babylon faithful to their duty and
their God. He regarded the exiles as representing all
that was best and noblest in the nation ; and he would
have been safe and honoured in the midst of them,
under the immediate protection of the great Babylonian
king. On the other hand, to return to Judæa was to
return to a defenceless and a distracted people, the
mere dregs of the true nation, the mere phantom of
what they once had been. Surely his life had earned
the blessing of repose ? But no ! The hopes of the

Chosen People, the seed of Abraham, God's servant, could not be dissevered from the Holy Land. Rest was not for him on this side of the grave. His only prayer must be, like that which Senancour had inscribed over his grave, " Éternité, deviens mon asile ! " The decision cost him a terrible struggle ; but duty called him, and he obeyed. It has been supposed by some critics[1] that the wild cry of Jer. xv. 10–21 expresses his anguish at the necessity of casting in his lot with the remnant ; the sense that they needed his protecting influence and prophetic guidance ; and the promise of God that his sacrifice should not be ineffectual for good to the miserable fragment of his nation, even though they should continue to struggle against him.

So with breaking heart he saw Nebuzaradan at Ramah marshalling the throng of captives for their long journey to the waters of Babylon. Before them, and before the little band which returned with him to the burnt Temple, the dismantled city, the desolate house, there lay an unknown future ; but in spite of the exiles' doom it looked brighter for them than for him, as with tears and sobs they parted from each other. Then it was that—

"A voice was heard in Ramah, lamentation, and bitter weeping ; Rachel weeping for her children refuseth to be comforted, because they are not. Thus saith the Lord, ' Refrain thy voice from weeping, and thine eyes from tears : for thy work shall be rewarded,' saith the Lord ; ' and they shall come again from the land of the enemy. And there is hope for thy time to come,' saith the Lord, ' that thy children shall come again to their own border.' "[2]

---

[1] So Grätz and Cheyne.   [2] Jer. xxxi. 15-17.

Disappointed in the fidelity of the royal house of Judah, Nebuchadrezzar had not attempted to place another of them on the throne. He appointed Gedaliah, the son of Ahikam, the son of Shaphan, his satrap (*pakîd*) over the poor remnant who were left in the land. In this appointment we probably trace the influence of Jeremiah. There is no one whom Nebuchadrezzar would have been so likely to consult. Gedaliah was the son of the prophet's old protector,[1] and his grandfather Shaphan had been a trusted minister of Josiah. He thoroughly justified the confidence reposed in him, and under his wise and prosperous rule there seemed to be every prospect that there would be at least some pale gleam of returning prosperity. The Jews, who during the period of the siege had fled into all the neighbouring countries, no sooner heard of his viceroyalty than they came flocking back from Moab, and Ammon, and Edom. They found themselves, perhaps for the first time in their lives, in possession of large estates, from which the exiles of Babylon had been dispossessed; and favoured by an abundant harvest, "they gathered wine and summer fruits very much."[2]

Jerusalem—dismantled, defenceless, burnt—was no longer habitable. It was all but deserted, so that jackals and hyænas prowled even over the mountain of the Lord's House. All attempt to refortify it would have been regarded as rebellion, and such a mere "lodge in a garden of cucumbers" would have been useless to repress the marauding incursions of the envious Moabites and Edomites, who had looked on with shouts at the destruction of the city, and exulted when her

---

[1] Jer. xxvi. 24.   [2] Jer. xl. 12.

carved work was broken down with axes and hammers. Gedaliah therefore fixed his headquarters at Mizpah, about six miles north of Jerusalem, of which the lofty eminence could be easily secured.[1] It was the watch-tower from which Titus caught his first glimpses of the Holy City, as many a traveller does to this day, and the point at which Richard I. averted his eyes with tears, saying that he was unworthy to look upon the city which he was unable to save. Here, then, Gedaliah lived, urging upon his subjects the policy which his friend and adviser Jeremiah had always supported, and promising them quietness and peace if they would but accept the logic of circumstances— if they would bow to the inevitable, and frankly acknowledge the suzerainty of Nebuchadrezzar. It was perhaps as a pledge of more independence in better days to come that Nebuzaradan had left Gedaliah in charge of the young daughters of King Zedekiah, who had with them some of their eunuch-attendants. As that unfortunate monarch was only thirty-two years old when he was blinded and carried away, the princesses were probably young girls ; and it has been conjectured that it was part of the Chaldæan king's plan for the future that in time Gedaliah should be permitted to marry one of them, and re-establish at least a collateral branch of the old royal house of David.

How long this respite continued we do not know. The language of Jeremiah xxxix 2, xli. 1, compared with 2 Kings xxv. 8, might seem to imply that it only lasted two months. But since Jeremiah does not mention the year in xli. 1, and as there seems to

---

[1] Some identify it with *Shaphat.* a mile from Jerusalem

have been yet another deportation of Jews by Nebuchadrezzar five years latter (Jer. lii. 30), which may
have been in revenge for the murder of his satrap,
some have supposed that Gedaliah's rule lasted four
years. All is uncertain, and the latter passage is of
doubtful authenticity ; but it is at least possible that the
vengeful atrocity committed by Ishmael followed almost
immediately after the Chaldæan forces were well out
of sight. Respecting these last days of Jewish independence, " History, leaning semisomnous on her pyramid,
muttereth something, but we know not what it is."

However this may be, there seem to have been
guerilla bands wandering through the country, partly
to get what they could, and partly to watch against
Bedouin marauders. Johanan, the son of Kareah, who
was one of the chief captains among them,[1] came with
others to Gedaliah, and warned him that Baalis, King
of Ammon, was intriguing against him, and trying to
induce a certain Ishmael, the son of Nethaniah, the
son of Elishama—who, in some way unknown to us,
represented, perhaps on the female side, the seed
royal[2]—to come and murder him. Gedaliah was of
a fine, unsuspicious temperament, and with rash
generosity he refused to believe in the existence of
a plot so ruinous and so useless. Astonished at his
noble incredulity, Johanan then had a secret interview
with him, and offered to murder Ishmael so secretly
that no one should know of it. " Why," he asked,
" should this man be suffered to ruin everything, and

---

[1] They are called *sari* (" princes ").

[2] There is no Elishama in the royal genealogy, except a son of
David. Ishmael may have been the son or grandson of some
Ammonite princess. An Elishama was scribe of Jehoiakim (Jer.
xxxvi. 12).

cause the final scattering of even the struggling handful of colonists at Mizpah and in Judah?" Gedaliah
forbad his intervention. "Thou shalt not do this," he
said : "thou speakest falsely of Ishmael."

But Johanan's story was only too true. Shortly
afterwards, Ishmael, with ten confederates,[1] came to
visit Gedaliah at Mizpah, perhaps on the pretext of
seeing his kinswomen, the daughters of Zedekiah.
Gedaliah welcomed this ambitious villain and his
murderous accomplices with open-handed hospitality.
He invited them all to a banquet in the fort of Mizpah ;
and after eating salt with him, Ishmael and his bravoes
first murdered him, and then put promiscuously to the
sword his soldiers, and the Chaldæans who had been
left to look after him.[2] The gates of the fort were
closed, and the bodies were flung into a deep well or
tank,[3] which had been constructed by Asa in the middle
of the courtyard, when he was fortifying Mizpah against
the attacks of Baasha, King of Israel.

For two days there was an unbroken silence, and
the peasants at Mizpah remained unaware of the
dreadful tragedy. On the third day a sad procession
was seen wending its way up the heights. There were
scattered Jews in Shiloh and Samaria who still remembered Zion ; and eighty pilgrims, weeping as they went,
came with shaven beards and rent garments to bring
a *minchah* and incense to the ruined shrine at Jerusalem.
In the depth of their woe they had even violated a law
(Lev. xix. 28, xxi. 5), of which they were perhaps

---

[1] The Hebrew text calls these ten ruffians *rabbi hammelech*, "chief
officers of the king" of Ammon.

[2] Josephus records or conjectures that the governor was over-
powered by wine, and had sunk into slumber (*Antt.*, X. ix. 2).

[3] In Jer. xli. 9, for "because of Gedaliah," the better reading is
"was a great pit" (LXX., φρέαρ μέγα).

unaware, by cutting themselves in sign of their misery.
Mizpah would be their last halting-place on the way to
Jerusalem ; and the hypocrite Ishmael came out to them
with an invitation to share the hospitality of the murdered satrap. No sooner had the gate of the charnel-
house closed upon them,[1] than Ishmael and his ten
ruffians began to murder this unoffending company.
Crimes more aimless and more brutal than those committed by this infinitely degenerate scion of the royal
house it is impossible to conceive. The place swam
with blood. The story " reads almost like a page from
the annals of the Indian Mutiny." Seventy of the
wretched pilgrims had been butchered and flung into
the tank, which must have been choked with corpses,
like the fatal well at Cawnpore,[2] when the ten survivors
pleaded for their lives by telling Ishmael that they had
large treasures of country produce stored in hidden
places, which should be at his disposal if he would
spare them.[3]

As it was useless to make any further attempt to
conceal his atrocities, Ishmael now took the young
princesses and the inhabitants of Mizpah with him,
and tried to make good his escape to his patron the
King of Ammon. But the watchful eye of Johanan,
the son of Kareah, had been upon him, and assembling
his band he went in swift pursuit. Ishmael had got
no farther than the Pool of Gibeon, when Johanan

---

[1] Ishmael—a marvel of craft and villainy—put into practice the
same stratagem which on a larger scale was employed by Mohammed
Ali in his massacre of the Mamelukes at Cairo in 1806 (Grove, *s.v*
Bibl. Dict.). For "the midst of the city " (Jer. xli. 7), we ought to
read " courtyard," as in Josephus.

[2] Comp. Jehu's treatment of the family of Ahaziah (2 Kings x. 14).

[3] The dark deed is still commemorated by a Jewish fast, as in the
days of Zechariah (Zech. vii. 3-5, viii. 19).

overtook him, to the intense joy of the prisoners. A scuffle ensued; but Ishmael and eight of his blood-stained desperadoes unhappily managed to make good their escape to the Ammonites. The wretch vanishes into the darkness, and we hear of him no more.

Even now the circumstances were desperate. Nebuchadrezzar could not in honour overlook the frustration of all his plans, and the murder, not only of his viceroy, but even of his Chaldæan commissioners. He would not be likely to accept any excuses. No course seemed open but that of flight. There was no temptation to return to Mizpah with its frightful memories and its corpse-choked tank. From Gibeon the survivors made their way to Bethlehem, which lay on the road to Egypt, and where they could be sheltered in the caravanscrai of Chimham. Many Jews had already taken refuge in Egypt. Colonies of them were living in Pathros, and at Migdol and Noph, under the kindly protection of Pharaoh Hophrah. Would it not be well to join them?

In utter perplexity Johanan and the other captains and all the people came to Jeremiah. How he had escaped the massacre at Mizpah we do not know; but now he seemed to be the only man left in whose prophetic guidance they could confide. They entreated him with pathetic earnestness to show them the will of Jehovah; and he promised to pray for insight, while they pledged themselves to obey implicitly his directions.

The anguish and vacillation of the prophet's mind is shown by the fact that for ten whole days no light came to him. It seemed as if Judah was under an irrevocable curse. Whither could they return? What temptation was there to return? Did not return mean fresh intolerable miseries? Would they not be torn to pieces by the robber bands from across the Jordan? And what could be the end of it but another deportation to Babylon, with perhaps further massacre and starvation?

All the arguments seemed against this course; and he could see very clearly that it would be against all the wishes of the down-trodden fugitives, who longed for Egypt, "where we shall see no war, nor hear the sound of the trumpet, nor have hunger of bread."

Yet Jeremiah could only give them the message which he believed to represent the will of God. He bade them return. He assured them that they need have no fear of the King of Babylon, and that God would bless them; whereas if they went to Egypt, they would die by the sword, the famine, and the pestilence. At the same time—doomed always to thwart the hopes of the multitude—he reproved the hypocrisy which had sent them to ask God's will when they never intended to do anything but follow their own.

Then their anger broke out against him. He was, as always, the prophet of evil, and they held him more than half responsible for being the *cause* of the ruin which he invariably predicted. Johanan and "all the proud men " (*zēdîm*) gave him the lie. They told him that the source of his prophesy was not Jehovah, but the meddling and pernicious Baruch. Perhaps some of them may have remembered the words of Isaiah, that a day should come when five cities, of which one should be called Kir-Cheres (" the City of Destruction ") —a play on the name Kir-Heres, "the City of the Sun," On or Heliopolis—should speak the language of Canaan and swear by the Lord of hosts, and there should be an altar in the land of Egypt and a *matstsebah* at its border in witness to Jehovah, and that though Egypt should be smitten she should also be healed.[1]

So they settled to go to Egypt; and taking with them Jeremian, and Baruch, and the king's daughters, and all the remnant, they made their way to Tahpanhes or Daphne,[2] an advanced post to guard the road to Syria. Mr. Flinders Petrie in 1886 discovered the site of the city at Tel Defenneh, and the ruins of the very palace which Pharaoh Hophrah placed at the disposal of the daughters of his ally Zedekiah. It is still known by the name of "The Castle of the Jew's Daughters"—*El Kasr el Bint el Jehudi.*[3]

In front of this palace was an elevated platform (*mastaba*) of brick, which still remains. In this brick-work Jeremiah was bidden by the word of Jehovah to place great stones, and to declare that on that very platform, over those very stones, Nebuchadrezzar should pitch his royal tent, when he came to wrap himself in the land of Egypt, as a shepherd wraps himself in his garment, and to burn the pillars of Heliopolis with fire.[4]

Jeremiah still had to face stormy times. At some great festival assembly at Tahpanhes he bitterly reproached the exiled Jews for their idolatries. He was extremely indignant with the women who burned incense to the Queen of Heaven. The multitude, and especially the women, openly defied him. "We will not hearken

---

[1] Isa. xix. 18–22.

[2] Jer. ii. 16, xliv. 1 ; Ezek. xxx. 18 ; Jer. xliii. 7, xlvi. 14 ; Herod., ii. 30.

[3] Fl. Petrie, *Memoir on Tanis* (Egypt. Explor. Fund, 4th memoir), 1888.

[4] Jer. xliii. 13, Beth-shemesh. Only one pillar of the Temple of the Sun is now standing. It is said to be four thousand years old. It is certain that Nebuchadrezzar invaded Egypt and defeated Amasis, the son of Hophrah, B.C. 565, reducing Egypt to "the basest of kingdoms" (Ezek. xxix. 14, 15). Three of Nebuchadrezzar's terra-cotta cylinders have been found at Tahpanhes.

to thee," they said. " We will continue to burn incense, and offer offerings to the Queen of Heaven, *as we have done, we, and our fathers, our kings, and our princes, in the cities of Judah, and in the streets of Jerusalem* ; for then had we plenty of victuals, and were well, and saw no evil. It is only since we have left off making cakes for her and honouring her that we have suffered hunger and desolation ; and our husbands were always well aware of our proceedings."

Never was there a more defiantly ostentatious revolt against God and against His prophet! Remonstrance seemed hopeless. What could Jeremiah do but menace them with the wrath of Heaven, and tell them that in sign of the truth of his words the fate of Pharaoh Hophrah should be the same as the fate of Zedekiah, King of Judah, and should be inflicted by the hand of Nebuchadrezzar.[1]

So on the colony of fugitives the curtain of revelation rushes down in storm. The prophet went on the troubled path which, if tradition be true, led him at last to martyrdom. He is said to have been stoned by his infuriated fellow-exiles. But his name lived in the memory of his people. It was he (they believed) who had hidden from the Chaldæans the Ark and the sacred fire, and some day he should return to reveal the place of their concealment.[2] When Christ asked His disciples six hundred years later, "Whom say the people that I am ?" one of the answers was, "Some say Jeremiah or one of the prophets." He became, so

---

[1] How far the prophecy was fulfilled we do not know. Assyrian and Egyptian fragments of record show that in the thirty-seventh year of his reign Nebuchadrezzar invaded Egypt and advanced to Syene (Ezek. xxix. 10).

[2] 2 Macc. ii. 1–8; comp. xv. 13–16. The tradition is singular when we recall the small store which Jeremiah set by the Ark (Jer. iii. 16).

to speak, the guardian saint of the land in which he had suffered such cruel persecutions.

But the historian of the Kings does not like to leave the close of his story in unbroken gloom. He wrote during the Exile. He has narrated with tears the sad fate of Jehoiachin; and though he does not care to dwell on the Exile itself, he is glad to narrate one touch of kindness on the part of the King of Babylon, which he doubtless regarded as a pledge of mercies yet to come. Twenty-six years had elapsed since the capture of Jerusalem, and thirty-seven since the captivity of the exiled king, when Evil-Merodach, the son and successor of Nebuchadrezzar, took pity on the imprisoned heir of the House of David.[1] He took Jehoiachin from his dungeon, changed his garments, spoke words of encouragement to him, gave him a place at his own table,[2] assigned to him a regular allowance from his own banquet,[3] and set his throne above the throne of all the other captive kings who were with him in Babylon. It might seem a trivial act of mercy, yet the Jews remembered in their records the very day of the month on which it had taken place, because they regarded it as a break in the clouds which overshadowed them—as "the first gleam of heaven's amber in the Eastern grey."

---

[1] Evil-Merodach (Avil-Marduk, "Man of Merodach") only reigned two years, and was then murdered by his brother-in-law Neriglissar (Berosus *ap.* Jos.: comp. *Ap.*, i. 20). The Rabbis have a story—perhaps founded on that of Gaius and Agrippa I.—that Evil-Merodach had been imprisoned by his father for wishing his death, and in prison formed a friendship for Jehoiachin.

[2] "Lifted up his head." Comp. Gen. xl. 13, 20.

[3] To be thus ὁμοτράπεζος, or σύσσιτος, of the king was a high honour (Herod., iii. 13, v. 24. Comp. Judg. i. 7; 2 Sam. ix. 13, etc.).

EPILOGUE

"On Jordan's banks the Arab's camels stray,
On Zion's hills the False One's votaries pray,
The Baal-adorer bows on Sinai's steep;
Yet there—e'en there—O God, Thy thunders sleep."

BYRON.

"God, Thou art Love: I build my faith on that."

BROWNING.

BEFORE concluding I should like to add a few words (1) on what some may regard as the too favourable attitude towards what is called the "Higher Criticism" adopted in this book ; and (2) on the deep, essential, eternal lessons which we have found in chapter after chapter of it.

1. As regards the first, I need only say that the one thing I seek, the sole thing I care for, is Truth,—truth, not tradition. Even St. Cyprian, devoted as he was to custom and tradition, warns us that "Custom without Truth is only antiquated error," and that what we believe must be established by reason, not prescribed by tradition.

And it cannot be laid down too clearly that the old view of Inspiration—which defined it as consisting in verbal dictation, which made the sacred writers "not only the penmen but the pens of the Holy Spirit," and which spoke of every sentence, word, syllable, and every letter of Scripture as Divine and infallible—was a dangerous and absolute falsity, and that any attempt in these days to enforce it as binding on the intellect and conscience of mankind could only lead to the utter shipwreck of all sincere and reasonable religion. "Not needlessly," says the learned author of *Italy and her Invaders*—himself an able opponent of many modern conclusions on the subject—"should I wish to shake even that faith which practically believes that the whole Bible, exactly in its present shape, yes, almost the English Bible just as we have it, came straight down from heaven. But we do want to get away from all mere theories as to the way in which God *might* have revealed Himself, and to learn as much as we can of the way in which He *has* revealed Himself in actual fact, and in real human lives." [1]

To do this has been one of my objects in this volume, and in the preceding volume on the First Book of Kings.

2. We have now only to cast one last glance on this book, and on the lessons which it is meant to teach.

Consider, first, its deep and varied interest. It has the combined value of History and of Biography; and, in dealing with both, its aim is to pass over all minor and earthly details, and to show the method of God's dealings both with nations and with the individual soul.

If we look at the book only as a History, it shows us in the briefest possible compass a series of

---

[1] T. Hodgkin, *Friends' Quarterly*, September 1893, p. 401.

national events of the greatest importance in the annals of mankind. We become witnesses of the fierce occasional struggles between Israel and Judah, and of the constant warfare of both with those wild surrounding nations—the people of Moab, and of Edom, Gebal, and Ammon, and Amalek, the Philistines also, and them that dwell at Tyre. We watch the indomitable resistance of Tyre to Assyria and Babylon. We see the Northern Kingdom of Israel rise into wealth, power, and luxury, only to sink into deep moral corruption, until, at last, the patience of God is exhausted, and He obliterates its very existence in an apparently final and irremediable overthrow. We witness the rise, culmination, and fall of Syria; the culmination and the crashing overthrow of Nineveh; the rise and the splendour of Babylon. We see the surging tide of the nomad Scythians and Cimmerians rise into flood and ebb away with spent and shallow waves. We see the petty fortress of Zion triumph in its defiance of the mighty hosts of Sennacherib because it is strong in reliance upon God, and we see it grow faithless to God until it succumbs to the captains of Nebuchadrezzar. Again and again we observe that the Almighty stills the raging of the sea, the noise of his waves, and the madness of the people.

The conviction is borne upon our soul with overwhelming power, as we read the pages of Amos, of Isaiah, and of Jeremiah, that, in spite of all their rage and tumult, and apparently irresistible dominance, God still sitteth above the water-floods, and God remaineth a King for ever.

Side by side with this spectacle of the dealing of God with nations, in which we see written in large letters, in characters of blood and of fire, His dealing with guilty nations, we have abundantly in these chapters the narrower yet more intense interest which arises from the contemplation of human nature—one and the same in its general elements, but infinitely varied in its conditions—in the lives of individual men. It is revealed to us as in a picture—it is brought home to us, not by didactic inferences, but with the silent conviction which springs from the evidence of facts—that wealth is nothing, and rank nothing, and power nothing, but that the only thing of essential importance in human lives is whether a man does that which is good or that which is evil in the sight of the Lord. Good kings and bad kings pass before us; and though the best kings, like Hezekiah and Josiah, were no more free from earthly misfortune than are any of the saints of God—though Hezekiah had to suffer anguish and humiliation, and Josiah died in defeat on the battle-field, —yet we are irresistibly led to the belief: "Say ye of the righteous that it shall be well with him; for they shall eat the fruit of their doings. Woe unto the wicked! It shall be ill with him; for the work of his hands shall be done to him."

We all have a guide in life. "We are not left to steer our course even by the stars, which the clouds of earth may dim. The ship has something on board which points towards the spiritual pole of the universe. I will not venture to call it an *infallible* guide. It wavers with tremulous sensitiveness; it may be deflected by disturbing influences; but still in the main it points with mysterious fidelity towards the pole of our spirits, even God. And what is this compass which we have for our guidance? Some would call it Conscience; but we call it by a holier name, and say that even as the needle is acted on by the magnetic

current, so our spiritual compass is the spirit of man
acted on by the Spirit of the living and infinite God."
The lesson of this book—of every book of biography or
of history—is that men are noble and useful in proportion
as they are true to that law of an enlightened conscience
which represents to them the will and the voice of
God.

Ahaziah and Jehoram of Judah, tainted with the
blood of Jezebel, and perverted by the example of
Ahab, live wretchedly, reign contemptibly, and perish
miserably; while good Jehoshaphat and pious Josiah
are richly blessed. In the vaunting elation of Amaziah,
in the blood-stained ferocity of Jehu, in the ruthless
examples of usurpation and murder set by king after
king in Israel, and in the consequences which befell
them, we see that "fruit is seed." Shallum, Menahem,
Pekah, Athaliah, have to pay a terrible price for brief
spells of troubled royalty; and the slow corruption and
disintegration of the people reflects the vile example of
their rulers. Like king, like people; like people, like
priest. We look on at a succession of thrilling scenes
—the horrors of beleaguered cities, the raptures of unexpected deliverance, the insulting vanities of triumph;
we hear the wail that rises from long lines of fettered
captives as they turn their backs weeping upon their
native land. And we are told "strange stories of the
deaths of kings." We see the King of Moab sacrificing
his eldest son to Chemosh upon the wall of Kir-Haraseth
in the sight of three invading hosts. We shudder to
think of Ahaz and Manasseh passing their children
through the fire before the grim bull-headed monster
in the valley of the children of Hinnom. We see the
two ghastly piles of the heads of young princes on
either side the gates of Jezreel. We see Jehu driving

31

his fierce chariot over the body of the painted Tyrian Queen. We catch a glimpse of the sackcloth under the purple of the King of Israel as he rends his clothes at the horrible cry of mothers who have devoured their babes. We see the child Joash standing with the high priest in the Temple amid the blast of trumpets, while the alien murderess is pushed out and hewn to the ground. We see Manasseh dragged with hooks to Babylon. We watch the haggard face of the miserable Zedekiah as his sons are slaughtered before the eyes which thenceforth are blinded for evermore. We burn with indignation to see the villain Ishmael close with corpses the well of Mizpah. But even when the phantasmagoria seems most appalling and most bloody, we watch the Day-star from on high begin to shed its glory over the grey east. In due time that Day-star was to rise in men's hearts and on the world, with healing in His wings; and we feel that somehow, beyond the smoke and stir of earth's anguish,

> " God's in His heaven,
> All's right with the world."

And like a Greek chorus amid the agonies of destiny stand the prophets, those clearest and greatest of moral teachers. They, in spite of their holiness and faithfulness, are not exempt from the calamities of life. Amos was insulted and expelled by the high priest of Bethel; Urijah was martyred; Hosea's prophecy is one long and almost unbroken wail; Isaiah was mocked and slandered by the priests of Jerusalem, and, if the tradition be true, sawn asunder; Micah, though spared, prophesied under imminent peril; Jeremiah, saddest of mankind, type of the suffering servant of Jehovah, was smitten in the face by the priest Pashur, thrust into the stocks for the general derision, flung into a deathful prison, let down into a miry well, hurried into exile, defied, denounced, insulted, at last in all probability martyred. Prophets in general were hated and disbelieved. They were the eternal antagonists of priests and mobs. With priests they had so little affinity, that when a prophet was born a priest, like Jeremiah and Ezekiel, he might count on the undying hatred and antagonism of his order. Priests, with scarcely an exception, under every erring or apostatising king, from Rehoboam to Ahaz, from Ahaz to Zedekiah, with a monotony of meanness, did nothing but acquiesce, careful mainly for their own rights and revenues; prophets did little but raise, against them and their party, an unavailing protest. When, in the days of the priest-regent Jehoiada, the priests had power, he had made a special ordinance that there should be overseers in the Temple whose function it should be to put in the stocks and the collar "every man that is mad, and that maketh himself a prophet";[1] and Shemaiah was quite indignant that there should be any delay in putting this convenient ordinance into force. Priests were chiefly absorbed in functions and futilities in the exact spirit of their guilty successors in the days of Christ. There could be little sympathy between them and the inspired messengers who spoke of such reliance on observances with almost passionate scorn, and to whom religion meant righteousness towards men and faith in the Living God.

This high lesson of Prophecy came into greater prominence with each succeeding generation. It had been taught by Amos, the first of the literary prophets,

---

[1] Jer. xxix. 25-27.

with emphatic distinctness. It was summarised by Hosea in words which our Saviour loved to quote: "Go ye and learn what that meaneth, I will have mercy, and not sacrifice." It had been uttered by Micah in an outburst of splendid poetry which summed up all that God requires. It was reiterated in many forms by Isaiah and by Jeremiah in words of richer moral value than all that came from the teaching of the priestly functionaries from the days when Aaron seduced Israel with his golden calf till the days when Caiaphas and Annas goaded the multitude to prefer Barabbas to Jesus, and to shout of their Messiah, "Let Him be crucified."

It was the richest fruit which sprang from the long Divine discipline of the nation,—the knowledge that outward things are of no avail to save any man; that God requires righteousness, that God looketh at the heart.

And the prophets themselves had to learn by the irony of events that no suppression of local sanctuaries under Hezekiah, no multiplication of ceremonies and acceptance of Deuteronomic Codes under Josiah, were deep enough to change men's hearts. Isaiah, like Amos, dwells with anger on the reliance upon vain ritual, which is so cheap a substitute for genuine holiness; and Jeremiah, despairing utterly of that reformation under Josiah of which he had once felt hopeful, had to denounce the new reliance on the Temple and its sacrifices. He ultimately felt no confidence in anything except in a new covenant in which God Himself would write His law upon men's hearts, and all should know Him from the least even to the greatest.

But the History of Prophecy also in this epoch is

marked by events of world-wide importance. In the days of Isaiah we see the change of Israel from a nation into a church of the faithful, for which alone he has any permanent hope. In him, too, we hear the first distinct utterances of the final form in which should be fulfilled the Messianic hope. Under Jeremiah there was still further advance. He points, as Joel does, to the epoch of the gift of the Holy Spirit, and shows that God does not only deal with men as nations, or as churches, or even as families, but as beings with individual souls.

This and much besides we have seen in the foregoing pages, in which we have endeavoured to point the lessons of the Books of Kings. The one main lesson which the narrative is meant to teach is absolute faith and trust in God, as an anchor which holds amid the wildest storms of ruin, and of apparently final failure. Not until we have realised that truth can we hear the words of God, or see the vision of the Almighty. When we have learnt it, we shall not fear, though the hills be moved and carried into the midst of the sea. It is the lesson which gets behind the meaning of failure, and raises us to a height from which we can look down on prosperity as a thing which—except in fatally delusive semblance—cannot exist apart from righteousness and faith. This is the lesson of life, the lesson of lessons. If it does not solve all problems on their intellectual side, it scatters all perplexities in the spiritual sphere. It shows us that duty is the reward of duty, and that there can be no happiness save for those who have learnt that duty and blessedness are one. And thus even by this book of annals—annals of wild deeds and troubled times—we may be taught the truths which find their perfect illustration and proof in the life and teaching of the Son of God.   When those truths are our real possession, the work of life is done. Then

> " Vigour may fail the towering fantasy,
> But yet the Will rolls onward, like a wheel
> In even motion by the love impelled
> That moves the sun in heaven, and all the stars."

APPENDIX I

THE KINGS OF ASSYRIA, AND SOME OF THEIR INSCRIPTIONS.

DATES from the *Eponym Canon* and the Assyrian Monuments; Schrader, *Cuneiform Inscriptions, and the Old Testament,* E. Tr., 1888, pp. 167-187.

B.C.

860.—Shalmaneser II.

854.—Battle of Karkar.   War with *Ahab* and *Benhadad.*

842.—War with Hazael.   Tribute of *Jehu.*

825.—Samsi-Ramman.[1]

812.—Ramman-Nirari.

783.—Shalmaneser III.

773.—Assur-dan III.

763.—June 15th.   Eclipse of the sun.

755.—Assur-Nirari.

745.—Tiglath-Pileser II.

742.—Azariah (Uzziah) heads a league of nineteen Hamathite districts against Assyria (?).

740.—Death of Uzziah (?).

738.—Tribute of Menahem, Rezin, and Hiram.

734.—Expedition to Palestine against Pekah.   Tribute of Ahaz.

732.—Capture of Damascus.   Death of Rezin.   First actual collision between Israel and Assyria.

728.—Hoshea refuses tribute.

727.—Shalmaneser IV.

724.—Siege of Samaria begun.

722.—Sargon.   Fall of Samaria.

---

[1] Up to the time of Tiglath-Pileser II., the Eponym Year (which is not here given) marks the second complete year of each king's reign.

B.C.

721.—Defeat of Merodach-Baladan.

720.—Battle of Raphia. Defeat of Sabaco, King of Egypt.

715.—Subjugated people deported to Samaria. Accession of Hezekiah.

711.—Capture of Ashdod.

707.—Building of great palace of Dur-Sarrukin.

709.—Sargon expels Merodach-Baladan, and becomes King of Babylon.

705.—Assassination (?) of Sargon.

705.—Sennacherib.

704.—Embassy of Merodach-Baladan to Hezekiah.

703.—Belibus made King of Babylon.

702.—Construction of the Bellino Cylinder.

721.—Siege of Ekron. Defeat of Egypt at Altaqu. Siege of Jerusalem. Campaign against Hezekiah and Tirhakah disastrously concluded at Pelusium and Jerusalem.

681.—Murder of Sennacherib.

681.—Esar-haddon.

676.—Manasseh pays tribute.

668.—Assur-bani-pal (Sardanapalus).

608.—Death of Josiah in the battle of Megiddo against Pharaoh Necho.

The dates and names of Assyrian kings as given in *Records of the Past* (ii. 207, 208) do not exactly accord with these in all cases.

	B.C.
Tiglath-Pileser II.	950
Assur-dan II.	930
Rimmon-Nirari II.	911
Tiglath-Uras II.	889
Assur-natzu-pal	883
Shalmaneser II.	858
Assur-dain-pal (a rebel)	825
Samsi-Rimmon II.	823
Rimmon-Nirari III.	810
Shalmaneser III.	781
Assur-dan III.	771
Assur-Nirari	753
Tiglath-Pileser III. (Pul)	745

	B.C.
Shalmaneser IV. (an usurper)	727
Sargon (Jareb?) (usurper)	722
Sennacherib	705
Esar-haddon I.	681
Assur-bani-pal	668

* * * * *

Destruction of Nineveh under Esar-haddon	
II., or Sarakos	606

INSCRIPTION OF SHALMANESER II. ON THE BLACK OBELISK IN THE BRITISH MUSEUM [1]

It begins with an invocation to the gods Rimmon, Adar, Merodach, Nergal, Beltis, Istar, and proceeds :—

"I am Shalmaneser, the strong king, king of all the four Zones of the Sun, the marcher over the whole world, . . . who has laid his yoke upon all lands hostile to him, and has swept them like a whirlwind."

It tells of his campaigns against the Hittites etc., etc.

The allusion to Jehu runs as follows :—

"The tribute of Yahua, son of Khumri, silver, gold, bowls of gold, vessels of gold, goblets of gold, pitchers of gold, lead, sceptres for the king's hand, staves, I received."

This inscription is supplemented by another on a monolith found at Karkh, twenty miles from Diarbekr (*Records*, iii. 81-100), which mentions the battle of Karkar, with its slaughter of fourteen thousand of the enemy, among whom was Akkabhu Sirlai—*i.e.*, Ahab of Israel.

II

TIGLATH-PILESER II. (CIRC. B.C. 739)

In his Records he mentions no less than five Hebrew kings— Azariah, Jehoahaz (Ahaz), Menahem, Pekah, Hoshea—as well as Rezin of Damascus, Hiram of Tyre, etc. His name perhaps means "He who puts his trust in Adar." See *Records of the*

---

[1] This Shalmaneser died about B.C. 825, after a reign of thirty-five years (Sayce in *Records of the Past*, v. 27-42 ; Oppert, *Hist. des Empires de Chaldée et d'Assyrie* ; Ménant, *Annales des Rois d'Assyrie*, 1874).

Past, v. 45-52 ; Schrader, *Keilinschr.*, pp. 149-151 ; G. Smith, *Assyrian Discoveries*, pp. 254-287.

Unfortunately the inscriptions are very mutilated and fragmentary.

III

Our chief knowledge of SARGON is from the great inscription in the Palace of Khorsabad. It is translated by Prof. Dr. Jules Oppert, *Records of the Past*, ix. 1-21. The king's inscription at Bavian, north-east of Mosul, is in the same volume, pp. 21-28, translated by Dr. T. G. Pinches. See, too, *id.*, vii. 21-56, xi. 15-40.

The Khorsabad inscription has these passages :—

"The great gods have made me happy by the constancy of their affection ; they have granted me the exercise of my sovereignty over all kings."

He says :—

"I besieged and occupied the town of Samaria ; I took twenty-seven thousand two hundred and eighty of its inhabitants captive. I took from them fifty chariots, but left them the rest of their belongings. I placed my lieutenants over them ; I renewed the obligations imposed upon them *by one of the kings who preceded me.*" [Tiglath-Pileser, whom Sargon does not choose to name.]

"Hanun, King of Gaza, and Sabaco, Sultan of Egypt, allied themselves at *Raphia* to oppose me. I put them to flight. Sabaco fled, and no one has seen any trace of him since. I imposed a tribute on Pharaoh, King of Egypt."

He tells us that he defeated the usurper Ilubid of Hamath, who had been a smith ; burnt Karkar ; and flayed Ilubid alive.

He defeated Azuri and Jaman of Ashdod, and his most persistent enemy, Merodach-Baladan, son of Jakin, King of Chaldæa.

He ends with a prayer that Assur may bless him.

IV

Bellino's Cylinder comprises the first two years of SENNACHERIB. It is translated by Mr. H. F. Talbot, *Records of the Past*, i. 22-32. It was published by Layard in the first volume of *British Museum Inscriptions*, pl. 63. The facsimile of it was made by Bellino.

It begins :—

" 'SENNACHERIB, the great king, the powerful king, the king of Assyria, the king unrivalled, the pious monarch, the worshipper of the great gods, . . . the noble warrior, the valiant hero, the first of all kings, the great punisher of unbelievers who are breakers of the holy festivals.

"Assur, my lord, has given me an unrivalled monarchy. Over all princes he has raised triumphantly my arms.

"In the beginning of my reign I defeated Marduk-Baladan, King of Babylon, and his allies the Elamites, in the plains near the city of Kish. He fled alone; he got into the marshes full of reeds and rushes, and so saved his life."

(He proceeds to narrate the spoiling of Marduk's camp, and his palace in Babylon, and how he carried off his wife, his harem, his nobles.)

We see here an illustration of the vaunting tones of this king which are so faithfully reproduced in 2 Kings xviii.

His Bull Inscription, chiefly relating to his defeats of Merodach-Baladan, is translated by Rev. J. M. Rodwell (*Records of the Past*, vii. 57-64).

V

The Taylor Cylinder, so called from its former possessor, is a hexagonal clay prism found at Nineveh in 1830, and now in the British Museum (translated by Mr. H. F. Talbot, *Records of the Past*, i. 33-53).

The first two campaigns of Sennacherib are related as on the Bellino Cylinder. The Taylor Cylinder narrates campaigns of his first eight years.

The story of the third campaign narrates the defeat of Elulæus, King of Sidon; the tribute of Menahem, King of Samaria; the defeat of Zidka, King of Askelon; the revolt of Ekron, which deposed the Assyrian vassal Padi, and sent him in iron chains to Hezekiah; the battle of Egypt and Ethiopia at Altaqu (Eltekon, Josh. xv. 59), and the capture of Timnath. Of Hezekiah the king says :—

"And Hezekiah, King of Judah, who had not bowed down at my feet, forty-six of his strong cities, castles, and smaller towns, with warlike engines, I captured; 200,500 people, small and great, male and female, horses, sheep, etc., without number, I carried off. Himself I shut up like a bird in a cage inside Jerusalem. Siege-towers against him I constructed. I gave his plundered cities to the kings of Ashdod, Ekron, and Gaza. I diminished his kingdom; I augmented his tribute. The fearful splendour of my majesty had overwhelmed him. The horsemen, soldiers, etc., which he had collected for the fortification of Jerusalem his royal city, now carried tribute, thirty talents of gold, eight hundred of silver, scarlet, embroidered woven cloth, large precious stones, ivory couches and thrones, skins, precious woods; his daughters, his harem, his male and female slaves, unto Nineveh, my royal city, after me he sent ; and to pay tribute he sent his envoy."

He then narrates his fourth, fifth, sixth, and seventh campaigns against Elam, etc. His eighth was against "the children of Babylon, wicked devils," etc. He ends by describing the splendour of the palace which he built.

VI

An inscription of ESAR-HADDON, found at Kouyunjik, now in the British Museum, mentions his receipt of the intelligence of his father's murder by his unnatural brothers, while he was commanding his father's army on the northern confines.

"From my heart I made a vow. My liver was inflamed with rage. Immediately I wrote letters, saying I assumed the sovereignty of my Father's House." He prayed to the gods and goddesses ; they encouraged him, and in spite of a great snowstorm he reached Nineveh, and defeated his brother, because Istar stood by his side and said to their army, " An unsparing deity am I" (*Records of the Past*, iii. 100-108).

VII

A terra-cotta cylinder of ASSUR-BANI-PAL (the Sardanapalus of the Greeks) is now in the British Museum. It is translated by Mr. G. Smith, *Records of the Past*, i. 55-106, ix. 37-64 ; Oppert, *Mémoire sur les Rapports de l'Egypte et l'Assyrie* ; and G. Smith, *Annals of Assur-bani-pal.*

Its most interesting parts relate to the campaign of his father Esar-haddon against Egypt, and how Tirhakah, King of Egypt and Ethiopia, reoccupied Memphis. He defeated the army of Tirhakah, who, to save his life, fled from Memphis to Thebes. The Assyrians then took Thebes, and restored Necho's father, Psamatik I., to Memphis and Sais, and other Egyptian kings, friends of Assyria, who had fled before Tirhakah. The kings, however, proved ungrateful, and made a league against him. He therefore threw them into fetters and had them brought to

Nineveh, but subsequently released Necho with splendid presents. Tirhakah fled to Ethiopia, where he " went to his place of night" —*i.e.*, died.

APPENDIX II

INSCRIPTION IN THE TUNNEL OF SILOAM

THE inscription of Siloam is the oldest known Hebrew inscription. " It is engraved on the rocky wall of the subterranean channel which conveys the water of the Virgin's Spring at Jerusalem into the Pool of Siloam. In the summer of 1880 one of the native pupils of Dr. Schick, a German architect, was playing with other lads in the Pool, and while wading up the subterranean channel slipped and fell into the water. On rising to the surface he noticed, in spite of the darkness, what looked like letters on the rock which formed the southern wall of the channel. Dr. Schick visited the spot, and found that an ancient inscription, concealed for the most part by the water, actually existed there." The level of the water was lowered, but the inscription had been partly filled up with a deposit of lime, and the first intelligible copy was made by Professor Sayce in February 1881, and six weeks later by Dr. Guthe. Professor Sayce had to sit for hours in the mud and water, working under masonry or earth. There can be little doubt that this work is alluded to in 2 Kings xx. 20 ; 2 Chron. xxxii. 30; Isa. viii. 6 ("the waters of Shiloah ["the tunnel"?] which flow softly ").

The alphabet is that used by the prophets before the exile, somewhat like that on the Moabite Stone, and on early Israelitish and Jewish seals. The language is pure Hebrew, with only one unknown word—*zadah*, in line three: perhaps "excess" or "obstacle."

Professor Sayce thinks that it proves that " the City of David " (Zion) must have been on the southern hill, the so-called Ophel. If so, the Valley of the Sons of Hinnom must be the rubbish-choked Tyropœon, under which must be the tombs of the kings, and the relics of the Temple and Palace destroyed by Nebuchadrezzar.

The inscription is:—

" The excavation ! Now this is the history of the excavation. While the excavators were lifting up the pick each towards his neighbour, and while there were yet three cubits [to excavate], there was heard the voice of one man calling to his neighbour, for there was an excess in the rock on the right hand [and on the left ?]. And after that on the day of excavating, the excavators had struck pick against pick, one against another, the water flowed from the spring [*môtsâ*, "exit," 2 Chron. xxxii. 30] to the Pool" (that of Siloam, which therefore was the only one which then existed) "for twelve hundred cubits. And [part] of a cubit was the height of the rock over the head of the excavators" (Sayce, *Records of the Past*, i. 169-175).

The letters are on an artificial tablet cut in the wall of rock, nineteen feet from where the subterranean conduit opens on the Pool of Siloam, and on the right-hand side. The conduit is at first sixteen feet high, but lessens in one place to no more than two feet. It is, according to Captain Conder, seventeen hundred and eight yards long, but not in a straight line, as there are two *culs-de-sac*, caused by faulty engineering. The engineers, beginning, as at Mount Cenis, from opposite ends, intended to meet in the middle, but failed. The floor has been rounded to allow the water to flow more easily. It is a splendid piece of engineering for that age.

The Pool of Siloam is at the south-east end of a hill which lies to the south of the Temple hill: the Virgin's Fountain is on the opposite side of the hill, more to the north, and is the only natural spring or "Gihon" near Jerusalem, so that its water was of supreme importance. Being outside the city wall, a conduit was necessary. Hezekiah "stopped all the fountains" (2 Chron. xxxii. 4)—*i.e.*, concealed them. By providing a subterranean channel for them, he saved them from the enemy and secured the water-supply of the besieged city.

APPENDIX III

WAS THERE A GOLDEN CALF AT DAN?

THE question might seem absurd, but for its solution I must refer to my paper on the subject in the *Expositor* for October 1893.

The *sole* authorities for a calf at Dan are 1 Kings xii. 28-30 ; 2 Kings x. 29. If in the former passage we alter *one letter*, and read האפד (the "ephod ") for האחד (the "one ")—as Klostermann suggests—we throw light on an obscure and perhaps corrupt passage. The allusion then would be to Micah's old idolatrous image (which *may* have been a calf) at Dan. The two words " and in Dan " in 2 Kings x. 29 may easily have been (as Klostermann thinks) an exegetical gloss added from the error of one letter in 1 Kings xii. 30.

Dan was a most unlikely place to select: for (1) It was a remote frontier town; and (2) there was no room, and no necessity there, for a new cultus beside the ancient one established some centuries earlier, and still served by priests who were direct lineal descendants of Moses (Judg. xviii. 30, 31).

This would further account for the absolute silence of prophets and historians about any golden calf at Dan; and it adds to the inherent probability, also supported by some evidence, that there were *two* cherubic calves at Bethel.

For further arguments I must refer to my paper.

APPENDIX IV

DATES OF THE KINGS OF ISRAEL AND JUDAH, AS GIVEN BY KITTEL AND OTHER MODERN CRITICS[1]

ISRAEL

		B.C.
Ahaziah	... ...	855—854
Jehoram	... ...	854—842
Jehu ...	... ...	842—814
Jehoahaz	... ...	814—797
Joash ...	... ...	797—781
Jeroboam II.	... ...	781—740
Zachariah	... ...	740
Shallum	... ...	740
Menahem	... ...	740—737
Pekahiah	... ...	737—735
Pekah	... ...	735—734
Hoshea	... ...	734—725

---

[1] Many of these dates can only be regarded as uncertain and approximate. Kamphausen dates the commencement of all the latter kings a year later (*Die Chronologie der hebräischen Könige*, Bonn, 1883).

JUDAH

	B.C.
Jehoram ben-Jehoshaphat	851—843
Ahaziah ben-Jehoram	843—842
Athaliah	842—836
Joash ben-Ahaziah	836—796
Amaziah	796—783
Amaziah-Uzziah	783—737
Jotham	737—735
Ahaz	735—715
Hezekiah	715—686
Manasseh	686—641
Amon	641—639
Josiah	639—608
Jehoahaz	608
Jehoiakim	608—597
Jehoiachin	597
Zedekiah	597—586

OTHER FINE VOLUMES AVAILABLE

1980-81

1101	Farrar, F. W.	The First Book of Kings	16.75
1201	Farrar, F. W.	The Second Book of Kings	16.75
1701	Raleigh, Alexander	The Book of Esther	9.00
1902	MacLaren, Alexander	The Psalms (3 vol.)	43.50
2001	Wardlaw, Ralph	Lectures on the Book of Proverbs	27.50
2702	Tatford, Frederick	Daniel and His Prophecy	8.25
4201	Kelly, William	The Gospel of Luke	16.95
4302	Hengstenberg, F. W.	Commentary on the Gospel of John (2 vol.)	34.95
7004	Adeney, Walter D.	The Books of Ezra and Nehemiah	11.50
7105	Stanley, Arthur	Epistles of Paul to the Corinthians	20.95
7106	Moule, H. C. G.	Colossian and Philemon Studies	10.50
7107	Fairbairn, Patrick	The Pastoral Epistles	14.95
8401	Blaikie, William G.	David, King of Israel	14.50
8402	Farrar, F. W.	The Life and Work of St. Paul (2 vol.)	43.95
9401	Warns, Johannes	Baptism	11.50
9502	Liddon, H.P. & Orr, J.	The Birth of Christ	13.95
9503	Bruce, A. B.	The Parables of Christ	12.50
9504	Bruce, A. B.	The Miracles of Christ	17.25
9505	Milligan, William	The Ascension of Christ	12.50
9506	Moule, H.C. & Orr, J.	The Resurrection of Christ	16.96

TITLES CURRENTLY AVAILABLE